The Triumph of Love

The Triumph of Love

Same-Sex Marriage *and the* Christian Love Ethic

Eric Reitan

CASCADE *Books* · Eugene, Oregon

THE TRIUMPH OF LOVE
Same-Sex Marriage and the Christian Love Ethic

Copyright © 2017 Eric Reitan. All rights reserved. Except for brief quotations in critical publications or reviews, no part of this book may be reproduced in any manner without prior written permission from the publisher. Write: Permissions, Wipf and Stock Publishers, 199 W. 8th Ave., Suite 3, Eugene, OR 97401.

Cascade Books
An Imprint of Wipf and Stock Publishers
199 W. 8th Ave., Suite 3
Eugene, OR 97401

www.wipfandstock.com

PAPERBACK ISBN: 978-1-4982-9625-0
HARDCOVER ISBN: 978-1-4982-9627-4
EBOOK ISBN: 978-1-4982-9626-7

Cataloguing-in-Publication data:

Names: Reitan, Eric.

Title: The triumph of love : same-sex marriage and the Christian love ethic / Eric Reitan.

Description: Eugene, OR: Cascade Books, 2017 | Includes bibliographical references and index.

Identifiers: ISBN 978-1-4982-9625-0 (paperback) | ISBN 978-1-4982-9627-4 (hardcover) | ISBN 978-1-4982-9626-7 (ebook)

Subjects: LCSH: Same-sex marriage—Religious aspects—Christianity | Love—Religious aspects—Christianity | Homosexuality—Religious aspects—Christianity | Queer theology

Classification: BT707.6 R45 2017 (paperback) | BT707.6 (ebook)

Manufactured in the U.S.A.   07/19/17

To John Kronen, whose steadfast friendship
I sometimes take for granted.
And to Phil, Randi, and Jake Reitan, whose commitment to fighting
for social change remains an enduring inspiration.

Contents

Preface | ix
Acknowledgements | xiii
Introduction | xv

 1 The Triumph of Same-Sex Marriage | 1

 2 Fred Phelps Is Not Dead | 19

 3 Christian Love | 35

 4 A Matter of Choice? | 61

 5 Homosexuality, Mental Health, and the Good of Children | 78

 6 Love the Sinner, Hate the Sin? | 106

 7 Stories of Identity | 124

 8 The Possibility and Promise of Same-Sex Marriage | 148

 9 The Scriptures of a Loving God | 171

10 Natural and Unnatural | 197

11 Slippery Slopes | 223

12 Disagreeing in a Spirit of Love | 243

Bibliography | 269
Index | 281

Preface

I was hard at work finishing the second draft of this book when, to the surprise of most and the horror of many, Donald Trump won the 2016 presidential election. Before that moment, many LGBT (Lesbian, Gay, Bisexual, and Transgender) persons and their allies had the sense of moving with an inevitable social tide. While more work needed to be done, the *Obergefell v. Hodges* Supreme Court decision marked a turning point in the history of the gay rights movement. Same-sex marriage was now the law of the land. The majority of Americans supported it. While a substantial part of the Christian community found these changes odious, for the first time in American history gays and lesbians were moving inexorably in the direction of full social equality.

For many, Trump's election victory shook that sense of inevitability, awakening them to the fragility of the changes that have occurred. Of course, important voices in the LGBT community have been pointing to that fragility for years. Mel White warned about the forces arrayed against LGBT equality long before Trump's victory. In the 2011 preface to his book, *Holy Terror*, he challenged the complacency that Obama's presidency seemed to be inspiring in many, pointing to the rise of the Tea Party and warning that "the civil and religious rights we have gained are easily reversed" if the forces represented in that movement were to gain ascendancy.[1] But after the landmark Supreme Court decision, many felt such warnings were more about fear than reality.

My sense of the LGBT community tells me that Trump's win changed that, but not because of Trump's own views on the matter. Few think Trump harbors strong opposition to same-sex marriage, and he stated quite

---

1. White, *Holy Terror*, xix.

explicitly in his post-election *60 Minutes* interview that he is "fine" with same-sex marriage and regards the issue as "settled."[2] But Trump's administration is, as I write this, increasingly filling up with cabinet members who have a history of opposing LGBT rights.[3] And Trump was nudged to victory in part by his ability to harness the support of people upset about progressive changes in the American landscape—changes such as the advent of same-sex marriage. Trump's victory is thus a reminder of the persistent influence and strength of those who desire to reverse what so many sexual minorities have struggled so long to achieve.

On a deeper level, there is the sense among many in the LGBT community that Trump's win has emboldened fringe elements of American society that embrace ideologies of hate—as if these elements have taken the election result as a sign that social taboos against overt bigotry and intolerance have been suspended or weakened. So far, the evidence for the truth of this has been anecdotal, but the rise in stories among people I know personally has forced me to take notice. Just a day after the election, a friend of mine was accosted by two men on his way into a store. They called him a faggot and told him his kind was no longer welcome. "Trump won!" they declared. It was time for him to scurry back into the closet.

His experience is part of what the Southern Poverty Law Center has characterized as a post-election wave of hateful graffiti, intimidation, and harassment.[4] Some may question the legitimacy of such reports, but whether a genuine increase or simply an increase in attention towards incidents of hate, the experience of minority groups has been of a society in which they are more likely to be targeted. Coming only a few months after the brutal mass murder in an Orlando night club, the perceived uptick in homophobic harassment has reminded gays and lesbians of their vulnerability in a very *embodied* way. There are people out there whose attitudes and ideologies prime them to physically assault sexual minorities. Such individuals are rare, but for every person on the brink of committing violence there are many more who, while they'd never lift a finger to inflict physical harm, would in a heartbeat restore that world where gays and lesbians live in a closet of secrecy and shame. A world where legalized same-sex marriage is nothing but a pipe dream.

And so for many, including myself, the world we confront today does not look like one in which same-sex marriage is a *fait accompli*. Rather, it looks like a world that stands poised between two alternative visions, with

2. Schultheis, "Trump Talks," para. 13–14.
3. Landsbaum, "Every One."
4. Eversley, "Post-Election Spate of Hate Crimes," para. 1–3.

social forces vying for and against same-sex marriage and neither outcome inevitable.

Christian ideas, values, and arguments are not the only forces at work in this social environment. But their influence cannot be ignored. Hence, it is imperative for all Christians to think carefully and honestly about how to use that influence. Which forces should we ally ourselves with? Which *shouldn't* we ally ourselves with? In which direction should we exert our efforts as disciples of Christ and instruments of the God of love?

This book is the culmination of decades of personal experiences, philosophical reflections, and theological struggle about just these questions. And although I do not pretend that it offers the final answers, my hope is that the perspective articulated here will advance the discussion—ensuring that as we strive to faithfully live out our calling at this moment in history, we do so with the kind of commitment to loving our gay and lesbian neighbors that, no matter what else we might think about homosexuality and same-sex marriage, Jesus' ethic of love unambiguously demands.

Acknowledgements

I would like to thank those who took the time to read portions of this book (or the whole thing!) and offer valuable feedback, especially John Kronen, Sally Houck, and Jenell Williams Paris. I would also like to thank my editor, Robin Parry, for allowing me to pester him remorselessly about formatting and house-style questions. I am also deeply indebted to all of those persons, too many to mention by name, who have shaped my understanding of the LGBT experience through the years. This book could not have been written without the guidance they have given both my intellect and my soul. Finally, I would like to thank my family: my wife, Tanya, who showed great patience as I buried myself in the task of writing; and my children, Evan and Izzie, who showed no such patience, but who filled me with the laughter and affection that help to fuel all my efforts.

Introduction

This is not a book about what the Bible does and does not say about homosexuality and same-sex marriage, although these are questions I explore later in the book. For those interested in books of that kind, there are plenty of excellent works on both sides of the issue.

This is not a book aimed at uncovering an overarching scriptural understanding of sexual ethics and the purposes of marriage, although these are issues I will need to wrestle with. Again, there are numerous books out there that do an excellent job of exploring these issues in depth.

Nor is this a memoir by a gay Christian man struggling to integrate his faith and his sexuality after growing up in a Christian community that tells him the two are incompatible. Such stories of struggle will need to be examined in this book, but as a straight man I am ill-equipped to write that kind of memoir. Again, there are excellent books out there written by those who are well-equipped to tell such stories with eloquence and power.

This book is about love—Christian love, to be precise, the kind of love that has come to be captured by the Greek work "agape." It is a book about that distinctive brand of love modeled by Jesus on the cross: an unconditional good will toward every person, friend and enemy alike; a concern for the needs of others without concern for whether they deserve it. This book begins by taking seriously the idea that such love lies at the center of the Christian moral life, and then asks the following question: What does Christian love for our gay and lesbian neighbors demand?

And that is not a question we can answer without looking up from the pages of our books—our theology texts, our Bible study guides, our sermon collections, even our Bibles themselves—to pay attention to our gay and lesbian neighbors. We cannot love our gay and lesbian neighbors in the Christian sense if we have no understanding—compassionate, empathic understanding—of what it is like to be them.

This requirement places the greatest burden on straight Christians like myself, since we do not inhabit the lives of sexual minorities and so must practice sustained listening and stretch our empathetic imaginations. But the requirement also has implications for LGBT Christians, since no two people have the same experiences, the same histories, the same struggles. Christian love calls us to love the neighbor, not some generic humanity or some general class. And the neighbor is a concrete individual with a unique set of circumstances and struggles.

That doesn't mean we can avoid looking at generalities. There are common themes in human experience that need to shape our thinking when we are making decisions that affect whole classes of people. And let's be clear: what Christians decide about homosexuality and same-sex marriage will affect a whole class of people. The Christian community has power, both to shape the lives of those who grow up within that community and to shape the wider culture. And so we need to think about the generalized impact that our choices have on classes of people who are most directly impacted by them. In the case of same-sex marriage, those most directly and powerfully impacted are our gay and lesbian neighbors.

So we need empathy for our gay and lesbian neighbors, and sometimes that means identifying common themes in the experiences of these neighbors. Many of these common themes can be understood with the help of the social and behavioral sciences and the conclusions reached by researchers in these fields. And so I will be digging into some of that research in this book. But we must always pair such generalized understanding with loving attention to the concrete neighbor. Love begins with attention. Moral reasoning within the context of the Christian love ethic has to be informed and infused by the lessons of such attention.

This brings me to another distinctive feature of this book: I am not, by training, a biblical scholar or a theologian. By training I am a philosopher, with specializations in moral philosophy and the philosophy of religion. I am also a Christian—a Lutheran Christian—and when I first began to seriously pursue a career in philosophy I had my own struggles with integrating my identity as a Christian with my love for rigorous philosophical reflection. My solution was to bring my philosophical training to bear on issues relating to my faith.

Moral philosophers develop moral theories and apply them to controversial moral problems, and so I decided to do that: to develop the moral theory that I saw at the heart of Scripture, and then apply it to a controversy I had enormous passion for. And so I wrote a PhD dissertation in which

I developed the Christian love ethic in the way philosophers do and then applied it to the dilemma of defensive violence: If Christians are supposed to love their neighbor without regard for whether the neighbor deserves it, then I am supposed to love both the unjust aggressor and the innocent victim. How do I do that?

This book is, for me, a kind of return to that sort of Christian moral philosophy—except that this time, I am applying the Christian love ethic to a different issue that I am passionate about: same-sex marriage. And this time I am writing with a much richer body of experience to draw from, as will soon become clear. Finally, this time I am writing not for a committee of professors who will decide whether I graduate, but for the Christian community—because I think the kind of approach to this issue that my training has prepared me for offers a valuable contribution to ongoing Christian conversations and debates.

In short, this is a book of Christian moral philosophy, written with deep attention to the lived experience of sexual minorities and in a style meant to be accessible to general readers. Occasionally, of course, the ideas and arguments I need to tackle get a little tricky, and I would do no one a favor by oversimplifying them. But even when tackling more challenging topics, my aim is to do so as accessibly as I can. I want all readers who care about the intersections of Christian moral life and homosexuality to be able to benefit from this book and the thoughts it contains.

But most of all, I want to inspire my readers to look up from their books, including this one, and pay attention to one another: the neighbors we are called to love.

1

The Triumph of Same-Sex Marriage

In August of 2009, a tornado swept over the General Assembly of the Evangelical Lutheran Church in America just before it voted to lift its ban on the ordination of partnered gays and lesbians. The tornado damaged the roof of the Minneapolis Convention Center where the General Assembly was meeting, as well as clipping the spire of Central Lutheran Church across the street. It also blew out the windows of the iconic Electric Fetus record store.

Few were surprised when conservative pundits declared it a judgment from God.[1] (The Electric *Fetus*? Any God with a modicum of decency would be appalled.) Nor was there much surprise when, like a metaphorical tornado, the ELCA vote swept through congregations, stirring conflict and inspiring individuals and more than six hundred congregations to leave in protest.[2]

A few years earlier, when the vote went the other way at the 2005 General Assembly, it was the progressives' turn to leave. I was one of those progressives. My family had been part of the struggle to change ELCA policy,

---

1. John Piper, for example, called it a "gentle but firm warning to the ELCA and all of us" to turn away from the sin of homosexuality. See Piper, "The Tornado" para. 20.

2. In the years immediately following the 2009 vote, 654 congregations voted to disaffiliate themselves from the ELCA. See Secretary of the ELCA, *2013 Pre-Assembly Report*, 10.

and when the 2005 vote came down, we were tired. The decision to become a Lutheran in exile was painful, and I didn't make it easily. For me, two considerations were especially influential. First, I wanted to give my whole self to my church community, but I didn't think I could freely give my time, talents, and resources to a church that, when confronted with this decision, consciously chose to perpetuate discrimination against people I loved.

Second, I needed spiritual renewal and support to recover from what had been an exhausting and ultimately disappointing struggle. My wife and I had been deeply invested in the local covenant group that met weekly to discuss the ELCA's materials on sexuality. Those weekly conversations had been trying and often anguished, and the final outcome for us was that our church had come to feel like the battleground. For spiritual renewal, we needed to look elsewhere.

It was a four-year exile, and because I live in Oklahoma—one of the states that has a claim on being the buckle of America's Bible Belt—it wasn't a simple matter to find a church nearby that accepted its LGBT members on an equal footing. And so, for four years, my family drove an hour every Sunday morning to attend church.

The first time I returned to my local ELCA congregation after the 2009 vote, the service was following a contemporary musical setting of the Lutheran liturgy that my wife calls the *Jesus Christ Superstar* setting (although I think it sounds more like *Godspell*). This small Oklahoma church was the only place I'd ever encountered that liturgy, and it had always been my favorite. The congregation had the musical talent—and the earnest energy—to do more than pull it off. When the cantor's rich baritone sang out, "Praying, let your spirit soar, as we're laying our burdens at God's door," it was enough to give me chills.

I tried to sing the responses, but I kept having to stop because I was crying too hard.

Accommodationists and Sell-Outs

Both then and now, many conservatives on this issue have treated my decisions and the decisions of people like me as a sad symptom of Christians selling out to secular culture, favoring its values over the clear teachings of Scripture and Christian tradition. And as the broader culture has undergone seismic changes on the issue of same-sex marriage—culminating in the June 2015 Supreme Court decision that legalized same-sex civil marriage throughout the US—those same conservative Christians have represented these social transformations as a *defeat* for Christian values.

Some have portrayed it as a defeat of staggering magnitude. Tim Wildmon of the American Family Association (a conservative Christian group) describes the Supreme Court decision as "a spiritual 9/11." As Wildmon sees it, "We have said to God Almighty, *We don't care what you say about marriage and your definition of what's natural and normal.*"[3] Bill Muehlenberg, writing for *BarbWire* (a right-wing Christian news site) declares that the majority-voting Supreme Court Justices "have declared war on marriage, on God, on morality, on family, and on our children."[4]

Waging war on children! What could be more un-Christ-like than that?

While most conservatives are less hyperbolic than Wildmon and Muehlenberg, they tend to share the conviction that this isn't merely a defeat for same-sex marriage opponents. It's a defeat for Christianity. The permissiveness of secular culture has prevailed over Christian values. The cultural indulgence in "whatever feels good" has rolled over the Christian forces fighting to preserve essential sexual constraints.

Underlying this conviction is the assumption that there can be no legitimate *Christian* case for same-sex marriage, no compelling argument rooted in Christianity and its values. If Christians disagree about homosexuality, it's because the Christians on the side of reform have lost touch with their faith, seduced by secular values or led astray by years of incremental accommodation.

The latter is the message of Lutheran theologian James Nestingen, who began a 2002 lecture on homosexuality and the Lutheran Church in the following way:

> Since cultural sexual standards began to shift in the 1960s, the basic approach of Lutherans in the ELCA tradition has been accommodation.... The current presenting issue is homosexual practice. The issue did not arise out of the larger Christian or a particularly Lutheran agenda.... It is a cultural conflict, a part of an ongoing North American societal undercutting of what were once commonly accepted sexual restraints, the expectation being that the church will continue to accommodate. The question is if there is anything left in our heritage that holds.[5]

On Nestingen's view of things, the whole of the ELCA has lost its moral footing, gradually accommodating secular culture more and more,

---

3. Tashman, "Conservatives React," para. 3.
4. Muehlenberg, "SCOTUS Declares War," para. 8.
5. Nestingen, "Is There a Law?" Although the conference proceedings were published, these opening remarks are excluded from the published version.

especially in the sexual domain. It's not just individual Christians who've surrendered their convictions. It's whole denominations.

Is this portrait correct? Does this conservative narrative offer an accurate depiction both of what lies behind the cultural shift toward accepting same-sex intimacy and what lies behind progressive Christian support for it? Is the recent triumph of the marriage equality movement best explained as the defeat of Christian values, and Christian support for these changes best seen as accommodation or capitulation?

I think not.

Same-Sex Marriage and Christian Love

When my best friend in graduate school came out to me, I probably didn't handle it in the *worst* conceivable way. I didn't reject him. I didn't start foaming at the mouth and calling him a filthy pervert. As I recall, the initial exchange went something like this:

John: "I'm gay."

Me (after an awkward silence): "Well, I'm not."

Fortunately, this not-quite-stellar testament to eloquence and sensitivity didn't put him off. We remained friends.

My ill-formed thoughts about homosexuality and Christian faith were shaped by that friendship. John is likely the reason I'm a Christian today, and certainly the reason I connected with the Lutheran side of my heritage. When I started graduate school I was conflicted about the relationship between my devotion to philosophy and my Christian beliefs, and it would have been easy to let the latter slip away amidst the agnosticism and atheism surrounding me. But John swept into my office on my first day, shaking hands and asking questions.

One of the things he wanted to know was whether I believed in God. I confessed that I did, and he was delighted. He began my education in the tradition of Christian philosophy, launching into brilliant monologues about Thomas Aquinas and Francisco Suarez. He opened up my appreciation for the rich historical synergy between serious philosophical inquiry and religious faith.

Soon, we became known among the graduate students as "the God Guys." Of the two of us, he was the more theologically conservative. And, as it turned out, he was the one who was gay. As our friendship deepened, he shared with me what that meant, in terms of his own lived experience. He told me what it was like to be a devout Lutheran who discovered in adolescence that he didn't have a lick of attraction for the opposite sex, but felt for boys all the romantic and tumultuous things that, in adolescence, I felt for girls. He told me about efforts to change his sexuality—including the efforts of well-meaning therapists who blamed his homosexuality for an attempted suicide. He told me about the failures of those efforts. He shared with me the distinctive struggles of a gay Christian who enters adulthood carrying the sense that his sexuality has no legitimate place in the world.

One of the common themes of conservative attacks on homosexuality is the emphasis on how much the gay community is riddled with promiscuity and casual sex. The message seems to be that gays are incapable of monogamous love. For them, it's all about hedonistic pleasure, all about throwing out normal standards of sexual restraint.

If there's a key lesson that John's stories drove home for me, it would be just how *backward* this conservative critique is. John tried to make that very point in correspondence with Nestingen not long after Nestingen's 2002 talk. Let me share a bit of that exchange:

> When I was young . . . homosexuality was hardly spoken of. What society, my parents, and the Church thought about it was not very encouraging to me as a young gay man. I could not bring myself to tell my parents I was gay, because I was so ashamed of that fact. But they had a book I found called *Everything You Wanted to Know about Sex But Were Afraid to Ask*. They kept it on a shelf in the closet in their bedroom (ironic, don't you think?). I don't remember how I came across it, but once, when they were gone, I read it because I wanted to know more about being gay (or being "a homosexual," as we said back then). I nervously turned to the section in it on homosexuality. The author of it related a lot of stories from gay men about their experiences. None of them spoke of committed, loving gay relationships. They were all about meaningless sexual encounters. One shocked me. It had to do with a gay man who went to the local bowling alley when he wanted sex. . . . The author of this book said that homosexuality is inherently unfulfilling. The penis really wants the vagina (he really *said* that—it is emblazoned on my memory), and so no homosexual *can ever find love with another man*.
>
> But I was passionately in love with my friend Billy. I thought about him all the time. I wanted to be with him all the time. I wanted to tell him I loved him. I wanted to kiss him above all. But he could not handle any of that . . . .[6]

---

6. Unpublished correspondence.

Billy, like John, was gay. But unlike John—who was visibly effeminate and ear-marked for bullying and gay-bashing from an early age—Billy could pass as straight. Like John, he was ashamed of his sexuality. Unlike John, he could pretend to the world that he was just like everyone else.

But he wasn't like everyone else. Where others' adolescent longings drew them toward members of the opposite sex, Billy's drew him toward the same-sex . . . and toward John. But, as John points out,

> Billy could not have imagined dating me, in the sense of taking me home to his parents, announcing that I was his boyfriend, etc. They would not have been happy about that, to say the least—nor would have my parents. But I loved him, and would have dated him secretly, pretending to the outside world we were just friends, but behaving like lovers in private. He couldn't do that even—he could not admit he was gay or he loved me.

Years later he did admit it, but at the time he couldn't, because "that would involve owning his gayness and somehow integrating it into his life, and Billy was not ready to do it." While John was more willing to "own his gayness," he was too frightened of rejection—by his parents foremost, but also by the broader community, including his faith community—to live his public and private lives in an integrated way.

And the social stigma that prevented Billy and John from integrating their sexuality into their lives combined with something else: the urgency and energy of adolescent sexuality. But that sexuality existed outside the parameters of society's norms. Society afforded it no legitimate space for expression, and so instead it became furtive. John describes how they would engage in sexual acts, and Billy would pretend to be doing something else: "looking in drawers or something." Afterward, they would pretend nothing had happened. Isolating their sexuality from the rest of their lives, cutting it off from the rest of their relationship, was their way of coping with the social condemnation of who they were.

John expresses the anguish of this social exclusion in the following way:

> In the midst of all this turmoil growing up, I remember walking by the dirty book store in town. Outside they advertised gay magazines. . . . I was intrigued because here, at least, was a magazine admitting the existence of people like me. Eventually I got the courage to go into the dirty book store. . . . I was filled with a vast array of conflicting emotions. I wanted love—I wanted *Billy*, in fact. I did not want a life of meaningless sex. But I was gay, I knew that, and I needed some kind of place, some

where in the world, I could *be* gay with other gay men. I needed some affirmation that there were people like me. This magazine did not condemn me for being gay—it proudly advertised that it had stories in it to make gay people like me "cum and cum again." So *that* attracted me, but I was repelled by the loveless objectifying nature of it all. But, I thought that I would probably just have to accept "the facts" about being gay. Gays are "queer," my class mates told me, they are "sick," they are "perverts." . . . I could not talk about any of this with my parents. . . . It would only make me feel more ashamed. Billy, whom I loved, would only have casual sex with me, sex in which he never looked at me, pretended to do other things. And even the psychologist who wrote the book *Everything You Always Wanted to Know about Sex But Were Afraid to Ask*, said that the penis wants the vagina, and so gays could never be happy, could never have lasting relationships. But I knew that I was gay, I knew I could never be straight (and why should I want to when most of the straight boys I knew growing up teased me, insisted that my love of history, of books, of beautiful objects, of opera, was all sick, and that real men play football, disdain art, etc.,—I *loathed* them), so I thought: "This is my fate, a life of meaningless sex. But it is better to have even that, rather than never to be able to be intimate with a man, never to touch a man in a sexual, and perhaps romantic way. And maybe, just maybe, it could be tender once in a while, and the man might look at me when we have sex, and kiss me, and say he loved me and sound like he meant it."

What my best friend never had were things I grew up taking for granted: a model for the responsible expression of my sexuality, a vision of how to live it out in ways that would nurture its healthy development and protect me from the volatility and vulnerability that human sexuality and romantic impulses can bring. I grew up assuming that sex could be part of a meaningful human relationship—indeed, that it *should* be part of something defined by enduring mutual love. John grew up with the message that his sexuality was essentially cut off from human love, and that any effort to nurture a meaningful relationship was the effort to nurture sin. While my parents supervised my earliest romantic relationships, imposing constraints and expectations, John couldn't even talk to his parents about his earliest romantic feelings, let alone bring his first love home for dinner.

I grew up expecting to one day fall in love and get married. John grew up hoping that, despite what society kept telling him about what it meant to be gay, he could one day savor a momentary pretense of love.

Denied what I had, John's sexuality evolved in a kind of moral vacuum—and the only thing that acknowledged him, that offered him a place, was an adult bookstore. Christianity and the rest of society had pushed him out into the cold. Like the little match girl, from the Hans Christian Andersen story of the same name, he looked in from the outside, shivering and alone, catching glimpses of a better world with the brief flickering warmth and light of each tiny match.

But unlike the little match girl, he didn't die. Instead, as he shivered in the alley, the pornographer came to him and said, "Here. Follow me." And having nowhere else to go, he did.

And then the conservative Christians all around him said, "See? They're promiscuous! They show no sexual restraint! Proof that their sexuality is essentially bad and wrong."

It wasn't secular values that shaped my thinking about homosexuality and Christian values. It was my friendship with a gay Christian. It wasn't the sexual permissiveness of the broader culture that convinced my conscience to support same-sex marriage. It was listening to and empathizing with the life experiences of my best friend. What he longed for wasn't sexual permissiveness. What he longed for was a society that imposed healthy boundaries on his sexuality, rather than throwing him out into the cold.

After listening to John I could see no way to "love the sinner but hate the sin." In the light of what I'd heard, I didn't know how to love my gay neighbors as myself while continuing to embrace the traditional view that *all* expressions of my friend's sexuality—even in the context of committed and faithful monogamy—were wrong.

I wrestled with these things as a budding moral philosopher specializing in Christian ethics (I eventually wrote my dissertation on the Christian love ethic and its implications for defensive violence). When my conscience said, "I can't love him as a Christian while condemning his loves," was I just falling prey to some sort of sentimentality? Or was my conscience giving voice to a rationally defensible conviction?

In later chapters I'll explain why I became convinced of the latter. For now, I just want to stress the following: if I'm right, then Christian supporters of same-sex marriage, far from being sell-outs or accommodationists, have reasons for their view rooted in the most fundamental Christian moral norm of all.

Those reasons need to be brought into critical conversation with the Christian arguments *against* same-sex marriage—such as arguments rooted in Natural Law and traditional readings of Scripture. Not everyone will be convinced, as I am, that the argument from Christian love is the stronger argument. But I hope, even so, that my readers will come to see that there is after all a *Christian* argument, rooted in *Christian* values, for same-sex marriage—an argument that a Christian could find convincing for reasons that have nothing to do with accommodating secular culture.

In saying this, I need to stress that it is *marriage* for same-sex couples, not some other framework for accepting their intimate relationships, that I think Christian love entails. If Christians are going to accept same-sex intimacy at all, they should do so *on the same terms with which they accept heterosexual intimacy*. And that means restricting it to and nurturing it within the context of monogamous, covenantal life-partnerships forged by vows of fidelity, commitment, and mutual love.

To hold up the institution of marriage as the framework for sexual holiness is not something Christians do out of prudishness or legalism. It's something we do out of love. Sexuality has enormous potential to enrich us, but it is also fraught with dangers. Marriage—to the extent that it approximates the Christian ideal—nurtures the potential and guards against the dangers. It is a gift of love, and to withhold that gift from gays and lesbians is to plunge them into a world of dangers.

In other words, there can be no Christian support for same-sex *sex* absent Christian support for same-sex *marriage*. Let us condemn homosexual promiscuity as forcefully as we condemn heterosexual promiscuity. Let us condemn infidelity and adultery and exploitative marriages wherever we find these things, whether in same-sex partnerships or heterosexual ones. But when it comes to committed monogamous love between two people of the same sex—the kind of love expressed in joining two lives together in partnership and mutual support—let us not call it sin. Because to call it sin is to wish for that cold dark place where my friend grew up, a place where he and other sexual minorities are cast like the match girl—an alley that some escape through suicide, some through drug addiction, some through sleazy alternatives to love, and some by breaking the window, climbing into the warmth and light, and insisting on a place at the table.

Love doesn't wait for them to crawl in through shattered glass. Love opens the door and offers them a chair.

I don't expect everyone to be convinced, but I do hope that critics will understand why growing numbers of their fellow Christians *are* convinced, and thereby come to see that these fellow Christians cannot be simply dismissed as abandoning Christian values.

Making this point is the main purpose of this book. But before turning to that point in detail, I want to explore a related point about what has helped motivate the astonishing social changes we've seen. I want to suggest that none of this could have happened if values *fundamentally Christian in character* hadn't prevailed over some deeply *un*-Christian forces fighting to perpetuate LGBT marginalization.

Put another way, I don't think we can understand what has happened in our culture by invoking secular permissivism and growing Christian accommodationism the way Nestingen and those like him do. *Even if you think that same-sex relationships are sinful, and even if you are convinced that Christians like me are mistaken about what love demands, when you look at the cultural changes that have precipitated growing social and legal acceptance of same-sex intimacy, you should* still *recognize and acknowledge an important way in which those changes reflect a victory for Christian values.*

Simply put: even assuming (as I do not) that same-sex marriage is a sin, the victory of same-sex marriage is a triumph for Christian love.

If you think this idea is crazy, bear with me.

Victories amidst Defeats

In our fallen world, victories rarely come without cost. And in a world governed by an almighty God, defeats are rarely so complete that no seeds of the divine purpose can be found amidst the ruins.

On the day I returned to my local ELCA church from my four-year exile, I noticed that Sam[7] wasn't there. In the weeks that followed, it became clear he wasn't coming back. Sam was someone I'd worked with in church leadership. Like me, he'd been part of our congregation's anguished discussions leading up to the 2005 vote. But when that vote came down as it did, he was—for the time being—on the winning side.

I remember once, during our covenant group meetings, talking passionately about the tangible human harms that the traditional condemnation of homosexuality had inflicted on people I love. During a break I saw him pacing the hall, his face awash in distress. He was struggling, I think, to come to terms with what I and others had said.

Later, he spoke to our group in a tone of confession. "I can't change my position on this," he said, "because it's *Paul* who condemns homosexual acts. I can't read Romans any other way. And Luther learned about salvation by grace through faith from *Paul*. Paul is just one step away from Jesus! I can't. I just can't." His voice trembled with emotion.

When I returned home after the 2009 vote, Sam made the same hard choice I'd made four years earlier. I think I know a little of what he went through in making that choice. I understand why he's gone, and I continue to respect him and his faith, even as I continue to think he's mistaken

---

7. Name changed for anonymity.

about homosexuality. And I hope that when I left, he understood why and continued to respect me and my faith, even as he continued to think I was mistaken.

The nature of the disagreement between us makes it hard to know how to organize a common worship life that reflects our competing values. Sam's convictions demand that worship exclude full participation of people that I think faithful worship requires us to include. This isn't just a case of finding the grace to worship alongside those with different ideas, because this debate is about how, in our common worship life, we are going to treat real human beings. The community must choose. And depending on the choice the community makes, one or the other of us will face a dilemma. Do we sacrifice our values so we can worship in peace? Do we keep fighting against the community's norms, never fully experiencing peace in our place of worship, constantly confronting the practices we think are wrong? Or do we walk away?

But even in the midst of disagreements with those kinds of stakes, it's possible to retain a spirit of mutual respect.

That Sam left the ELCA after the 2009 vote is a tangible cost of something that, for me, was an important victory. But costs can be more or less serious. It is one thing for me or Sam to make the decision to worship elsewhere. It would be something else to lose the bonds of mutual respect and love that can unite those who confront such differences. The former may reflect the inevitable trade-offs of pursuing the demands of conscience in a fallen world. But the latter?

Suppose that, after years of conflict, same-sex marriage finally wins the day throughout the Christian community. And suppose I'm right about what Christian values call for: when Christians generally come to accept same-sex marriage, Christian values—at least on this issue—will have prevailed. But imagine that this victory comes at the cost, not just of some Christians like Sam choosing to worship elsewhere, but of the Christian majority no longer respecting and reaching out to Sam and those like him, no longer pursuing fellowship with them in a spirit of sincerity and love—no longer seeing them as brothers and sisters in Christ.

If that were to happen, then Christian values would have prevailed on the matter of same-sex marriage at the cost of shattering mutual respect and fellowship across lines of disagreement. And that would mean a telling defeat for Christian love. Sometimes a victory can come at a cost so high that the victory is hollow and the truth is that everyone has lost.

This is one reason why, as I make my arguments in this book and elsewhere, I am committed to doing so in a way that is fair and honest about opposing perspectives, a way that resists the urge to make false generalizations.

That said, I don't intend to hold back or sugar-coat my arguments. If I think my opponents are making choices that betray Christian values, I will say so and say why. I may be blunt about practices I find egregious. But I hope to express my convictions in a spirit of openness and respect.

Victories can be won in ways that make everyone lose something precious. And just as there can be defeats in the midst of victory, so can there be deep victories in the midst of defeats. In fact, sometimes a defeat can spring from transformations so valuable that the defeat is trivial compared to what everyone has won.

Seeing those deeper victories amidst defeat often requires the same spirit of mutual respect I've been talking about. In a narrow sense, of course, the SCOTUS ruling and the broadening cultural acceptance of same-sex relationships are victories only for more progressive Christians like me. For conservatives, these changes represent a defeat. But not necessarily a defeat for *all* their values. Not necessarily a defeat for the values that matter most.

If a budding democracy cements its commitment to democratic methods, establishes a foundation for fair elections into the future and, through the first such election, chooses the candidate with the better hair, we ought to see that as a victory for democracy. And it will be a victory for democratic ideals even for those who think the winning candidate is only paying lip service to democratic ideals and doesn't represent them the way the losing candidate does.

Likewise, I'm convinced that Christian values have won something important in the cultural struggles culminating in legalized same-sex marriage—whether or not one thinks that same-sex marriage *as such* constitutes a victory.

Marriage Victorious

There are at least two reasons why this is so. One is this: as the gay community has sought access to marriage, they have been actively seeking for themselves the very constraints on sexual expression that Christianity has long taught are essential. This is an important and under-appreciated way in which Christian values have—as a result of the fight for same-sex marriage—expanded their reach and their perceived importance.

We need to remember that a number of scholars and gay rights activists on the far left have been strongly critical of marriage and hence opposed to the pursuit of marriage equality. Some of these critics are primarily worried about the patriarchy they see as inextricably bound up with traditional marriage. But for others, marriage as such is too confining, imposing limits on sexual expression that they don't want to see imposed. Gay rights leader Paula Ettelbrick argued in 1989 that marriage "runs contrary to two primary goals of the lesbian and gay movement: the affirmation of gay identity and culture and the validation of many forms of relationships."[8]

Some of Ettelbrick's concerns are ones I am inclined to embrace—for example, her worry that in practice the extension of legal marriage rights to same-sex couples will simply mean that "a simple certificate of the state, regardless of whether the spouses love, respect, or even see each other on a regular basis, dominates and is supported."[9] Surely most Christians would share the concern that what matters is not a legal certificate but the actual practice of flawed partners trying to live out a marital covenant with commitment and grace. But when Ettelbrick endorses "the goals of providing true alternatives to marriage and of radically reordering society's views of family,"[10] she is rejecting the central importance that Christians have given to marriage.

But the marriage-equality movement has lifted up that centrality. The triumph of that movement has been a triumph for the idea that marriage matters, that it offers a uniquely valuable if not indispensable space within which couples can safely express their sexuality and grow in love for one another. Wherever same-sex marriage has been legalized, same-sex couples have flocked to county clerk's offices for their licenses, waited in line to get married, celebrated the joyous union with friends and family—in short, treated marriage as the good that Christianity has always taken it to be.

But while I think this is an important victory for Christian values, it is not the most important one. Gays and lesbians have historically been treated as "other" in much the same way as blacks and Jews. That is, they have been targeted as a group for systematic marginalization and abuse. Dismissed as "sick" and "perverted," their very existence has been seen as something disgusting that needs to be hidden—and when gays and lesbians have refused to stay quietly in the closet, they've been targeted for overt harassment and violence. What such "othering" cannot allow is for gays and lesbians to have a public voice, one that people listen to with empathy and compassion.

All of this is antithetical to Christian love. And whatever else can be said about recent changes, the path to social acceptance of same-sex marriage was paved by a growing number of people, within the straight majority, refusing to participate in the ideological *othering* of their gay and lesbian

---

8. Paula Ettelbrick, "Since When," 124.
9. Ibid., 127.
10. Ibid., 128.

neighbors, choosing instead to acknowledge them and their stories, to hear them, to respond with compassion and empathy.

In other words, to love their gay and lesbian neighbors as themselves.

Love Victorious

Gays and lesbians are a small minority of the population. Without the help and support of the heterosexual majority, the cause of marriage equality would never have gotten off the ground. If there's been a triumph of same-sex marriage in the US and elsewhere, it's because the straight community has had a change of heart.

Many conservatives try to explain that change of heart in terms of the growing sexual permissiveness and moral laxness of secular culture. They think same-sex marriage is the result of decades of anything-goes relativism that's worn away at traditional restraints on sexual expression.

But does that story make sense?

Clearly, Western society has a problem with permissiveness and moral laxness. We don't help the poor nearly as much as we should. We indulge in meaningless entertainments and luxuries while children starve. We think the command to love our neighbors as ourselves is satisfied if we bring the new people next door a plate of home-baked cookies.

Americans routinely fail to live up to the demanding ethic of Christianity—and even those of us who self-identify as Christian typically shrug off these failures as if they were nothing. But while laxness and permissiveness can account for the gradual bleeding away of standards, they can't be what motivates an active effort to transform entrenched social institutions to include people who have been historically excluded.

Of course, laxness and permissiveness might, when combined with a sufficiently widespread desire for self-indulgence, motivate people to eliminate barriers to self-indulgence. But there are two problems with seeing this as an adequate explanation for the rise of same-sex marriage. First, marriage *imposes* barriers on self-indulgence. Access to marriage is about having access to an institution aimed at *reining in* sexuality, focusing it, limiting its expression to a single other human being.

But the deeper issue here is this: If you aren't gay, none of your self-indulgent motives could conceivably inspire you to work toward eliminating the barriers to same-sex intimacy. Because if you aren't gay, you won't want to have gay sex.

So even when laxness and permissiveness are combined with a penchant for self-indulgence, we won't get the social energy to drive the large-scale cultural and legal movement that we've witnessed. There aren't enough gay people out there for that.

Perhaps a defender of the conservative narrative might argue that a small, energized minority can effect substantial change without the help of the majority, so long as the majority doesn't care one way or the other about what the minority is doing. All that's needed from the majority is *apathy*.

But what we've witnessed is not a growing indifference to same-sex marriage. What we've witnessed is growing *support*. I've been teaching this topic in Oklahoma for fifteen years. In all that time, I have yet to meet a class of students that was largely indifferent about it. That hasn't changed over time. If anything, students have become more interested, more passionate, more engaged in this issue. At the same time, they have come out increasingly in favor of same-sex marriage.

And there is a deeper issue, one I'll return to in chapter 2: If homosexuality is the Big Sin, then most of us can avoid the Big Sin without any effort. The heterosexual majority is let off the moral hook without having to *do* anything. We can feel good about ourselves even as we buy a new widescreen TV with money that might have saved the lives of starving children. At least we're not gay.

A deliberate cultural shift toward accepting homosexuality amounts to a deliberate decision to wipe away an easy *cover* for moral laxness. If we want to explain why gays and lesbians are for the first time in history confronting the prospect of full social inclusion, we need to do it by appeal to the motives of a majority with no interest in having gay sex themselves— and who might actually use the condemnation of gay sex as a convenient mask for self-indulgence.

What could that motive be?

When I reflect on my own experience as a straight ally, the answer is clear. I became an ally because of my love for friends who came out to me, who told me their stories—stories that moved me, stories that enabled me to understand their experiences in a way I hadn't before. I have since then connected with many other allies, and they all say the same thing. They took up the cause out of compassion for their gay and lesbian neighbors.

On a weekend when the Oklahoma Ku Klux Klan abandoned its plan to protest a theologically progressive church because the weather was too cold, I shivered with dozens of others in a vigil line, holding images of gays and lesbians who'd been murdered or driven to suicide by social rejection. We stood together, gay and straight, outside a church that condemned homosexuality with such force that a congregant was inspired to attempt to have her grandchildren forcibly removed from her own daughter's home just because her daughter was living in a stable lesbian relationship.

Where hate failed to inspire the KKK to endure the cold, we stood shivering through two worship services. It wasn't permissiveness that inspired us to do that. And it wasn't self-indulgent impulses that made us return month after month, inviting dialogue, reaching out to congregants and deacons and clergy in an effort to help them understand the human impact of their more pugnacious rhetoric.

It wasn't moral laxness that led my wife and me to travel across the country the following spring—despite fighting a stomach virus—to join with hundreds of others to protest a denomination putting one of its clergy on trial because of whom she loved.

The kind of grassroots activism that inspires social change doesn't get its energy from libertinism and licentiousness. So where does it get that energy? One answer is from a sense of *justice*—but not justice in the abstract, and certainly not in the retributive sense that drives many to want to inflict harm. Rather, it is the sense of justice that springs from witnessing the suffering of others, the sense of justice that inspires us to act on their behalf.

It's the cry of the mother whose child has been hurt, of the brother whose sister has been knocked down. In other words, it's the justice that is a species of love.

I became an ally because I loved my gay friends, and because as I heard their stories and saw the impact of traditional teachings on their lives, I thought, "This is wrong."

I didn't think, "Right and wrong is all relative, so people should be free to do whatever they want." I thought, "This is wrong—absolutely, objectively *wrong*. This violates the law of love. This defies the fundamental moral truth that Jesus held up to the world two thousand years ago and is uncompromising in what it calls us to be."

Not all straight allies put things in such Christian language. Not all of them explicitly identify the urgings of conscience with the Christian law of love. But if there is a reason the straight majority has come to increasingly reject the historic condemnation of homosexuality, it has to do with our human capacity to identify with and empathize with those who are different from us. It has to do with the fact that not only have gays and lesbians been coming out of the closet more and more to tell their stories, but more and more straight people have been listening.

They've heard stories like the ones John told me, and like the ones that Mel White tells in *Stranger at the Gate: To Be Gay and Christian in America*. They've heard about what it's like to grow up at the margins, silenced and alone, forced to live a lie and constantly subjected to prejudicial assumptions about perversity and depravity that crush their longing for human love. What has increasingly happened in Western culture is that gays and lesbians have been telling their stories—and instead of ignoring or dismissing or denouncing them, instead of throwing up ideological walls against them, people have *paid attention*.

To pay attention to the neighbor, rather than hurrying by, is the first thing the Good Samaritan does. Christian love *starts* with attention and so must stand opposed to the common practice of othering—of identifying a whole class of people as unworthy not merely of equality but of the effort to see them as they are, to recognize their plight, to hear their anguished cries. If we want to understand why our culture changed its mind on same-sex marriage, the answer lies with this: growing attention to *what it's like to be gay*. As the majority came to empathize more deeply, they increasingly rejected the marginalization, the disdain, the gut-level disgust and ideological hatred that, for so long, has inspired the overt offenses of bullies and gay bashers as well as more subtle and systemic forms of marginalization.

Of course, conservatives might be convinced that society has reached the wrong conclusions. They could argue that while greater neighbor-love for gays and lesbians is commendable, same-sex marriage isn't what such love demands. They might be convinced (as I am not) that genuine love for gays and lesbians is compatible with the continued denunciation of their loving relationships and tender intimacies.

But even if this is true, it doesn't erase the greater love. And the growth of such love is a victory for the most important Christian value of all.

The spread of responsive, attentive, empathic concern for the good of our neighbors is, simply put, the spread of something Jesus singled out among all the virtues. We are a far cry from living out an ethic of love faithfully in this world. There are probably many ways in which we've become worse at it. But there are moments when the spirit of love makes itself felt on a social level, when it has the power to tip the scales in favor of changes that don't serve the interests of the majority, but instead favor a marginalized minority.

This book is premised on an important idea: all Christians, whatever they think about same-sex marriage, are called to be on the same side when it comes to loving our gay and lesbian neighbors and when it comes to opposing forces that promulgate hatred and division. This means that all Christians, whatever they think about same-sex marriage, should affirm the neighbor-love that has fueled the passions of social reformers, motivated straight allies in growing numbers, and shifted the consciences of witnesses. It means that all Christians should guard against unwittingly allying themselves with the dark forces that love contends against: the deep human tendency to perpetuate division, to exclude and scapegoat those who are different, and to reach for easy righteousness through the Pharisee's comforting mantra, "At least I'm not one of *them*" (Luke 18:11).

A first step toward achieving this common mission is understanding the ideas and psychological impulses that lie behind such forces of division and hate.

It is this subject I turn to next.

2

Fred Phelps Is Not Dead

According to the news reports, Fred Phelps—controversial founder and pastor of the hate-filled Westboro Baptist Church—died on March 19, 2014, at the age of eighty-four. After decades of preaching that "God hates fags" and leading protests at the funerals of gays and lesbians and (more recently) soldiers, Phelps was finally gone.

That's what they say. But Fred Phelps isn't dead.

Okay, technically he's dead. But I'm not talking about clinical death.

And I'm not talking about his immortal soul. I like to imagine that, in whatever post-mortem realm awaits us, Phelps has been moved to silent weeping by the radically inclusive love of God, and that the self-loathing he tried to slather onto others here on earth has started flaking off under the force of that love. I like to imagine that his old hateful mantra has been replaced by a new one: "Even me? You love *even me*?"

But when I say that Fred Phelps isn't dead, I mean that the signature Phelpsian hatred—wrapped up in a message of divine mandate, bow-tied with Bible-verses, and then shoved in our faces as if it were the gift of Christ to humanity—is alive and well.

And it comes at us in more and less blatant forms.

Thick Black Ink

Shortly after an essay of mine, "Gay Suicide and the Ethic of Love," appeared in an issue of *The Humanist*, I received a handwritten letter from someone named William who called himself a pastor. I've saved the letter. It's written in a thick black scrawl, as if the author's rage forced him to push the pen into the paper with as much force as he could muster. He frequently capitalized words and phrases for emphasis, and even more frequently underlined them (sometimes even resorting to double underlining).

On two occasions he drew frowny-faces in the margins. They're almost amusing if you can avoid reading what's written next to them.

William's letter is a testament to conviction. At one point he announces that "2+2 forever equals 4, not the 3, 7, 11 or 18 that you come up with." His aim, of course, is to express his unswerving certainty that his take on the issue of homosexuality is as beyond dispute as simple arithmetic. Those who think otherwise are voicing absurdities. Phrases like "phoney-baloney CRAP" (the underlining and capitalization are his) characterize his treatment of views that diverge from his own.

The heart of his message is captured in the following paragraphs, which I reproduce here in their entirety (with underlining and capitalization preserved):

> Despite the bully sinning against Zach Harrington, his deathstyle killed him. To blame us for revealing the evil of homosexuality and trying to protect society (especially children) is retarded insanity or simply willful sinning. Am I full of "self-righteous intolerance" for simply believing God and trying to obey him? NO, the blood is on your hands, Mr. Progressive Christian.
>
> Your cotton candy "law of love" is simply 1960's Situation Ethics warmed up. Who defines love, you and other progressives? To support and encourage people to engage in homosexuality (and other LGBT depravity) is to actually HATE people like Zach. I wonder if you are actually defending your own lifestyle. Well?
>
> Their love should be condemned, just like the "love" of incest, rape, bestiality and Muslims having up to 4 wives. And, of course, they CAN "change their intimate feelings" since NO ONE is born homosexual. One either chooses the lifestyle or is seduced into it. Ever hear the mantra "sex before eight or it is too late." How come only 2% of our population is homosexual, yet commit 33% of child sexual abuse??

Something of William's rage—not to mention the hatred and intolerance that he explicitly disavows—is lost when these paragraphs are typed, when the thick black ink, the palpable pressure against the paper, is severed from the words. But I suspect most readers will still feel the vitriol, and perhaps even shudder as I did the first time I opened the envelope and began to read.

I must confess that curiosity inspired me to Google his full name, which quickly produced a number of letters-to-the-editor, mostly on the subject of HIV/AIDS. His main point in these letters is this: we should only care about "the innocent victims of HIV/AIDS, not the immoral ones who bring this venereal disease on themselves."

Put another way, we should truncate the scope of our compassion. Before we reach out to those ravaged by a disease, we should investigate how they got it. And if sin is involved we should turn away in disgust, but not before blaming them for the misery and death of the innocent—as if the line between villain and victim could be drawn in thick black ink.

Sinners vs. Sin

William is not representative of Christians who condemn homosexuality. I know many Christians who have no trace of homophobia, who feel fondness and friendship for gays and lesbians, who would happily devote hours of compassionate care to an AIDS victim no matter how they contracted the disease—but who, when asked, would say they think homosexuality is a sin. It's a conclusion they're led to, sometimes grudgingly, by what they find in the Bible or in their theological tradition. These are the Christians who, when they say "love the sinner but hate the sin," actually sound sincere (at least about the "love the sinner" part; when it comes to the "hate the sin" part, it sometimes seems as if they are struggling—forcing out the words when pressed while trying to hide the tone of apology).

That used to be me. Once, in college, a friend and I were heading into the cafeteria from a Bible study group, and during small talk with the woman who ran our ID cards we identified ourselves as members of the InterVarsity Christian Fellowship on campus.

"Does that mean," she asked pointedly, "that you think all homosexuals are going to hell?"

The question made me cringe. This was a topic I'd rather avoid. But my friend gamely jumped into the silence, explaining that *of course* we didn't think all homosexuals were going to hell.

"So you don't think it's a sin?" she asked.

"Well, you know," I said, trying for a confidence I didn't feel, "we're all sinners."

"Homosexuality is a sin," my friend said, more willing than I to voice that message directly. "But so are lots of other things. God loves us in spite of our sins, and forgives us on account of Christ. We're supposed to do the same: love the sinner but hate the sin. It's what it means to be a Christian."

And I nodded my head enthusiastically. I almost breathed a sigh of relief, as if I'd gotten off the hook. *I was still a loving guy.*

And I went on my way, happily avoiding the issue for another few years.

I suspect that for every Pastor William there are dozens who are more like what I used to be: striving to love their "homosexual neighbors" while condemning the "sin" of homosexuality—and addressing the tensions embedded in that view by avoiding the topic.

It was only because I *couldn't* avoid the topic—because my best friend in graduate school came out to me as gay—that I found myself having to honestly confront what I believed. And when I did, my uneasy invocation of the "love the sinner" mantra crumbled (and rather quickly, I might add) before the practical implications of categorically condemning all homosexual sex. I couldn't do it. I couldn't live out those implications, because it seemed obvious to me that doing so would be a failure of love. But why that's so is an issue I will explore more fully in the chapters to come.

My point here is that many Christians sincerely want to love their gay and lesbian neighbors, and they recognize that the ugliness we find in William's words is deeply at odds with the spirit of Christian love.

But none of that means we can simply ignore William's letter. While most Christians, regardless of what they think about homosexuality and same-sex marriage, will quickly distance themselves from such venomous ideas, what they are distancing themselves from is a *distillation*. It's a purified form of something that usually wears a nicer face and hides behind gentler language. Most of the time it keeps company with kinder sentiments, wiser ideas, and more loving practices. And so it can be hard to see it for what it is. In a way, William's letter and Westboro's hateful signs do us a favor. They expose something that's most insidious when hidden.

Ideologies of Division

What they expose is ideological hate, a phenomenon whose structure and psychological underpinnings are beautifully characterized by Jean-Paul Sartre in *Anti-Semite and Jew*. Sartre points out that taking responsibility for creating meaningful lives can be frightening. It is hard work fraught with the risk of failure. And so we try to hide from it, and one common hiding place is in mythologies of division: anti-Semitism and racism and other ideologies that divide the world into in-groups and out-groups, Children of Light and Children of Darkness.

This mythology has a pair of crucial elements. The first is the notion that you have value simply by belonging to the right group. But notice that the conferred value is comparative. There needs to be a *wrong* group: the outsiders, the Children of Darkness. In the face of all our failings, this mythology allows us to say, "Well, at least I'm not one of *them*." Sartre expresses this idea in the following way:

> By treating the Jew as an inferior and pernicious being, I affirm at the same time that I belong to the elite. This elite, in contrast to those of modern times which are based on merit or labor, closely resembles an aristocracy of birth. There is nothing I have to do to merit superiority, and neither can I lose it. It is given once and for all.[1]

The second key element of this mythology has to do with scapegoating. If you're especially valuable just because of belonging to the chosen group, then you should be uniquely happy as well, even if you do nothing to achieve it. Unless, that is, there's some evil systematically operating to thwart your happiness.

And that is precisely what the Children of Darkness are: the evil that menaces the happiness of the Children of Light. "Underneath the bitterness of the anti-Semite," Sartre writes, "is concealed the optimistic belief that harmony will be re-established of itself, once Evil is eliminated."[2] For anti-Semites, of course, Jews are this evil, and destroying them or beating them down is the solution.

This sort of thinking is seductive. It's so much easier to destroy than to create. If our happiness depends on our own creative effort, we only have ourselves to blame for our misery. How much easier to imagine that it's the fault of an enemy, and that joy and peace will bloom all around us, all on its own, once the enemy is crushed.

Christianity is, by its nature, ill-suited to this sort of bifurcating ideology. First of all, the Christian faith teaches that we are, all of us, in bondage to sin and cannot free ourselves. And it teaches that all of us carry the stamp of our perfect creator: the image of God. We're all stuck in this common

---

1. Jean Paul Sartre, *Anti-Semite and Jew*, 27.
2. Ibid., 43

human dilemma, characterized by an essence that's profoundly good and a lived reality that falls so far short of our potential.

More profoundly, Christianity teaches that when it comes to the creative effort to build meaningful lives, we aren't alone after all. The fear of failure is mitigated by the promise of cosmic redemption. Working for the good isn't a way to *earn* our happiness or salvation. It's an effect of embracing the unmerited gift of God's grace. The solution to our imperfection isn't scapegoating but divine forgiveness. And when it comes to the daunting project of creating the good despite our inadequacies, it isn't accomplished by pretending all we need is to destroy some enemy. It's achieved by becoming instruments of a God of love, channeling that love into the world.

Christians, unlike Sartre, do not believe that we face the burden of human existence all alone. For Christians, Sartre's existential predicament, the one that drives fearful people to hide behind hateful ideologies, is an illusion. And so, from a Christian standpoint, those who seek self-worth by vilifying others are further from the truth that even Sartre took them to be. For Sartre, anti-Semites are fleeing their existential predicament rather than facing it honestly. For Christians, anti-Semites are fleeing something that doesn't even exist. Where Sartre saw one error—the decision to hide from responsibility for our lives—Christians must posit a second: imagining we face that responsibility in a world without God.

It's naïve to think Christians are immune to these errors. The impulse to divide the world into the good and the bad is strong. One might even say we're in bondage to it. And the condemnation of homosexuality offers a distinctive opportunity for this impulse to creep into our lives, put on Christian clothes, and undermine the Christian hope by masquerading as it.

What is distinctive about homosexuality is that it names both a pattern of behavior and an inner disposition. The latter is more basic. Possessing a homosexual orientation—a stable and unchosen disposition to be attracted sexually and romantically to the same sex—is a fact about who gays and lesbians are, just as heterosexual orientation is a fact about who straight people are (and bisexual orientation is a fact about who bisexuals are). Whether it's a fact central to *identity* is a different matter. I can be something—white, say, or Norwegian—without it defining me. The place of sexuality in our identity is something I'll explore in chapter 7. For now, it's enough to point out that in its basic sense, being gay or lesbian is something you *are*, not something you *do*.

There is something disingenuous in Pastor William's insistence that sexual orientation is chosen rather than discovered. While there are complexities to this question of choice that I'll take up in chapter 4 (including questions about whether sexual orientation can be changed once it is discovered), most of us intuitively grasp that none of us decided one day to be attracted to the same sex or the opposite sex (or both). Gays and lesbians don't choose to be gay, and it isn't just the psychological community that's convinced of this. Adolescent gay bashers—euphemistically called "bullies"—know it. They target the "faggots" in their midst long before those targets have become sexually active; long before they've "chosen a homosexual lifestyle." It's who those young gay men *are* that these bashers loathe—not what they do.

But to have a homosexual orientation is to have the disposition to *do* certain things, namely what goes along with romantic and sexual attraction: falling in love, making love, snuggling, uttering vows of devotion, forming partnerships, experiencing break-ups and heartbreak, pining with unrequited longing, writing absurd love poems. It's the disposition to do all the things that human beings are inclined to do in love, but with members of one's own sex.

Because homosexuality straddles the line between something gays and lesbians *are* and something they *do*, it becomes possible to despise the former in the guise of denouncing the latter. It becomes possible, in other words, to do all the things that Sartre sees the anti-Semite do: first, divide the world between *us* and *them* and make our worth hinge on not being one of *them*; second, make *them* the scapegoats for our failures and disappointments. It becomes possible to do all of this in the guise of taking a stand against immoral *behavior*.

Progressives on this issue often puzzle over why conservative Christians single out homosexuality for such attention and moral outrage when it is barely mentioned in the Bible and there are stronger biblical grounds for condemning a pastor who spends money on a new car while children are starving in Bangladesh.

Here, I think, is the reason: as with the majority of the population, most Christians aren't gay or bisexual. In other words, most Christians aren't sexually attracted to members of the same sex. And this means that, for most Christians, it is *incredibly easy* to avoid the supposed sin of same-sex sex. It requires no effort. For most of us, the prohibition on such activity is a call to refrain from doing something that, because of our innate sexuality, we have no temptation to do.

For me, as a straight man, avoiding gay sex requires about as much will-power as avoiding the consumption of raw sea cucumbers—something I was once required by etiquette to sample. I gagged on the first bite and hope never to have to confront one of those slimy, cartilaginous lumps of embodied nausea again. At least not on a plate.

The point is this: if the moral injunction not to have gay sex is the one that *really matters*, most Christians can feel great about themselves without having to do anything. They can be among the people favored by God without effort—just because they have the good luck to be straight. Gays and lesbians have to be thrown to the wolves, of course, but the bigotry here can be obscured in a way that more conventional racist bigotry cannot. It's *what they do* that puts them beyond the pale. If they only made a better choice, they could be good like us.

Every time homosexuality gets treated as an especially grievous sin—every time a Christian buys new designer shoes with money that could have fed starving people, and then shakes their head at what the world is coming to when a gay couple seeks the right to marry—we witness the easy righteousness that comes from the mythology of division. The Aristocracy of Heterosexuality: "At least I'm not one of them."

What about the second element, the scapegoating that treats the failures of the chosen group as the outsiders' fault? You needn't look far to see this element at work in conservative Christianity. And I'm not referring to Westboro Baptist Church here, or Pastor William. I'm referring to James Dobson and Focus on the Family, the conservative Christian organization Dobson founded.

Division with a Loving Face

Focus on the Family's stated purpose is to provide Christian resources for building healthier and happier families. Not long ago I was on a road trip and, while station-hopping on the radio, heard the name "James Dobson." I paused, because for me the name is fraught with significance. What I got was advice on what to do if your child suddenly declares, "I hate you!"

The advice struck me as excellent. It modeled a compassionate response that affirmed the child's feelings but distinguished those feelings from the way they'd been expressed, inviting the child to apply the Golden Rule, to think about how it would feel to be told, "I hate you."

What I was listening to was a message played on a Christian radio station and put out by Focus on the Family. I found myself thinking that here, in this message, was a beautiful modeling of how Christ's love ethic might be communicated between a parent and child at a moment of conflict and hurt. And so I must stress that, whatever my complaints about Focus on the Family, there are dimensions of this organization that embody the spirit of love, that attend sensitively and helpfully to child-rearing issues and to challenges that married couples face. Dobson and Focus on the Family are not Phelps and Westboro Baptist Church.

But parts of their message are disturbingly similar. If we look carefully at the range of advice coming from Dobson and Focus on the Family, what we find is guidance for building a family that fits a very specific *blueprint*. The elements of that blueprint shouldn't come as a surprise: traditional gender roles for husbands and wives, differential child-rearing of boys and girls, and—above all else—monogamous *heterosexual* partnership as the bedrock of every family. Families that don't fit this blueprint are defective. No matter how nurturing, how compassionate, how faithful and monogamous and mutually supportive same-sex partners are, they can't be "real families" at all.

But the message goes deeper than this. Despite the Christian love that characterizes some of Dobson's teachings and rhetoric, something like Pastor William's overt divisiveness breaks through when the topic turns to homosexuality. "For more than 40 years," Dobson claims, "the homosexual activist movement has sought to implement a master plan that has had as its centerpiece the utter destruction of the family."[3]

Utter destruction! And it is the mere existence of socially recognized same-sex families that will accomplish this destruction: "Traditional marriage between one man and one woman cannot co-exist with homosexual marriage. It will destroy the family."[4]

Arguments for something like this view, expressed in less catastrophic terms, have been offered—and I will explore later why I find them uncompelling. But even the strongest versions of such arguments cannot justify Dobson's rhetoric of calamity. What such rhetoric conveys is the urgency and divisiveness of war: *we* are threatened by *them*. A same-sex couple rearing children with tenderness and care is not a family but a *threat* to it. The survival of the heterosexual family depends upon breaking those homosexual families apart or, failing that, at least denying them social and legal legitimacy.

Dobson's rhetoric goes deeper still. In his book *Bringing Up Boys*, he maintains that one of the keys to raising healthy boys is protecting them from the pernicious influence of "homosexuals." According to Dobson, homosexuals have an agenda and a movement, and its goal is nothing short of sexual access to children, especially boys, for the sake of converting them to homosexuality. He warns about the homosexual "movement" pursuing

3. Statement appeared in the April 2004 *Focus on the Family Newsletter.* Quoted in Lutes, *A False Focus,* 6.

4. Stated during a May 23, 2004 television address, "The Battle for Marriage," simulcast to hundreds of churches. Quoted in ibid.

its "desire to gain access to boys" by, for example, purportedly campaigning to lower the legal age of sexual consent.[5] The rhetoric here is designed to inspire fear: fear of the other, fear of those who are different. "Moms and dads, are you listening?" he says. "This movement is *the* greatest threat to your children. It is a particular danger to your wide-eyed boys, who have no idea what demoralization is planned for them."[6]

We have here the same identification of homosexuality with pedophilia that we found in Pastor William's letter. This is no accident. William actually sent me a booklet, "The Top Ten Myths about Homosexuality," put out by the Family Research Council, a conservative Christian group founded by Dobson and devoted to opposing legal or social recognition for families that don't fit its norm. William's claim about the rate of homosexual child molestation comes directly from this booklet.

The booklet's author, Peter Sprigg, supports this conclusion not by appeal to a particular study (there isn't one, although there are studies that contest it) but by engaging in a confusing and confused inferential process based on statistics drawn from tangentially-related studies linked with the help of dubious assumptions and equivocation. I'm not exaggerating. The reasoning really is that flawed—and in chapter 5 I will take Sprigg's argument seriously enough to show just how much of a waste of time it was to expend the intellectual energy to take it seriously. For now, I want to focus on how this linkage between homosexuality and pedophilia works to subvert parental protective instincts and direct them against gays and lesbians. The focus on vulnerable, wide-eyed *boys* (even though girls are more often the victims of childhood sexual abuse) also taps into patriarchal sentiments about male sexuality and its debasement.

The thinking generated by this kind of rhetoric is predictable. The primary task of parenting becomes a pugnacious one: destroy the enemies who threaten our children. And Dobson is clear who these enemies are. The greatest threat to our children isn't drugs or school violence or poor educational systems or a rapidly degrading natural environment. It isn't neglect or abuse. *It's homosexuals.*

As a father, I know that parenting is hard and frustrating work. And so it's easy for me to see the allure of this kind of message. The mystery and distress of *not knowing what to do* is taken out of parenting. In the midst of our wrestling to find the balance between overindulging our children and being too strict, Dobson says, "Look here. Here is the enemy." As we anguish over how to simultaneously nurture independence and impose

---

5. Dobson, *Bringing Up Boys*, 125.
6. Ibid., 127.

healthy boundaries, Dobson offers a simpler channel for our energies: *keep the perverts out of our schools.*

The Christian answer to these human struggles is the promise that God is with us, wise where we are foolish, loving our children through us even where we fall short, and redeeming our failures. And to be fair, Dobson knows this and preaches this. But that message is combined with and thereby diminished by the competing answer offered by divisive ideology, which points to a different refuge from the anguish of the human condition: it's us versus them. We have an enemy to blame.

Cloaked in Christian language and embedded in parenting and marital advice that is genuinely helpful, we have here a mythology of division that in itself has nothing to do with building healthy families and everything to do with vilifying gays and lesbians and the families they create. In the hermetically-sealed environment of such an ideology, any home that does not fit the paradigm *cannot* be healthy or happy, no matter how much laughter and love fill its walls.

It is for all of these reasons that, on May 2, 2005, Soulforce paid a visit to Focus on the Family's Colorado Springs headquarters. Soulforce is a national organization committed to using the nonviolent methods pioneered by Gandhi and King to end what they call "spiritual violence" against sexual minorities. Their aim that day was to express the ways in which Dobson's anti-gay rhetoric was harming real-world families. At the head of the Soulforce group was one family in particular: Phil and Randi Reitan and their son Jake.

Phil is my first cousin, and Phil and Randi are the godparents of my son. Their son, Jake, is a bright, talented young man with a profound vision for social justice and the courage and commitment to act on that vision. He is also gay. And because of the kinds of teachings coming out of organizations such as Focus on the Family, Jake was being systematically denied social and legal privileges that heterosexuals take for granted—such as the right, in most states, to legally marry the person he loves, or to become a rostered minister in most church denominations.

And so my relatives stood before the entrance to the Focus on the Family complex, and Randi read aloud a letter in which she pleaded with Dobson to soften his harmful rhetoric. In the letter, she talked about the love that was alive in their family, and the pride they had for Jake, "a courageous young man who feels a passion for justice." And she talked about her fears for him. "We have had 'fag' scrawled on our driveway, raw eggs in our mailbox, pink paint balls peppering the front of our home, lamp posts broken, unsigned letters filled with terrible messages mailed to our home and Jake's car window smashed into a million pieces."

It was these fears that brought Phil and Randi and Jake to Focus on the Family's doors. "People are taught to hate," Randi said. "People are taught to be intolerant. As Christians, we must teach God's love for all his beloved children by our love and our actions."

When she finished reading, the three of them moved forward to hand-deliver the letter.

They were promptly arrested for trespassing.[7]

A Battle for Christianity's Soul

My point is that the message found in Pastor William's letter is not so far removed from messages emerging from a large and highly influential conservative Christian organization. In both, we find the mythology of division. As my cousins faced arrest at the doors of the Focus on the Family complex, they were engaged in something far more significant than a dispute over an isolated teaching or a quibble about the meaning of Romans 1:26–27. They were part of a fight for the soul of Christianity.

It isn't a fight between good guys and bad guys, between Children of Light and Children of Darkness, in-groups and out-groups. Rather, it's a battle between the spirit of compassion and the spirit of division, between love and hate, between exclusion and embrace. The enemy isn't Dobson, but the ideology of division that, at least when he turns his thoughts to homosexuality, has taken possession of him. The hero isn't Randi Reitan, entreating Dobson to speak with a more compassionate voice. The hero is the love that is moving in and through her as she speaks. It's not a war between people, the good and the bad. It's a war between the opposing forces that live and move in every one of us.

There are many sincere Christians who, in this struggle, would sooner side with my cousins, pleading for compassion at a silent gate, than with the purveyors of divisiveness—but who, nevertheless, insist that homosexuality is a sin. In an important sense these Christians are on the same side of the struggle that I find myself on. This is one of the reasons I think the current conflict in the church, while occasioned by the question of homosexuality's moral status, touches on a struggle far more important. Whatever you think of same-sex relationships, the legal and social acceptance of them is a lesser evil, surely, than a Christianity recast in the image of racism and anti-Semitism, a Christianity transformed by the ideology of hate.

---

7. These events were covered by various news sources (for example, see Emery, "Family Arrested"), but the details of Randi Reitan's letter were not included in these reports.

In other words, it is crucial that as Christians struggle with how to respond to the burgeoning cultural acceptance of same-sex relationships, they do so in a way that prioritizes the law of love. Ideological hatred has latched onto homosexuality. It can be tempting for those who think same-sex marriage is wrong to reach for ideas that serve their cause, without thinking carefully enough about the deeper implications of those ideas. Ideological hate has power. It has a track record of firing up groups, of mobilizing them into action—albeit action that destroys rather than creates, that builds walls instead of bridges, that forges enmity instead of fellowship.

Even if conservative Christians oppose same-sex marriage for reasons that have nothing to do with such ideological hate, it can be tempting to ally themselves with forces that display this kind of mobilizing power. But to do that is to lend strength to something that challenges the heart of Christianity more fundamentally than any question about who gets to build a romantic partnership with whom.

By the same token, however, progressives on this issue need to resist the temptation to lump every Christian conservative in with those whose ideas and messages have been shaped by ideological hate. Not long ago I read a thought-provoking and beautifully-written book by Jenell Williams Paris, *The End of Sexual Identity*. Paris is an anthropologist at Messiah College, and a devout Christian. Her experiences with gay friends—including the loss of a friend, who defensively called her a homophobe when Paris "stood up for her faith" by declaring homosexuality a sin—have led Paris to a deep concern for the ideological divisiveness that defines much Christian discourse about sexuality.

At one point in her book, she explicitly addresses the dangers of divisive ideology. As she puts it, "Processes of 'othering' should alert us to probable injustice."[8] Talking about the pervasive human tendency for groups to "create 'us' and 'them' categories" in which "they" deserve less than "us" and "may even receive disregard and violence," Paris makes a point in tune with the ones I've been making here: "Regardless of our moral stances regarding same-sex sex, Christians should be aware of and attentive to ways in which sexual others are at risk for cruelty, discrimination, and violence."[9] To address these dangers, Paris calls for a "post-sexual identity church" in which "there's no moral high ground for heterosexuals and no closet for homosexuals. There's just people, each of whom is lover and loved."[10]

---

8. Paris, 71.
9. Ibid.
10. Ibid., 92

But in *The End of Sexual Identity,* Paris expresses this call to transcend divisive categories and to love across differences from a personal stance that remains conservative with respect to sexual ethics. Here's how she expresses her position:

> My views are conservative—I'm a "sex only within marriage between a man and a woman" kind of Christian—but I am well aware that Christians of good faith disagree about the meaning of personal sexual holiness. Maligning those with whom we disagree, even to the point of questioning the validity of their faith or salvation, is counterproductive and damages the witness of our religion as a whole, which is supposed to be comprised of believers from many times and places united in their devotion to Jesus, not to a set of beliefs about sexuality.[11]

I disagree with the conservative view of same-sex relationships. I think love demands that we set aside the categorical condemnation of homosexuality, for reasons I will develop in detail in the coming chapters. But it is clear that the perspective Paris articulates in *The End of Sexual Identity* is motivated by a sincere desire to do what love demands. And this includes a sincere desire to love her gay and lesbian neighbors as herself.

She is not homophobic. She is not endorsing an ideology of hate. And to treat her as if her outlook were no different from Pastor William's, to put her in the same category as Fred Phelps just because she says "I am a 'sex only within marriage between a man and a woman' kind of Christian," smacks of ideological division: it's us against them, and she's said the one thing sufficient to make her one of *them.*

A hallmark of ideological division is the tendency to see our neighbors, not as unique human beings in all their individual complexity, but as nothing but members of the reviled group: Jews or faggots. Or, as the case may be, homophobes.

Let me be clear: I think that even divorced from ideological hate, the belief that all same-sex intimacy is sinful does harm to gays and lesbians. It pushes them toward personal identity narratives defined by inner and outer struggle over their sexuality, as I argue in chapter 7; and it not only deprives them of the distinctive array of goods that marriage provides but in so doing puts them at the margins of society, as I argue in chapter 8. This is why I think obedience to the love command requires us to abandon the categorical condemnation of homosexuality. But one can try to make that case without mischaracterizing the motives and convictions of those Christians who are conscious of the dangers of divisive ideologies, who warn against

---

11. Ibid., 85

them even as they confess conservative beliefs about the ethics of same-sex intimacy, and who repeatedly stress the primacy of a love that cares about and seeks fellowship with gays and lesbians.

Love can and does call us to disagree when we think our neighbor is wrong—but it calls us to disagree in a distinctive way. The disagreement must be shaped and informed by compassionate attention, by an understanding of our neighbor's actual convictions and what lies behind them. To refuse to see how Jenell Williams Paris is different from James Dobson—or, for that matter, how James Dobson is different from Fred Phelps—betrays a failure of such attention. As soon as we glibly lump together those who disagree with us on an issue, we have moved away from the stance that love demands. We have drifted, instead, toward the kind of crude *othering* that is the first step toward ideological hate.

Those who embrace the perspective Paris lays out in *The End of Sexual Identity* are on the same side as I am with respect to the struggle that matters most—the struggle against ideological hate, the struggle to live out the ethic of love with integrity. And here's another point about that struggle, one we cannot forget on pain of losing the struggle before we've begun: *those who promulgate ideologies of hate do not comprise an out-group that we should define ourselves against.*[12] We must, no matter what our beliefs, resist the temptation to say, "At least I'm not one of those homophobes."

Progressives are not immune to the subtle lure of hatred-in-disguise. It would be painfully easy for progressive Christians to treat Fred Phelps, Pastor William, James Dobson, and the rest as Children of Darkness, to fall prey to the idea that if only we can cast the fundamentalists down from their places of influence, human happiness will blossom on its own.

What Christian love demands is that we reject the vitriol of Pastor William, not that we reject *him*. What Christian love demands is that we say *no* to the pattern of scapegoating that Dobson endorses in some of his rhetoric, not that we say no to Dobson. It also demands that when I walk into my daughter's gymnastics studio (chewing a granola bar, as it happens) and see a beautiful quote from Dobson printed on the whiteboard as the day's inspirational message, I be willing to concede, "James Dobson is more than the ideology that he falls prey to when he thinks about homosexuality."

And this very point leads me to reflect back critically on the title of this chapter, and the rhetoric that started my reflection: the identification of ideological hatred with Fred Phelps. There is a tragic truth lying behind that

---

12. Of course, we *can* define ourselves against hate and acts of hate without defining ourselves against the persons who are gripped by hate. And as Christians, that is something I believe we *must* do.

identification: Fred Phelps became consumed by his hate. Divisive ideology charted the course of his life and defined his legacy.

But Fred Phelps remains a beloved child of God. And that makes him far more than his legacy of hate. If his spirit is alive in Pastor William and others, it is only in this sense: the force that took hold of his life lies in each of us. It is at work in each of us, including me. Part of what it means to be Christian is to acknowledge this, but also to see that force as something we can and must resist with the help of God.

Phelps and his Westboro congregation have, for years now, taken very public delight in the thought of gays and lesbians roasting in eternal torment. And to the extent that any of us takes delight in the thought of Fred Phelps roasting in a fire just as hot, we do our part to keep his spirit alive.

3

Christian Love

What does is it look like to love your neighbor as yourself?
When I'm teaching Christian ethics and ask this of my students, they'll typically mention such things as mowing the elderly neighbor's lawn or sitting with grandma in the nursing home. That's what comes to mind first for them: caring for the elderly and infirm. What doesn't come to mind first is this: hanging on a cross, dying in agony for the sake of saving the angry, jeering crowd that wants you dead.

I don't hold this against my students. There may be reasons why the crucifixion shouldn't be the first thing that comes to mind when we picture loving our neighbors as ourselves. Christians are called not to be saviors but *disciples* of the savior—not to die for the sins of the world but to embody in this time and place, amidst all our merely human flaws, the transforming love that blazes down from the cross.

To know what that looks like, we might need an *intermediate* role model, someone who exemplifies what it's like for flawed and finite people to strive to live out a spirit of love. For me, especially when it comes to the controversies over homosexuality and same-sex marriage, that role model is a little gay man named Don.

Love from the Easement

In January of 2002, Soulforce in Oklahoma—a local chapter of the national organization devoted to nonviolently promoting social justice for sexual minorities—lined up on a city easement. They stood across the street from a large Southern Baptist congregation in the Oklahoma City area, Village Baptist Church, holding signs and a banner urging the end of "spiritual violence against God's lesbian, gay, bisexual, and transgendered children." For several cold hours they sang Christian songs like "Yes, Jesus Loves Me" and protest songs like "We Shall Overcome." They stood in silent prayer for the people of Village Baptist Church. They took turns at a microphone telling stories of how anti-gay teachings had impacted their lives.

I say "they." I should say "we." My wife and I were among the roughly fifty people who stood, shivering, on that easement. So was our friend Don.

Don is a gay Quaker I got to know when we co-facilitated several Alternatives to Violence workshops. A small, white-bearded man who'd look at home in Santa's workshop, Don has a kind of quiet dignity that's warm and melancholy at once, as if he's always just shy of crying for all the beauty and tragedy in the world. When you meet him, you want to hug him. It was because of Don's connections to Soulforce that my wife and I first became involved with that group and, ultimately, with the monthly vigils at Village Baptist Church. The first vigil that January was the culmination of months of effort to engage church leaders in dialogue about their teachings on homosexuality.

Several months before, a member of the church sought to have her grandchildren forcibly removed from her daughter's home. Not because the children were being abused or neglected, but because their mother was in a lesbian relationship. The grandmother was inspired by the teachings of her pastor, who was in turn reflecting Southern Baptist teachings. She was sincerely afraid that a lesbian relationship posed an imminent threat to the welfare of her grandchildren, a fear fueled by what she learned in church.

Soulforce sought out the church leadership with a proposal: pursue a joint, monthly study group, where members of the Village Baptist Church community could sit down with members of Soulforce to discuss homosexuality. Leading these efforts was Karen, the president of Soulforce in Oklahoma, who had a personal stake in the case: it was her sister who'd faced the prospect of having her children torn from her; and it was her mother who'd sought to have it done. Karen wrote letters and met with the pastor, and for a while it seemed as if the study group might actually happen. But then negotiations broke down.

And so the vigils began. Once a month, as best we could, we pursued dialogue from the easement. Some of us wrote letters, and in response to mine the pastor agreed to meet with me. We had a long conversation in his office. He referred to the protesters as "them" as if I weren't one of them—perhaps because he knew I was straight. "You can't talk to those people," he said, even though he was talking to me.

It became quickly apparent he had no intention of permitting a joint study group in his church. For him, any such group would only risk leading church members astray. As he put it, "The Bible is clear."

At one point I invited him to imagine an adolescent boy in his church who was just discovering he was gay, a boy who'd never acted on his sexuality but whose feelings were unambiguous. He was romantically drawn not to girls but to other boys, and those feelings persisted in the face of the Southern Baptist teaching that "even desire to engage in a homosexual sexual relationship is always sinful, impure, degrading, shameful, unnatural, indecent and perverted."[1]

What would the pastor say to an adolescent secretly carrying those labels, perhaps berating himself with them day after day? "*I* am sinful; *I* am impure; *I* am unnatural, indecent, perverted." What might he do to help that boy avoid the path of suicidal despair that so many gay teens stumble down?

I asked him to imagine a gay *boy*, not a lesbian girl, because I thought it might be easier for him. I was, I think, being condescending: I didn't take him for a man especially skilled at empathy, at least not toward those very different from himself.

As I recall, he answered my question by saying he'd listen to the boy's struggles and advise him to find a solution in the Word and Will of God. He left the substance of his advice as vague as that, with only one clarification: he'd remind the boy that under no conditions could he act on his feelings.

His answer struck me as naïve. Even if the pastor's door was open, I doubted the boy I had in mind would walk through it. I thought, *Maybe that's why the pastor can be so vague about what he'd say and do. Because he knows that all of this is purely hypothetical.* No gay child would ever dare approach him, for fear of having the pastor's voice add depth and resonance to all that self-loathing, all those soul-crushing words the child told himself each day.

I walked away from the meeting trembling with emotions I couldn't name. But in hindsight there is something I must confess. I walked into that meeting expecting to meet the self-righteous Pharisee. And that prejudicial expectation never wavered. Perhaps his carefully schooled mannerisms and

---

1. Southern Baptist Convention, "Resolution," para. 11.

scripted words made it easy: he played a role and never let it drop, while I imposed a stereotype and never let it drop. Our meeting was a ritual. There were ideas and arguments, but there was no human connection. His full humanity never encountered mine.

I did not love him as myself.

One vigil Sunday, a member of our group, Danny, decided that he needed to worship with the congregation. "I had to know for myself," he said. "Did they really hate us—me—so much?"[2]

But his decision to visit was also about the courage to face a painful past. Danny had grown up Southern Baptist. His father had thrown him out when he was fifteen. As he approached the church, memories flooded in: "As I walked up the VBC steps I remembered my childhood, and as I did each step seemed heavier. Would I make it to the top? I wanted to turn and run. *I can't do this."*

But he did it. Greeters seized his hands, their welcome feeling almost like an attack.

Before and during the service, he imagined that the darting glances were about recognition: they knew he was one of the protesters. An old woman sat next to him and held his hand. That gesture—I imagine mottled fingers enclosing his, a pat on the knuckles, maybe the scent of sweet perfume—was surely meant to comfort and welcome. But for Danny, it meant that if things became unbearable, it would be harder to escape.

During the sermon, it seemed to Danny that the pastor's eyes kept returning to him "every time he landed hard on the word 'sinner.'" He distracted himself by looking at the stained-glass windows:

> So beautiful. Yet, the more I looked, the more I realized I wanted to be on the outside of those windows, with people whom I loved and I knew loved me. I knew the only romantic love I would ever experience was with another man, and that fact, how I am able to love, was condemned by those around me.

After the service he almost fled the sanctuary. What was for others like a second home was for him oppressive, and he breathed relief when Karen greeted him from the vigil line, when he could join his friends on the easement. For some the windy margins feel more like home, because the love of friends who welcome you as you are is more beautiful than stained glass.

The monthly vigils continued. Every month we smiled and greeted congregants as they passed us on their way in and out of church. Many watched through windows and doorways as we sang, prayed, and stood in

---

2. Quotes are from unpublished correspondence.

silence, but especially as we shared our stories and reflections from the strip of grass beside the road.

Once, on a particularly cold winter day, the deacons came out with hot drinks. Coffee or cocoa, I can't remember which. Sometimes we had conversations with congregants after church. Some made plans to meet for coffee. When Mel White, founder of Soulforce, joined us one Sunday morning, his presence brought out the pastor, who invited him in for worship.

It's hard, in retrospect, to decide how much of this was real human connection, and how much pretense: I smile at you, you bring me coffee, we'll prove to each other how much we live out Christ's command to love our enemies.

I'm sure there was plenty of pretense.

But there was also Don. Don knew no pretense. He shamed me with the authenticity of his love. After every vigil we'd meet at an open and affirming church to debrief and reflect. At one of those meetings Don talked about the faces of those he saw going in and out of Village Baptist Church: human faces, mothers and fathers, grandmothers and clumsy children. Like so many, Don's history with churches like this did not lead him to think of them as places of hope. What they offered wasn't the gospel but soul-crushing rejection. He joined the vigils because he believed in standing up against oppression. But what Don saw from the vigil line was humanity.

And he wept. He stood amidst our group, this tiny man, and he wept at the humanity of his oppressors. No pretense. No prejudices. Just the heart of a man beating with shared humanity.

He also wept for the gay and lesbian adolescents who were part of that congregation. He talked about seeing a boy in the doorway, watching us in fascination and wonder. What were we to him? People who self-identified as Christian, who sang hymns and prayed and spoke about the inclusive love of God from the edge of the road. "Maybe it's the first time that boy has ever believed it was possible, to be acceptable to God even though he's gay. That's why we do this. That's why we can't stop."

The boy I'd asked the pastor to imagine wasn't hypothetical at all. Don had seen him watching us from the doorway. And Don knew—we all knew because of stories like Danny's—something about what it's like to be that boy.

Don returned to the vigil line every month out of love: love for those who looked at the stained glass windows, so beautiful, and longed to be in some imagined world beyond the glass, where how they were able to love didn't trigger condemnation. Danny knew that other world was there, but for that unnamed boy in the doorway the vigil line was his first inkling it might be real.

Don never wavered in his conviction that Village Baptist's teachings were wrong. The congregation perpetuated them without understanding their effects, blind to the children who were pushed ever closer to despair. And yet he saw in their faces a humanity like his own, and he felt that fellowship so deeply he wept.

Then, one hot summer morning in late June, Don and his friend Rob decided it was time to worship at Village Baptists Church. It wasn't a vigil day, and they didn't come anonymously. They wore small Soulforce pins, and by then their faces were familiar. Don—the endearing little white-bearded man in denim overalls—isn't easy to forget. And Rob is blind and so might have been remembered for that reason. When they walked in the doors, everyone knew: these were members of the group that had stood vigil outside Village Baptist Church, in snow and rain and heat, for six months.

For Danny, attending worship had been an exercise in courage: a journey like his namesake's, into the lion's den. For Don and Rob, it was an extension of what had made Don weep. Don and Rob came to pursue fellowship with those whose teachings they found oppressive. An exercise in shared humanity across lines of conflict.

"For the last six months," Don told the Sunday School class they attended, "we've been outside with the Soulforce vigils. We wanted to come *inside* so we could meet and get to know some of the church members."[3]

They were greeted warmly. Several people invited them to sit with them during worship. As the service started, Don marveled at the size of the choir and the orchestra, and what he called the "karaoke-style" singing, with lyrics projected on a screen. It wasn't until the sermon that the trouble began.

As the pastor rose to the pulpit, the title of his sermon was projected on the screen:

Identifying and Destroying the Enemies of God. First Samuel 17

Don felt a rising dread. The pastor announced that this week he was taking a break from his sermon series to talk about something different: the protesters who'd been coming once a month. "They want a study group," he said. *"There will be no study group!"*

He said it with the kind of strident power that's meant to fire up a crowd. And it worked. The congregation surged to its feet in applause. As far as Don could tell, only he and Rob remained sitting.

And then the pastor walked the congregation through the clobber passages.

---

3. Quotations taken from unpublished correspondence.

That's what Don calls them. It's what sexual minorities typically call them: the familiar litany of passages, about half a dozen depending on how you count. A mere handful of sentences, but for friends of mine like Don these are the passages they've heard more than any others. Over and over again, a litany of conversation-stoppers designed to trump their experience, their cries of anguish, their suicidal thoughts, all their efforts to be heard. None of it matters because of Leviticus 18:22 or Romans 1:26–27.

The Bible transformed into a weapon.

This is surely not the intent of everyone who quotes these passages. But it's the experience of gays and lesbians. They're called "clobber passages" because, in the lives of sexual minorities, they function time and again like cudgels.

While he sat in the pews, a helpful neighbor shared a Bible with Don so he could read along as the pastor used the clobber passages to "identify the enemies of God." And Don felt it rising up inside him, the voice of indignation, of protest. "As we headed for the Corinthian passage," Don recalls, "I felt my pulse throbbing on both sides of my neck. I really don't recall what the last thing he said was. All I remember was that I was on my feet and had just said in a loud voice, 'I am proud to be gay!'"

Things happened quickly after that. Several large men, "all of whom had been sitting close behind us, immediately grabbed both of us and started pushing us out of the church." Don struggled to say something, to make some statement about what he'd felt, what he believed, "but I feel sure that it was not very coherent at this point."

Meanwhile, his friend Rob was in panic. "Being blind and not knowing what he was being pushed and shoved towards must have been extremely frightening. By the time we got to the back of the church I was able to assure Rob that I had hold of him."

Outside the church, Don tried again to speak. One of the men who'd dragged them from the sanctuary said the pastor was "entitled to his beliefs."

"I'm at a loss," Don answered, "as to how to communicate with someone holding such beliefs."

That's what he wanted, even then: to communicate. To find a way to do what I hadn't even tried to do in the pastor's office: to establish that human connection, that authentic encounter where love and truth are found.

That's the space in which Don tried to live his life—that place of human connection, that place where his true self could not stay silent in the face of what he could only describe as abuse. Even when the rules demanded something else—the pastor speaks, everyone else listens; the pastor is entitled to his beliefs, and the lone voice that cries out in protest is shoved into the wilderness—even then he could not stay silent.

He could not stop caring. He could not stop pursuing fellowship. And he could not stop saying no.

The God of Love and the Ethics of Love

It may seem subversive to choose, as my model of Christian love, a gay man who had the temerity to rise up in the middle of a sermon and announce that he was proud to be gay.

It is.

But I don't do it just to be subversive. At the end of this chapter I want to explore more fully why Don strikes me as such a helpful model, at least when we're thinking about Christians caught up in contemporary disputes about homosexuality and same-sex marriage. I also need to look more closely at the most seminal Christian model of love—Jesus on the cross—to see how and why Don's actions embody many of its lessons.

But first I want to step back and think about Christian love in a more general way. While examples of love in action take us to the heart of the concept, we need a broader framework to understand what diverse examples have in common, to see which features of the examples are essential and which aren't.

The fourth chapter of 1 John offers a powerful starting point for just such an overview. It's here we find the powerful assertion that God *is* love. The chapter also helps to make sense of something puzzling Jesus says in the Gospels. When asked to name the greatest commandment, Jesus identifies two: "You shall love the Lord your God with all your heart, and with all your soul, and with all your mind," and "You shall love your neighbor as yourself" (Matt 22:37–38). What is most puzzling here is that he says the second is *like* the first.

It doesn't take much reflection to see why this is puzzling. As Paul Ramsey points out, a call to love your neighbor as you love yourself is a call to pursue your neighbor's good whether your neighbor deserves it or not, because that is how you love yourself: "You naturally love yourself for your own sake. You wish your own good, and you do so even when you may have a certain distaste for the kind of person you are."[4] Self-love, Ramsey notes, "does not wait on worth."[5] Hence, neither does Christian neighbor-love.

But while it is surely possible to honor God's worth, to value God for God's greatness, it isn't possible to *pursue God's good*. God is infinitely beyond our reach. Nothing we do can harm *or* benefit God. When it comes to

---

4. Ramsey, *Basic Christian Ethics*, 100.
5. Ibid.

loving God, what we *can* do—respond to God's value—is the very thing that *isn't* supposed to be part of neighbor-love. It's what we *can't* do in relation to God that forms the heart of neighbor-love—namely pursuing the loved one's good. Seen in this light, love for God and love for neighbor appear to be nothing alike.

But 1 John offers a link between neighbor-love and love for God that might resolve the puzzle. That link is their common root in God's love for us: "This is love: not that we loved God, but that he loved us and sent his Son as an atoning sacrifice for our sins" (1 John 4:10). On account of this divine love for us, we are called to "love one another" (1 John 4:11). When we do so, "God lives in us and his love is made complete in us" (1 John 4:12).

The idea here is astonishing: when we respond to God's love for us by loving our neighbors, God *lives in us*. In all of Scripture, there is no portrait of intimacy with God more complete than this: when we allow God to make us into instruments of his love, God *inhabits* us. Whatever closeness we can achieve through prayer and worship, whatever mystical encounters we can realized by groping for a God who is out there beyond our finite reach, the greatest closeness comes from loving our neighbor—when God fills us from within. Neighbor-love is also the visible sign of our love for God: "Whoever claims to love God yet hates a brother or sister is a liar. For whoever does not love their brother and sister, whom they have seen, cannot love God, whom they have not seen. And he has given us this command: Anyone who loves God must also love their brother and sister" (1 John 4:20–21).

The idea is this: we love God by allowing divine love to inhabit us and flow through us into the world. Loving God and loving neighbor become two dimensions of the *same* act. First we open ourselves to the source of love and make ourselves its vessel; then we express that in relation to our neighbor. If this is right, then we should expect the ethical life to be wholly comprehended in showing love to our neighbors—which is precisely what Paul claims when he says that all of the commandments are "briefly comprehended" in the "commandment to love your neighbor as yourself" (Rom 13:10). For Paul, the love command is the foundational moral principle: all of morality follows from it.

First John clarifies that this foundational love originates in God's very nature, and we understand love by looking at God's most profound revelatory act: God "sent his Son as an atoning sacrifice for our sins." Christian love is here revealed to be a giving of the self for the other's sake, without regard for self-interested motives or whether the neighbor deserves it. What is revealed on the cross is also revealed in creation, which Gustav Aulen describes as "primarily the life-giving work of sovereign divine love."[6] Creation bestows the gift of existence, the fundamental good and the precondition for all other goods. Like Christ's atoning sacrifice, creation represents a divine love that gives freely for the other's sake. The gift of existence certainly can't be earned, since before being created there is no one there to deserve anything.

As Stanley Grenz puts it, "Because God is love, God is self-giving. Because God is self-giving, God willingly creates the world."[7] Karl Barth sums up his understanding of Christian love in similar terms: "Love is a free action: the self-giving of one to another without interest, intention or goal; the spontaneous self-giving of the one to the other just because the other is there and confronts him."[8]

This *giving*-love needs to be distinguished from the sort of love Scrooge has for his money: the covetous desire to possess. Anders Nygren used two ancient Greek terms to distinguish these kinds of love: *eros* and *agape*. *Eros* names the desiring love that longs to possess an object (or person, who thereby is treated like an object), whereas *agape* is the self-giving love that Barth identifies with God's nature and picks out as genuinely Christian.

We love our neighbors in the agape sense by giving of our time and resources to promote their good. But as already noted, we can't love God like that. What we can do is give our *wills* over to God, relinquish our worldly aims, and allow God's aims to become ours. This is why Nygren argues that human love for God is about submitting our wills to God's will: it remains a self-giving love, rather than a covetous love, but what we give to God is our whole selves, for God to do with as God wills. And what God wills is for us to love as God loves, to love each other as God has first loved us.[9] We love God by making ourselves instruments of God's love, channeling that love toward our neighbors.[10]

This perspective answers anyone claiming that love for God might require obedience to purported divine commands that harm our neighbors. Although Nygren stresses that love for God is about obedience to God's

---

6. Aulen, *Faith of the Christian Church*, 181.

7. Grenz, *Theology for the Community of God*, 101. See also Aquinas, *Summa Theologica* I, Q. 20, Art. 2.

8. Karl Barth, *Church Dogmatics* IV/2, §68, 752.

9. This is *not* to say that our love for one another is *just* an expression of our love for God. To love my neighbor for *God's sake*, rather than for my neighbor's, is to fail to love my neighbor as God does, and hence to fail to properly love God. To love as God loves, I need to care about my neighbor's good for my *neighbor's* sake, as a free and unmerited gift.

10. Nygren, *Agape and Eros*, 94–96.

will, such obedience means loving our neighbors as ourselves. This is why Jesus could say the command to love God is "like" the command to love our neighbors: although the former is about giving our wills over to God in obedience, and the latter is about giving of our time and resources to promote the neighbor's good, in practice the two acts of self-giving converge upon the same thing. There will be no divine command contrary to neighbor-love, because God is love. And we cannot hope to love our neighbors as ourselves unless we give our wills over to the God whose love is pure and perfect in a way that the love born of our unaided human wills could never hope to be.

This fact gives rise to an important principle for those who embrace the Christian love ethic. *If I have compelling reason to think that some purported command of God would, if obeyed, do my neighbors no good but instead do only harm, then I have compelling reasons to think that the purported divine command does not in fact come from the God of love. In other words, I have compelling reason to take it to be false prophecy.*

Who Is My Neighbor?

But if Christian ethics is essentially about making ourselves instruments of God's love, we must understand the scope of that love. Who exactly is my neighbor? In the Parable of the Good Samaritan, Jesus turns that question on its head. As Paul Ramsey notes, the parable *challenges* those who ask it. "Who is my neighbor?" is, for Jesus, the wrong question. The questioner should "revise entirely his point of view, reformulating the question first asked so as to require neighborliness of himself rather than anything of his neighbor."[11] A person doesn't have to pass some test to qualify as a proper object of Christian love. The Samaritan—a member of a marginalized and despised group—makes the injured victim on the road *into* a neighbor by his love. And we are called to do likewise.

My neighbor, then, is any concrete person I encounter—even my enemy, as Jesus himself makes plain (Matt 5:43–45). Christian love, because it is an unconditioned gift, makes every person it meets into a neighbor; but especially those in need, the wounded and the victims, as the Good Samaritan parable reveals. In this sense, Christian love has a universal scope—but not, as Ramsey warns, in the sense that what I love is some generic humanity.[12]

---

11. Ramsey, *Basic Christian Ethics*, 93.
12. Ibid., 94–5.

Christian love is universal in the sense that *each* individual human I encounter is the proper object of my love.[13]

This fact distinguishes the Christian love ethic from two of the most important modern philosophical theories of ethics: Kant's ethics and utilitarianism. Kant held that we should treat the humanity *in* ourselves and our neighbors as an end, not merely as a means. For Kant, humanity is defined by rationality and the capacity to live as rationally autonomous agents; this rational nature demands respect. But for Christian ethics, it is the concrete neighbor who needs to be respected and valued, not the generic humanity within them. It *does* matter that these neighbors have a human nature, one that includes a capacity for rational deliberation and autonomy. But this matters because it tells us how to value and respect the concrete neighbor, how to promote the neighbor's good. While Christians should agree with Kant that we shouldn't treat people as mere means to our own ends, as nothing but tools or things, the reason is because of our love for them as individuals, not respect for their abstract humanity.

Utilitarianism, like the Christian love ethic, is concerned about promoting the welfare of others. But for utilitarianism, the moral act is identified with whatever maximizes the overall happiness of the majority. Christian love cares about each concrete neighbor, not some collective within which individual needs and interests can be lost. Whereas utilitarianism cares only about the forest—"the greatest general happiness"—Christian love focuses on each tree. Utilitarianism risks reducing individual neighbors into "happiness containers" and caring about them only as vessels that might (or might not) contain some of the happiness that results from the happiness-maximizing choice. But Christian love cannot neglect the individual in favor of the majority in this way. While hard calls have to be made in a fallen world, and while there are limits to the good we can do for our neighbors, the focus on each individual neighbor means that these difficult choices cannot be reduced to a numbers game. For example, a policy that seeks to do good for all, even if it has a low chance of success, may be preferred over a policy that guarantees the suffering of one neighbor to ensure a high probability of happiness for many. The former policy shows love for *each* neighbor in a way that the latter simply can't. From the standpoint of love, this difference is crucial.

But there are limits to human love, and this fact does create dilemmas. First of all, while God can give endlessly, we cannot do so without depleting ourselves—a fact that generates tough questions about how Christian love

---

13. Ibid., 95.

relates to self-love.[14] Ramsey, for example, argues that Christian love is really self-love "inverted": it redirects the kind of love we usually focus inward onto our neighbor instead.[15] If this is right, we should consistently favor our neighbor's good over our own.

But consider the following: I am the only person who can actively enjoy the goods of my life. And if I refuse to do so, then no one—not even God—can effectively pursue my good. Agapic love is thwarted if the loved one refuses to enjoy the goods of existence that love offers. Furthermore, if God loves me and I'm supposed to love as God loves, then doesn't it follow that I should love myself as God does?[16] To give to my neighbor endlessly without attending to my own needs would not only cut back my capacity to love by depleting my resources, but would fail to show for myself the love God has for me. I'd fall short of making God's will my own. Hence, contrary to Ramsey's view, there is a place for self-love within the Christian love ethic. The scope of neighbor love includes myself.

Our limitations raise other difficulties aside from those tied to self-love. Even if we nurture our capacity to give, the sea of human need will exceed us. We *cannot* show the fullness of agapic love for everyone. What we *can* do for everyone is hope and pray for their welfare and refrain from inflicting harm.[17] But when it comes to actively pursuing their good, we must be selective. The selection isn't always up to us. If we are walking on the Jericho road and come across a man stripped and beaten and half-dead, the weight of our neighbor's need impresses itself on us in a way love cannot ignore. The person we encounter is the neighbor we are called to love, whether friend or foe; and if that person is in need and cannot provide for him- or herself, then neighbor-love calls us to step across the road and give as we can. This is true even if stopping makes us miss a fundraising campaign that could have saved lives. Neighbor love begins with the concrete person we encounter and reaches out from there, to the broader sea of suffering humanity, as we are able. Perhaps utilitarian considerations about maximizing

14. For a review of the American debate on this issue, see Post, "Disinterested Benevolence," 356–68.

15. Ramsey, *Basic Christian Ethics*, 100.

16. Aquinas makes this point as follows: "Secondly, we may speak of charity in respect of its specific nature, namely as denoting man's friendship with God in the first place, and, consequently, with the things of God, among which things is man himself who has charity. Hence, among these other things which he loves out of charity because they pertain to God, he loves also himself out of charity" (*Summa Theologica*, II-II, Q. 25, Art. 4).

17. With the possible exception of cases where pursuing the good of an innocent victim seems to require harming the aggressor. Such cases underlie the ongoing Christian debate over the justifiability of violence.

welfare might come into play when we are pursuing such charitable work, when we are deciding where to send our donation check or which homeless shelter to donate time to, but it does not justify walking past the concrete person in need. My neighbor is first and foremost the living person I confront and interact with, whoever that may be.

Showing Love: Attention and Empathy

Sometimes what people need is to take care of things themselves or get help from someone other than us, someone they know and trust. Just because we can help doesn't mean that *our* helping is what will do the most to meet our neighbor's needs. Since our resources are limited, it would misuse them to help those whose welfare would be better served if they took care of themselves, or if a loved one able and willing to help did so. Furthermore, what shows love for one person may not show love for another, since these things may be a function of personal circumstances not everyone shares. Thus, we need to notice those circumstances so that our loving motives don't misfire.

In short, love requires the kind of discernment that comes from compassionate attention. The first thing the Good Samaritan did on the road to Jericho was *pay attention*. He recognized this battered soul as a fellow human being, wounded and in need. Ramsey describes well what neighbor-love should look like if we are to love our neighbor as we love ourselves, but there is something important he misses about self-love: *we pay attention to ourselves*. We inhabit ourselves and our needs. We may not always understand our needs, but we feel them pressing into our consciousness, driving us to act. What would it look like to be comparably conscious of our neighbor's needs? For the French philosopher and mystic Simone Weil, that sort of consciousness is a product of attention. To love others, we must know that they exist in the same way that we ourselves exist—as subjects who suffer and need, not as mere things that litter the landscape. "The poet," she says, "produces the beautiful by fixing his attention on something real. It is the same with the act of love. To know that this man who is hungry and thirsty really exists as much as I do—that is enough, the rest follows by itself."[18]

Love calls for the kind of attention that inspires empathy, and to empathize with our neighbors we often need to hear their stories enough to inhabit their perspective. We need to listen compassionately, perhaps beyond the actual words they speak. Such attention helps us see the needs of those around us and identify the best way to allocate our limited resources

---

18. Simone Weil, *Gravity and Grace*, 173.

to help meet those needs, but it also is a gift in its own right. To receive such attention, to be known by others, is a fundamental human need.

Mutual Love and Fellowship

The call to love our enemies makes it clear that, as Christians, we are to love our neighbors whether or not they love us back. But that doesn't mean we shouldn't *pursue* mutuality. Mutual love forges bonds of understanding and affection, overcomes alienation, and unites people and God together in a way that unreciprocated love never can. Such bonds of fellowship are among the greatest joys that creatures can experience. Thus, Miroslav Volf insists that "the *goal* of self-giving love is mutuality of perfect love."[19] The kingdom of God is not a kingdom of unrequited love but of mutuality, a community in which God and creatures are bonded to one another through reciprocal love. It is this "beloved community" that inspired Martin Luther King Jr.'s moral vision and efforts of social change.[20] When we look at what it is to be human, community and fellowship turn out to be fundamental to our welfare. As such, one of the greatest gifts we can offer is fellowship or friendship.

In authentic fellowship, we both give and receive. As we give the gift of compassionate attention, we receive the gift of another self: their experiences, feelings, and convictions. As we give the gift of ourselves, we receive the gift of attention. The gap between self and other is bridged while preserving the integrity of each. On classical Christian theology, God is a being whose very essence embodies such unity-in-diversity. Not only is God's very nature love, but it is mutual and reciprocal love. It is loving *fellowship*. This means that when, among humans, self-giving love becomes mutual, God inhabits the entire relationship, bringing persons together in a way that mirrors the triune nature of the divine.

We can't bring about such reciprocal love alone. It requires a free response. But we can try to inspire it. And the best way to inspire it is to love even where it isn't reciprocated, to persistently reach for that in our neighbor which bears the image of God.

Again, there are limits. We cannot in this life nurture fellowship with the sea of humanity. What we can do is remain open to fellowship with those we meet and interact with. But being open to fellowship does not

---

19. Miroslav Volf, *Exclusion and Embrace*, 190.

20. I borrow the phrase "beloved community" from Martin Luther King Jr., who used it to describe the goal of self-giving Christian love. For an especially nice articulation, see King, "Advice for Living," 106.

mean enduring relationships that are defined by abuse and exploitation. I can be open to fellowship while protecting myself from abuse. I can be realistic enough to know when something dysfunctional is all I am likely to get. Since I can only cultivate a finite number of relationships in this life, I am justified in pursuing fellowship where, in my best judgment, doing so is most likely to bear fruit. Furthermore, imposing conditions on a relationship can sometimes be not just a matter of self-care but an expression of agapic love, such as when loving parents impose rehab as a condition for welcoming a drug-addicted child. This does not mean that the parents' *love* is conditional, since unconditional love might be the very thing motivating the condition.

But not all conditions on relationship fit this description. If I'm open to friendship with a blind neighbor only on the condition that she acquire the power to see, my openness is a sham. Even if we concede that meeting the condition is good for her, there is nothing my neighbor can do to meet it. If, instead, I am open to friendship *only* if you become blind, there *is* something you could do about it: you could maim yourself. But the mere fact that you can meet my condition doesn't mean I'm open to fellowship in the way love requires. I'm forcing you to choose between your welfare and a relationship with me, and love does not impose such choices. Love cares about welfare *and* fellowship.

In real life the conditions we impose on our relationships are (usually) less overtly gruesome. But suppose a young man experiences nothing but coldness from his father except when he forsakes his dreams to live out his father's instead—giving up drama club, say, to join the football team. Or suppose a lesbian woman is not welcome in church unless she ends the most important, life-enriching relationship of her life. We will return to examples like this last one in later chapters. For now the point is this: *Christian love entails an openness to fellowship that is incompatible with imposing conditions that our neighbors either can't meet at all or can't meet without harming themselves.*

Love and Intrinsic Value

Some theologians argue that Christian love should be indifferent to *all* value assessments. Nygren, for example, claims that God's agape "does not recognize value, but creates it. Agape loves and imparts value by loving. The man who is loved by God has no value in himself; what gives him value is precisely the fact that God loves him."[21] He concludes that if we are to love

---

21. Nygren, *Agape and Eros*, 78.

as God loves, our love must likewise be of a sort that creates rather than responds to value. But unlike God, human beings do not create the neighbors they're called to love. When Nygren speaks of human agape, he skirts the significance of this fact by noting that human agape does not respond to fellowship but creates it.[22] This is an important way our love can reflect the creative dimension of God's love. But what we are called to love is the *neighbor* not the fellowship we help create. While God's love creates the very object of love, our love does not. The love expressed in God's creative act *can't* respond to the loved one's merit, because prior to the act nothing exists to merit it. But human acts of love are not like this. Every human act of love is directed to the neighbor who already exists and possesses intrinsic value.

There is a way Christian love remains unmotivated by value assessments: we must not withhold it based on our neighbors' moral character, talents and abilities, or likelihood of reciprocation. But Jesus called us to love our *neighbors*, not diamonds or potato salad. And part of the reason, surely, is that our neighbors have an intrinsic value that inanimate things don't possess—what traditional theology calls the image of God. Of course, it's also true that Christian love promotes our neighbors' good, and this is possible only because our neighbors are beings who can suffer or flourish, stagnate or grow in wisdom, fall into vice or cultivate virtue in ways that diamonds can't. But what makes it possible to pursue our neighbors' good in a way we can't pursue a rock's good is the very thing that makes our neighbors more intrinsically valuable than rocks. People (and arguably animals) are proper objects of agapic love only because of *what* they are. And what they are *has* value by virtue of God's creative work. No matter how vile or dull, our neighbors bear inherent dignity and worth. Failing to honor this is one way we harm our neighbors. It is not good for people to be treated like mere things.

The Cross as Symbol of Love

All of these ideas about Christian love are enriched when we reflect on the most central Christian example of love: the cross. But in addition to being the most central example, for several reasons it's also one of the most difficult. First, if we're groping for a model to live by, the cross hits us like a repudiation. It's one thing to die for Christ or for the Christian community as the early martyrs did, or for our children as so many parents are prepared to do. But what Christ did on the cross is more akin to *leaping in front of a bullet to save the life of the sexual predator who murdered our child.*

22. Ibid., 102.

In this sense the cross convicts us all. It reminds us of our inadequacy in the face of God's perfect love. But even if we were able to follow the model of the cross, how often are we positioned to live out the love ethic in such astonishing ways? We aren't Jesus. We aren't the saviors of the world, and most of the time love doesn't call us to accept a martyr's death.

There is also a more theologically pressing reason not to focus too narrowly on the cross: when we do, we're in danger of drawing the wrong lessons. In her remarkable little book, *Victimization: Examining Christian Complicity*, Christine Gudorf worries that when we focus too narrowly on Christ's death and resurrection, making it "the central, and perhaps only, paradigm for life," we risk romanticizing victims in ways that make us complicit in their victimization.[23]

One way this happens is by implicitly encouraging victims to accept abuse by falsely equating love with sacrificial suffering. When we see Christ's suffering not as an example of the lengths to which love will go but as the chief model of what it means to love, we're in danger of teaching a lesson that, as Gudorf notes, has been rightly rejected by those most focused on the plight of marginalized and disempowered groups. Both feminist thinkers and Latin American liberation theologians have stressed that we should regard the value of sacrificial suffering as "instrumental," as "good not in itself but only when its object is mutual love."[24]

But Gudorf makes an even deeper point. If following Christ is *just* about taking up our cross, *just* about following the path through suffering and death to the resurrection that waits on the far side, we are in danger of thinking that "real life, joy, and kingdom can only emerge from suffering."[25] We identify life with *resurrected* life, the life born in the aftermath of affliction. And so we see suffering not as an evil to be overcome but as the path from false life to real life.

This perspective is dangerous for two reasons. First, it loses sight of the fact that suffering is not intrinsically redemptive. The nature of suffering is *subverted* by the cross, not represented in it. Gudorf puts the point this way:

> History continues to demonstrate that if there is a lesson to be learned from suffering, it is that many violated persons become violent, that those treated inhumanely often become inhumane, and that some, when left without hope, kill themselves

---

23 Gudorf, *Victimization*, 71.
24 Ibid.
25 Ibid., 72

in despair. Suffering both kills and deforms. The message of the gospel is a hope-filled response to this truth—not a negation of it.[26]

Secondly, Gudorf notes that much of what we know to be good in life does not arise out of suffering and death but "from love and friendship, from creative work, and from interaction with nature." If we look beyond the cross to the life Jesus lived and the message he preached, we learn that "it is good for all to eat and drink together, to bake and fish, to sow and harvest, to celebrate weddings, to cherish children, to pray, and to do these things together, without judgment or exclusion."[27] These goods "are born naturally into our lives, not resurrected."[28]

Put concretely, portraying suffering as the primary path to the most valuable goods may convince the abused wife that, instead of escaping her abuser, she should accept the battery as her cross, her path to resurrection. We imply that the cyclical explosions of violence are the road to some romanticized salvation—of herself, her husband, their relationship. Since domestic violence follows a cycle in which bursts of overt violence are followed by remorse and a so-called "honeymoon" period, the abused wife may entertain the false hope that each such honeymoon marks the moment of resurrection, of new life finally arrived—something truer and more beautiful than anything she could hope to realize in, say, a relationship defined by mutual care and concern and respect. Until, of course, the abuse cycles up anew.

Such romanticization of suffering puts us in danger of encouraging victims to submit to abuse in the name of "costly discipleship," as if the way of the cross were about seeking out ways to be crucified.

Salvation through suffering is not natural. It's a miracle. It is God enduring what mere humans cannot, bringing life and joy out of what, in the ordinary course of human life, brings distortion, destruction, and despair. In the cross we see a divine promise of cosmic companionship amidst suffering, the promise that affliction's corrupting power is defeated by God's redeeming love.

In short, Christ's redemptive *accomplishment* on the cross is beyond us. That God can always bring good out of suffering doesn't mean we can, and it surely doesn't mean that suffering is always good. This fact carries important lessons. First, loving as Jesus loved does not mean submitting to abuse and injustice, suffering quietly, and waiting for the resurrection to

26. Ibid.
27. Ibid., 73.
28. Ibid., 72.

come. When we do that, we aren't taking up our crosses and following Jesus, because what Jesus accomplished on the cross is profoundly different from what we could accomplish through silent submission to abuse. While there are diverse theories of the atonement, they agree that on the cross Jesus *overcame* sin and death. The cross has thus become God's cosmic repudiation of sin and death, a resounding *no* echoing through history. To follow Christ, we too must say *no* to the evils of sin and death and to all the other evils Jesus vocally repudiated through his ministry: the hatred and oppression and injustice that harms the neighbors we're called to love.

Taking up our cross and following Jesus does not mean simply enduring abuse, because most of the time simply enduring abuse gives it tacit permission to continue. Christian love confronts and renounces the powers that stand arrayed against the spirit of love; and unlike the infinite God, we are not usually in a position to do that by submitting ourselves to crucifixion.

None of this is to say that Christ's followers are never called to suffer, even to die. What it means is that for us, living in the natural world, the good is most often served through such things as feeding the hungry, healing the sick, building understanding amidst differences, and speaking truth to power—not by hanging on a cross. While we are called to *risk* suffering and loss and even death as we do these things, our crucifixion is not the *way* to new life. In that sense, the cross is not so much a model for us to live by as it is a hope we can take with us as we face life's struggles. It does not tell us what Christian love most typically looks like.

Nevertheless, it tells us something that deepens our understanding of love. First, Christ's crucifixion represents the extreme to which Christian love is prepared to go for the neighbor's good. We may not ordinarily be called to die, but Christian love is prepared to go that far when necessary. Secondly, the cross offers a portrait of what it means to live out Christ's command to love our enemies by dramatizing love at its most unconditional. On the cross, we learn that loving enemies means not just working for the good of those who don't deserve it, but facing *even death* for those who despise us and wish us dead, if that is what is required to save them.

The cross also demonstrates that this sort of love has a transforming power. Those for whom Christ died did not have the moral worth that could make them deserve such sacrifice, but traditional theology teaches that this undeserved act of love freed humanity from bondage to sin. However we work out the theology here, the core message is that love has the power to transform those who are loved, to open up pathways to redemption and sanctification that did not exist before. We love our neighbors whether or not they deserve it; but by loving them, we can hope to inspire astonishing moral transformations.

This leads to a third lesson of the cross. If the love displayed on the cross has the power to transform individual hearts, it does so with a broader communal aim of restoring fellowship, of reconciling human beings to one another and their creator, of achieving the kingdom of God. The cross reinforces the point that while Christian love may not be conditioned by reciprocity, its *aim* is reciprocal fellowship and the beloved community.

A final lesson of the cross relates to Christ's broader teachings on opposing evil. Many Christian thinkers have found in the cross a profoundly nonviolent message, one that defies standard ideas about the right to self-defense. The message, in brief, is this: *It is better to endure the violence our enemies throw at us than to prevent it by doing violence in return.*

This is not the same as saying we should never act to prevent violence or that we should endure it without reason. To prefer *enduring* violence to *meting it out* is not the same as treating violence as acceptable. Violence damages the physical and psychological integrity of its victims even as it threatens the humanity of its agents. If both the victims and agents of violence are neighbors we're called to love, we must repudiate the violence that does this harm. What has inspired Christian advocates of nonviolence is the conviction that repudiating violence means *both* refusing to do it *and* acting to prevent it in nonviolent ways.

Jesus taught that there are creative ways to repudiate evil without doing harm to its perpetrators, ways to overcome death without dealing death, and ways to build a kingdom of love without wielding a sword against those who stand in the way. Walter Wink has argued that this message of creative resistance to evil is central to Jesus' Sermon on the Mount. Christ's injunction to turn the other cheek (Matt 5:39) has often been seen as a kind of non-resisting meekness in the face of violence. But for Wink, that couldn't be farther from the truth:

> "If anyone strikes you on the right cheek, turn the other one to him as well." Why the right cheek? A blow by the right fist in that right-handed world would land on the left cheek of the opponent. An open-handed slap would also strike the left cheek. To hit the right cheek with a fist would require using the left hand.... The only way one could naturally strike the right cheek with the right hand would be with the back of the hand. We are dealing here with insult, not a fistfight. The intention is clearly not to injure but to humiliate.... Masters backhanded slaves; husbands, wives; parents, children; men, women; Romans, Jews. We have here a set of unequal relations, in each of which retaliation would invite retribution. The only normal response would be cowering submission. Why then does he counsel those

already humiliated people to turn the other cheek? Because this action robs the oppressor of the power to humiliate. The person who turns the other cheek is saying, in effect, "Try again. Your first blow failed to achieve its intended effect. I deny you the power to humiliate me. I am a human being just like you. Your status does not alter that fact. You cannot demean me."[29]

By turning the other cheek, a symbolic act aimed at humiliation is stripped of the capacity to achieve that aim. And the crucifixion represents, in historical terms, something very similar. For the Roman Empire, the cross was not just a tool of torture and death but of humiliation. It symbolized the degradation of Rome's enemies. But that symbolic meaning has been transformed. What was once a symbol of humiliation has become a symbol of courage and love. Jesus did not simply put up with contempt and degradation, *he exposed it for what it was.*

To believe that Jesus was the incarnate God is to believe that the very creator of the world became the object of humiliation. If the victims of humiliating violence truly are rendered worthless by the degrading acts that seek to turn them into things, then the very creator of the world, *the most infinitely valuable thing in the universe*, is rendered worthless, too. But, of course, the incarnate God cannot be rendered worthless by any human act. By stepping into the victim's place, Jesus exposed these acts of contempt and violence as empty gestures incapable of achieving what they aim to achieve. On the cross God stood in solidarity with all victims, declaring, "What you do to the least of these, you do to me." And, we might add, "What your gestures of contempt fail to do to me, they fail to do to the least of these." Murderous violence aims to turn people into things in the most literal way of all: by turning them into corpses. But even this effort to strip the value from God's creatures is undermined, the hollow impotence of such violence laid bare in the form of an empty tomb.

In my experience, the first time people hear Wink's account of Jesus' call to turn the other cheek, they are astonished. But the cross represents an even more astonishing example of creative nonviolence: a way for God to repudiate human abusiveness and cruelty on a global scale without doing violence to the perpetrators; a way of asserting the dignity and worth of every victim in the face of forces that would crush them, not by striking back in kind, but by exposing the other cheek—or in this case the other nature, the divine nature, of Christ.

Whether Christians must foreswear violence altogether is an ancient controversy and not one I mean to answer here. Sometimes it seems that in

---

29. Wink, *Engaging the Powers*, 175–76.

this fallen human world we are forced to choose between allowing innocent victims to suffer and intervening in violent ways. Given an ethic that calls us to love both victims and aggressors, this choice represents a dilemma with no easy solutions. But we cannot look at the cross without recognizing a profound call to seek alternatives to violence, and a strong message to the effect that creative alternatives to violence are available more broadly than our limited imaginations typically suppose.

In sum, when we look to the cross as a symbol of Christian love, we see a love that is prepared, when necessary, to sacrifice for the good of others, and to do so in ways that call attention to and actively repudiate evil and injustice; a love that seeks the neighbor's good without regard for their moral worth or whether they are inclined to love us back; a love that affirms the dignity of all persons, especially in the face of the forces that would violate them, and does so in a way that exposes the impotence of violence to destroy what comes from God; a love that refuses to violate or degrade the perpetrators of evil, but reaches out instead in a spirit of compassion and forgiveness. "Forgive them, for they know not what they do."

Love amidst Conflict

Models of Christian love are all too rare when we look at human conflicts and debates. Instead of loving each other, we vilify our opponents or ridicule them. Instead of loving opponent-neighbors in a way that does not wait on their worth, we try to show that they aren't worth much. Instead of reaching across the divide of differences with empathetic listening and honest sharing, we try to thump each other into silence with zinger arguments, clever slogans, or biblical clobber passages. Instead of internalizing the message that we should stop asking who our neighbor is and ask instead how we can show neighbor-love, we give sermons on how to identify God's enemies.

We see each other through lenses of stereotype and prejudice, and instead of seeking each other's good as human beings, we seek victory for our side. While it's not hard to find examples of loving gestures strategically deployed to prove how much better we are than our opponents, it's rare to find such gestures as part of sincere efforts to work for the kingdom of God.

Don stands out for me because, of all those I saw involved in the confrontation between Soulforce and Village Baptist Church, he came closest to representing the kind of love that reaches across the gap of disagreement, that honors shared humanity in the midst of enmity, that desires good both for those injured and those inflicting injury, that seeks to cultivate fellowship where it is absent, and that does all this without compromising the commitment to saying no to what is inimical to love. Don modeled for me Christ's way of repudiating evil, especially in that moment that many will see as the most troubling—that moment when he stood up in the pews and cried out, "I'm proud to be gay."

To call this act an example of Christ-like love may strike many as more than just subversive. It may seem outrageous. Doesn't saying this beg the question by assuming the very thing that needs to be proved—namely, that homosexuality isn't sinful? Don't Don's actions look completely different if we assume that conservatives are right about homosexuality? On that assumption, can't we say that the lesbian woman whose relationship triggered the conflict was actually pursuing a sinful lifestyle, and that the grandmother was right to be concerned? Doesn't it follow that Soulforce was protesting Village Baptist Church for preaching the truth and that the pastor was right to worry about a joint study group that could lead his congregants astray? And on that fateful Sunday morning in June, doesn't it follow that Don's words just amount to him announcing that he's proud to be a sinner?

Maybe if we assume that homosexuality isn't a sin, Don's actions look like taking a loving stand against injustice. But don't these same actions looked unloving as soon as we assume that homosexuality is a sin?

There is an important truth in these questions: perspective matters. But that truth needs to be paired with another one: in the human world, truth can be elusive. Unlike God, human beings are not infallible. Our perspective might be wrong.

This fact has two important implications. First, when we think about Christian love we need to draw a distinction between loving acts and loving motives. If I intend what is good for you for your own sake, then my motive is loving. But suppose I'm mistaken about what is good for you and that my actions, rather than benefiting you, do you harm. In that case, what I am doing is something that, given my motives, *I would reject if only I knew the truth*. One way to describe this is to say that while my motives are loving, my actions are not. A loving act, in this sense, is what a person with loving motives *would* do if they knew the truth.

When we don't know which perspective is true, we may not be able to say much about whether an *act* is loving. We may only be able to speak to the motives of the agents, *given their perspective*. The question, then, is not what Don's actions look like from the perspective of those who disagree with Don, but what they look like from the perspective he inhabits. When our aim is to determine whether someone has loving motives, the proper perspective to adopt is *theirs*. This is not begging the question.

That said, loving agents don't merely care about having loving motives. They care about what is actually good for their neighbor. Which means they aspire to do loving acts. This means they care about the truth, about adopting the *right* perspective. The question is how we do that.

When Mahatma Gandhi justified his commitment to nonviolence as a means of social change, he was aware that the perspective from which we act might be partially or even wholly mistaken. Nevertheless, if we are convinced about a matter of justice, our conscience calls us to act. We can't and shouldn't be paralyzed by the mere possibility of error. Instead, we should pursue our cause using means that will prevail in the long run only if truth is on our side. We should avoid methods that are indifferent to truth, methods just as likely to work if our perspective is wrong. For Gandhi, one problem with violence lies precisely in this: whether it works doesn't depend on the truth of your position but on whether you've got more guns.

From Don's perspective, Village Baptist Church was teaching things harmful to his gay and lesbian brothers and sisters. That was why he was on that vigil line—the same reason I was there. And all of us were committed to the nonviolent methods of Gandhi and King. But Don did a better job of living out Gandhi's insight than I did. Don saw the humanity on the far side of that line, and he knew that wherever there are diverse human experiences, there are perspectives we can learn from, perspectives that offer insight into a reality that transcends us all. While human fallibility did not paralyze Don into inaction or keep him from speaking out against what he saw to be error, he sought out those whose views were opposed to his own. He went into their midst, ready to encounter their perspective.

Violence is not the only strategy of conflict resolution that's indifferent to the truth. Others include insulating your community from lucid articulations of opposing views, or using the power of the pulpit to impose a uniform perspective that allows no dissent. If you love your neighbors as yourself, you want to know the truth about your neighbors. You want to be informed about their experiences, their stories, their insights and arguments. And so you will refuse to rely on methods that shut down such insight. But you won't just refuse to use them yourself. You will say *no* to them. You will seek strategies that stand against such methods while affirming your own understanding of the truth.

This is what Don did when he rose in the pews that June morning. When he walked into that church, he modeled an openness to communication, to learning from one another. But when the Bible was used to silence him and others like him, to render them unworthy of a hearing because they are "the enemies of God," he felt the fire of justice and surged from his seat. He cut through the conventions that demanded his silence, and he spoke.

But what about the words he spoke? *I am proud to be gay.* Isn't pride a vice, a kind of self-love that stands in the way of loving our neighbors as ourselves?

It is helpful here to think of the difference between "White Pride" and "Black Pride." A movement that espouses black pride occurs in a context of systemic oppression that, based on race, degrades the dignity of an entire class of people. When racism pervades a society, the marginalized group is treated as worth less, as having a value below that of other human beings. In the face of this, black pride isn't about blacks puffing themselves up but about rejecting messages and practices that would beat them down. It is a way of saying no to injustice, a way of affirming their inherent dignity in the face of a system that tries to strip it away. And they speak not just for themselves but for a group—for all the neighbors who are victims of oppression, who might internalize the degrading message. It is a way of saying, "Don't believe it. Don't allow yourself to be beaten down. Don't take it in silence, because it is not something you deserve."

"White pride" is an entirely different thing, because it occurs in a context of white privilege. Given that context, it is a way of claiming that privilege for oneself, as opposed to standing up for the victims of injustice and oppression. This is the kind of pride that is a vaunting of the self. This is the kind of pride that stands in the way of Christian love.

So what was Don doing—what did he intend to do—when he surged to his feet at that moment in that church? Like many others, Don had joined the protests at Village Baptist Church because, from his perspective, Southern Baptist teachings and practices were harming his gay and lesbian brothers and sisters. Although he had found a life in which he could largely avoid the reach of those teachings and practices, he chose not to stay in his place of safety but to cross the road. He chose not only to reach out to help those who were hurt, but to stand against those who would inflict such harm. But not with violence. And from a vigil line of prayerful and nonviolent protest he saw the humanity of those on the other side. He saw past the harm to the human souls beneath, and felt the connection deeply enough to bring tears to his eyes.

And so he sought fellowship across the line of difference, risking himself by stepping into their world. And when, in their midst, he was struck by verbal blows akin to the back-handed slap that a master gives a slave, he did what Jesus said to do: he turned the cheek of equal dignity by rising from the pews.

4

A Matter of Choice?

One day as I stood in the vigil line outside Village Baptist Church, I overheard a conversation between a church deacon and a fellow vigil-keeper.

"If you could prove to me scientifically that homosexuality isn't a choice," the deacon said, "I might rethink my position. But there's no proof!"

The vigiler, a gay man, responded in a way that made perfect sense to me: "I'm not an expert in the science, but I know my own experience. I didn't choose to be attracted to other men. I just am. Did you choose to be attracted to women? Was that ever a *choice* for you? Or was that something you just discovered?"

The deacon seemed troubled by that answer. I suspect he found himself introspecting about his own sexuality and, in the process, empathizing a little with what it's like to be gay.

If we want to love our gay and lesbian neighbors, that is one thing we need: to understand is what it's like to be gay. How do my gay and lesbian neighbors experience their sexuality and their romantic relationships? How are their lives impacted by conservative condemnations of homosexuality and by the daily pressures of living in a society that is overwhelmingly straight? How has the historic exclusion from access to marriage affected them?

And then there's the question raised by the church deacon: do gays and lesbians choose to be that way?

Love and Science

Next to what my gay neighbors tell me about what it's like to be gay, scientific evidence has long been of secondary importance to me. It's not just more interesting to listen compassionately to my gay friends than to read scientific journals; it's a more direct expression of Christian love. But when I think about what scientists do, I can't treat their work as divorced from the work of love. Neighbor-love begins with *attention*, and one thing scientists do is pay attention.

Scientists try, imperfectly, to see the world as it is in all its details and variety, and to honestly describe what they find without the filters of presuppositions and prejudice. Social and behavioral scientists focus that sort of attention on our fellow human beings, the very neighbors we're supposed to love. Their work is informed not only by surveys and controlled experiments, social observations and statistical analyses, but also by insights gleaned from qualitative interviews and the observations of those in psychological counseling professions who listen to the stories and experiences of others.

The gaze of love is different from the scientific gaze; but the level of honest attention that scientists try to bring to their subjects isn't something to be *avoided* by those trying to love their neighbors as themselves. Where loving attention differs from scientific attention isn't in the depth or honesty of the attention, but in the reasons behind it. Scientific attention can be motivated by any number of things—from mere curiosity to the desire for fame and fortune. But for the gaze of love it's always about doing good for the concrete neighbor, especially the neighbor in need. Love asks, "How can I help?"

This question isn't always easy to answer. We're limited. We miss things. Despite our best efforts, we're misled by our presuppositions. But it's important to do the best we can. To use a distinction from the last chapter, neighbor love isn't just about having loving *motives* but also about doing loving *acts*. If we love our neighbors as ourselves, we don't want our ignorance to inspire well-meaning choices that cause harm.

Relevant scientific knowledge—gleaned from the cumulative efforts of scientists to make careful and accurate observations—can enrich our understanding of those Christ has called us to love. This is especially true when we're talking about community teachings, practices, and policies that affect many people, not all of whom we can pay attention to personally. The fruits of science can also help dispel prejudices and errors that lead us to misinterpret what we see in our neighbors even when we're *trying* to pay attention. As such, science might even help us see the people right in front of us more clearly than we did before.

Those committed to loving their gay and lesbian neighbors thus have reason to pay attention to scientific research into homosexuality. *How* scientific findings should affect our ethics is a more complex question. The Village Baptist deacon seemed convinced that scientific "proof" that "homosexuality isn't a choice" would have important implications for the ethics of same-sex relationships. I take it he had in mind proof of two interrelated things: first, that no one deliberately adopts a homosexual orientation the way one chooses home décor; second, that there is no reliable mechanism for changing sexual orientation once you've discovered yours. In other words, sexual orientation falls outside the scope of what we can voluntarily control. Of course, we can't expect scientific research to *prove* this in the way I can prove I have only two beers in my fridge. Science offers evidence of greater or lesser strength, rarely proof. My best guess is that what the deacon meant to say is that, if scientific research offered strong evidence that sexual orientation falls outside the scope of voluntary control, this would be relevant for deciding the ethics of homosexuality.

Some scholars are skeptical of this claim. Stanton Jones and Mark Yarhouse have argued that whether a behavioral disposition toward homosexuality falls outside of voluntary control has little bearing on whether the behavior itself is right or wrong. Here's how they put it:

> Homosexual persons are not subhuman robots whose acts are predetermined. They are moral agents who inherit tendencies from biology and environment, and who share in shaping their character by the responses they make to their life situations. Like all persons, they must ask, "This is what I want to do, but is it what I should do?" The existence of inclinations or predispositions does not erase the need for moral evaluation of those inclinations.[1]

Jones and Yarhouse are right that no act becomes moral just because we have an unchosen disposition to do it. By the same token, no act becomes immoral just because it's in our power to eliminate a disposition toward it. But let's suppose it's true that sexual orientation falls outside the scope of voluntary control. That fact will affect gays and lesbians. And those effects will have implications for Christian love.

Suppose for a moment that you are gay. If your sexual orientation falls outside the scope of your voluntary control, then laws restricting marriage to heterosexual couples will affect you differently than it will affect

---

1. Jones and Yarhouse, *Homosexuality*, 90.

heterosexuals. Heterosexuals will be free to marry the people they can and do fall in love with. The law will prevent them from marrying people they have no interest in marrying anyway, but who cares? That's no restriction worth bothering about. You, however, will only be allowed to marry people you *can't* fall in love with—that is, the people you have no interest in marrying. The people you can form romantic pair bonds with are precisely those you aren't allowed to marry. Something available to heterosexuals and usually treated as a life-enriching good won't be available to you.

When trying to love our gay and lesbian neighbors as ourselves, these sorts of impacts are relevant. The question of whether sexual orientation falls outside the scope of voluntary control is therefore relevant—and scientific evidence that speaks to this question becomes relevant, too.

Other things that science speaks to may also be relevant. To love my gay neighbors is to want what is good for them. But many conservatives argue that homosexuality harms gays and lesbians because it is associated with mental disorders. For example, Peter Sprigg writes in a Family Research Council booklet, *The Top Ten Myths about Homosexuality*, that "regardless of whether one considers homosexuality itself to be a mental disorder, there can be no question that it is associated with higher levels of a whole range of mental disorders."[2] Being gay, according to Sprigg, is bad for gay people. And so, if they can change their sexuality, we should encourage them to do so. Maybe even force them into change therapies if we're their parents. What we should not do is tell them they are fine just the way they are. For Sprigg, that would be like telling alcoholics to keep on swigging the booze.

So what does the broader scientific community have to say about this? Is homosexuality, like alcoholism, tied to mental health problems and troubled lives? If so, is the source of those problems homosexuality as such or is it, rather, an effect of the social stigmatization of homosexuality? Is being gay harmful, or is it more harmful to be *condemned* for being gay?

Another issue that conservatives often raise is the supposed danger gays and lesbians pose to others. While the Christian love ethic calls us to love our gay and lesbian neighbors, it doesn't call us to love *only* them. Conservatives frequently argue that gays and lesbians pose a threat to our children. Some argue that it's bad for kids to grow up in families with same-sex parents. Others insinuate that homosexuality is linked to pedophilia and child sexual abuse—the idea being that persons with a homosexual orientation are somehow predisposed toward child rape. Both claims are endorsed

---

2. Sprigg, *Top Ten Myths*, 22–25.

by Sprigg in the *Top Ten Myths* pamphlet,[3] but is there any credible scientific support for these contentions?

These are the issues I will focus on in the next two chapters, starting with the question of how much our sexual orientation falls within the scope of voluntary control. But if my aim here is to explore what scientific research can tell us about homosexuality, some will notice something missing from the list: the question of what *causes* homosexuality.

There are several reasons why I don't intend to explore this question in detail. First, no one asks what causes people to be straight. But just because something is "normal" doesn't mean its origins are any less mysterious. I remember my first exposure to sex education in grade school. I learned how babies were made with the help of cartoon images showing (in the sketchiest terms) how the sperm got to the egg. I wondered why anyone would want to *do* that. I even asked my friend's mother. She smiled and answered, "In a few years you'll know."

She was right. But do we really understand how the hormones in the bodies of adolescents change their brains so that grade-school kids puzzled by the whole thing suddenly find themselves swimming in a sea of sexual and romantic desires—usually for the opposite sex, but sometimes for the same sex (and sometimes both)? Why is it, after all, that I found myself in adolescence noticing girls in a way that I didn't notice boys? Why did I suddenly find myself wrestling with desires to kiss and touch and profess undying love for girls, but not boys?

The real question isn't how some people end up with a homosexual orientation, but how and why each one of us ends up with the sexual orientation we have. To frame it as simply a question about what causes *homosexuality* is an effect of heterosexual privilege. Straight people are the majority, and our sexuality is presupposed in the fairy tales we listen to as children, the movies we watch, and countless other cultural tropes and institutions. Because it's presupposed, we never question it.

But the matter of causes is mysterious regardless of the sex of those we find ourselves attracted to, and scientific research is only beginning to find answers. There is some evidence—drawn from identical twin studies—that genetics plays a role, especially for men, but that the role is not decisive.[4] Gestational environment—including hormone exposure during pregnancy—appears to be very significant.[5] Differences in male sexual orientation

3. Ibid., 30–39.

4. Eckert et al., "Homosexuality in Monozygotic Twins," 421–25; Whitam et al., "Homosexual Orientation in Twins," 187–206; Kendler et al., "Sexual Orientation," 1843–46; J. Bailey et al., "Heritable Factors," 217–23.

5. Hines, "Prenatal endocrine influences," 170–82; Hines et al., "Androgen and

have been correlated with physical differences in the brain.[6] But, as the American Psychological Association notes, "No empirical studies or peer-reviewed research support theories attributing same-sex sexual orientation to family dysfunction or trauma."[7] In short, there is evidence of a range of causes, sufficient at least to undercut the idea that same-sex attraction is nothing but a perverse choice or the product of bad parenting.

But if my aim is to love my gay and lesbian neighbors as myself, the actual causes of sexual orientation matter far less than the fact that our sexuality is generally something we discover about ourselves rather than something we choose, and not something we can simply change by an act of will. It comes to us as a fact about ourselves that we must decide what to do about. If we have the good fortune to be straight, not much agonized decision-making is required: we follow our attractions and desires, and the moral question is when and where and how we should pursue them. If our orientation is gay or bisexual, then—at least given the world in which we live—the choices become more difficult.

While the question of underlying causes may loom large if I look at sexual orientation through the eyes of scientific curiosity, through the eyes of love the question is this: What now? Now that you are here, with the sexuality that you have, how should I treat you? What should I encourage you to do with your life? Which choices, if I encouraged you to make them, would enrich your life? Which would involve little more than futile gestures only likely to culminate in pretense or despair? What choices are real options for you, and among these, which will do the most to help you realize a good and praiseworthy human life?

From the standpoint of Christian love, the question isn't about causes but about choices.

Sexual Orientation and the Issue of Choice

When we ask whether homosexuality is a matter of choice, we need to be careful, because the term "homosexuality" is ambiguous. It names several things. First, there is sexual *behavior*: Who do you have sex with? Who do you choose to cultivate romantic relationships with? Second, there is sexual *orientation*: Who are you attracted to, sexually and romantically? Who *can* you, given your unchosen dispositions, successfully cultivate a romantic

---

Psychosexual Development," 75–81; Sanders and Ross-Field, "Neuropsychological Development," 1–16 and "Sexual Orientation," 459–70.

    6. LeVay, "A Difference in Hypothalamic Structure," 1034–37.

    7. American Psychological Association Task Force, *Report*, 63.

relationship with? Third, there is sexual *identity*: How do you define or understand yourself in relation to your sexual and romantic feelings and behaviors?

Unless we are controlled by pathological impulses, our sexual and romantic *behavior* falls within the scope of voluntary control: I can choose to act on my desires or resist them, to do things I have no desire to do or to refrain. Sexual identity, likewise, involves deliberate personal choice: I choose to identify myself in a particular way and with a particular community, to treat some personal feature—in this case my sexuality—as central to my self-understanding.

But these choices about behavior and identity may be strongly influenced by facts about ourselves that fall beyond the scope of personal choice. Sexual orientation is generally understood to fall into that category. The American Psychological Association defines sexual orientation as follows:

> Sexual orientation refers to the sex of those to whom one is sexually and romantically attracted. Categories of sexual orientation typically have included attraction to members of one's own sex (gay men or lesbians), attraction to members of the other sex (heterosexuals), and attraction to members of both sexes (bisexuals).[8]

In a more extensive report, the APA defines it as follows:

> ... sexual orientation refers to an individual's patterns of sexual, romantic, and affectional arousal and desire for other persons based on those persons' gender and sex characteristics. Sexual orientation is tied to physiological drives and biological systems that are beyond conscious choice and involve profound emotional feelings, such as "falling in love." Other dimensions commonly attributed to sexual orientation (e.g., sexual behavior with men and/or women; social affiliations with LGB or heterosexual individuals and communities, emotional attachment preferences for men or women, gender role and identity, lifestyle choices) are potential correlates of sexual orientation rather than principal dimensions of the construct.[9]

In other words, sexual orientation is about dispositions regarding romantic and sexual attraction, not primarily about behavior or social identities.[10] Your sexual orientation means your disposition to be romantically

---

8. American Psychological Association, "Guidelines," 11.
9. American Psychological Association Task Force, *Report*, 30.
10. Fritz Klein has developed a model of what he calls sexual orientation that

and sexually attracted only to members of the same sex, the opposite sex, or both. There is also a growing trend toward treating asexuality—defined as a stable disposition to be attracted to neither sex—as a fourth orientation.[11]

Social scientists generally agree that what these categories name are actually points along a continuum. As traditionally understood, that continuum runs along a line from heterosexuality to homosexuality, with bisexuality falling in the middle. However, if asexuality is included among orientations, it might be more useful to imagine sexual orientations as falling within a field defined by two variables: degree of opposite sex attraction, and degree of same-sex attraction. Those who have a high degree of one but not the other would qualify as gay or straight, those with a high degree of both as bisexual, and those with little or no attraction to either sex as asexual.

While it's generally agreed that sexual orientation is not chosen, there is some evidence of fluidity of sexual orientation, at least in some people (more commonly women than men).[12] Fluidity, however, is not the same as voluntary control. One might find at one point in life that one is equally attracted to both sexes, and later that one is more strongly oriented toward one sex over another. These changes may be influenced by environmental circumstances. But change over time, even change in response to environmental influences, does not entail choice. If it did, many people who currently grow older would stay forever young. Furthermore, the fact that *some* people exhibit such change over time does not mean such fluidity can be universalized to all who self-identify as gay and lesbian.

As already noted, sexual *behavior* and *identity* are much more influenced by the choices we make than is orientation. But orientation impacts which choices are available to us in these areas, as well as their consequences. If I have a stable heterosexual orientation but engage in gay sex, the sex act won't have the propensity to nurture a romantic bond or connection with my sexual partner. I may even have to close my eyes and imagine that my sexual partner is someone of the opposite sex in order to sustain arousal.

---

includes not just sexual and romantic attraction but also behavior and identity, as well as non-sexual/romantic preferences such as with whom one likes to socialize. See Klein, *The Bisexual Option*, 16–20. This model, in which so many varied phenomena are included under one heading, is useful for highlighting the complexity of human sexuality but less helpful for clear thinking about its distinct aspects. Hence, I will follow the more conventional approach expressed by the APA.

11. See, for example, Scutti, "Asexuality is Real."

12. See Diamond, *Sexual Fluidity*; Baumeister, "Gender Differences in Erotic Plasticity."

Rather than being an expression of intimacy, it becomes merely about the pleasurable physical sensations of sexual stimulation and release.

It is easy to imagine hedonists who are interested solely in physical pleasure deciding to pursue sex with a willing partner even though they aren't attracted to them. They might know tricks for sustaining the arousal required to experience physical pleasure, even with someone who doesn't turn them on. For them, sex would amount to a kind of mutual masturbation, a cooperative self-pleasuring rather than a romantic bonding experience.

I often hear people characterize homosexual sex in precisely these terms—as sex that's only about physical pleasure, about using another person's body for hedonistic self-gratification. And that's exactly what homosexual sex would amount to *if you have a heterosexual orientation*. By the same token, however, that is exactly what *heterosexual* sex would amount to if you have a homosexual orientation.[13] I often wonder if those who describe all homosexual sex as just about hedonistic self-gratification do so because they are straight and haven't been able to imagine any other possibility. They are imagining what would motivate *them* to have sex with someone of the same sex, whom they couldn't have romantic feelings for. And they think, "I'd do that only if *all* I were interested in were satisfying a base appetite for pleasurable sensations."

In other words, they are failing to admit the existence of a homosexual orientation. They are assuming that gays and lesbians actually have a heterosexual orientation, but for some reason have decided that pursuing physical pleasure with people they aren't attracted to is preferable to pursuing the emotionally complex richness that's possible in sexual union with someone they are drawn to both romantically and sexually. Such an assumption is false. It cannot survive even a few moments of compassionate listening to our gay and lesbian neighbors.

The point, however, is this: our sexual orientation determines the meaning that sexual activity can have with persons of the same and opposite sexes. For those of us who are straight, heterosexual sex can be an integral part of an emotionally rich romantic relationship (although it isn't always), whereas homosexual sex cannot. At best, the latter could only be about physical pleasure. But if your orientation is homosexual, the categories are reversed: only homosexual sex can be an integral part of an emotionally bonding and meaningful romantic partnership. If you pursue heterosexual sex, it will be cut off from these things.

---

13. Unless, of course, it's done out of duty to a spouse you aren't attracted to but have unwisely decided to marry.

Sexual orientation also impacts the meaning of sexual identity choices. Suppose that I—a heterosexual man—find deep personal connections with the gay community and make the (crazy) decision to adopt a gay identity. This choice would have very different implications for me than it would for someone with a homosexual orientation. To fit into the community as a self-identified gay man, I would need to *pretend* to have attractions and emotional dispositions I don't actually have. Relationships formed with others in the community would be shaped by that pretense, likely culminating in emotional hurt and feelings of betrayal. I would, in short, be "living a lie." It goes without saying that the reverse is also true: if someone has a stable homosexual orientation but chooses to identify as straight, perhaps pursuing a heterosexual marriage and the like, the result would be a life of pretense: living a lie whose consequences could prove quite tragic.

So, while sexual behavior and sexual identity are subject to choice, the issue of *which* choices are available, as well as what their consequences will be, is shaped by something that isn't chosen but discovered—namely sexual orientation. A bisexual orientation clearly affords the most room for personal choice. Bisexuals can pursue romantic and sexual intimacy in either heterosexual or homosexual partnerships, making choices about both behavior and identity that are exclusively heterosexual, exclusively homosexual, or both. But even if a bisexual orientation affords this level of flexibility with respect to behavioral and identity choices, the bisexual orientation *itself* is not chosen. In this respect, bisexuality is just like homosexuality, heterosexuality, and asexuality.

But while human experience and social science agree that our sexual orientation is something we discover about ourselves rather than something we adopt by choice, this fact does not *as such* imply that we could never voluntarily *change* the sexuality we discover. Many gays and lesbians, motivated by the belief that their sexual dispositions are unwholesome, have tried to change them, sometimes by seeking out conversion therapies offered by mental health providers (in defiance of current professional standards of care), sometimes by joining so-called ex-gay ministries that promise religious resources for change. Psychologists call such projects of self-transformation Sexual Orientation Change Efforts, or SOCE.

Do such efforts work? Here, we have to be suspicious of any therapies that measure success in terms of changing, not underlying dispositions and attractions, but dominant *behavior* patterns. Philosopher Frederick Suppe explains well why any such therapy, even if it achieves the result of exclusively heterosexual *behavior*, doesn't amount to a change in sexual *orientation*.

Suppe asks us to consider the case of a man named Michael, whose sexual arousal cues—both visual and tactile—are firmly tied to men.

Essentially, the things that arouse him sexually are physical traits possessed by (some) men and not by women. At least as significant is the fact that Michael's sexual arousal is *inhibited* by physical traits typical of women. Nevertheless, Michael has been able to perform sexually with a woman— but it required that he close his eyes to avoid off-putting visual cues while engaging in some bodily contortion to limit off-putting tactile ones (while maintaining enough of the right kind of contact to preserve arousal). In other words, it was difficult to do. He had to trick himself into thinking his sexual partner was someone other than she was—a man rather than a woman.[14]

Now imagine that Michael becomes quite good at this routine as part of a "conversion therapy" regimen. Maybe he's able to tone down some of his knee-jerk revulsion to heterosexual sex, so that inadvertent reminders of who he's actually having sex with won't kill his arousal. And suppose he is able to "muster sufficient will-power to not engage in sex with any . . . males." As a result, his outward behavior becomes consistently and exclusively heterosexual. "But," Suppe asks, "what if he has to fantasize his partner is a male to effect coitus or resort to masturbation with homosexual fantasies as the major component of his sexual outlet?" And suppose, furthermore, that "his cue-response pattern is just the same as it was before 'conversion'; only now he has learned enough gymnastics with an adept and willing partner to circumvent them."[15] Has such a person been successfully converted from gay to straight?

Of course not. "What we want to say here," Suppe notes, "is that he still is a homosexual, one who has learned to fake (bizarrely) heterosexual coitus through mastery of sensory deprivation and gymnastic techniques."[16]

The question, then, is whether more than this can be achieved through SOCE. The general consensus among social scientists today is one of deep skepticism. Most hold that conversion therapy is largely ineffective and has the potential to do harm.[17] One long-term study conducted by Kurt Freund helps explain why. Freund performed a "therapeutic experiment" on gay men who came to him "of their own accord to ask for help." The treatment involved both aversion therapy and "positive conditioning toward females" and resulted in 20 percent of the clients getting married and starting families. But over the course of the study, "Virtually not one 'cure' remained a

14. Suppe, "Curing Homosexuality," 396–97.

15. Ibid., 398.

16. Ibid.

17. For a summary of the relevant research conclusions on this issue, see Green, "The Immutability of (Homo)Sexual Orientation," and Haldeman, "Sexual Orientation Conversion Therapy."

cure."[18] Freund concluded that what his therapies succeeded in doing over the long term was nothing good. His therapy merely "helped clients to enter into marriages that later became unbearable or almost unbearable."[19]

Training gays and lesbians to repress homosexual desire and engage only in heterosexual sex, if the underlying attraction remains unchanged, amounts to training them to engage in sexual activity only with persons toward whom they cannot develop and sustain intimate feelings—and hence with whom sexual *intimacy* is impossible. Sexual intimacy is a sharing of selves in a very physical way. If Michael has to pretend that Mary is Mark in order to sustain the level of arousal required to have sex with her, he is not pursuing intimacy with Mary. He *can't*. Imagine, then, the long-term psychological toll—on both Michael and on Mary—of a marriage built around such pretense. Even if some level of opposite-sex attraction could be cultivated—and same-sex attraction resisted—through sustained, ongoing effort to counteract the pull of one's orientation, the long-term stress and strain of such efforts would force Michael's attention inward. He would be focused on trying to make himself continually *capable* of loving his spouse instead of working on building that love. Imagine what it would be like to be the spouse of someone who has to continually work that hard to build up some modicum of attraction to you.

Nevertheless, in the Family Research Council booklet on supposed "myths" about homosexuality (which should perhaps be renamed "The Top Ten Truths about Homosexuality that We at the Family Research Council Would Really Like to Call Myths"), Sprigg insists that those who say conversion therapy is ineffective are misleading us. Part of his strategy is to point out how sexual behavior can change (while adopting a definition of sexual orientation that *includes* behavior so that he can say that change has been observed "in some aspects of sexual orientation, particularly behavior"[20]). When it comes to the matter of change in attraction, Sprigg concedes that this is "undoubtedly the most difficult aspect of 'sexual orientation' to change." In other words, the "aspect" of sexual orientation that actually *is* sexual orientation (as that term is typically used) is, he admits, difficult to change, even though the aspects of it that *aren't* actually sexual orientation can be modified more successfully (perhaps through the combination of fantasy and physical gymnastics that Suppe talks about).

But despite conceding the difficulty of changing the aspect of sexual orientation *that's actually sexual orientation*, he nevertheless believes it can

---

18. Freund, "Should Homosexuality Arouse Therapeutic Concern?" 238.
19. Ibid., 239.
20. Sprigg, *Top Ten Myths*, 9.

A Matter of Choice?

be done. To support this, he cites a handful of sources, mostly drawn from the publications of NARTH (National Association for Research and Therapy of Homosexuality). NARTH is an organization born out of opposition to the APA's decision to stop treating homosexuality as a mental illness. The members of NARTH are committed to the pursuit of therapeutic "cures" of homosexuality in defiance of the prevailing view that such cures are ineffective and unwise. In short, NARTH exists for the expressed purpose of opposing the dominant view that conversion therapies are ineffective and unwise—and it promotes research aimed at supporting its very reason for existence.

Given this agenda, the impartiality and objectivity of research reports emerging out of NARTH are understandably suspect. The Southern Poverty Law Center's magazine, *The Intelligence Report*, recently described NARTH as pushing ex-gay therapy "with the zeal of a religious movement," such that it "has emerged as the preeminent source of what many regard as 'junk science' . . . that underpins the anti-gay movement's fervent opposition to equal rights and stigmatizes LGBT people as mentally sick."[21] Perhaps for that reason, Sprigg places most of the weight of his argument on two studies that don't come from NARTH. The one he pays most attention to is a 2003 study by Robert Spitzer.[22]

For this study, Spitzer interviewed 200 persons who had undergone some form of conversion therapy. Most of the participants were drawn from two sources: "ex-gay" ministries that used religious practices such as prayer to influence change, and (who else?) NARTH. So what did Spitzer conclude? Essentially, that *some* degree of change in "core aspects of sexual orientation" such as "sexual attraction, arousal, fantasy, yearning, and being bothered by homosexual feelings" was possible (not guaranteed) for highly motivated individuals (such as those driven by religious convictions to view homosexuality as a sin).[23]

Spitzer's interpretation of his data was not only at odds with the dominant conclusions of social scientists but was strongly challenged by a range of scholars in the field who found serious methodological and conceptual problems with the study.[24] Spitzer himself, in fact, became convinced by these challenges. Not only has he publicly stated that he now agrees with his

---

21. Lenz, "NARTH," para. 5–6.
22. Spitzer, "Can Some Gay Men and Lesbians Change," 403–17.
23. Ibid., 413.
24. Many of these critiques are collected in Drescher and Zucker, *Ex-Gay Research*, and summarized by Morrow and Beckstead, "Conversion Therapies," 644–45.

critics, but he has offered an apology to the LGBT community for his deeply flawed study and the harm it has done.[25]

But what about the other study? In 2007, Stanton L. Jones and Mark A. Yarhouse—an evangelical Christian research team—published a book, *Ex-Gays?*, reporting on a multi-year study of gays and lesbians who sought to change their sexual orientation through the help of ex-gay ministries. Like the Spitzer study, success was measured in terms of the self-reports of study participants. One person claiming to be a participant in the study wrote about his experience in an Amazon review of the book, and what he has to say is interesting:

> There were numerous instances when the interviewer would ask that I clarify an answer to one of the items on the assessment, usually when my original response was not in support of reparative therapies. After some years I began to experience deep anxiety over answering the questionnaire and dreading the interactions with the interviewer(s). When I decided to drop out of the study I received a call from one of the authors who told me that if I pulled out from this study completely there would be "eternal consequences." I remember him clearly stating that the "souls of an entire generation" could be affected if I did not continue and stay with my initial course of answers—which were born out of intense pressure put upon me by the church and ex-gay ministries I attended. When I finally found the courage to stand up to the institutions representing ex-gay and reparative therapies they all responded in much the same manner, with condemnation and instillment of fear. I am not aware whether or not my responses were ever included in the final study but I was one of those who attempted to withdraw and had to suffer judgement and being chastised by one of the so-called leaders of this study.[26]

This self-report, if authentic, highlights one possible concern about the Jones and Yarhouse study: it was conducted by researchers whose personal convictions gave them an interest in finding evidence of the success of ex-gay ministries. This concern, by itself, would not undermine the study—but the American Psychological Association identified a range of methodological problems, including "the absence of a control or comparison group and the threats to internal, external, construct, and statistical validity." They go on:

---

25. See Carey, "Psychiatry Giant Sorry." The apology letter can be found at Becker, "Exclusive," para. 2–5.

26. Gutierrez, "Customer Review," lines 6–22.

Best-practice analytical techniques were not performed in the study, and there are significant deficiencies in the analysis of longitudinal data, use of statistical measures, and choice of assessment measures. The authors' claim of finding change in sexual orientation is unpersuasive due to their study's methodological problems.[27]

But let's set aside these objections and assume that the Jones and Yarhouse study is reliable. On that assumption, what does it show? Here, we can't do better than to look at what Jones and Yarhouse actually have to say about the study's findings in their most recent peer-reviewed discussion of it. One thing they concede is that there are reasons to think that the self-reports of the study participants might not reflect changes in sexual orientation at all, but rather in sexual identity.[28] Furthermore, if this worry is set aside, only 23 percent of their final study population reported successful "conversion" of sexual orientation. But this number is the percentage that remained in the study after drop-outs. Jones and Yarhouse concede that under certain assumptions, "only 9% of the sample achieved success."[29] In other words, depending on one's assumptions, the religiously-based SOCE that Jones and Yarhouse studied had an 80–90 percent failure rate among highly-motivated self-selected research subjects who urgently wanted to change their sexuality in order to better align with their religious convictions.

Let's put it this way. There's a sense in which Jones and Yarhouse answer *yes* to the question, "Can gays and lesbians change their orientation?" But it's a yes-answer in the same way that we would answer yes to the question, "Can you, using two unweighted dice, roll double-sixes four times in a row within half an hour of trying?" Sure, it can happen. But if you try it, even if you're dedicated and do nothing else for the next half hour, you'll probably fail.

Furthermore, the Christian psychologist Warren Throckmorten has pointed out that the reported 23 percent success rate may be better described as a *shift* from homosexual-leaning bisexuality toward heterosexual-leaning bisexuality, rather than a conversion from homosexuality to heterosexuality. As he puts it, "An alternative way of describing the outcome is that the participants went from one end of the bisexual spectrum to the other. On average, the group rating indicated both heterosexual and homosexual attractions at the beginning, middle and end of the study."[30]

27. American Psychological Association Task Force, *Report*, 90 n. 71.
28. Jones and Yarhouse, "A Longitudinal Study," 423.
29. Ibid., 424.
30. Throckmorten, "The Jones and Yarhouse Study," para. 12.

In other words, the Jones and Yarhouse case for the success of SOCE, when all the methodological complaints are ignored and assumed to be unconvincing, tells us that SOCE has an 80 to 90 percent failure rate, that its few successes may not involve changes in sexual orientation at all (but only changes in identity), and that if its reported successes are treated as involving sexual orientation they may be better described as inspiring a small minority of highly motivated individuals to shift from being homosexual-leaning bisexuals to being heterosexual-leaning bisexuals.

If we claim that this study shows that change is possible, we can honestly do so only if, by "change is possible," we mean the following: "If you try really hard to change and are deeply dedicated to the effort, you will probably fail—but failure isn't *guaranteed*."

Even this modest conclusion rests on the assumption that we can trust the self-reports that served as a primary measure of successful conversion. And here, we need to remember that those offering these reports come from a distinctive belief-framework in which successful conversion is seen by many as a sign of having a right relationship with God. Self-deception for the sake of holding up a favorable self-image would be unsurprising. And reports by *ex*-ex-gays—people who claimed to have been successfully converted only to concede later that they were not—suggests that such deception is not a mere possibility but a reality. The most notorious case of such ex-ex-gay stories comes from one of the founders of the most important of the ex-gay organizations, Exodus International. In a statement of apology for his work in creating and sustaining Exodus, founder Michael Bussee described his experience with the program this way:

> Some simply dropped out and were never heard from again. I think they were the lucky ones. Others became very self-destructive. One young man got drunk and deliberately drove his car into a tree. Another (a fellow leader of the ex-gay movement) told me that he had left EXODUS and was now going to straight bars—looking for someone to beat him up. He said the beatings made him feel less guilty—atoning for his sin. One of my most dedicated clients, Mark, took a razor blade to his genitals, slashed himself repeatedly, and then poured drain-cleaner on the wounds—because after months of celibacy he had a "fall."
>
> In the midst of all of this, my own faith in the EXODUS movement was crumbling. No one was really becoming "ex-gay." Who were we fooling? As one current EXODUS leader admitted, we were just "Christians *with* homosexual tendencies who would rather not have those tendencies." By calling ourselves

"ex-gay" we were *lying to ourselves and to others*. We were *hurting people*.

In 1979, another EXODUS pioneer (Gary Cooper) and I decided to leave EXODUS—and our wives. For years, we had both firmly believed that the EXODUS process would make us straight. Instead, we realized we had fallen in love with each other! We came out publicly against EXODUS in 1991. Our story is featured in the documentary "One Nation Under God." Gary died of AIDS shortly before the film was completed.[31]

Stories like this one are hardly unique. They raise questions about the extent to which the self-reports of those undergoing SOCE are trustworthy descriptions of what is really happening and the extent to which they are, instead, hopeful expressions of what participants would like to be true of themselves. Once we factor in these possibilities, Jones's and Yarhouse's poor success rate for conversion starts to look like an unrealistically optimistic reading of the evidence.

In short, it is deeply misleading for Sprigg to claim that research shows gays and lesbians can change their sexual orientation. At best, what the research shows is that highly motivated people who commit to changing their sexual orientation and devote themselves to this project in a concerted way will *almost* always fail. To say, in this context, that change is possible is simply to say that given the current evidence, we can't confidently remove the "almost."

What we can say with confidence is that changing one's sexual orientation will not be a viable choice for most gays and lesbians—and arguably not for any of them. If we recommend such a change, what we will be recommending is that they invest personal resources into a project of self-transformation that isn't likely to work. Since those motivated to seek SOCE are largely driven by the urge to resolve the strong dissonance between their sexuality and their religious values, urging them to invest effort into a project that will almost certainly fail seems like a recipe for disappointment. Add that disappointment to the existing self-loathing that comes from having a sexuality your religious community condemns, and we shouldn't be surprised if some people take a razor to their own genitals.

---

31. Bussee, "Statement of Apology," para. 11–13.

5

Homosexuality, Mental Health, and the Good of Children

So far I have argued that sexual orientation is not chosen and, according to the best research, not the sort of thing we can ordinarily expect to be able to change. Even granted the optimistic view that a small percentage can change their sexuality through dedicated effort, the majority who try will fail.

This has important implications for what it means to love our gay and lesbian neighbors. To *categorically* condemn homosexuality—to condemn *every* expression of it including marital ones—is to impose on gays and lesbians a grim set of options. They can pursue a straight marriage defined by pretense, lack of real intimacy, and a sex life cut off from romantic love and facilitated by pretense—in other words, sex that defies the values underlying the Christian commitment to confining sex to marriage. Those who take this option would be depriving both themselves and their spouse of authentic intimacy. Given the love ethic, this would be a very difficult option to recommend (although we should show compassion toward those who, out of desperation, make that choice).

The other alternative, given the categorical condemnation of homosexuality, is *suppression*: gays and lesbians can attempt to never have sex, *ever*, from the moment of their sexual awakening until they die. They can attempt to reject every single opportunity for romantic love that ever comes their way for the entirety of their mortal lives, even if they meet that soulmate who makes their heart sing. In short, the categorical condemnation of homosexuality imposes on gays and lesbians (or most of them, if you embrace Jones's and Yarhouse's conclusions) a moral requirement to make a lifelong sacrifice heterosexuals aren't obligated to make, one that almost everyone I know, gay or straight, would find enormously burdensome.

What is called for here is different from the celibacy of Roman Catholic clergy, who voluntarily adopt celibacy as part of their vocation. Heterosexual clergy could decide not to enter the priesthood and instead pursue a different career that allows them to marry. If they don't think celibacy is something they can handle, that's what they should do. But the celibacy that conservative Christianity foists on gays and lesbians is not part of a vocational choice. Since their sexuality is supposedly defective no matter how it's expressed, they must either change it or suppress it. And since change is a miracle God seems thrifty with, they're left with suppression.

Imposing such a burden does not seem compatible with the love ethic *unless* it does some good, either for gays and lesbians themselves or for others who might be affected (such as, for example, children). Does it? In this chapter, I will consider what behavioral and social sciences research has to say on this question. More precisely, I want to explore whether empirical research supports the following claim: *homosexuality should be categorically condemned, despite the hardships this imposes on gays and lesbians, because suppressing a homosexual orientation is good for either gays and lesbians or affected third parties.* My conclusion will be that the research offers no such support. If Christians want to support the view that suppressing homosexuality is good for people, they'll have to look elsewhere.

Homosexuality and Mental Health

In his *Top Ten Myths* booklet, Peter Sprigg argues that "regardless of whether one considers homosexuality *itself* to be a mental disorder, there can be no question that it is *associated* with higher levels of a whole range of mental disorders."[1] The implication is that it's bad for you to be gay. Sprigg, of course, thinks the solution is for gays and lesbians to make themselves straight; but were he to concede the unviability of this solution he might urge celibacy on the grounds that this is better for the mental health of gays and lesbians than any expression of their sexuality, even monogamy.

There are those who do urge precisely this—including some gay and lesbian Christians who have accepted the categorical condemnation of

1. Sprigg, *Top Ten Myths*, 22.

homosexuality and have sought to live a life of sexual abstinence. Some, such as Wesley Hill, have earnestly sought a path of meaning and joy in such a life by, in part, cultivating alternative, non-sexual sources of intimacy to fill the void: a life in which "spiritual friendship"—notably chaste friendship that is covenanted, cemented by vows—replaces a sexually-intimate life partnership.[2]

There is no reason to suppose that Hill and others who advocate for this life are lying about the value and richness it offers them. But to suppose that all people are cut from the same cloth and can equally attain to such a life is another matter. Clearly, we need (platonic) friendship, especially when we are without a romantic partnership. But it does not follow that foregoing romantic intimacy for a lifetime is no sacrifice for those with intimate friends, or that it does not diminish the quality of our lives. And for some, it may be more than just a disappointment that can be readily borne in the course of an otherwise satisfying life.

In some cases, personal history plays a role. It is one thing to ask someone who hasn't found the love of their life—a partner for whom they feel intense romantic and sexual attraction in addition to deep compatibility—to abstain from seeking an intimate romantic partnership akin to marriage. To demand this of those who have found such a person is quite different. The agony such a demand can generate is dramatized in literary form in Annie Proulx's story, "Brokeback Mountain,"[3] as well as in the movie it inspired.

But aside from such matters of personal history, it is a mistake to assume that all persons have the same gifts with respect to suppressing or setting aside human drives as potent as sexuality. There is a long Christian tradition, stretching back to St. Paul, that lifts up the celibate life as potentially rich and satisfying *for those who have the gift for it*. But as Paul points out (1 Cor 7:1–9), most people *don't* have that gift, and for them sexual expression in marriage is the better choice. Since it would be foolish to suppose that, unlike heterosexuals, *all* gays and lesbians have been blessed with the gift of celibacy, one might suppose that Paul's advice should apply to gays and lesbians, too: for those who don't have the gift, marriage is the better choice.

Paul's advice here reflects a loving responsiveness to human diversity: not everyone has the same gifts (1 Cor 7:7), and we can't expect everyone to be able to live the life Paul can live. At least in part, Paul's view can be

---

2. Hill, *Spiritual Friendship*.

3. Of course, in this story Jack and Ennis do not attempt celibacy in lieu of a relationship with one another. Rather, they pursue pretense-filled and loveless marriages with women and, with each other, something far less (and far less satisfying) than marriage.

couched in the language of mental health: *if you lack the gift of celibacy, it is better for your mental health to enter into marriage and express your sexuality in that context than to struggle all your life to suppress your sexual desires.* Conservatives who want to invoke the mental health of gays and lesbians as a reason for a celibacy requirement would have to deny that this Pauline principle applies to gays and lesbians. They would have to say that for gays and lesbians who lack the gift of celibacy, it is better for their mental health to fight their sexual and romantic yearnings all their lives, to burn with unfulfilled desires and risk stumbling into unplanned sexual encounters out of weakness of will, than to channel their sexuality into a monogamous relationship with someone they love.

Stated in these terms, the claim sounds staggeringly implausible—the sort of claim that, absent strong evidence for its truth, we ought to reject. Does the research provide such evidence?

Hardly. In fact, research indicates that gays who express their sexuality in monogamous or primarily monogamous same-sex relationships are better off, in terms of mental health, than those who remain single or are in open relationships.[4] According to that research, it isn't better for their mental health to remain single (nor is it better for them to be promiscuous or in "open" relationships). What is best for their mental health is the same-sex equivalent of marriage.

To be fair, this research doesn't distinguish between celibate and non-celibate singles, and so we can't confidently say based on this research alone that monogamous gays are better off than those gay singles who succeed at remaining celibate, even if they are better off than gay singles as a broader class. Maybe celibate gays are better off than monogamous ones, but non-celibate single gays are so much worse off that they bring down the average.

But even if we were to grant this assumption for the sake of argument, there's the fact that most people don't have the gift of celibacy. Human beings aren't generally very successful at maintaining a commitment to sexual abstinence. It's hard enough to manage it until marriage.[5] One philosophical opponent of same-sex sex, in trying to explicate the nature of human sexuality, notes that "we are built in such a way that sexual arousal is hard to resist and occurs very frequently."[6] To suppose that most gays and lesbians will succeed at suppressing their sexuality for a lifetime defies the evidence

4. Parsons, "Alternatives to Monogamy," 303–12.

5. For example, research indicates that teens who make a pledge of premarital sexual abstinence/virginity display essentially the same patterns of premarital sexual activity as comparable teens who do not make such pledges, with the majority in both groups having had premarital sex. See Rosenbaum, "Patient Teenagers?" 110–20.

6. Feser, "The Role of Nature in Sexual Ethics," 71.

of human nature. And of the non-celibate options, monogamy is best for mental health. What follows, all else being equal, is that Christians who care about the mental health of gays and lesbians, at least those who lack the gift of celibacy (which will be most of them), should urge them to do what Christians have long said heterosexuals without the gift of celibacy should do: restrict their sexual expression to marriage.

In fact, contrary to Sprigg and the Family Research Council, the consensus among social scientists is that homosexuality as such is not maladaptive.[7] They do not deny Sprigg's claim that homosexuality is linked to a "range of mental disorders," but they argue that on the evidence, these correlations are best explained as effects of the social *stigmatization* of homosexuality and bisexuality.

The American Psychological Association defines "stigma" according to four key elements:

> (a) individual differences are labeled; (b) these differences are linked to undesirable traits or negative stereotypes; (c) labeled individuals are placed in distinct categories that separate them from the mainstream; and (d) labeled persons experience discrimination and loss of status that lead to unequal access to social, economic, and political power.[8]

When stigma in this sense targets people based on sexual orientation, it is usually called "sexual stigma," and most social scientists agree (the members of NARTH being a glaring exception) that the distinctive psychological health issues faced by sexual minorities arise from this kind stigma, especially when it becomes internalized—what is called "internalized homophobia" or "self-stigma."[9]

For gays and lesbians, stigmatization begins primarily in adolescence—with homophobic teasing and bullying and other forms of social marginalization.[10] Gays and lesbians are thus subjected to negative social pressures at a vulnerable time in their development, resulting in a range of problems including higher risks of depression, suicidal tendencies, drug and

---

7. The groundbreaking work in support of this was made by Evelyn Hooker, "The Adjustment of the Male Overt Homosexual," 18–31. For an overview of the rationale for the decision to remove homosexuality from the list of recognized disorders, see Gonsiorek, "The Empirical Basis," 115–36. See also Pillard, "Sexual Orientation and Mental Disorder," 52–56.

8. American Psychological Association Task Force, *Report*, 15.

9. Ibid., 15–16.

10. Martin and Hetrick, "Stigmatization," 163–83.

alcohol abuse, and school truancy.[11] But the risks associated with such stigmatization are significantly reduced by supportive environments at home or at school.[12] In other words, while there are negative mental health effects correlated with homosexuality, these diminish to the extent that communities important to sexual minority children—most notably their schools and families—do not tolerate their stigmatization but actively nurture and support them.

The most plausible way to account for this data is to say that the mental health problems correlated with homosexuality don't result from being gay, but from being stigmatized for being gay. One study made the following observation:

> It is noteworthy how similar LGB student scores are to heterosexual students when in a positive school climate and when not experiencing homophobic harassment. This suggests that schools with low homophobic teasing and a positive school climate will drastically reduce the prevalence of negative outcomes in LGB youth.[13]

If this is right, there is clear reason for Christians who care about the mental health of gays and lesbians to stand against sexual stigmatization. There is no comparable reason to urge sexual suppression, especially given the presumptive implausibility of the view that such suppression would be good for mental health.

Furthermore, there are reasons to worry that condemning homosexuality *contributes* to the stigmatization of gays and lesbians. It is true that condemning behavior is not the same as stigmatizing persons. It is also true that you can call homosexuality a sin without bullying or teasing gay and lesbian adolescents. Nevertheless, a degree of stigma is an inevitable consequence of condemning *every* expression of a homosexual orientation (even committed monogamy).

If a homosexual orientation is unchosen and efforts to change it generally fail, this means that their orientation is a fact about gays and lesbians, a given in their lives, that makes them different from the majority. The

---

11. See Munoz-Plaza et al., "Lesbian, Gay, Bisexual and Transgender Students," 52–63; Treadway and Yoakam, "Creating a Safer School Environment," 352–57; and three articles by Rivers: "Social Exclusion," 13–18; "The Bullying of Sexual Minorities," 33–46; "Recollections of Bullying," 169–75.

12. Espelage et al., "Homophobic Teasing," 202–16; Birkett and Espelage, "LGB and Questioning Students," 989–1000; Needham and Austin, "Sexual Orientation, Parental Support, and Health," 1189–98.

13. Birkett and Espelage, "LGB and Questioning Students," 997.

difference will be one they are often painfully conscious of, especially when they first discover it. Especially in adolescence, those who are sharply different from the majority often experience that difference as a mark against them—they are outsiders, they don't "fit in"—unless they are actively affirmed and celebrated precisely at that point of difference. To condemn all homosexual behavior is not just to refrain from affirming gays and lesbians at this point of difference. And it can't be restricted to a critique of nothing but external behavior. If every expression of a homosexual orientation is wrong, even committed monogamy, then the very sexuality of gays and lesbians is defective in the sense that it is *oriented essentially toward sin*. In other words, their very sexuality is morally bad in a way that the sexuality of others is not. They are not merely different from the majority. They are worse.

If your very sexuality is so broken that any time you pursue love in the romantic sense you have *committed a sin*—if that part of you responsible for one of the most meaningful kinds of human connection must always and everywhere be suppressed on pain of moral condemnation—then it is your sexual orientation itself and not just sexual behavior that is being judged in negative terms. As I will argue more fully in chapter 7, such judgment pushes sexuality to the forefront of your personal story. You won't be able to treat it as something marginal like eye-color. Just as skin-color becomes part of the identity of blacks in societies where racism is a significant force, so too with sexuality: if your community condemns your sexual orientation, your whole sexual self takes on a significance in your self-understanding it might not otherwise have. It becomes part of your identity. Part of *who you are* is condemned.

Condemning homosexuality is thus fundamentally unlike condemning adultery, say, or promiscuity. Adultery and promiscuity are ways of expressing sexuality. When we condemn those behaviors, we do not say that the underlying sexuality of the person who commits them has no legitimate expression. We tell adulterers to go back to their spouses. We tell the promiscuous to commit themselves to a single partner in monogamous marriage. By contrast, we tell gays and lesbians that unless they are somehow able to achieve the miracle of changing it, they must completely suppress the sexual side of their being—because any way of expressing it is a sin.

In fact, if same-sex intimacy is sinful *even* when expressed in the context of a nurturing, tender, committed relationship, then gays and lesbians who form committed monogamous partnerships may actually be judged *worse* than those gays and lesbians who lose themselves in impermanent and promiscuous encounters—because the former are (according to the conservative view) *making a lifelong commitment to sin*; whereas the latter can simply be seen as succumbing to weakness of will.

Imagine being an adolescent who has stable homosexual attractions and who grows up hearing the message that all homosexual acts are sinful. That message doesn't tell the adolescent *how* to develop her sexuality, *which* expressions of it to cultivate and nurture and which to avoid. Rather, it tells her *she can't express it at all* because her sexuality itself is unacceptable.

For bisexuals the story is a bit different, but in many ways the same. Even though their sexuality admits of accepted expressions, when "even the desire" for same-sex intimacy is wrong (as the Southern Baptist Convention explicitly insists), something about their sexuality is being stigmatized. Unlike their heterosexual peers, they can't expect their community to celebrate with them when they finally fall in love with someone who not only returns the feeling but is a good match in terms of interests, temperament, values, and life goals. They can't expect their community to be empathetic comforters when romantic losses break their hearts. They can't expect these things because the community's support for their loving relationships is conditioned by whether, this time around, they happen to fall in love with a person of the right sex.

For heterosexuals this condition is met automatically, whenever and wherever they fall in love. For bisexuals it isn't. And so, even though bisexuals, unlike gays and lesbians, have ways of expressing their sexuality that don't violate the traditional norm, their sexuality nevertheless puts them out of step with any community that embraces that norm. We never really know when we're going to meet the love of our lives, but if we're straight we know it will be someone of the opposite sex, and so we never face the risk that conforming to the community's values will require us to walk away from the beloved. Bisexuals do face that risk. For gays and lesbians, it is a certainty: if they *ever* fall in love with *anyone*, they will be required to walk away from love.

The condemnation of homosexuality does not say, "Shape up and behave yourself sexually!" To gays and lesbians it says, "You're not allowed to express your sexuality at all. Who you are sexually is unacceptable no matter how you express it." While the message to bisexuals may be less bleak, it nevertheless singles them out as different from the heterosexual majority in a way that is judged bad.

When it comes to the condemnation of adultery, *all of us can stand in solidarity with one another, supporting each other in living up to a shared constraint*—because all of us have the potential to be attracted to someone who isn't our spouse. But a social norm condemning homosexual sex does not generate solidarity. It creates us/them divisions. When a community condemns homosexuality, the heterosexual majority is *imposing a constraint on* a minority group, demanding sacrifices that the majority doesn't need to make. It is a demand that those who are different either conform or hide their difference: "This is what we, the majority, are like. If you can't be like this, you need to pretend like you are or suppress who you are." Gays, lesbians, and bisexuals are thereby singled out and judged defective based on their sexuality.

To convey this message is not, of course, the same as teasing and bullying and systematic social exclusion (although it can easily serve as a breeding ground for such overt abuse—and in a fallen world, almost certainly will). A community can categorically condemn homosexuality without calling gays and lesbians faggots or beating them up; but the community cannot categorically condemn homosexuality without telling sexual minorities that a part of who they are is fundamentally bad. A community can categorically condemn homosexuality without ostracizing gays and lesbians from all meaningful social relationships; but they cannot do so without excluding them from such important aspects of social life as celebration of romantic love, empathy for its loss, and access to marriage.

Furthermore, psychological research suggests that the mental health issues associated with stigma are compounded when gays and lesbians internalize this stigmatization, when they embrace for themselves the idea that their sexuality is essentially bad.[14] Common sense suggests that belonging to conservative religious communities that condemn homosexuality leads to a higher rate of internalized stigma, and what research has been done tends to supports this.[15] It would seem to follow that, all else being equal, a religious community that categorically condemns homosexuality

---

14. The role of such self-stigma or internalized homophobia in the development of gays and lesbians is explored in a series of articles by Malyon: "The Homosexual Adolescent," 321–30; "Biphasic Aspects," 335–40; and "Psychotherapeutic Implications," 59–69. See also Warwick et al., "Sexuality and Mental Health Promotion," 131–46; Gonsiorek and Rudolph, "Homosexual Identity," 161–76; Meyer and Dean, "Internalized Homophobia," 160–86; and Hershberger and D'Augelli, "The Impact of Victimization," 65–74.

15. Barnes and Meyer, "Religious Affiliation, Internalized Homophobia," 505–15. Wagner et al., "Integration," 91–110; Schuck and Liddle, "Religious Conflicts," 63–82; Mahaffy, "Cognitive Dissonance," 392–402. But the complex dimensions of religious communities and the variable ways individuals relate to them has generated some mixed findings. One research team found that higher level of religious commitment and scriptural literalism—factors often associated with conservative religion—had little impact on internalized homophobia. But a tendency to think for oneself about religious questions rather than defer to authority reduced the level of internalized homophobia. See Harris et al., "Religious Attitudes, Internalized Homophobia," 205–25.

is engaged in a practice that is bad for the mental health of the gays and lesbians in their midst.

Of course, all is not always equal. One study found that although immersion in "non-affirming religious environments" is correlated with "higher internalized homophobia," it was not associated with a higher incidence of mental health problems.[16] But a deeper look at the evidence led the researchers to conclude that "internalized homophobia may have suppressed the otherwise positive effect that exposure to religion can have on mental health."[17] This conclusion is supported by an Austrian study, which concluded that while religion is generally known to serve as a protective factor against suicide, in the case of gays and lesbians religion had mixed effects by virtue of the higher rates of internalized homophobia among those who belong to religious communities. For gays and lesbians, religion serves as *both* a protective factor *and* a risk factor for suicide.[18]

The implications for Christian ethical reflection are not straightforward, and I don't mean to draw the conclusion (yet) that because condemning homosexuality stigmatizes sexual minorities, it's immoral to condemn homosexuality. Reaching that conclusion will require more work. The main conclusion at this point is that correlations between homosexuality and mental health problems are caused not by being gay but by being stigmatized for being gay—especially when the stigma is internalized. While belonging to a religious community that condemns homosexuality tends to increase internalized stigma, religious belonging may also provide mental health benefits that offset the negative impacts. But this very fact puts sexual minorities into a difficult position that heterosexuals don't generally face: *the benefits of religious belonging come at a cost, a payment that their heterosexual peers don't need to pay*. If the benefits are truly great, then the cost of rejecting one's sexuality—and perhaps struggling valiantly (if fruitlessly) to change it—may seem worth it. The question the community needs to ask is whether it is fair or loving to selectively impose such costs.

In sum, being gay or lesbian does not, as such, damage mental health. But gays and lesbians are more likely to experience social stigma. They are more likely to be told that their intimate relationships are an abomination. They are more likely to find that those around them condemn their life partnerships rather than support them. They are more likely to be bullied. They are more likely to be the victims of gay-bashing. They are more likely to be pushed out of their communities of origin, rejected by their families,

---

16. Barnes and Meyer, "Religious Affiliation, Internalized Homophobia," 509–11.
17. Ibid., 512.
18. Kralovec et al., "Religion and Suicide Risk," 413–23.

treated as someone who doesn't belong. They are more likely to face the hard choice between being accepted by an otherwise nurturing community that demands they reject their sexuality, or accepting their sexuality and so earning the community's repudiation. If they make the latter choice, they may face the further choice between keeping the truth about themselves a secret so they can enjoy the benefits of community while living a lie, or being honest about who they are and facing exclusion or marginalization.

And even if none of these social costs are imposed, the lack of sufficient welcome and acceptance can, for adolescents conscious of their difference, set them on a troubling trajectory. That is, some differences in mental health outcomes may result, even absent overt stigmatization. It can be enough that society blithely assumes everyone's heterosexuality (as society for so long has blithely assumed right-handedness) in a way that makes gay and lesbian adolescents vividly conscious of their difference. For adolescents yearning to find their place, the sense of not fitting in can result in higher frequencies of substance abuse and depression, even absent overt stigmatization, unless there is a sufficiently clear expression of welcome. We might call the lack of such a welcome "heterosexist neglect." And despite all the changes that have happened over the last few decades, we still live in a world where expressions of welcome are mixed with heavy doses of heterosexist neglect *and* overt stigmatization.

In his *Ten Myths* booklet, Sprigg recognizes that so-called "homosexual activists" blame the mental health problems of sexual minorities on "homophobic discrimination" (although he fails to note that it's the majority of *social scientists* who do so, not just his so-called activists). But he quickly dismisses this view by appealing to a single study out of the Netherlands. In what Sprigg describes as "perhaps the most 'gay-friendly' country in the world," there apparently remains a link between being gay and higher rates of mental health problems.[19]

For Sprigg, this is enough to throw out the prevailing consensus among social scientists. His thinking seems to be this: if stigma were the reason for these mental health issues, then we wouldn't see *any* such issues in the Netherlands—*because, presumably, in the Netherlands sexual minorities experience no stigmatization at all, no heterosexist neglect, only an unqualified welcome*. Higher frequencies of depression, anxiety, substance abuse and the like must therefore be essential features of being gay.

For that argument to work, the Netherlands would need to be an island of gay acceptance untouched by the homophobic and heterosexist forces in play elsewhere in the world. So, is the Netherlands such an insulated gay

19. Sprigg, *Ten Myths*, 25.

utopia? Not according to a 2006 study for the Netherland's Sociaal Cutlural Planbureau.[20] The English summary of the report by the Netherlands Institute of Social Research indicates that "the majority of gays and lesbians have encountered negative experiences, on the streets or in nightlife centres, but also from family members, at work and in sport." Included among these negative experiences were such things as "denigrating comments about homosexuality or homosexuals, malicious gossip or bullying, and verbal or sometimes even physical violence. 'Faggot' is a widely used insult at work and in sport."[21] The summary also notes that 42 percent of Dutch respondents in one survey said they found two men kissing in public "repugnant," while 31 percent were offended by the public kissing of two women. This repugnance wasn't the result of some cultural abhorrence of public displays of affection, however, since only 8 percent were similarly offended by the public kissing of heterosexual pairs.[22]

Furthermore, same-sex marriage became legal in the Netherlands in 2001, whereas heterosexual marriage became legal . . . well, it has *always* been legal. The change from legally excluding gays and lesbians from the most important social institution to including them is only a few years old. To suppose that some legal magic wand can make a multi-generational legacy of social marginalization vanish overnight is worse than naïve.

One final point. Let's suppose Sprigg is right. Let's assume, for the sake of argument, that there are mental health problems linked to sexual orientation itself, apart from stigma and heterosexist neglect. If sexual orientation is unchosen and can't ordinarily be changed, we won't help gays and lesbians by *adding* stigma to their situation. Under this assumption, the question is how we can best address the mental health issues supposedly linked to homosexuality. To suppose that lifelong suppression of intimacy, lifelong denial of romantic love, lifelong exclusion from marriage, will somehow make things *better* verges on preposterous. If there is something about being gay that generates a propensity for depression and anxiety and substance abuse, then there is all the more reason to provide gays and lesbians with the kinds of goods—such as the support and security and comfort of marriage—that can help guard against these propensities; and there is all the more reason to avoid heaping on gays and lesbians even more and greater psychological stressors, such as the stigma that accompanies the categorical condemnation of homosexuality, and the burden of attempting lifelong suppression of sexuality when one lacks the gift of celibacy.

20. Kuyper and Bakker, *De Houding ten Opzichte*.
21. Netherlands Institute of Social, "Acceptance," para. 7.
22. Ibid., para. 15.

Harming Children

So far we have seen that, based on the prevailing research, there is no reason to think it is good for the mental health of gays and lesbians to suppress their sexuality altogether rather than pursue monogamy. Rather, the research *problematizes* the condemnation of homosexuality because of the link it draws between mental health problems and sexual stigma. So, if Christians want to argue that concern for the welfare of gays and lesbians justifies the condemnation of homosexuality, they need to look somewhere other than the mental health research for support.

But none of this is the end of the story. From the standpoint of love, we need to consider not only how expressing or suppressing homosexual dispositions affects gays and lesbians. We also need to consider the welfare of others. Perhaps the base-level stigmatization of a minority group is an unavoidable cost of showing the right kind of love for *everyone* affected.

A critic might point out, for example, that the categorical condemnation of sex with children singles out a minority group—namely pedophiles—based on their unchosen desires, communicating that their sexuality is essentially broken and that they must pursue suppression if they can't fix it. But, clearly, we still want to condemn sex with children. In fact, an ethic of love would demand that we do so, *because sex with children harms them.* Out of love for children, we must insist that pedophiles resist acting on their desires. No resulting stigma, however inevitable, should stop us.

In short, most would agree that we should communicate to pedophiles a message *exactly analogous to the message that conservative Christians direct toward gays and lesbians.* Communicating this message to pedophiles is appropriate even though a society that does so inevitably stigmatizes pedophiles, at least in the base-level sense. We might think we should refrain from imposing any stigma *greater* than necessary. But if a pedophile feels left out because he isn't allowed to marry the toddler of his choice, then so be it.

All of this is right. But gays and lesbians are not pedophiles. Imposing the same draconian requirements on them that we impose on pedophiles trivializes the profound differences between consenting adult same-sex monogamy and the sexual exploitation of children. While all people, gay or straight, need to observe constraints on the expression of their sexuality to avoid exploitation and harm, when an adult gay couple enters into a consensual monogamous relationship defined by reciprocal care and support, this is not a matter of exploitation or harm but of mutual love. As we've seen, no compelling empirical research suggests that gay and lesbian adults suffer mental harm when they pursue such consensual relationships. But that means they don't harm the mental health of their partner, either, since their partner would be *another* gay or lesbian adult pursuing such a relationship.

When pedophiles act on their sexual urges, *they violate children*. It almost pains me to have to point out this difference. Of course there are adults, gay and straight, who aren't pedophiles but find themselves attracted to physically mature teens, and if they act on these attractions they violate children, too. The violation of children is not the exclusive purview of pedophiles. What follows is that we should condemn all adults who act on attractions to children, whether they be pedophiles or straight men chasing their teen daughters' friends—or gay men chasing after teenage boys at a gay dance club. But no such condemnation implies the condemnation of loving marriages between consenting adults.

Put simply, when consenting adults marry one another and pursue a marriage of mutual care without abuse or exploitation, there is no victim. Someone might argue that when those consenting adults are of the same sex, there are spiritual harms that behavioral and social scientists can't measure. I will consider hypotheses about such empirically untestable harms in chapter 10. For now, the point is this: such supposed spiritual harms aside, the same-sex equivalent of a happy marriage has no direct victims.

But what about *indirect* ones? Is it possible that a society that accepts same-sex relationships would thereby indirectly hurt third parties? One common claim among conservatives is that socially accepting same-sex relationships—especially by legalizing same-sex marriage—threatens the institution of marriage, thereby undermining a bedrock social institution. However, this prediction of calamity is not based on empirical research but on slippery slope fears, which I will explore in chapter 11.

There is, however, another pool of indirect victims that Sprigg and the Family Research Council point to: our children. But how are children harmed—even indirectly—by the private behavior of consenting adults? There are two arguments. The first is this: if society comes to accept same-sex relationships, then more children will end up being raised by same-sex couples; but children raised by same-sex couples are worse off than children raised by heterosexual ones. The second argument, roughly, is this: there is (supposedly) a positive correlation between homosexuality and pedophilia: gays are more likely to be pedophiles. To accept homosexuality will therefore increase the frequency of pedophilia in society, resulting in more child victims.

Both arguments are terrible. They fail *even if we grant the empirical claims on which they are based*. But furthermore, the research does not support the empirical claims on which they are based. This doesn't stop Sprigg from concocting pseudo-evidence for the sake of linking gays and lesbians to pedophilia, and in the process bearing false witness against gays and lesbians in a way that is egregiously at odds with the love command.

But before turning to the child molestation charge, let's consider the milder argument, which rests on the claim that same-sex couples are worse parents than heterosexual ones. This claim is rejected in official statements by a wide range of professional organizations concerned with mental health and child welfare, including (but not limited to) the American Academy of Child and Adolescent Psychology, the American Academy of Pediatrics, the American Psychoanalytic Association, the American Psychological Association, and the Child Welfare League of America.[23] All assert that same-sex couples are as capable of being effective parents as heterosexual ones, appealing to relevant research to support their claim. Are all of these organizations lying or mistaken about what the research shows?

Sprigg, in his booklet, calls their assertion a "myth." In making the case for this view, he follows a strategy of mischaracterizing research, a strategy pioneered by James Dobson in a 2006 op-ed for *Time Magazine*, "Two Mommies Is One Too Many." In the essay, Dobson begins by claiming that, according to the research, "children do best on every measure of well-being when raised by their married mother and father." He then argues that gender differences matter in parenting, and cites the work of two scholars to support this: Kyle Pruett and Carol Gilligan.[24]

Both Pruett and Gilligan were outraged by Dobson's invocation of their research.[25] Both wrote letters to *Time Magazine* and Dobson complaining that he had distorted their work. Gilligan not only denounced Dobson's interpretation of her research in a letter but in a YouTube video, in which she described his use of her work as "distorted use of science," as a "caricature," and as "disrespectful."[26] Pruett, accusing Dobson of cherry-picking for discriminatory purposes in a manner "condemned in real science, common though it may be in pseudo-science circles," concludes his letter as follows:

> There is nothing in my longitudinal research or any of my writings to support such conclusions. On page 134 of the book you cite in your piece, I wrote, "What we do know is that there is no reason for concern about the development or psychological

---

23. Human Rights Campaign, "Professional Organizations on LGBTQ Parenting."
24. Dobson, "Two Mommies," 123.
25. Thacker, "Fighting a Distortion."
26. The YouTube Video can be found at https://www.youtube.com/watch?v=9NHdSVknB5Q.

competence of children living with gay fathers. It is love that binds relationships, not sex."[27]

Perhaps because of the moral force of Gilligan's video repudiation of Dobson's use of her work—and her explicit request in both the video and letter that he "cease and desist" from citing her work for his discriminatory goals—Gilligan is not quoted in Sprigg's *Ten Myths* booklet. Pruett, however, is still invoked—in precisely the way Dobson invoked him, in support of the very conclusion Pruett said there was "nothing in my longitudinal research or any of my writings" to support.

Like Dobson, Sprigg also begins by making the claim that children do best when raised by a married mother and father. Sprigg does so by quoting from a Child Trends Research Brief that says children do best when raised "by two biological parents who are in a low-conflict marriage."[28] In other words, children do better (all else being equal) when they are raised by two parents rather than one, when the marriage is low-conflict, and when the parents are the biological ones rather than, say, foster parents or one biological parent and a step-parent. But the research says nothing *as such* about the benefits of a two-*sex* parenting structure. Of course, the biological parents will *be* male and female unless one parent is transgender, but is it *this* fact or the fact that the children are being raised by their *biological* parents that matters?

Sprigg doesn't explore this issue, as important as it is. Instead, he sifts through the weight of the research to locate a single study in which children of (unmarried) same-sex couples did worse than comparable (unmarried) heterosexual couples. This 1996 study, by Soterios Sarantakos, is an outlier.[29] The American Psychological Association, in its 2005 report on gay and lesbian parenting, says that "Not a single study has found children of lesbian or gay parents to be disadvantaged in any significant respect relative to children of heterosexual parents."[30] Sociologist Paul Amato, in a mild critique of this statement, says that this is a somewhat unfortunate sentence, "given the

27. Besen, "Yale Professor," para. 4.

28. Moore et al., "Marriage from a Child's Perspective," 1. Current versions of the brief available for download now include a prefatory remark on an unnumbered lead-page from the lead author and Child Trends president, which says the following: "This Child Trends brief summarizes research conducted in 2002, when neither same-sex parents nor adoptive parents were identified in large national surveys. Therefore, no conclusions can be drawn from this research about the wellbeing of children raised by same-sex parents or adoptive parents." This disclaimer was presumably motivated by the kind of misuse to which Dobson and Sprigg put the brief.

29. Sarantakos, "Children in Three Contexts," 23–31.

30. American Psychological Association, *Lesbian and Gay Parenting*, 15.

existence of the Sarantakos (1996) study," and hence recommends that the sentence be revised as follows: "Studies overwhelmingly show that children of lesbian and gay parents are not disadvantaged . . . ."[31] In short, what the Sarantakos study shows is not that children of gay and lesbian couples do worse than children of heterosexual couples. What it shows is that among the studies into the subject, the conclusion that children of same-sex couples are not disadvantaged is *overwhelming* rather than *unanimous*. In other words, Sprigg had to search through a body of research that contradicted his conclusion before he could find one that offered modest support. Furthermore, the anomalous Sarantakos finding might be explained as an effect of the greater social stigma faced by children of same-sex couples—as a more recent Australian study would indicate.[32]

Despite the weight of contrary evidence, the conservative argument got a bit of a boost a few years after Sprigg wrote his booklet when a second study, published by Mark Regnerus, apparently supported the conclusion Sprigg favors.[33] But this study has been widely criticized. John Corvino concisely explains the chief problem with the Regnerus study this way:

> Regnerus' "Lesbian Mother" and "Gay Father" categories (unlike the "Intact Biological Family" Category) included children of adoptive parents, step-parents, single parents, and, notably, a large number from divorced parents. Regnerus then observes in the resulting data that the children of his "Lesbian Mothers" and "Gay Fathers" look less like children of married biological parents than they do like children of adoptive parents, step-parents, single parents, and divorced parents. Well, duh.[34]

In other words, Regnerus did not compare children raised by stable, long-term, committed same-sex partners with children raised by intact biological families. Instead, he compared children raised in *any* family structure that involved gay and lesbian parents (which could including everything from children raised by single prostitutes to children coming out of broken homes) with those raised by intact biological families.

Furthermore, we once again face the fact that if there is a disadvantage when all else is equal, the issue might have nothing to do with having two parents of the same sex and everything to do with the adult caretakers not being the biological parents. But suppose we could demonstrate that, on average, children raised by adoptive parents have more psychological health

31. Amato, "Well-being of Children," 771.
32. Crouch et al., "Parent-Reported Measures," para. 39.
33. Regnerus, "How different," 752–70.
34. Corvino, "Are Gay Parents Really Worse?" para. 11.

problems than do children raised by their biological mothers and fathers. Could we conclude from this that adoption is bad for children and ought not to be allowed? Of course not.

Adoptive parents can and do raise healthy, well-adjusted children. If there's anything that might reasonably be claimed, it's that being raised by both biological parents is better *all else being equal*. If a child has the option of being raised by their biological parents or by adoptive parents who are in all other respects equally competent and capable, there would be reason to prefer the biological parents. But to get from this to the conclusion that adoption is harmful and should be prohibited, we'd need to assume a whole lot of things that we wouldn't be justified in assuming—and our conclusion would clearly be false.

We'd have to assume, first, that when we allow adoption, there will be children who *would* have been raised by their biological parents who instead end up being raised by adoptive parents. Now this assumption might be true in rare cases, but mainly in ones where being raised by adoptive parents counts as an improvement. If adoption is outlawed, then children who come out of biological families characterized by *extreme parental negligence or abuse*, who might otherwise have ended up adopted by a loving family, could get stuck in abusive homes.

The point is this: even if children raised by their biological parents are better off, all else being equal, than adopted children, all else is not always equal. The reason we think it's a good idea to allow adoption in our society is because adoption is generally *good for the kids who are adopted*—and this is true even if there are challenges faced by adopted children that comparable non-adopted children don't need to struggle with.

Even if being raised by stable and loving biological parents is slightly better for developmental health than being raised by stable and loving adoptive parents, being raised by stable and loving adoptive parents is *far* better than being raised by unstable, abusive, or negligent biological ones or, in the case of orphans, by no parents at all. Having in place a system of adoption provides important social goods that would not otherwise be available, and on the whole is good for children—*even if* a comparison of comparable adoptive and biological families gives the latter an edge.

This adoption analogy makes it clear why the "bad for children" argument against same-sex marriage has to make so many dubious assumptions, even if we grant what the research gives us little reason to grant, namely that children do better (all else being equal) with both biological parents than with a same-sex parenting team (at least one of whom won't be the biological parent). The fact is that same-sex couples can and do raise healthy, well-adjusted children—and that remains true even if we grant the assumption that a parenting team made up of the biological parents is the *best* arrangement, all else being equal. As John Corvino humorously points out, what follows from this assumption is that "gay and lesbian couples should not kidnap children from their own married biological parents."[35]

Children being raised by same-sex couples today haven't been stolen from loving biological parents. It's not as if they would've had the benefits of being raised by both biological parents *if only they hadn't been forcibly removed from their biological homes and put into the hands of a same-sex couple*. And the legalization of same-sex marriage won't change that, because legalizing same-sex marriage doesn't amount to legalizing child-abduction.

What it does is extend the legal supports of marriage to families where children are being raised by same-sex couples. These supports increase the likelihood that the same-sex parents will stay together and provide a stable child-rearing environment. The kids actually being raised by same-sex couples are better off when those couples are married—and hence benefit when same-sex marriage is a real social and legal option.

There might be a *few* cases where children are raised by same-sex parents who might have been raised by their biological parents had same-sex marriage remained illegal. The cases I have in mind are ones involving ill-advised marriages between gay men and straight women, or straight men and lesbians—marriages entered into out of a misplaced belief that this will provide the "cure" for someone's homosexuality. In a world where same-sex marriage is legal, some of these tragic marriages might break up sooner, resulting in children being raised by one biological parent and a same-sex step-parent.

But where same-sex marriage is available and socially accepted, there will be fewer ill-advised marriages of this sort to begin with. Gays and lesbians will feel less need to hide from their homosexuality by entering into straight marriages. Fewer children will come into the world in the context of a marriage where one party has no romantic feelings for the other while the other party senses the lack of authentic intimacy and is hurt by it. In other words, fewer children will be born into marriages virtually destined for unhappiness and careening toward divorce. Fewer such marriages means fewer children growing up in such unstable homes.

---

35. Corvino and Gallagher, *Debating Same-Sex Marriage*, 48.

Child Molestation

In the wake of the June 2016 mass shooting at Pulse, a gay nightclub in Orlando, Florida, Pastor Steven Anderson of the Faithful Word Baptist Church had this to say (in a video that YouTube quickly took down):

> The good news is that there's fifty less pedophiles in this world, because, you know, these homosexuals are a bunch of disgusting perverts and pedophiles. That's who was a victim here, are a bunch of, just, disgusting homosexuals at a gay bar, okay?[36]

Anderson goes on to say that while Christians ought to endorse the killing of gays and lesbians, the killing ought to be done by the justice system rather than lone vigilantes, since that is what the Bible teaches. So while Anderson celebrates the mass shooting's outcome, he's critical of the means. Instead of lone vigilantes killing dozens, the government should round them up by the thousands and execute them. Since this would overrun our current death row, I can only suppose Anderson envisions concentration camps. Maybe he'd advocate using gas chambers for the sake of efficiency. Stoning, while more biblical, would be unworkable when you're trying to exterminate hundreds of thousands of people.

Anderson, of course, represents an extreme that few conservative Christians would support, but his claim that gays are prone to pedophilia is more widely endorsed—including by Sprigg and the Family Research Council in their *Ten Myths* booklet. The consensus among social and behavioral scientists is that no such link exists, but Sprigg misrepresents the research to fabricate support for the opposite conclusion.

For an explanation of the consensus Sprigg rejects, UC Davis psychologist Gregory Herek offers one of the most accessible introductions to the research findings.[37] While I cannot improve on his review, I can offer an overview of some of its main insights and consider the implications for the kinds of contrary claims that Sprigg and those like him want to make.

Seminal research into child molestation shows that child sexual abusers—most of whom are men—fall into one of two main classes, what researchers Groth and Birnbaum call "fixated" and "regressed" molesters.[38] Fixated molesters have an exclusive sexual interest in children and have no

---

36. Video and transcript preserved on the Friendly Atheist blog. See Mehta, "Christian Pastor Celebrates," para. 3.

37. Herek, "Facts about Homosexuality and Child Molestation."

38. Groth and Birnbaum, "Adult Sexual Orientation and Attraction to Underage Persons," 176–77.

sexual attraction to adults. Thus, they do not have what we would think of as either a heterosexual or a homosexual orientation. As Herek puts it,

> . . . many child molesters cannot be meaningfully described as homosexuals, heterosexuals, or bisexuals (in the usual sense of those terms) because they are not really capable of a relationship with an adult man or woman. Instead of gender, their sexual attractions are based primarily on age. These individuals—who are often characterized as fixated—are attracted to children, not to men or women.[39]

Fixated child molesters are thus what we typically think of when we think of pedophiles (although we should remember that not all pedophiles act on their urges). Regressed molesters, by contrast, do have an adult sexual orientation: they are attracted to men or women and have in the past formed adult sexual relationships. In Herek's words, "Regressed offenders have developed an adult sexual orientation but under certain conditions (such as extreme stress) they return to an earlier, less mature psychological state and engage in sexual contact with children."[40]

It is a mistake to describe fixated child molesters as either gay or straight, as if they had an adult sexual orientation. They don't. It is thus similarly a mistake to say that fixated child molesters who target boys are gay. To get a sense of the kind of mistake, imagine there's a class of fetishists in society who don't like to *eat* frozen desserts but do get a thrill from pouring them down their shirts. Suppose some of these fetishists prefer the feel of snow cones over ice cream. Would it make sense to call them snow cone lovers? One could do so, I suppose, but it would be misleading, since it would class them with people who actually like to *eat* snow cones, which is a different thing altogether. Likewise, the disposition to form intimate romantic and sexual relationships with adults is a very different thing from the disposition to molest children.

Sprigg's case for saying that gay men are more likely than straight men to molest children rests on making this mistake. His case is based almost completely on the fact that roughly 30 percent of child molestation victims are boys (and 70 percent girls), whereas the number of men who are gay falls well below 30 percent (research suggests that about 3.5 percent of the population self-identifies as gay, lesbian, or bisexual[41]). He reasons that this

---

39. Herek, "Facts," para. 24.

40. Ibid., para. 22.

41. See Gates, "How Many?" 1. Note, however, that this figure represents the percentage who self-identify as LGB, not the percentage of individuals with a homosexual orientation. Given the stigma that attaches to homosexuality, many with such an

discrepancy is explained by the fact that gay men are drawn to molesting children at a much higher rate than straight men are.

But this inference is wrong for all sorts of reasons. One problem is that the ratio of male to female victims—which may be roughly 30/70, as Sprigg says[42]—may not reflect the ratio of male-targeting to female-targeting victimizers. For example, suppose that molesters who target boys are far more apt to have multiple victims than those who target girls.[43] This might happen in a society less likely to entrust girls than boys to mere acquaintances. Or suppose the percentages among *known* child molesters doesn't accurately reflect the percentages among all child molesters, known and unknown. Again, this could happen in a society where parents are less inclined to entrust their girls to the care of those they don't know well. In such a society, molesters who target girls may be forced to focus their predations on the children close to them, such as relatives—and family dynamics being what they are, such cases may go unreported more often than cases where a camp counsellor or scout leader is the offender.

To make the point clear, imagine there are ten child abusers, nine who target girls, and one who targets boys. Suppose the nine have to work hard to build parental trust. Hence, they gain access to only one child each. The one who abuses boys, meanwhile, targets nine victims at a summer camp. In this case, half of the victims are boys even though only one of ten offenders targets boys.

But let's side aside these issues and grant that the ratio of boy-targeting pedophiles to girl-targeting ones is higher than the ratio of gays to heterosexuals. The ratio is almost certainly not three male-targeting pedophiles for every seven female-targeting ones, as Sprigg would have it. But there is one study which puts the ratio at one to eleven, which is still somewhat higher than the ratio of gays to straights in the general population.[44] Does Sprigg's conclusion—that men who are attracted to other men are more drawn to child-molestation—follow from this?

No. To see why not, let's return to an earlier analogy. Suppose 95 percent of Americans who eat frozen treats prefer ice cream to snow cones, while 5 percent favor snow cones. Now imagine that, among our fetishists who like pouring frozen treats down their shirts, 90 percent would rather pour ice cream down their shirts, while ten percent favor the chill feel of

---

orientation may resist self-identifying as gay.

42. One review study puts the percentage of male victims at between 22 and 29 percent. Putnam, "Ten-Year Research Update Review," 270.

43. Research supports this supposition. See Abel et al., "Self-Reported Sex Crimes," 15–17.

44. Freund and Watson, "The Proportions," 40.

a snow cone. Does it follow from this that people who prefer to *eat* snow-cones are more prone toward this brand of messy fetishism than people who prefer to *eat* ice cream?

Of course not. There could be all sorts of reasons why, among our fetishists, the ratio of ice-cream dumpers to snow-cone dumpers doesn't correspond to the ratio of ice-cream lovers to snow-cone lovers. It would be silly to insist that this difference could *only* be explained by the fact that people who prefer *eating* snow cones are somehow primed for this bizarre fetish in a way that ice-cream lovers aren't.

Or take a different example. Suppose vampires are real, and tend to favor victims of one sex over another. And suppose we learned that, although only 5 percent of ordinary (non-undead) men are gay, 10 percent of male vampires prefer to drink the blood of male victims. Is the only reasonable conclusion here that gay men are somehow more prone, because of their homosexual orientation, to becoming vampires? Of course not. There could be all kinds of reasons. Maybe male blood is slightly sweeter, and 10 percent of vampires have a sweet tooth. Or sweet fang.

Likewise, a difference between the ratio of male-to-female victims among child molesters and the ratio of heterosexuality to homosexuality among men with adult sexual orientations could be explained in many ways. *One* explanation is that being gay—that is, being attracted to the hairier, broader-shouldered, more muscular of the sexes—primes you for being sexually drawn to hairless, narrow-shouldered, not-very-muscular children.

Not only is this explanation highly implausible on its merits,[45] *but the research does not support it*. Sprigg tries to support it by referencing a single assertion from one study, which says that 86 percent of male-on-male child molesters described themselves as homosexual or bisexual.[46] But the study from which he extracts the relevant sentence isn't a study *about* the sexual orientation of offenders.[47] The study pursues none of the research precision needed to judge whether this is a significant finding. Instead, it's a passing remark. For all we know, the researchers had their subjects fill out a form

---

45. In fact, Groth and Birnbaum try to explain the observed absence of child molestation among adult gay men by the fact that "the heterosexual male is sexually attracted to masculine qualities whereas the heterosexual male is sexually attracted to feminine characteristics, and the sexually immature child's qualities are more feminine than masculine." See Groth and Birnbaum, "Adult Sexual Orientation," 180–81.

46. Sprigg, *Top Ten Myths*, 36. The quoted percentage comes from Erickson et al., "Behavior Patterns," 83.

47. It's about the behavior patterns of offenders—that is, the kinds of offenses they commit against children.

where respondents were asked to put a check mark next to "homosexual" or "heterosexual" or "bisexual," and the fixated molesters with *no* adult orientation chose the box that conformed to the direction of their pedophilic urges without being able to point out that they lacked any attraction to adults of either sex. Since the study wasn't *about* this issue, the researchers provided no information that could enable us to assess the meaning for the remark. Apparently, in digging for evidence to support his view, Sprigg couldn't find any in the body of research that's actually *about* the issue. So he had to settle for an evidentially meaningless throw-away sentence in a research paper exploring something else.

The research that actually tackles the issue, by contrast, consistently *repudiates* Sprigg's claim. When Groth and Birnbaum looked at regressed child molesters—that is, those child molesters who *do* have an adult sexual orientation—they found no evidence to support the claim that male homosexuals are more likely to molest boys. In fact, they found *the opposite*. Here's how they summarize their findings:

> All regressed offenders, whether their victims were male or female children, were heterosexual in their adult orientation. There were no examples of regression to child victims among peer-oriented, homosexual males. The possibility emerges that homosexuality and homosexual pedophilia may be mutually exclusive and that the adult heterosexual male constitutes a greater risk to the underage child than does the adult homosexual male.[48]

In another study, all the child sex abuse cases at Denver Children's Hospital from 1991 to 1992 were examined. Of the 269 cases where the molester could be identified, only two (one man and one woman) could plausibly be said to have an adult homosexual orientation.[49] That's less than 1 percent. Should we conclude, therefore, that gay men are *less* likely to molest children than are heterosexual men? That would show more fidelity to the research than Sprigg shows.

Finally, a 1989 study of the arousal patterns of gay and straight men found that there was no higher rate of arousal to children among gays than among heterosexual men.[50] An interesting thing about this 1989 study, however, is that Sprigg cites it to support his assertion that "although heterosexuals outnumber homosexuals by a ratio of at least 20 to 1, homosexual pedophiles commit about one-third of the total number of child

48. Groth and Birnbaum, "Adult Sexual Orientation," 175.
49. Jenny, "Are Children at Risk?" 42.
50. Freund, "Heterosexuality," 107–17.

sex offenses."[51] But what that study aimed to do was determine whether the rate of male-on-male child abuse could be explained by a higher rate of pedophilic attraction among men with a homosexual orientation. The study found that it could *not*. In other words, Sprigg misleadingly cites this study to give the impression that research *opposing* his view supports it. He is so committed to slandering gay men in the most horrifying way that he is willing to egregiously misrepresent research to provide the illusion that his slander is backed by science. The result is an abuse of science for the purpose of bearing false witness.

There's a reason why overtly homophobic bigots like Pastor Steven Anderson so glibly and insistently link homosexuality to pedophilia. The sexual abuse of children is one of the most horrific and unthinkable crimes most of us can imagine. The attempt to link gays and lesbians to this crime is a way of *othering* them, a way of making them something less than ordinary humans. We see this clearly in the quote from Pastor Anderson that started this section. The mass murder of human beings is trivialized because the victims are gay. Their lives don't matter the way other lives matter "because, you know, these homosexuals are a bunch of disgusting perverts and pedophiles."

By twisting research to create the false impression that gay men are prone to pedophilia, Sprigg and the Family Research Council not only slander their gay and lesbian neighbors, but do so in a way that serves the aim of marginalization. It would be an understatement to say this falls short of Christian love. It is an egregious violation of love, having far more in common with racism and anti-Semitism and other divisive ideologies of the sort described in chapter 2.

But one lingering issue remains. As noted above, one study suggests that among fixated male pedophiles, the percentage who are fixated on boys is higher (a bit less than 10 percent) than the percentage of adult men who are gay (a bit less than 5 percent). While the research also shows that men with an adult homosexual orientation are not prone toward pedophilia (certainly no more prone to it than straight men, and arguably less), one still wonders what might cause the higher rate of male-targeting among fixated pedophiles who lack an adult sexual orientation. The researchers who noted this difference suggested the following hypothesis (although with scant evidence): maybe there is something about the process of homosexual development that makes it more likely to get twisted or stunted, so that a higher percentage of those who go through it never develop into gay

---

51. Sprigg, *Top Ten Myths*, 36.

men but become fixated pedophiles.⁵² The idea is that even though those who develop an adult homosexual orientation are no more likely to target children than straights, adolescents with a biological disposition to develop a homosexual orientation are somewhat more prone toward some kind of failure or distortion of normal development.

But if there is something about the adolescent sexual development of gays that makes the development process more likely to get twisted or stunted, the most obvious candidate for that "something" would be *the social stigmatization of homosexuality itself.* In a powerfully insightful essay on the problem of pedophilic priests targeting vulnerable boys in the Catholic Church, Andrew Sullivan (a gay Catholic) offers the following assessment:

> A young Catholic who finds out he's gay therefore simultaneously finds out that his church regards him as sick and inherently evil, for something he doesn't experience as a choice. That's a distorting and deeply, deeply damaging psychic wound. Young Catholic gay boys, tormented by this seemingly ineradicable sinfulness, often seek religious authority as a way to cope with the despair and loneliness their sexual orientation can create. (Trust me on this; it was my life.) So this self-loathing kid both abstracts himself from sexual relationships with peers, idolizes those "normal" peers he sees as he reaches post-pubescence, and is simultaneously terrified by these desires and so seeks both solace and cover for not getting married by entering the priesthood.
>
> None of this is conceivable without the shame and distortion of the closet, or the church's hideously misinformed and distorted view of homosexual orientation. And look at the age at which you are most likely to enter total sexual panic and arrest: exactly the age of the young teens these priests remain attracted to and abuse.
>
> That's the age when the shame deepens into despair; that's when sexuality is arrested; that's where the psyche gets stunted. In some ways, I suspect, these molesters feel as if they are playing with equals—because emotionally they remain in the early teens. I'm not excusing this in any way; just trying to understand how such evil can be committed.⁵³

---

52. Freund and Watson, "The Proportions of Heterosexual and Homosexual Pedophiles among Sex Offenders against Children," 41.

53. Sullivan, "It's the Gays' Fault," para. 7–9.

Sullivan's analysis here applies to any children who internalize the social message that their sexuality is "sick" or "sinful" and respond by trying to suppress it at all costs—not just to those who become pedophilic priests. When the vulnerable psychology of an adolescent is assaulted by socially-induced self-loathing and juvenile efforts to completely stifle their impulses toward romantic love, the results are unpredictable, but predictably bad.

As we've seen, the evidence clearly shows that persons with adult homosexual orientations are not attracted to children and are not disposed to molest them. But as we've seen, gays and lesbians who grow up in communities that stigmatize them suffer a wide range of negative psychological effects. Many suffer in their ability to form intimate partnerships—since they see their sexuality as ugly and so have difficulty allowing themselves to express it in relationships that are loving and nurturing and beautiful. If these stigmatizing forces can cripple the sexuality of some so badly that they end up with a sexuality stunted at childhood in the way Sullivan describes, this is not what happens for the overwhelming majority of gays and lesbians. But it is possible that the blame for *some* instances of pedophilia rests with the social practice of stigmatizing homosexuality.

Of course, this is psychological speculation. But that is the point. We know that being an adult gay or lesbian does not entail a propensity to molest children. We do not know what forces create the psychology of the child molester. And if, as the one study suggests, the ratio of male-victimizing to female-victimizing male pedophiles is somewhat different from the ratio of gays to straights, we don't know why that is true, either. But the explanation that stigmatization is part of the problem—given how obviously harmful stigma is to healthy psychological development in so many other ways—seems entirely plausible. It's certainly far more plausible than the notion that something about being attracted to the hairier, broader-shouldered, more muscular sex primes one for being attracted to hairless, narrow-shoulder, non-muscular children.

As such, trying to *justify* anti-gay stigma by appeal to child molestation is irrational. It's a bit like those in a sexist society trying to argue that women who have been historically deprived of an education should continue to be deprived, since an education would be "wasted on them"—and then offering, as proof of this, the fact that women in the society don't exhibit the same level of intellectual erudition as the well-educated men. Using the likely effects of bigotry to justify bigotry is the kind of argument only people gripped by bigotry find compelling.

Finally, for reasons I will address is chapter 8, I think Christians are right about the value of marriage in providing a safe and healthy context for sexual expression. I think they are right that we do everyone a favor, including impressionable adolescents during their volatile sexual awakenings, when we urge a respect for human sexuality that sees it as properly dignified and expressed in loving, monogamous life-partnerships. This vision of sexuality can help shape the sexual development of adolescents—*but it will not do so for gays and lesbians if they are excluded from it.* Since they have been historically excluded, we should be unsurprised if gays and lesbians suffer ill effects at a rate higher than those who haven't been excluded. But that is a reason to include them, not a reason to make the problem worse by perpetuating exclusion.

The point is this: there is no good evidence for the charge that gays and lesbians are somehow intrinsically prone toward child molestation. But beyond that, it would be an invalid leap to conclude what conservatives typically want to conclude—namely, that homosexuality should be stigmatized and gays and lesbians denied access to the goods of marriage.

The pedophilia argument, then, is bad in just about *every conceivable way*. It embodies a gross mischaracterization of research in the service of an unsound argument with the morally pernicious effect of dehumanizing a class of people. If we were compiling a list of good examples of how *not* to love our gay and lesbian neighbors as ourselves, this would surely feature prominently on that list. When the name of Christianity is attached to this pedophilia argument, we can add abuse of Christianity to the list of abuses on offer. For those who have committed these abuses, the only fitting Christian response, I think, is public apology and repentance.

6

Love the Sinner, Hate the Sin?

The story is common enough. Joe and Mary are walking out of a college classroom where the topic of homosexuality just came up. Joe, a conservative Christian convinced that all homosexual sex is sinful, expressed this conviction during the class discussion. Mary, a lesbian, isn't quite ready to let that go. She's tired of staying quiet.

"You really think I should break up with my girlfriend," she says, "even though we love each other?"

"The Bible says it's wrong. I can't go against that."

"But what about *love your neighbor as yourself*? Isn't that in the Bible, too? You really think it's *loving* to break apart people who love each other?"

"I'm not breaking you apart. You've got to decide to do that for yourself."

"But you think we *ought* to break up. You would encourage us to break up."

"That's what God says."

"You really know what *God* says? How arrogant can you be!"

"I . . . it's in the Bible. I don't have anything against you or your girlfriend, but the Bible is clear. What you're doing is a sin, and I can't condone sin."

"This is the most meaningful relationship of my life. Anyone who knows me knows what ending it would do . . . it would be—" She breaks off, seething with frustration. She doesn't know how to say it. He seems to her like a wall of righteousness. She gropes for words: "If you think the world would be improved by Katy and me breaking up, what you really think is that the world would be better if both Katy and I lost the most meaningful, beautiful, loving relationship either of us has ever known. You think the world would be a better place if this beautiful thing were destroyed, if it were taken away from us, if both of us were left heartbroken. How is that love? How can you claim to love me and Katy if that's what you think should happen? You think it would be loving to tell a happily married couple they should divorce, that it would be wrong for them to grow old together? You think it would be *loving* to call what they have an abomination?"

"I didn't use that word."

"You didn't have to."

"But it's not the same thing. A married couple—"

"It is the same thing!"

"It's not! One's a sin and the other isn't!"

"I'm telling you that Katy and I have something beautiful together, and wanting to tear us apart is wanting to destroy something that makes our lives better. That's not love."

"I don't want to tear you apart. That's not what I'm saying."

"You don't? So you think it's fine for us to stay together?"

"No! I'm saying I'm supposed to love the sinner while hating the sin."

"That's a f**king copout!" she shouts. "If you hate my relationship enough to insist it should end, you don't love me and you don't love Katy. You can't call what we have a sin and still love us. That's bulls**t!"

Mary storms away. Joe stands there, shaking a little in the aftermath of her fury.

So is Joe right that he can love Mary while condemning as sin her most intimate relationship? Is Mary right that to hate her relationship is incompatible with loving her?

The question is important. Setting aside extremists like Fred Phelps with his "God Hates Fags" signs, conservative Christians typically agree that we ought to love our gay and lesbian neighbors as ourselves. But they typically hold that such love is fully compatible with condemning homosexuality—because we can "love the sinner but hate the sin."

For many of my gay and lesbian acquaintances, they've heard this phrase so much it has become an emotional trigger. They react as if it were nothing but a smokescreen for perpetuating hateful practices and policies, a false promise of love to make the reality of hate more palatable (that is, more palatable to the agents of hate and third-party observers, not to the victims).

In a recent Tulsa World op-ed, Mike Jones expresses just this sort of cynicism. He concedes that the "love the sinner, hate the sin" phrase could be used in beneficial ways. "But what can be a helpful, even comforting phrase, under the right circumstances," he says, "has been hijacked by those whose purpose is to hand down judgments . . . ."[1] And instead of being a general remark about sin and sinners, it has acquired a focus. In Jones's experience, the phrase "is used now almost exclusively for those who disapprove of the lesbian, gay, bisexual, transgender community."[2]

The widespread LGBT suspicion of the phrase doesn't spring out of nowhere. James Dobson, for example, repeatedly says that we should love our gay and lesbian neighbors as ourselves. The following statement is typical:

> Christians have a scriptural mandate to love and care for all the people of the world. Even those who are living in immoral circumstances are entitled to be treated with dignity and respect. There is no place for hatred, hurtful jokes, or other forms of rejection toward those who are gay.[3]

But as we've already seen, Dobson has persistently used rhetoric that feeds anti-gay ideologies of division, including claims that homosexuals are a threat to children. Dobson founded the Family Research Council and remains closely tied to it—the same Family Research Council that published the slanderous booklet we looked at in the last chapter, where homosexuality was falsely linked to pedophilia through egregious misrepresentation of research.

When public figures pay lip service to loving gays and lesbians at the same time that they pursue and support unloving practices, it is not surprising that when gays and lesbians hear "love the sinner but hate the sin," they find it a kind of disingenuous double-speak that is mostly about making hateful practices tolerable to the wider public by wrapping it up in loving words.

But in my experience, most individual Christians who talk about loving the sinner while hating the sin are sincere. There was a time when I used the phrase myself in relation to my gay and lesbian neighbors—and I was earnest enough when I did so. My problem wasn't that I didn't mean it. My problem was that I didn't wrestle with what it means to show love for gays and lesbians. The phrase became a mantra that I could fall back on to avoid confronting a real difficulty—the difficulty highlighted in the exchange between Joe and Mary. What is involved in believing that homosexuality is a sin—really believing it, acting as if it were true? And what is

---

1. Jones, "The Problem We Have with Sin," para. 4.
2. Ibid., para. 7.
3. Dobson, "Q&A," para. 2.

involved in really loving my gay and lesbian neighbors? And are these things compatible?

There is a tension here, and conservative Christians who invoke the "love the sinner, hate the sin" dictum are often dodging that tension. The dictum becomes an easy conversation-stopper, a way to hide from challenging questions about what it means to show love. Gays and lesbians have every right to complain when Christians do that.

Nevertheless, I think the dictum is an indispensable part of the Christian moral life. No Christian who seeks to live by the ethic of love can deny that we must love sinners while hating sin. The problem doesn't lie with the dictum itself, but with how it is invoked and with the challenge of figuring out what it implies.

The Importance of Loving Sinners while Hating Sin

When Christians talk about hating sin, they mean condemning it *with feeling* (as opposed to an abstract intellectual rejection). When you hate sin, your emotions are involved. Consider two responses to a news story about a brutal case of child abuse. One person hears the story, continues to sip his scotch, and says mildly, "People ought not to do that sort of thing." Then he goes back to reading his book. The other person turns white, trembles with outrage and declares, "That's awful! It's horrible!" For the rest of the evening, she can't get the story out of her mind. Her spirit is unsettled. She thinks about the abused child and wants to cry.

Both are condemning the child abuse, but only the latter person hates it. And the former person's response seems to be missing something important. If our emotional selves aren't involved, then we aren't standing against the moral horror with our *whole selves*. Child abuse *ought* to unsettle us. A negative emotional response is fitting, and the failure to have that sort of response displays a flaw in our character.

The idea here is that a good moral character—a virtuous character—involves having emotional responses that are in tune with moral reality. To have a good moral character means having the disposition to become angry when the situation calls for anger, and the disposition to grieve when it is appropriate to grieve. This is a view of the ethical life that was powerfully developed by the philosopher Aristotle and, for good reasons, has been taken up by some of the greatest Christian moral thinkers. If we aren't outraged by child abuse, then our emotional dispositions aren't accurately tracking the moral landscape.

Of course, all of us exhibit such failures. We overreact to relatively minor slights and underreact to the tragedy of mass starvation. All of us have room to grow. But the point is that moral growth involves our emotions and dispositions, not just our actions. It involves our tendency to feel joy or anger or outrage.

For Christians, sin is the name for what disrupts God's loving plan for creation. Sin is what damages the world that God has made, poisons the hearts of God's children, keeps us from loving our neighbors as ourselves, and impedes the flourishing of the beloved community. Sin is, in short, the enemy of love, born out of our alienation from the God who is love—our alienation from *love itself*. If we align ourselves with the God of love, we must stand against the forces that threaten love. "Sin" is the Christian name for those forces.

Whether we do or not, we *ought* to hate sin, in the sense of standing against it, repudiating it, with our whole selves—including our emotional selves.[4] But if we are to love our neighbors as ourselves, we ought to hate sin while unconditionally loving each and every person who commits sin. And if our hatred of sin spills over onto the sinner even the tiniest bit, we are guilty of the very thing we must hate. We must therefore hate even the tiniest spill, the minutest overflow, because it is the enemy of love.

As difficult as it may be to carry out in practice, I am convinced that the "love the sinner/hate the sin" precept is one of the most fundamental guiding principles of the Christian life. I believe this because Christians are called to do two things: reject and repudiate sin with our whole selves, and love unconditionally every neighbor regardless of who they are and what they have done. But in a world where (as Christianity also teaches) *everyone* sins, we can only meet this two-fold call by mastering the trick of loving sinners while hating sin. As sinners, we will of course find such mastery elusive. But we must strive for it nonetheless.

Applying the Love Sinners/Hate Sin Precept to Homosexuality

Armed with something like this perspective, many conservative Christians argue that no matter how difficult it may be to authentically love our gay and lesbian neighbors while hating homosexual sex, doing so is possible, and it

---

4. However, if we hate sin because we hate certain *people* and our hatred of them spills over onto the things they do, our hatred of their sin isn't something to be praised. Because it is motivated by our failure to love our neighbors as ourselves, the hatred of sin in such a case is itself sinful.

is something we must struggle to do if we want to live up to our Christian calling.

Robert Griffith, a Baptist preacher in Australia, doesn't merely pay lip service to this idea but, in a powerful sermon, offers an impassioned plea for it.[5] He is honest about the scope of Christian failure to love gays and lesbians, and shares a story about his mentor, Alan—the man who brought him to Jesus. Griffith talks about how this man, after years of marriage, left his wife for another man and was rejected by essentially everyone from his former life. Griffith had a vivid dream of Alan standing in a crowd of people, all of their backs to him, and was moved to reach out to his former mentor. When he did, Alan wept. Later, Griffith invited Alan into his home *without hiding the children away* (apparently, Griffith and his wife considered doing this). He describes the encounter as follows:

> Before going to bed, our children talked with him. He nursed them and played with them and I saw the dad that I always admired and wanted to imitate. Alan cried when the children went to bed and said that we were the first people in seven years of hell, who had let him anywhere near their children.
>
> He went on to tell us of the judgement and condemnation that had come from the Church and former friends in the Church. He was bitter—no doubt about it—but he was brokenhearted too. His best friend, an elder in the Church in which they both served for years, cut Alan off the moment he heard of his homosexual orientation. He even had his phone number changed to a new silent number so Alan couldn't call him.[6]

Drawing from this experience, Griffith struggles to define the proper Christian stance toward people such as Alan. For reasons having to do with Scripture and natural law—topics I will explore in later chapters—Griffith cannot accept the progressive view that homosexual behavior is not a sin. But neither can he accept the rejection and exclusion from the community of faith that has been so often the fate of gays and lesbians. While he insists that God *can* cure gays of their homosexuality, he concedes that many prayers for healing from illness and injury are never answered in this lifetime, and that in this life none of us are purged of all our sinful dispositions no matter how fervently we pray for deliverance. And for Griffith, homosexuality is one sin among many—no worse, he says, than gossip. We all struggle with sin. What we are called to do is speak out against sin while embracing and

---

5. Robert Griffith, "Homosexuality, A Christian Perspective."
6. Ibid., para. 21–22.

communing with our fellow sinners, trusting in God's grace to bring us ever closer to the purity he desires for our lives.

Griffith sums up his perspective in the following way:

> To those of you who until now have adopted a harsh attitude towards homosexuals, or worse still, one of indifference, I plead with you in the name of Jesus to repent of that indifference or that judgemental spirit. It may be the hardest road you ever travel, but it is possible to love and accept sinners without condoning their sin. It is possible to make it clear to a practicing homosexual that their lifestyle is contrary to God's creative purpose for them and that they are inviting Satan to sow seeds of pain and destruction into their lives. It is possible to make that clear *but* at the same time give them a hug and tell them we love them in the Lord and accept them just as they are and will relate to them as one sinner to another.[7]

Notice just how different Griffith's approach is from what we saw in the last chapter, where slanderous twisting of research was used to "other" gays and lesbians through false links to pedophilia. While those advancing such slander *say* we should treat gays and lesbians with respect, what follows their "but" has more to do with ideologies of division than love. But Griffith's words are no mere lip service to love. He sincerely seeks to love his gay and lesbian neighbors as himself—while remaining convinced that all homosexual acts are sinful. For Griffith, this conviction operates like a fixed given he must accommodate in his sincere efforts to love his gay and lesbian neighbors. Those who, like me, don't think this trick is possible should not allow our skepticism to prevent us from acknowledging the sincerity of the attempt.

Another impassioned defender of this attempt is Stanton Jones—the same Stanton Jones who, as we saw in chapter 3, has been on the forefront of efforts to prove that ex-gay ministries can change sexual orientation. Jones lays out his ethical perspective in an often-reprinted essay, "The Loving Opposition." After developing his case for why Christians should continue to condemn all homosexual acts, Jones describe what it looks like (in his eyes, at least) to love gays and lesbians while hating homosexuality.

First, he points to what he sees as a "revulsion to homosexual acts" that is "natural for heterosexuals" (although I and many other straight people I know don't feel it).[8] While he thinks we should be thankful "that there

---

7. Ibid., para. 87.

8. Jones, "Loving Opposition," 25. All the following quotations from Jones are from the same page.

are at least some sinful actions to which we are not naturally drawn," we need to ensure that our revulsion toward homosexual behavior does not lead to revulsion of homosexual persons. "If you cannot empathize with a homosexual person because of fear of, or revulsion to, them, then you are failing our Lord." He goes on to say that we must refrain from and repudiate "negative responses to homosexual people" such as "queer jokes and insults" as well as "violence and intolerance." And the church, he maintains, needs to be a place "where those who feel homosexual desire can be welcomed, . . . a sanctuary where repentant men and women can share with others the sexual desires they feel and still receive prayerful support and acceptance." Christians, Jones says, must be willing to knowingly "pray with, eat with, hug and comfort, share life with" their gay and lesbian neighbors.

But in the midst of this, Jones insists that "compassion in no way entails an acceptance of the gay lifestyle any more than it entails affirming an adulterer's infidelity." Here, it is worth noting that Jones's insistence that churches welcome and offer sanctuary appears to be conditioned: it is "repentant" men and woman who are welcomed in this way.

Jones seems to think that part of what it means to love gays and lesbians is to invite them to see their sexuality as an affliction from which they might hope to be healed. "As people with homosexual inclination follow our Lord down the narrow road," he says, "they can pray and hope for healing." It is no surprise—given Jones's ongoing efforts to prove that ex-gay ministries and change therapies actually work—that he claims "healing" is a real possibility. But even when his research with Yarhouse is interpreted in the terms most favorable to the view they're striving to prove, the most optimistic conclusion is that not everyone is doomed to fail at orientation-change efforts. Only the *majority* of highly motivated persons, sincerely dedicated to the attempt, will fail.

And so Jones has to concede that "we do not have certainty about how much healing and change is possible for any particular homosexual person" (I would rephrase that as "for each particular homosexual person, we can be quite confident that efforts to change will be met with disappointment, perhaps *bitter* disappointment"). For this reason, he says that we need to "balance a Christian triumphalism with a theology of suffering, a recognition that we are a hurting and beaten-down race." He stresses that there is "dignity and purpose in suffering." He speaks about a gay friend, Mark, whose prayers for healing have not been answered and who has lived a celibate life for fifteen years while enduring enormous psychological pain. Part of what the "love the sinner/hate the sin" dictum calls for, according to Jones, is that Mark "needs to be assured by the church of the meaningfulness of his pilgrimage." This assurance comes, at least in part, from remembering "that Christians witness to their faith not just in their strength and triumph, but also in their brokenness."

In short, Jones concedes that the categorical condemnation of homosexuality will inevitably generate for (many of) the gays and lesbians who embrace it a life of significant suffering that includes a persistent experience of brokenness. Jones believes that to be faithful Christians, gays and lesbians must *see* their sexuality as an affliction, a kind of spiritual disease that God has refused to heal them of for God's inscrutable reasons.

But this sense of being broken, of living with an affliction God won't heal, isn't an inevitable feature of being gay. Rather, it comes when gays and lesbians *see their sexuality in the way Jones favors*. In other words, Jones is recommending that gays and lesbians adopt a viewpoint about themselves that *produces* this anguished sense of brokenness. And even if gays and lesbians can't change their sexual orientation, they can change how they think about that orientation. Gays and lesbians can choose to live at war with their own sexuality—a choice that Jones lifts up in terms that should remind us of Christine Gudorf's warning against romanticizing affliction. Or they can choose a different path. This is a matter of choice, even if sexual orientation is not.

Many gay and lesbian Christians have internalized the understanding of homosexuality that Jones favors, only to have a kind of conversion experience in which they come to see their anguish as unnecessary. They set aside the narrative of affliction and, in its place, accept their sexuality on different terms. Instead of struggling to change or striving to be celibate and beating themselves up every time they fail, they adopt a more positive attitude that puts their sexuality on the same moral footing Christianity applies to heterosexuality: a gift of God meant to be expressed in faithful love within the context of a marital union.

I cannot tell you how many of my gay and lesbian friends tell a story featuring just this sort of transformation, experienced as a liberation from a soul-crushing burden. And among those who are Christian, they also tend to describe this moment of self-acceptance as a transformative moment in their *spiritual* lives. They come *closer* to God, as if a barrier between themselves and their creator had been lifted away.

We'll look more closely at some of these stories in the next chapter. For now the point is this: to adopt the view that Stanton Jones endorses is to condemn this transformation, to repudiate this alternative way of seeing homosexuality. Jones believes it is sinful to make the kind of choice made by my most emotionally balanced and spiritually joyful gay friends. For him, morality requires that gays and lesbians choose a much more painful path. The anguish and "costly discipleship" isn't some inevitable feature of having a homosexual orientation. It is a feature of internalizing the negative understanding of homosexuality that Jones thinks Christians are duty-bound to embrace.

To call homosexuality a sin is, in other words, to morally require that gays and lesbians take on a psychological burden that their straight brothers and sisters needn't carry. Jones sees the imposition of this burden as an inescapable implication of Christian ethics—but he imagines that when that implication is presented to gays and lesbians in the right light, it can be experienced as heroic and meaningful rather than gratuitous and alienating. When the church demands that gay and lesbians follow the burdensome path, the path of personal anguish and struggle, Jones says that it should also assure them that their suffering has a purpose in God's design. The church should provide a space where gays and lesbians—at least those who internalize the categorical condemnation of homosexuality and "repent" any past failures to live up to its demands—can come together and find some support and relief from the burden.

This, then, is how Jones thinks we love gays and lesbians while hating homosexual sex: we point them down a path of suffering and brokenness and away from the path that promises greater joy and wholeness; insist that those who follower the brighter path are sinners who are taking the easy way instead of the right way, but then assure them that their suffering has purpose and provide fellowship and spiritual support to those who take on the mandated sacrifice. For enduring such hardship, they should be treated with honor . . . by the privileged heterosexual Christians who don't need to worry about that kind of thing.

Here's another rhetorical way to frame Jones's perspective: privileged heterosexual Christians show love for their gay and lesbian neighbors, not by pointing them down the path of wholeness and joy, but by calling that sunny path a sinful one, insisting they follow the path of pain and hardship, but then saying, "You're my hero!" from the sidelines (or, more likely, from the sunny path of wholeness and joy that they are following themselves).

If my rhetoric implies skepticism, it's because I'm skeptical. Imagine, if you will, that the burden of poverty were treated in the same way—not as an affliction that the privileged have a duty to *alleviate* as best they can, but as one that the privileged expect the unfortunate to endure while the rich continue to enjoy their privilege. While wealthy Christians drive their air-conditioned cars to church, they show their love for the sweltering poor by pointing them down the path of continued poverty while assuring them that their suffering has a purpose in God's design and offering a place where they can receive hugs and prayers from the wealthy. Instead of feeding the hungry, what wealthy Christians should do is advise the poor that

"Christians witness to their faith not just in their financial prosperity, but in their starvation," and then honor the "costly discipleship" of those morally required to follow the path of malnutrition.

While this analogy does a good job of explaining how I see Jones's recommendations, it does not show that this way of seeing Jones's recommendations is the proper one. Certainly, *Jones* does not see his recommendations in this way. I'm certainly not saying that Jones and those like him *mean* to perpetuate needless suffering. I'm fairly confident, at least in Jones's case, that his refusal to describe his behavior in these terms isn't just a case willful self-deception to make himself feel better about perpetuating an ideology that makes his friend Mark's life so hard. There *are* people like that: religious insiders, respected leaders of the community who benefit personally from perpetuating an ideology that imposes a yoke of suffering on others. Since *they* aren't among those who suffer, they devise a comforting story that enables them to continue to enjoy their privilege while still being able to tell themselves they are loving the victims of the system that benefits them.

I don't think this is going on with Jones. And I certainly don't think that Griffith means to harm his gay and lesbian neighbors and parishioners. I think he sincerely and honestly desires their good. But sometimes you can truly believe something that's false. Sometimes you can perpetuate a system that harms a class of people, even if you believe that it doesn't.

When Is It Unloving to Take Something to Be a Sin?

Let's step back and consider the key principle at issue in both Griffith's and Jones's thinking—the idea that we can love gays and lesbians while hating all homosexual sex. The problem here is that both Griffith and Jones treat this principles as a straightforward application of the idea that we can love sinners while hating sin.

But even though I accept that we can (indeed, that we must) love sinners while hating sin, it doesn't follow that we can, for any given practice, love those who engage in that practice while hating the practice. For example, diabetics engage in the practice of taking insulin. Can we love diabetics while condemning (with feeling) any and every use of insulin?

Just because it is possible to love sinners while hating sin doesn't mean we can love violinists while insisting that it is always and everywhere immoral for anyone to play the violin. It doesn't mean we can love air-breathers (like you and me) while categorically condemning the practice of breathing. It doesn't mean we can love people who marry their soul mates while despising their marriages. And it doesn't mean we can love gays and lesbians while hating all homosexual intimacy.

Hating all homosexual sex shows love for gays and lesbians only if all homosexual sex *really is sinful*. If it's not, then hating all homosexual sex may be as damaging to gays and lesbians as condemning insulin injections is to diabetics.

Of course, it is quite possible to do many loving things toward gays and lesbians while condemning all homosexual sex: we could feed and clothe our poor gay neighbors, welcome them to our table, and in all sorts of ways show love. But the question isn't whether we can love our gay and lesbian neighbors in many ways while condemning all homosexual sex. The question is whether condemning all homosexual sex is *itself* a loving thing to do.

And to answer that, we need to think about not only the isolated act of *saying* that all homosexual sex is sinful, but also the broader systemic practices that would be implemented by a society that endorsed such a condemnation: excluding gay and lesbian couples from access to marriage; demanding lifelong abstinence if orientation-change is impossible; demanding that those who have fallen in love and formed loving same-sex relationships "repent of their sin" (that, in other words, they treat what may be their most life-enriching relationship as an evil to which they've succumbed and from which they should turn away). If you think all homosexual acts are sinful, you must also believe that the morally best society will treat it as such. And so you believe that in the best society—the society you aspire to bring about—gays and lesbians would grow up, live, and die immersed in the teaching that their sexuality is intrinsically defective. You believe that they *should* live their lives with a sense of being broken, that when it comes to romantic love and marital intimacy they *should* live at the margins, watching as their straight friends fall in love, form partnerships, and cement those partnerships in marriage—forever excluded from these things themselves.

Is *that* loving?

It's clearly possible, of course, for someone with loving *motives* to condemn all homosexual sex. Many Christians sincerely believe that homosexuality is akin to alcoholism, involving destructive impulses that must be purged or restrained. They think that just as love for alcoholics requires a strong stand against the alcohol abuse that's destroying their lives and harming those around them, so too does love for gays and lesbians require a strong moral stand against homosexuality.

But consider a different analogy. Imagine a father who sincerely believes it's sinful for his three-year-old daughter to *play*—that play will plunge his child into moral ruin. And so, out of concern for his child, he prohibits all play. Any child psychologist can tell you that this will radically undermine the child's healthy development. If the father has loving motives, then his misguided beliefs are leading him to do things he would *condemn* if he knew the truth. We need to keep in mind here the distinction made in chapter 3 between loving *motives* and loving *acts*, where loving acts are what people motivated by love *would* do if fully informed. Just because something is done from a motive of love doesn't mean that the act itself is a loving one.

So what kinds of *acts* are loving in the Christian sense? In chapter 3 I argued that loving our neighbors in the Christian sense involves caring about their welfare (*at least* to the extent that we avoid harming them) and being open to fellowship with them (in *at least* the sense that we don't put conditions on a relationship that it would be harmful to meet). Of course, Christian love often requires more—even, perhaps, that we sacrifice our lives for the sake of people who despise us. But at a minimum it requires that we care enough not to harm and are open enough not to impose conditions on fellowship that would cause harm if met.

Our *motives* are minimally loving if we *mean* to do these things. Our *actions*, however, might not be—as the example of our hypothetical father makes clear. The father wants to promote his daughter's welfare, but he's seriously misguided about what will do this. And so he denies his child something essential for healthy development. Such denial isn't an *act* of love, no matter what the underlying motives.

Of course, the daughter will be harmed only if the father is *able* to enforce his no-play policy. Under some conditions that might be impossible to do. The child might be able to sever her relationship with him. Or she might find ways to play in secret and then lie about it. In that case we'd no longer have an authentic relationship between father and daughter. Rather, the father's relationship would be with a pretense, an *image* of the child radically different from what the child is really like. What this shows is that the father's prohibition has forced the child to choose among bad alternatives: an inauthentic father-child relationship, no relationship at all, or being deprived of a condition for healthy development. And this means the no-play policy is unloving even if the father can't enforce it.

What this example shows us is this: the fact that we can love sinners while hating sin doesn't tell us whether we can love our gay and lesbian neighbors properly while condemning all same-sex sex and marriage. It doesn't tell us this because sometimes it's unloving to *take* an act to be sinful in the first place. Our hypothetical father will treat childhood play as sinful *either* because he's badly mistaken about the impact of play on his child's life *or* because condemning play is more important to him than loving his child. In short, there are cases where treating an act as sinful is possible only if you either believe falsehoods or abandon love. And so, if you care about both love and truth, the only reasonable conclusion is that the behavior isn't a sin at all.

As difficult as it may sometimes be, it is always possible to love a sinner while hating their sin—assuming that what we are hating *really is a sin*. But it doesn't follow that we can take any behavior whatsoever *to be* a sin and still love people as you should. Sometimes, taking an act to be sinful involves needlessly denouncing options there's no reason for our fellow human beings not to explore—such as, for example, deciding that violin-playing is a sin. In these cases, we'd be imposing needless constraints that might shut out life-enriching opportunities. Most people might be fine with a rule against violin-playing, but suppose a little girl one day hears the violin and falls in love with it. The sound sings to her soul, and she asks her parents if she can take violin lessons at school. Imagine that her parents shut down her dreams because "violin-playing is a sin." Now raise the stakes: imagine that the child has mild autism and has found in the violin a distinctive way to express her inner self, a pathway to self-expression she has so far been unable to find anywhere else.

In other cases—as in the case of our hypothetical father who condemns all childhood play—taking the behavior to be a sin would put us at odds with human welfare in a more general way. In cases like these, it's the act of *condemning* the behavior that violates the love ethic. It's not the child at play who is sinning, but the father who condemns it. Put simply, *sometimes it's sinful to call something a sin*.

For these reasons, the "love the sinner, hate the sin" dictum is perhaps best stated as follows: *if some practice or behavior really is a sin, then it is possible to hate that practice or behavior while loving those who do it*.

When clarified in this way, the dictum actually cuts in two directions. We might argue, *granted* the sinfulness of homosexuality, that it must be possible to love gays and lesbians while condemning all homosexuality since it is always possible to hate sinful acts while still loving those who do them. But we might instead reverse the reasoning and argue that, since condemning all homosexuality damages the life prospects of gays and lesbians in ways that love can't countenance, homosexuality cannot be a sin—since, if it *were* a sin, then it *would* be possible to hate it while loving gays and lesbians.

In other words, if we begin by assuming that homosexual acts are always sinful, the "love the sinner/hate the sin" principle will lead us to conclude that loving gays and lesbians while hating homosexuality *must* be possible. But if our starting point is that hating all homosexual acts has implications contrary to what love for gays and lesbians requires, the same principle will lead us to conclude that homosexual acts cannot be sinful after all. Both arguments accept that it is possible to love sinners while hating what really is a sin, but they reason in opposing directions.

These two opposing trajectories of argument may explain what really divides Christians who genuinely want to love their gay and lesbian neighbors as themselves. Conservatives have become convinced that homosexuality is a sin, and on that basis conclude that condemning homosexuality *must* be compatible with loving their gay and lesbian neighbors, no matter how difficult combining these things might be in practice. Progressives on this issue, by contrast, have become convinced that it's impossible to love their gay and lesbian neighbors as they should be loved if one takes up the cause of condemning all homosexual sex. Although not necessarily expressed in these terms, many progressives have come to use the "love the sinner/hate the sin" dictum as a kind of *test* for whether homosexuality really is a sin. We might put it this way: if homosexuality were a sin, it should be possible to condemn it without thereby compromising our capacity to love our gay and lesbian neighbors; but since that isn't possible, it must not be a sin after all.

Compassionate and Empathetic Attention

How do we determine when a behavior is sinful? How do we determine when the real sin lies in *calling* the behavior sinful in the first place? Consider again the father who thinks it's a sin for his daughter to play. In his case there's a sharp disconnect between what he *means* to do and what he *in fact* does. People who love others want to avoid such a disconnect by avoiding false beliefs about what's good for others. And people who love others pay attention to them. There's an obvious connection between these two things: paying attention to our neighbors gives us information about them that can help us discern what will promote their welfare and what won't.

When we love others, we are especially called to pay attention to how *our behavior* affects them. We are called to be empathetic enough to determine the impact of our choices on them and compassionate enough to be responsive to what we learn. In a sense, this combination of empathy and compassionate responsiveness lies at the heart of living out the Golden Rule. For Jesus, there appears to be an intimate connection between the command to love and the command to do unto others as we would have them do unto us (see Luke 6:27–31).[9] This may be because the latter offers a way to decide how to love our neighbors: Would we want that done to us? But the Golden Rule does not mean we should arrange a leap-from-behind-the-furniture

---

9. For deeper discussions of the connection between love and the Golden Rule, see Wattles, "Levels of Meaning," and Kirk, "Love Your Enemies."

surprise party for someone with post-traumatic stress disorder just because *we* like that kind of surprise. If they experience hours of adrenalin-fueled anxiety every time they're surprised, it doesn't matter that *we* would have enjoyed it. What matters is how our behavior actually affects them, and whether we would appreciate having others impose those kinds of effects on us. Empathetic and compassionate attention is what informs us about these effects. Without it, the Golden Rule is blind.

I think this is why it's so hard to believe that our hypothetical father's primary motivation really is love for his daughter. A loving father would *pay attention* to his child. He'd take her experience seriously. Were she suffering, he'd try to find out why, in part by asking for her perspective. This might lead him to consider how childhood play factors into the lives of other children (perhaps inspiring him to consult the best available research). Unless some motive *other than love* is in control, it's hard to fathom any father doing these things while continuing to endorse the no-play policy. Perhaps the father's primary motive is allegiance to some guru who teaches that play is wrong, and maintaining that allegiance matters more to him than loving his child—but he wants to preserve the illusion of love. So he hides from the evidence, even as it shows that his prohibition is driving his child to the brink of despair.

When we love others, we pay attention. But there's a difference between paying attention to a person's preferences and paying attention to *how their lives go*. My children would prefer to eat candy and ice cream all day long and never touch a vegetable (unless it's deep-fried). But if I look at how people's lives go, I see that people are best off, not when they grow up shamelessly indulging their sweet tooth, and not when they grow up under fascist dietary prohibitions, but when they grow up learning the right balance between dietary restraint and occasional indulgence. When we focus on how people's lives actually go—observing what gives long-term meaning as opposed to temporary pleasure, what builds character rather than breaking it down, what deepens a spiritual connection to God and what shatters faith—what we learn is often the best evidence for what is beneficial and harmful.

Such compassionate attention is not only a good way of deciding how to show love. It's also a loving way to make decisions—a *way of deciding* that shows love. Loving others as ourselves begins with paying attention to them as we pay attention to ourselves: empathetically inhabiting their experience as if it were our own. We learn things when we do that. Part of what it means to love our neighbors as ourselves is that we take seriously what we learn.

It's based on such attention that we know that some people have a disposition toward alcoholism and that if they drink, they are heading down a path of mounting suffering, broken relationships, and damaged lives. Based on such observations, we are justified in concluding that they *should not drink*—even if others, who lack a propensity for alcoholism, aren't burdened by such a constraint. They shouldn't drink even though drinking satisfies their short-term desires, because when they drink their lives and the lives of others can become a living hell. And sometimes it's not even a *living* hell. Sometimes it's a spiral toward suicide or a slow death from liver failure. Sometimes it's a terrible moment, stumbling out of a car to stare at the corpse of the child hit during a drunken drive home.

Because of this evidence of how their lives go, we can confidently say that hatred of their drinking is not only consistent with loving them, but an essential expression of that love. This same sort of compassionate attention to how people's lives go can help us learn when love requires that we treat something as a sin and when love precludes it (and when it does neither). At the very least, such attention has to be *part* of what informs us when, as people who love our neighbors as ourselves, we make decisions about what to condemn and what not to condemn, which behaviors to hate and which to affirm. If we pursue such decisions without any regard for how they impact our neighbors' lives, can we really claim to be living by an ethic of love? If we decide that homosexuality is a sin without paying any attention to how this prohibition impacts gays and lesbians—and then ignore their cries of protest, their stories of suffering, their final desperate acts of self-destruction—can we honestly say we are living up to the demands of love?

Not every Christian who has paid compassionate attention to gays and lesbians has decided that homosexuality is not sinful after all. But most Christians who are progressive on this issue (certainly all who have shared with me their journeys) have arrived at their progressive stance at least in part by doing something the Christian love ethic calls for: paying attention to their gay and lesbian neighbors, especially to how the traditional view that homosexuality is sinful affects their lives, including their spiritual relationship with God. To be shaped by such attention is to be shaped by something that the love ethic calls us to be shaped by—and so it is not a treasonous betrayal of biblical values to allow such attention to move us. It is, rather, fidelity to the biblical ethic of love.

In sum, the fact that we can love sinners while hating sin does not tell us that it is possible to love gays and lesbians while hating homosexuality. Rather, it tells us only that this is possible *if homosexuality really is sinful*. Many Christian progressives on this issue have, implicitly if not explicitly, used this principle as a *test* for whether homosexuality is a sin—and their testing ground has been *the lived experience of their gay and lesbian neighbors*. They have listened compassionately to the life stories of gays and lesbians, empathized with their struggles, and concluded that the condemnation of homosexuality is doing them harm. They've found it impossible to reconcile their love for their gay and lesbian neighbors with the continued condemnation of homosexuality. But since it is always possible to love the sinner while hating the sin, they've been led to the conclusion that homosexuality must not be a sin after all.

I am among those Christians led to this conclusion by compassionate attention to the stories of our gay and lesbian neighbors. In the next chapter, I want to explore some of those stories and reflect on the lessons I have taken from them—especially lessons about *identity*.

7

Stories of Identity

What does it mean for gays and lesbians to live their lives as part of a community that categorically condemns their sexuality? What implications does that have for their life prospects? For their mental health? For their sense of who they are?

In this chapter I want to pay special attention to the last of these questions. We all have a sense of who we are, a story we tell ourselves *about* ourselves. These stories feature some personal traits as especially important: physical characteristics or group memberships, intimate relationships or vocational activities. We say, "I *am* a writer" or "I *am* an American," and these things become part of our identity.

We're not always *conscious* of these stories. They may operate in our lives as a kind of unconscious subtext. But whether conscious or unconscious, our lives are profoundly shaped by them. If our lives are spiraling toward depression or plagued by disappointments, it may be because the story we're telling ourselves about who we are is leading us astray.[1]

Identity in this sense is a subjective affair. While the size of my nose is an objective fact about me, whether it features into my self-understanding is a function of the story I tell myself about my life. For me, my nose is too

---

1. For an accessible introduction to the concept of narrative identity and its place in psychology, see Singer, "Narrative Identity and Meaning Making." For a good discussions of the role of narrative identity in psychological health and happiness, see Bauer et al., "Narrative Identity and Eudaimonic Well-Being."

trivial to factor into my story, but for the titular character in Edmond Rostand's play, *Cyrano de Bergerac*, it's life-defining. Despite his eloquence and talents with a sword, Cyrano dares not woo Roxane, the woman he loves. The source of his self-doubt is his whopping big honker. Instead of courting her himself, he lends his eloquence to the handsome-but-dense cadet, Christian. Cyrano writes letters on Christian's behalf, and Roxane falls for Christian on account of these. When she concedes that even were Christian ugly she would love him for the inner beauty he's displayed in those writings, this admission leads to no happy ending for Cyrano. Christian is killed in battle, and Cyrano hides what they've done so that Roxane's love for the deceased won't be tarnished. It isn't until Cyrano's dying moments that Roxane guesses the truth.

One moral to this story is that Cyrano has given too much prominence to his prominent proboscis. Roxane would have loved him for his eloquence and his spirit, despite his outsized snout. But by the time he realizes this, his honor won't let him undo the choices his distorted self-understanding has led him to make. In short, it matters what kind of identity we adopt, because our welfare—perhaps the entire trajectory of our life—can hinge on it. And so we ought to be clear about what our story is and how it affects our capacity to lead the best life we can.

Of course, it's not wholly Cyrano's fault that his nose features so significantly into his story. His nose has been attracting attention (and mockery) for his whole life. When society pays so much attention to something about us, it's hard to keep it from becoming part of our self-understanding. We don't construct our identity in isolation but in a social context. And what society has to say about us will influence our personal narrative and emergent identity. It takes great strength of character to defy dominant social messages—and when we display such strength, *that* becomes part of our story. If Joe lives in a society that attaches great significance to his nose's dimensions, his decision to *defy* this message may become a defining feature of who Joe is. Hence, even though the social message doesn't shape Joe's identity in the same way that it shaped Cyrano's, it still has a crucial impact. Whether we define ourselves *in terms of* dominant social standards or *against* them, the social standards shape our story.

For these reasons, communities committed to the love ethic should think about how the messages they send will impact the personal narratives of individuals. They need to use their power to shape identity-stories wisely, in ways that enhance rather than diminish life prospects.

Gays and lesbians don't have a singular life story, any more than heterosexuals do. They construct their identities from a variety of personal traits, group memberships, relationships, and meaningful activities. But for most gays and lesbians, their sexuality factors into their story. This may not be true for everyone. Some—those who border on asexuality, for example—may attach to their sexuality the kind of marginal significance I attach to the dimensions of my nose. And not every gay or lesbian who attaches significance to their sexuality will do so in the same way. Nevertheless, we live in a social context where it is hard for gays and lesbians to avoid being at least partly defined by their sexuality. This is especially true in any society that categorically condemns all homosexual acts. *In any such society, persons with a homosexual orientation will typically find that their sexuality acquires the prominence of Cyrano's nose.* They can internalize the condemnation or defy it, but either way it will profoundly shape them.

The question is what kinds of life stories this traditional teaching inspires, and whether these stories enhance or diminish the life prospects of our gay and lesbian neighbors.

The Common Story and Its Implications for Identity

Given the facts about sexual orientation and the realities of what it means for a community to categorically condemn all homosexual acts, there will be some common features to the stories of gays and lesbians who belong to such communities. Many of these features have already emerged in earlier chapters, but it will be helpful to bring together diverse threads into a more unified picture.

To begin, persons with a homosexual orientation can find fulfilling sexual and romantic relationships only with members of the same sex, and they neither choose this sexual orientation nor have the power to effectively change it, whatever religious or clinical approaches they might employ. While there is no evidence that having a homosexual orientation makes one more prone to mental health problems, there is evidence that the *stigmatization* of homosexuality has a negative impact on the mental health of gays and lesbians, especially when internalized.

Many of these mental health issues are surely caused by stigmatization that rises to the level of overt discrimination, marginalization, and abuse—but even when a community refrains from such excesses, the categorical condemnation of homosexuality carries an *inherent* stigma, insofar as it reaches beyond the mere stigmatization of outward behavior to the very sexuality of gays and lesbians. To see every expression of their sexuality as illegitimate is to see their sexuality itself as inherently bad. When change therapies or ministries are pursued, the message of defectiveness can be compounded by disillusionment and self-blame when these efforts fail.

When combined with the inefficacy of SOCE efforts, the categorical condemnation of homosexuality leaves gays and lesbians with only one "legitimate" option: suppression of their sexuality. Although monogamy appears to be best for the mental health of most, the categorical condemnation of homosexuality precludes this option. If they pursue it anyway, the categorical condemnation of homosexuality entails that this relationship ought to end, no matter how meaningful, loving, and satisfying the relationship is for the parties involved.

This sacrifice is mandated absent any clear link to tangible benefits for others. When gays and lesbians enter into romantic partnerships, there are no obvious victims. On the contrary, it's when they turn away from same-sex intimacy based on the condemnation of homosexuality that human beings appear to suffer—namely themselves. Their stories become about missed opportunities, typically paired with guilt feelings when they fail to resist sexual temptation—when, after denying themselves sexual expression in the context of love and intimacy, they furtively seek some surrogate in degrading encounters.

This is not the kind of life story that psychologists would typically dub "healthy." But it is the kind of life story that, for many gays and lesbians, is the narrative outcome of internalizing the message that homosexuality is a sin.

They could, of course, reject this message, refuse to make it part of their value system, and instead deliberately embrace their distinctive sexuality. If the community teaches the categorical condemnation of homosexuality, that choice means standing against the community's values, affirming what the community condemns, and facing the repercussions of that choice.

The End of Sexual Identity?

The choice to embrace a sexuality that one's society condemns is a choice that, among other consequences, lends to one's sexuality a prominence it's unlikely to have for the non-stigmatized majority. This phenomenon is easily seen in the case of racial minorities. When blackness is stigmatized, the effort to shake off the harmful effects of that stigma requires affirming what society has invested with negative value. To reclaim their dignity in the face of a racist system, blacks must claim their blackness, lifting it up in defiance of the negative message.

For those in the white majority, things are different. Because their race doesn't serve as a stumbling block to a positive self-understanding, racial categories can remain in the background of their story. This is why "black pride" makes sense as an act of self-affirmation, while "white pride" sounds like a euphemism for racism. To lift up what is beaten down is to stand against racism. To lift up what is already privileged is to affirm the system of racial privilege, and thus endorse racism. For those whites who aren't overtly racist, then, their whiteness is just a fact about themselves, not something they actively lift up in telling their story. For blacks in a racist society, their race inevitably features into their self-understanding whether they internalize the dominant social message or fight against it. But it's typically those who fight against it who we think of as *claiming* for themselves a black identity. Whether they claim it or not, the silence about race that is possible for whites is simply not an option for blacks. When no one is saying "no," you don't need to say "yes." But when the "no" is an ever-present feature of you social environment, the defiant "yes" becomes an essential act of self-respect. In its absence, what follows isn't a story in which one's race doesn't feature, but a story in which one's race features in the manner of Cyrano's nose.

Similarly, in a society that condemns homosexuality, gays and lesbians who choose to affirm their sexuality are engaged in a significant narrative act: they are choosing to tell a story about themselves that runs contrary to the dominant social message. They are lifting up something about themselves that society condemns. Ordinarily when we think about a gay identity, this is what we think about. Hence, *Christians* with a gay identity are those who, in defiance of traditional Christian teachings, treat their sexuality not as a curse but as a blessing from God, a gift to be treated with due reverence by expressing it in a context that nurtures rather than degrades it.

Fiction writers and other storytellers will tell you that at the heart of every good story are the *conflicts* that drive the protagonist's journey. There are differences, of course, between works of fiction and our identity-forming stories. A good novel will have much more conflict than a good life. But it remains true that our identity-forming stories can't *ignore* the points of conflict in our lives. Any trait that puts us at odds with our community becomes, almost inevitably, central to our narrative. And so it is for the sexuality of gays and lesbians who affirm their sexuality in a society that condemns it. As sociologist Jeffrey Weeks has pointed out, a core reason why gays and lesbians "have mobilized around their sense of sexual identity" is because "it was in their sexuality that they felt most powerfully invalidated."[2]

But what about those who don't defy the social condemnation of homosexuality but internalize it? Given the struggles described above, it's doubtful these gays and lesbians can tell their story in a way that treats their

---

2. Weeks, "Questions of Identity," 42.

sexuality as insignificant. Here, the conflict is internal rather than external—a war with their own sexuality rather than with their community. But whether internal or external, important conflicts gravitate to the center of our identity-forming stories.

Put simply, gays and lesbians who live in communities that categorically condemn homosexuality face an existential choice between self-denial for the sake of social acceptability and social condemnation for the sake of romantic and sexual fulfillment. No such existential choice can be peripheral to one's life story, no matter which choice one makes—even if sexuality were imbued with less cultural weight than in Western culture today.

In short, the categorical condemnation of homosexuality *creates the very conditions* under which homosexual orientation *migrates to the center of someone's personal narrative.*

Jenell Williams Paris, in her lovely book, *The End of Sexual Identity*, invites us to imagine a world where people *don't* define themselves and each other in terms of their sexuality. She notes that we are socialized to think that sexual desire "is identity-constituting, and that people who experience persistent same-sex attraction are a distinct category of persons in society."[3] She notes that sexual identity categories "lay a grid of meaning over our created natures . . . ."[4] This grid has a tendency to artificially lump diverse people together and treat a single trait as significant in a way Christians should resist. For Christians, a different basis for identity is required: "What you want is not a message about who you are. Human identity links directly to God, the creation to its Creator. From beginning to end, Scripture persuades us that we are God's beloved."[5] She likens us to bags of groceries full of diverse items. Which items should define us and serve as the label for the bag? Paris answers, "If 'beloved' were the label on every bag, then identity would be secure, regardless of the items in the bag or their condition."[6]

Paris's vision can be seen as a vivid elaboration of Paul's transformative message, in Galatians 3:28, that in Christ all terrestrial categories fall away: we are neither Jew nor Greek, male nor female, slave nor free. But in the world we live in, this is an aspirational vision, not a lived reality. Paris is right that Christians should strive for a world where our identities aren't built around race or sex or sexuality but around our status as beloved children of God. But in the actual world our churches are largely segregated by race—and where racism persists, African-Americans may *need* a refuge on

---

3. Paris, *The End of Sexual Identity*, 56.
4. Ibid., 74.
5. Ibid., 96.
6. Ibid., 97.

Sunday mornings, a place where they can join in solidarity with others who know what they are going through. Young gays and lesbians, too, are often driven to seek refuge with others who share their experience—especially if they grow up in communities teaching the categorical condemnation of homosexuality. In what may be one of the most deeply unfortunate facts of history for sexual minorities, at least those prone toward alcoholism, the most visible place of refuge has been the gay bar.

From a Christian standpoint, there is an important truth in the call to set aside sexual (and other) identities in favor of a Christian one centered around our relationship to God and Christ. But the path to such an identity is much easier for those whose sexuality isn't stigmatized. It is one thing to ask heterosexuals, who live in a society that takes their sexuality for granted, not to attach great significance to being straight. To ask those whose sexuality is condemned to do likewise is to invite them to leave out of their life story a defining source of struggle. Christians who want to preserve the condemnation of homosexual acts but urge the end of sexual identity may be inadvertently setting up their gay and lesbian neighbors for just another way to fail.

None of this is to say that Paris is wrong that Christians should aspire to form communities in which sexuality no longer serves as an identity marker. The question is how to move closer to that. At one point in her book, Paris gestures to the problem I'm highlight here. She says,

> It just doesn't make sense to lump diverse individuals together as "homosexuals" and then claim the Bible has a single message of condemnation that covers each of their situations; doing so reduces the complexity of a human life to a single abominable term. By condemning homosexuality with such vehemence, Christians have arguably contributed to the cementing of sexual desire as central to human identity.[7]

But it isn't just condemning homosexuality "with such vehemence" that drives gays and lesbians into a corner when it comes to defining themselves. Teaching that homosexual sex is always sinful, regardless of the context and motives of the participants, cuts to the very sexuality of gays and lesbians and puts it and everything that goes with it—romantic love and intimate life-partnerships—at odds with the broader community. Paris rightly points out that all intimate partnerships fall short of holiness in a world where each of us is flawed. But for gay and lesbian Christians, the teaching that homosexuality is a sin means that their intimate partnerships won't fall short just in *contingent* ways that can be fixed or healed. While

7. Ibid., 70.

straight couples can always aspire to be more attentive, more caring, more emotionally or sexually faithful than they have been, gay couples can never aspire to make their relationship less gay. The only way to overcome *that* so-called "sin" in their relationship is by *ending the relationship*.

To accept this teaching is to accept the idea that all of their intimate romantic partnerships will be *essentially* bad, not just accidentally bad in the ways that all heterosexual marriages are, ways that could be fixed by greater devotion and commitment. To be told that homosexuality is a sin isn't to be told that they will always need to work on overcoming this sin in their intimate partnerships. It's to be told that to overcome this sin, they must end any intimate partnership they have and commit to never having one again.

When Paul concedes that most of his brothers and sisters in Christ lack his gift for celibacy and ought to marry instead of burn with suppressed desires, he is offering a path whereby the majority of Christians can focus on Christ without being distracted by their sexuality. He is, in other words, offering a means whereby it becomes easier to adopt a Christ-centered identity, easier to transcend the terrestrial labels we carry in our mortal lives.

Marriage offers a *way* of situating our sexuality into our life story that puts our sexuality into perspective, enabling us to focus on the more important things, the more eternal things. For gays and lesbians who accept the traditional teaching about homosexuality, this path is blocked.

Ironically, the positive affirmation of a gay identity may be, in the face of the social stigmatization of homosexuality, the closest that gays and lesbians can come to adopting an identity where sexuality can be put into the perspective Paul and Paris recommend. If Christian communities want an end to sexual identity, this goal seems unattainable so long as homosexuality continues to be categorically condemned. Until that condemnation is a thing of the past, gay and lesbian Christians who want to approximate Paris's (and Paul's) vision may find they are best served by doing two things: first, adopting a gay identity in which they no longer live in a state of perpetual conflict with their own sexuality but recognize monogamous love as a legitimate context for its expression; second, seeking out a Christian community that affirms gay identity, thereby removing external conflict about sexuality from their immediate Christian environment. Freed from the inner and outer conflicts that can drive sexuality to the front of their narratives, they will be better able to focus on other things—such as serving the poor or deepening their relationship with God.

Paying Attention to Life Stories

These points become more compelling the closer we look at the stories of gays and lesbians immersed in communities that teach the traditional condemnation. Bernadette Barton, in one qualitative study, explores forty-six such stories through interviews with gays and lesbians from the American Bible Belt. Barton's cumulative impression is that these stories describe "living through spirit-crushing experiences of isolation, abuse, and self-loathing."[8] One study participant was a lesbian woman, Carol, from rural Kentucky. Unlike many in the Bible Belt, Carol did not experience overt homophobia from her parents. She was not subjected to the kind of scathing remark that met John, another study participant, when he came out to his mother. According to John, "she said that God destroyed a city over that and that it was evil and I made her sick."[9]

Carol's parents, by contrast, simply "deferred to the authority of the local churches and preachers in matter of social and moral issues."[10] And what her church told her was that homosexuality was wicked:

> The preacher would preach on homosexuality. He would always group us in with the so-called perverts, you know, like child molesters and just awful people. Of course, since I was having feelings about me being different, I felt like I needed to go to the altar and just pray and ask God to forgive me every Sunday. And every Sunday I would get on my knees and just cry and pray.[11]

The prayers didn't change her, and she felt destined for damnation. "I just knew that I was going to roast in hell, and had been taught this all my life."[12] The long-term implications were substantial. Barton summarizes Carol's journey as follows:

> What this combination of fundamentalist indoctrination and parental passivity added up to in Carol's life was an ongoing struggle with low self-esteem based in the belief that because she was gay, god did not love her, no one would love her, and that she was literally unlovable. In desperation, Carol tried an ex-gay program hoping they would have some secret formula to "fix" her. . . . When the Exodus therapy failed to eliminate her romantic and sexual feelings for women, Carol resigned herself

---

8. Barton, "'Abomination,'" 465.
9. Ibid., 473.
10. Ibid., 476.
11. Ibid., 472.
12. Ibid., 473.

to being damned and alone. It took two decades of suffering, counseling with a lesbian therapist, and meeting her partner Jennifer for Carol to emerge part way out of the wasteland of depression, anxiety, and hopelessness within which her religious upbringing had stranded her.[13]

For others, the pathway out of deep psychological distress comes through rethinking and eventually rejecting the church's claim that homosexuality is sinful. Laura, another of Barton's research informants, describes how this process evolved in her own life:

> I went through a whole struggle with God over it because of the way I was raised. God's very important to me . . . and, it was hard . . . it was very hard. But I started doing research. I realized I needed to stop looking at the Bible the way people told me to look at it, and I need to start looking at it as though I've never seen it before, and make my own interpretations of what I see there. Let God talk to me. He doesn't need any human beings' help to tell me what he has to say.[14]

Laura describes an extended process of study—"hours and hours and days and days and days just pouring over linguistic, theological, cultural research" with two copies of the Bible next to her at the computer—culminating in the conclusion that "God doesn't condemn homosexuality, at all. He has nothing negative to say about it."[15]

What Laura describes is an instance of what other qualitative researchers, looking into the lives of gay and lesbian Christians, have termed "identity integration." Psychological researchers Rodriguez and Ouellette identify this as one of four options for gay and lesbian Christians. The other three are to reject the religious identity, to reject the homosexual identity (through the pursuit of orientation change and, failing that, sexual abstinence), and to compartmentalize—a risky strategy that will work in preventing "identity dissonance" only if the individuals can manage to rigidly divide the two aspects of their lives.[16] Those who achieve integration, by contrast, are able to achieve "a single, new, workable understanding of the self" without turning their backs on their faith or struggling to suppress or change their sexuality. They "hold a positive gay identity, a positive religious identity, and do not feel conflict between the two." Furthermore, they "have no self-imposed

---

13. Ibid., 476–77.
14. Ibid., 478.
15. Ibid.
16. Rodriguez and Ouellette, "Gay and Lesbian Christians," 334.

walls between their homosexuality and their religious beliefs, and perceive societally-imposed barriers as surmountable."[17] Instead of feeling broken or fractured or dishonest with themselves, they feel whole—and they discover that feeling *without* throwing out their faith.

For many, achieving this kind of integrated identity is the outcome of years of struggle in which other options are tried first. Sometimes, the grimness of the other alternatives—a life without their faith (turning away from a Christian identity that's important to them), a life without romantic love (seeking to suppress their sexuality), and a life without integrity (compartmentalizing and pretending that the two have nothing to do with each other)—leads gay and lesbian Christians to the brink of suicide. Some tragically act on the self-destructive impulse. But for others—such as Darren, one of the informants in Gerald Walton's study of integrated gay Christians—it becomes a turning point:

> The catalyst [for me in accepting that I was gay] was me coming to the point where I was going to kill myself. At that point, I thought, "No, this isn't what God wants for me . . . ." At that point, that's where the freedom was. I realized that for so long I was mad at God, and I had embraced the church. But at that point, I realized that it's not God that I should be mad at. It's the church that I should be mad at. I was able to embrace God. . . . The church was totally abandoned.[18]

This narrative is hardly unique. A friend of mine, Corey, tells a story similar to Darren's. When he first discovered his sexual orientation, he was an adolescent growing up in a Pentecostal community. There was no place for expressing his sexuality in that community, but he also had profound religious experiences, the sense of being seized by the Holy Spirit, the joy of accepting Jesus as his Lord and Savior. Like many young charismatic Christians, he was on fire for God. He saw his future in the ministry, bringing souls to Christ. The hiccup in that vision came in adolescence, when he realized he was attracted not to women but to men.

And so he followed the dominant advice offered by the evangelical Christian world to young gays and lesbians. He sought to change his orientation. He hoped and prayed for what Stanton Jones tells gays and lesbians to hope and pray for: healing.

He was so motivated to change this thing inside him, this "broken" sexuality, that he pretended success. He pretended it as much to himself, the first target of his deceit, as to anyone else. He was healed! Instead of being

---

17. Ibid., 334–35.
18. Walton, "'Fag Church,'" 10.

an impediment to his imagined life in evangelical ministry, his sexuality became an asset. More precisely, his story of being an ex-gay, someone whom God had cured of homosexuality, became a pathway to ministry. The evangelical world, hungry to believe that such healing is possible, embraced him.

But it was a lie. The lie brought him to the brink of marriage with a friend he hoped he could love, a woman who might cure him of the persistent feelings he suppressed and denied. But then he read Mel White's *Stranger at the Gate: Being Gay and Christian in America.* There were differences between Mel's story and his own: Mel never declared himself an ex-gay, because he never came out as gay at all until, later in life, he was ready to embrace his sexuality. Instead, for years he denied his feelings and struggled to be straight, to find healing through prayer or, failing that, marriage to a good woman who'd make him straight. But the biggest difference between Corey's story and Mel's was that Mel had already gone down that path: straight marriage, children, building a life around a lie only to see it become increasingly intolerable. In Mel's story Corey saw his own future, a future pretending to be something, someone, he was not. In contemplating it, the lie Corey had been telling himself was exposed.

Mel's personal narrative spared Corey's would-be wife the anguish of marrying a man who couldn't love her back, but for Corey the struggle wasn't over. He'd been too deeply taught the sinfulness of homosexuality to shake it off. He'd tried to deny his homosexuality, but couldn't. And although it felt as if God had rejected him, Corey couldn't return the favor. His faith, his memories of being touched by the Holy Spirit, were too strong. The trick of compartmentalizing these forces eluded him. And so he edged ever closer to suicidal despair.

But one day he visited a church he didn't belong to, part of a denomination he knew little about. As he listened to the message of grace, he confronted his belief that God had rejected him for being gay. And he saw it for a lie. A deeper and more potent lie than any he'd perpetrated on himself and others as he pretended he was straight. The reason he couldn't reject God was because God had never rejected him. The reason he couldn't shake off the memory of the Holy Spirit seizing hold of him was because the Spirit had never let go. The church's message of rejection had obscured that divine presence, but in that moment it broke through anew.

He experienced God's complete acceptance and love, and for Corey this acceptance did not exclude his sexuality—not in the way that, for example, it excluded his more mean-spirited human impulses toward jealousy or cruelty or selfishness. Instead, that love embraced his sexuality and affirmed it as part of how God had made him.

Today, Corey pursues a life of ministry in an open and affirming church. The scars from his struggle remain, but he no longer sees his sexuality as a stain or stumbling block. That was lifted away by religious experiences that said, "Your sexuality is neither a sickness nor a sin."

Was it a delusional experience, a case of false prophecy? Labeling it as such is one way for conservatives to set aside Corey's story and others like it. But Christians have long taught that the test of prophecy lies in its fruits. And what were the fruits of Corey's experience? A deeper sense of God's presence in his life. Dedication to a life of ministry and sharing God's love with the world. Spiritual resources for fighting depression and despair.

None of this settles the argument. The point is this: if we pay compassionate attention to the stories of our gay and lesbian neighbors, we find that the categorical condemnation of homosexuality is not just something that gays and lesbians *resent* the way that alcoholics resent those who tell them they need to give up drinking. The condemnation of homosexuality is something that, when they internalize it and try to live it out, becomes an ongoing source of personal anguish. Rather than enabling them to focus on loving God and their neighbors, this condemnation functions as a kind of cage for their sexuality—but their sexuality isn't a quiet prisoner. Out of allegiance to conservative teachings, they struggle daily to push their sexuality into the cage, turn the key, and keep it contained. But it doesn't go away. Instead, this process of ongoing suppression makes it, like the proverbial elephant in the room, an ever-more-bloated presence that blocks every sight-line.

For alcoholics, living sober is a discipline, but a liberating one. They are free from the scourge of alcoholism. Some gay men caught up in sexual addiction and promiscuity find a discipline of sexual abstinence similarly liberating—but only because it frees them from destructive expressions of their sexuality. Some gays and lesbians, because their community affords them no pathway to a legitimate expression of their sexuality, find themselves cast adrift. Since the social norms offer no viable path to healthy sexuality, they land in a sexual world completely outside these norms. They fall into promiscuity, furtively expressing themselves with strangers in bathroom stalls. It becomes a kind of addiction as they grope for some alternative to the loving intimacy that their community says can never be theirs. They feel sick inside, and sometimes ex-gay communities—which provide some of the same twelve-step resources offered by other addiction recovery groups—offer a promise of liberation from sexual addiction.

But there is no similar liberation that comes from choosing celibacy over intimacy with a beloved life partner. There is no similar liberation that flows from struggling to remain sexually abstinent for a lifetime instead of expressing sexuality in the context of loving marriage. The insistence that gays and lesbians give up romantic love because (supposedly) their sexuality is intrinsically defective doesn't lift them up and renew their hope for the future. While ex-gay ministries sometimes offer a moment of hope, as people escape the degrading clutches of anonymous sex in bathroom stalls, when the false promise of orientation change proves empty and no healthy alternative path to sexual expression is offered, what begins to appear is a barren future: a future without romantic love, without the intimate touch of the beloved, without even the potential for these things. All that they are offered is a life in which they keep pushing their sexuality back into the cage. In the face of that prospect, no gay or lesbian person I know who has chosen same-sex marriage with a suitable partner describes that choice as even remotely like "falling off the wagon."

By contrast, conservative Christian communities offer only the chimerical hope of orientation change or the heavy demand of lifelong abstinence—the former no real option at all, the latter no real option for those who lack the gift of celibacy. As their straight friends fall in love and get married and move forward in life with an intimate life partner to share the journey, they are told to remain forever outside such human intimacies.

For some, this message is anti-evangelical, driving them away from the Christian faith. Others struggle to remain and to meet the grim demand. Instead of serving the poor alongside a same-sex life-partner equally committed to service, they are struggling to make themselves ex-gay. Instead of sharing the good news alongside a partner they love, they are visiting counsellors and therapists in an effort to nurture attraction to the opposite-sex partner they decided to marry in an effort to fit in. Whereas married straight couples join the church's mission work together in a spirit of joyful service, lonely gays and lesbians join as a distraction, as a way not to think about what they are suppressing, as a way to get over the heartache of turning their backs on love—and then grit their teeth when they find themselves working next to someone who fills them with a longing they've sworn to resist.

What Stanton Jones calls "costly discipleship" is in fact a struggle whose costs, for many, include being distracted from discipleship.

What conservative Christian communities rule out, what they persist in refusing to the gays and lesbians in their midst, is identity integration—the kind embodied by Ruth, a forty-seven-year-old Black lesbian who belongs to a gay-positive church. Ruth describes her sense of self as follows:

> Lesbian and Christian, it's like breathing, they work together, there's nothing separate about it. I love my spouse, but if I'm

walking down the street and I see somebody who needs my help, if I can possibly help them I will help them. That's being Christian. It doesn't take away from the fact that I'm also a lesbian.[19]

Such integration isn't accompanied by a sense of do-whatever-you-want licentiousness. Rather, it's accompanied by the sense of liberation from oppressive bonds that comes from lifting away the kind of crushing constraint that our hypothetical father in chapter 6 imposes on a child who wants to play.

Hating Identities

In the last chapter I argued that rote invocations of the "love the sinner, hate the sin" mantra don't show that condemning homosexuality is compatible with loving our gay and lesbian neighbors. If we hate all homosexual behavior, we hate the very sexuality of gays and lesbians—and that hatred has potentially costly implications for their lives. As we begin to see now, these costly implications may reach beyond sexuality to the domain of *human identity*.

But let me be clear. Were I to hate the sexuality of my gay and lesbian neighbors, I wouldn't *necessarily* end up hating their very identities. That would depend on whether they hate their own sexuality as much as I do. If they do—if they adopt an identity-story defined by inner conflict—then they would join me in loathing this piece of who they are. If I categorically condemned homosexuality, I could still embrace such *self-rejecting identities*—the identities of gays and lesbians who internalize the condemnation, grit their teeth, and look for comfort in conservative admiration of their costly discipleship. What I couldn't do is embrace *self-affirming gay and lesbian identities*—the identities of those gays and lesbians who choose to affirm their sexuality rather than live in a constant state of war with it. I wouldn't be able to listen to the kind of story Ruth tells—a story of wholeness and integration—and say, "I'm happy for you." Instead, I'd need to treat her story the way we're inclined to treat the stories of self-congratulatory racists who compound their unjust behavior with personal narratives that valorize and celebrate their offenses. Our loathing extends beyond what they've done to their very sense of self.

Likewise, anyone who categorically condemns homosexuality must, to be consistent, loathe the very identity of those gays and lesbians who

---

19. Rodriguez and Ouellette, "Gay and Lesbian Christians," 341.

adopt a self-affirming narrative. Hatred of homosexual behavior cuts not only to their sexuality, but to their identity. And if behavioral scientists are right about the negative implications of internalizing the stigma against homosexuality, what this means is that the conservative Christian community is thereby imposing on gays and lesbians a kind of ultimatum: "Either tell yourself a story about who you are that magnifies the hardship and depression in your life, or we will hate not just what you do but your very sense of who you are."

There are times and places where such an ultimatum makes sense, such as in the case of the overt racists mentioned above. Such racists are very different from well-meaning people who harbor implicit racial biases that lead them to unknowingly commit injustices against their minority neighbors. If we hate racism, we won't hate the identity of people who see their racist dispositions as a problem to be overcome. Instead, we stand in solidarity with their struggle. But we *will* hate the identity of those "self-affirming racists" who shamelessly embrace their racism.

In hating the racist identity of the latter, we don't hate their basic humanity. Our hatred doesn't cut to their deepest self because they can adopt a new identity-story that doesn't put them at odds with racial minorities, a story that would be good for everyone: good for the racist, good for the targets of racial bias, good for the advancement of the beloved community. Hating someone's identity *can* express Christian love if the identity is damaging and the hatred of it is accompanied by a deeper affirmation that urges a shift toward something healthier. Given how destructive a self-affirming racist identity is, hating the very identity of such racists can show deep Christian love. But that doesn't mean the same is true of hating a self-affirming gay identity. Given the body of evidence I've confronted, it appears that the self-*rejecting* identity is the most destructive, and the self-affirming one the healthiest. And given this conclusion, my love for my gay and lesbian neighbors will not permit me to hate the identity of those who affirm their sexuality.

For me, this conclusion springs more from listening to my gay and lesbian neighbors than from studying the social sciences research (although the latter reinforces my experience). I have listened to story after story, and the lesson is the same: it's the self-rejecting narrative that is damaging, and the self-accepting one that promotes wholeness and community and love. When conservative Christians categorically condemn homosexuality, they are (perhaps unwittingly) urging gays and lesbians to adopt a life-stunting identity-story as the prerequisite for full Christian embrace.

It's like telling Cyrano de Bergerac, "Yes, having a big nose really is a big deal. You should fixate on it and make it the centerpiece of your personal story. Deciding not to court Roxane was the right choice, because your nose makes you an unsuitable romantic partner. You should never even consider afflicting any woman with you and your unsightly conk. If you think otherwise, repent!"

Stanton Jones's Stories

But not every Christian who has listened to the stories of gays and lesbians comes away with this impression, even though it hits me with such irresistible force. Stanton Jones is among those Christians who recognizes the importance of listening to our gay and lesbian neighbors. "To think about homosexuality," he says, "is to think about people—people whom I have known as acquaintances and a few well enough to love."[20]

And so he begins his essay, "The Loving Opposition," with five stories about gays and lesbians he knows. The first is Tom, who fell into a life of promiscuous and anonymous sex and eventually died of AIDS. Then there is Gail, who is in a happy lesbian relationship. She and her partner have a child with the help of a sperm donor, but Gail's expression of the Christian faith has left all traces of orthodoxy behind, replacing God with a "god force" within us all and leaving no room for repentance and forgiveness. Third we have Fred, who was molested by an older brother, "threw himself . . . into a highly promiscuous gay subculture" until he became a Christian, and then forsook homosexuality and married Debbie, struggling hard to build sexual feelings for her and eventually finding himself "completely healed of his homosexual inclinations." Fourth is Peter, who pursued a similar path as Fred, but instead of achieving the miracle of orientation change fell into homosexual affairs and divorced his wife Denise after fifteen years, leaving her furious and betrayed while he pursued monogamy with a man. And finally we have Mark, whom I've already talked about. He's the one who, failing to achieve the miracle of orientation change, pursued a path of "costly discipleship" by living a life of complete sexual abstinence, a life that Jones admits is full of enormous pain.[21]

One kind of story that's missing from this list is the kind Corey represents: someone who, despite early struggles, integrates his sexuality and his Christian faith while still young, before he tries to cure himself through years in an unhappy heterosexual marriage, and who still believes in God and Christ and the Holy Spirit. Also missing is a story that parallels the life journey of so many heterosexual Christians. I have in mind that boring but

20. Jones, "The Loving Opposition," 19.
21. Ibid.

satisfying tale of growing up without any gut-wrenching conflicts between faith and sexuality, drawing lessons from the former on how to express the latter, falling in love, getting married, growing old together despite the inevitable challenges of negotiating a life together, and sticking it out in part because the church provides support and encouragement through the tough times. That's the story that heterosexual Christians take for granted—not necessarily as a lived reality, but as a real possibility. It's also the story that facilitates the sort of Christian community Jenell Williams Paris endorses, where sexuality neither defines nor divides us.

It's a story that's pretty rare for gay and lesbian Christians who live their lives in the kind of conservative Christian world that Stanton Jones inhabits. What makes it rare is the influence of the categorical condemnation of homosexuality. Some shake off that influence and achieve Ruth's kind of integration without much struggle. But for many more, that harmonious integration of faith and sexuality, which heterosexual Christians take for granted, needs to be fought for and worked for in the face of staunch resistance. It comes, sometimes, after "hours and hours and days and days and days just pouring over linguistic, theological, cultural research," as it did for Laura. Or to comes after a steady descent into suicidal despair, as it did for Darren and Corey. Or it comes after years of closeted pretense, as it did for Mel White.

What heterosexual Christians take for granted is, for most gays and lesbians growing up in conservative Christian communities, the climax of a crucial chapter in a life story shaped by struggle around sexuality and faith. In other words, the categorical condemnation of homosexual sex operates to exclude the very stories that, unsurprisingly, are missing from Stanton Jones's collection. Because Jones lives immersed in a world that takes as given the fittingness of imposing on gays and lesbians substantial impediments to integration and wholeness, the stories he is most familiar with are ones characterized by struggle, by the heightened significance of sexuality, and by integration achieved through dispensing with central tenets of the Christian faith. It can be easy under those conditions to erroneously conclude that homosexuality itself is the source of these problems. But that is the wrong conclusion.

Consider the story in Jones's collection that is least fraught with struggle. Gail sounds as if she is satisfied with her life, although she has distanced herself in symbolically potent ways from the evangelical Christian world. The dissatisfaction in the case of Gail's story doesn't come from Gail, but from Jones, who as a conservative evangelical is understandably unhappy about her rejection of traditional Christian theology. Gail's strategy for overcoming inner struggle involves standing *against* much of what Jones's evangelical community stands *for*. When it comes to overcoming outer struggle, her strategy appears to involve distancing herself from that community. Others in Gail's situation choose silence about who they really are to minimize the outer struggle. Either strategy impedes real fellowship with the community. As we have seen, conservative Christianity's condemnation of homosexuality forces gays and lesbians to choose among defective options: inner struggle with their own sexuality, outer struggle with the conservative Christian community, or abandoning fellowship with it altogether.

To achieve her happy ending, Gail appears to have chosen the final option. Jones does, of course, tell another happy-ending story that doesn't involve conflict with or distance from the conservative evangelical community to which Jones belongs—namely Fred's (purportedly) successful ex-gay story. But while this story has a happy ending in Jones's telling, it was not achieved without years of Fred struggling inwardly with his sexuality:

> After a couple of years of costly discipleship and growth, Fred felt called by God to marry Debbie, and she him, in full knowledge of his problem. Only towards the end of their engagement did he begin to experience any sexual attraction to her whatsoever. Now, after 14 years of marriage, much prayer and counseling, Fred feels almost completely healed of his homosexual inclinations.[22]

As Jones tells it, Fred's story of inner struggle culminates in a successful and happy marriage to Debbie. But if so, Fred is a remarkable exception to the rule. The more common conclusion is what we find in Peter's story—a marriage falling apart after fifteen years of living a lie. Perhaps Jones was a bit premature, only fourteen years on, to declare a happy ending for Fred and Debbie. Or perhaps not. Perhaps Fred was a gay-leaning bisexual who was able to nurture his nascent heterosexual attractions enough to find love with Debbie. What is clear is that even if Fred's story does have a happy ending, it would be irresponsible given the evidence to recommend that others follow Fred's example. Doing so would be a recipe for heartbreak, broken homes, and bitterness—a tragedy not just for the gays and lesbians in such marriages, but for their spouses, wedded to those who can't love them back the way they long to be loved.

In other words, among the stories Jones shares it is the story of Gail—who rejects traditional Christian teachings on a number of fronts—that represents the only *realistic* option for a happy ending. This may explain why conservative Christian communities are so apt to invoke the threat of hell with respect to homosexuality. Despite the ubiquity of human sin, why

22. Ibid.

do gays and lesbians, who just want to love each other, get disproportionately slapped with the message that they're damned? Perhaps it's because *hell is the ultimate unhappy ending*. When the only narrative that promises this-worldly happiness requires rejecting the teachings of the church, the church may want to defend those teachings by promising the worst possible epilogue for those who are lured by the promise of happiness in this lifetime.

Be that as it may, it's clear that Jones's stories leave out cases like that of my friend John: not merely a nominal integration of Christian and gay identities, but an integration that embraces traditional Christian creeds, that affirms core theological doctrines with confident faith. Both John and I are Lutherans, but John is the more theologically conservative. While I tend to drift toward more liberal and progressive expressions of the Christian faith, John serves as a steady countercurrent in my life, reminding me of the deep beauty and power of the tradition and its more conservative theological ideas.

And he's a self-accepting gay man who has been with his partner well over twenty years. For Jones, it seems as if no such story is possible. But the reality is more subtle than that. Someone *can* reject the notion that homosexuality is categorically sinful while being quite conservative in other ways—about the Trinity and the atonement, about sin and redemption, repentance and forgiveness. Believing in a personal God who calls us to repent from our sins does not logically require that we also believe that same-sex marriage is one of those sins for which repentance is required. You can reject the latter without rejecting the former.

Gail rejects both, and among gays and lesbians she's hardly alone. Many gay and lesbian Christians have learned that their distinctive voices, rooted in their experiences as sexual minorities, are unwelcome. They've internalized the message that when their faith communities have moral and theological conversations, they had best stay silent or risk being silenced by rote invocations of biblical clobber passages. And so, as they pursue an integration of their faith and their lived experience as sexual minorities, they do it *apart* from that faith community. Since the community doesn't listen to them, they stop listening to the community.

It's not hard to see why a gay or lesbian Christian might reject the language of repentance as Gail does. When the call to repent is combined with the insistence that what you should repent *from* is the most meaningful, loving, and enriching relationship of your life, that call can feel like an attack. When you try to explain why it feels that way and no one listens, no one seriously entertains the possibility that there is actual wisdom to be gained from your experience, the doubling-down on the demand for repentance becomes a psychological violation. *You* are discounted. If the call to repent has come to mean *you don't count*, you're likely to grope toward a version of the Christian faith that doesn't invoke the language of repentance. Likewise, when God the Father becomes too closely identified with a church whose relationship to gays and lesbians is defined by the refusal to listen, it's not surprising if sexual minorities, as they try to integrate their faith and sexuality, look for a conception of God that is less cruel.

Once gays and lesbians have found their way to a more palatable faith on their own, it doesn't do much good to point out that a personal God needn't be cruel, or that dispensing with repentance means we should no longer demand that rapists and murderers turn from their evil and beg forgiveness. Christian conservatives in the best sense of that term—those Christian voices whose concern is with preserving what is good and beautiful within the tradition—lose their power to rein in the progressive critic's enthusiasm for change when their first move is to deny the critic a place at the table. The critic then pursues their criticism liberated from all conservative cautions against throwing away too much.

When the conservative pays no heed to the anguished cries of those being crushed by inherited teachings, it is no surprise when those being crushed, as they shake off what is crushing them, shake off more than they need to. I am utterly convinced that the church needs both progressive and conservative voices—progressive voices that identify injustices and other problems within the church and call for change, and conservative voices that lift up tradition and warn that it is far easier to destroy than to create and that a fervor for change may ruin in a day great and beautiful things that it took generations to build.

But the church also needs these voices to talk to each other, to take each others' concerns seriously, with an openness to being moved. This is especially true when the conversation is about real people—such as gays and lesbians—who are part of the church and who are in pain. If the conservative voices fail to listen honestly to their concerns, they aren't just opposing a progressive challenge to orthodoxy. They are shutting out a class of people from the community of faith. It should be entirely unsurprising when those who aren't heard replace, in their personal theologies, a personal God of abiding love with an impersonal god force in each of us. If this change is a mistake, I doubt the God of love will be holding Gail to task for her error.

In summary, the stories of gay and lesbian Christians that Stanton Jones surveys are not the only stories out there. The happy-ending stories are not limited to stories of gay heretics who fall in love and throw out tradition and those rare (or imaginary) stories of ex-gay successes in which years of struggle end in orientation change instead of divorce. It may look to Jones as if these are the options, but if so, that is because he is deeply immersed in a community whose very teachings about homosexuality make more hopeful alternatives rare. If we turn our eyes to open and affirming churches and listen to the stories of gay and lesbian Christians who have landed in these gay-positive congregations, we find other narrative possibilities.

This is certainly what researchers Rodriguez and Ouellette found when they interviewed members of the Metropolitan Community Church of New York (MCC/NY). They found those like Ruth, whose integration of her sexuality with her Christian faith is "like breathing." And those like Timothy, who is just beginning his journey out of internalized homophobia:

> It's a recent thing, the past couple of years. The religious right forced me to come up with a way to justify my life [as a gay Christian] in a real way, not a cosmetic way, but in a way that's unified, that both go together and equal the whole that is me. As I said, it's recent, and it was a struggle, but I've had to do it for my own self-esteem.[23]

Rodriguez and Ouellette point out that the open and affirming church itself (in this case MCC/NY) plays a vital role in helping congregants find integration of their Christian and gay identities. "In participants' narratives," they explain, "MCC/NY emerges as a very special, indeed sacred, space for identity work."[24] For them, the words of Esther capture the dominant sentiment well:

> I think I'm blessed. Sometimes I can't express how blessed I feel. That God lives [at MCC/NY], God is at home here. I have a chance every Sunday to come here and be with God. Here I've a sense of connectedness and of belonging, and of being one with my community and with God at the same time. And what a double blessing that is for me.[25]

What we have in Esther's words is a happy-ending story, but the happy ending isn't about romantic love at all. It's about God. It's about the blessedness of being part of a community of faith where God is alive. And that joyous encounter with God happens for Esther and those like her at a church that rejects the traditional Christian teaching on homosexuality—in a way that wasn't able to happen for them at a church that accepted it. This may be what is most conspicuously missing from Jones's stories of gay and lesbian Christians: the stories of those for whom God came alive *because they were finally able to escape the stumbling block to faith that the categorical*

23. Rodriguez and Ouellette, "Gay and Lesbian Christians," 341.
24. Ibid., 343.
25. Ibid., 344.

condemnation of homosexuality imposed. In Esther's words there is blessing, there is grace, found in and through the integration of her identities. She is free to focus on God, to be with God, without the distraction of the "costly discipleship" whose biggest cost may be discipleship itself.

Concluding Remarks

Christian communities that set aside the traditional condemnation of homosexuality open up for gays and lesbians identity-stories that more traditional communities shut down. In faith communities like MCC/NY, what is missing from Stanton Jones's catalogue of gay Christian lives becomes a lived reality: stories that integrate sexuality and faith in the way that Christian churches have long sought for heterosexuals with the help of marriage. In stories such as these, sexuality is freed of the ponderous weight it carries when it's a source of lifelong struggle, and so can fall into the background. When Paul offered marriage as a living alternative to celibacy, it was because he saw that for those who lacked the gift for it, the effort to pursue celibacy would inspire a struggle not merely doomed to failure, but potentially distracting from the Christian life.

The life stories of our gay and lesbian neighbors reveals that what Paul believed to be true of his fellow Christians is no less true of gay and lesbian Christians. Esther and those like her, unburdened by the condemnation that requires them to adopt an identity-story of inner struggle, are free to focus on God's presence and the life of faith. And when this happens in churches that aren't segregated by sexuality—like some of the open and affirming churches to which I've belonged, where straight and gay worship side by side—Paris's vision of the end of sexual identity starts to become more than a pipe dream.

Stanton Jones doesn't include such stories in his survey of gay and lesbian Christians, not because they aren't possible, but because the categorical condemnation of homosexuality to which he and his community are committed rules them out. The question is whether ruling them out is a loving thing to do. After listening widely to my gay and lesbian neighbors, some of whose stories I've shared here, I've become convinced that the answer is no.

But I've reached this answer from the starting point of loving attention to my gay and lesbian neighbors. From this starting point, it appears unloving to demand that gays and lesbians forego a self-accepting identity. From this starting point, Jones' call to honor the "costly discipleship" of those who live at war with their sexuality strikes me as obscuring the poisonous fruits of a teaching by romanticizing the suffering of its victims. From this starting point, it does not look like love to condemn those who turn from that path of self-rejection to find joy and wholeness and the sense of God's living presence in churches that don't demand such anguish.

But there are other starting points. Many Christians start with Scripture or natural law arguments (or some combination of these) to arrive at conclusions at odds with the ones I reach from the starting point of loving attention. And as Christians wrestle with this subject, we cannot ignore Scripture and the legacy of traditional moral theology expressed in natural law theory. My point so far is that we also cannot ignore the lessons of loving attention, not if we claim to love our neighbors as ourselves. When we look at Scripture and tradition, we must do so in a way that makes the lessons of loving attention an integral part of our deliberations.

But before turning to Scripture and natural law, I want to look more closely at marriage itself. Marriage has always offered, for Christians, the primary framework for sexual holiness. As such, the most conservative Christian alternative to a categorical condemnation of homosexuality would be same-sex marriage: the formation of a covenantal space within which gays and lesbians can express their sexuality in monogamous love.

8

The Possibility and Promise of Same-Sex Marriage

I suspect most Christians who condemn same-sex marriage think along the following lines: "All homosexual sex is sinful, so same-sex marriage would lift up sin and enshrine it in the bonds of matrimony. To do that would be wrong." But some critics of same-sex marriage take a different approach. They argue that same-sex marriage isn't even possible, since marriage is by definition a union between one man and one woman. If so, gay sex can never be anything but extra-marital sex. If only *marital* sex is morally legitimate, gay sex is always wrong.

For me, one of the most surreal moments in the 2011–12 presidential election season came when Senator Rick Santorum, running for the Republican nomination, started waving napkins from the stump. While his napkin-waving might have looked a bit silly, his purpose was to highlight what he took to be the silliness of same-sex marriage. "You can call a napkin a car," he said, "but it doesn't make it a car. You can call a paper towel a chair, but it doesn't make it a chair. Marriage is what marriage is."[1] For Santorum, calling a same-sex partnership a marriage is as absurd as calling a napkin a car. A napkin just can't *be* a car, because it doesn't have what it takes to be one. Likewise, a same-sex union just can't *be* a marriage.

---

1. Mandell, "GOP Presidential Candidate," para. 4.

Santorum isn't alone in making this kind of claim. Conservative blogger and pundit Matt Walsh puts it this way:

> Some people have accused me of being against marriage equality. This is completely unfair. I'm not against it. I'm not anti-it. I don't oppose it. . . . I have no problem with marriage equality—except that it doesn't exist. It can't exist. It never has existed. It never will exist. . . . How would I oppose that which cannot be? That's like trying to pass a law to deny Santa Claus his voting rights.[2]

It's one thing to oppose same-sex marriage based on the conviction that homosexuality is a sin, something else to declare that same-sex marriage isn't possible. Those who say the latter sidestep the charge that they are discriminating against gays and lesbians, denying them goods they might otherwise have. It's not a failure to love your gay and lesbian neighbors if you deny them what is impossible for them anyway.

So what should we make of these sorts of claims?

Conservative Christians routinely say that marriage "has always been" a relationship between one man and one woman. Rick Santorum, in his napkin-flapping stump speech, declared that it has been this way "from the very beginning of time" (a phrase that always makes me cringe, largely because so many undergraduate term papers begin with it).[3]

One way to understand this claim is to see it as about God's design-plan for creation: from the moment God created humanity, he designed them to form *heterosexual* pair-bonds, and "marriage" is our word for this divinely ordained relationship. Defenders of this idea support it both by appeals to Scripture and by appeals to what is called "the natural law," and I will explore the arguments rooted in these foundations in later chapters. In this chapter, however, I want to make the case that all such arguments are best understood as arguments about what we should and shouldn't do, not as arguments about what is possible or impossible.

Conservatives can and do argue that we *should* reserve marriage for the procreative pair-bond between one man and one woman. They can and do argue that the reason is because doing otherwise defies God's intentions. But there's a big difference between saying that we *shouldn't* deviate from a strictly heterosexual approach to marriage, and claiming that we *can't*.

---

2. Matt Walsh, "There is No Such Thing," para. 1–3. It is clear in the essay that it isn't just full equality between same-sex marriages and heterosexual ones that Walsh finds impossible. Such equality is impossible, on his view, because same-sex marriage is impossible.

3. Edwards, "Karen Santorum," para. 11.

Doing the latter invokes the language of necessity in a way that almost seems to be about avoiding responsibility for the hurtful implications of withholding same-sex marriage. But the love ethic demands that we take seriously the potential harms of excluding gays and lesbians from marriage. To the extent that people deny that any exclusionary activity is going on, it becomes harder to explore the implications of the love ethic.

A Complex Cultural History

One way to approach this issue is historically. It is certainly true that in most human societies you find long-term sexual pair-bonds between men and women, and that in *most* societies, *most* marriages have been heterosexual. But as Stephanie Coontz notes, the history and cultural diversity of marriage practices belies the notion that marriage is simply the recognition of some "biological imperative" written into the nature of our species:

> The rules governing who can marry whom have varied immensely from group to group. In some societies, marriages between first cousins have been prohibited. In others, such unions have been preferred. Some societies have encouraged polygamy. Others strictly prohibit it. Such a contradictory hodgepodge of social rules could not have sprung from some universal biological imperative.[4]

The variability in marriage practices doesn't just apply to rules about who gets to marry whom, but to cultural principles governing "how marriage should be organized and what its main purpose should be."[5] To give a sense of this variability, Coontz offers a range of examples of marriage practices that defy the norm of the one-man-one-woman-child-producing-pair-bond:

> There are West African societies in which a woman may be married to another woman as a "female husband." In these cultures, if the wife brings children with her to the marriage or subsequently bears children by a lover, those children are counted as the descendants and heirs of the female "husband" and her extended family. And numerous African and Native American societies recognize male-male marriages.
>
> What about traditional Chinese and Sudanese ghost or spirit marriages, in which one of the partners is actually dead? In these societies a youth might be given in marriage to the dead

---

4. Coontz, *Marriage, a History*, 26.
5. Ibid.

son or daughter of another family, in order to forge closer ties between the two sets of relatives.[6]

Coontz notes that in many cultures, the most common form of marriage historically "was that between a man and several women," while more rarely it would "unite a woman and several men."[7] And while it's true that stable heterosexual partnerships that produce children have been found all over the world despite these variations, "many societies prohibit some people from marrying even if they have stable, mated relationships that produce children, but allow other people to marry even if they do not engage in sexual intercourse or cannot bear children."[8]

As for the idea that marriage is something that's been around in a particular form since humanity's beginnings, Coontz offers the following run-down of dominant theories of early human social organization, before "marriage" was invented:

> Some researchers believe that early humans lived in female-centered groups made up of mothers, sister, and their young, accompanied by temporary male companions.... Other scholars argue that the needs of defense would have encouraged the formation of groups based on male kin, in which fathers, brothers, and sons, along with their female mates, stayed together. ... A third group of researchers theorize that hominid groups were organized around one male mating with several females and traveling with them and their offspring.[9]

What is not taken seriously, says Coontz, is the idea that "the male-female pair was the fundamental unit of economic survival and cooperation." Given that arrangement, "no one could have survived very long in the Paleolithic world."[10]

To say, as Rick Santorum does, that "marriage is what marriage is," doesn't help us very much in the face of such a complex story. As Coontz puts it,

> ... marriage has taken so many different forms in history that trying to define it by its most frequently encountered functions does not really help us understand what any particular society's marriage system is or how and why such a system changes over

---

6. Ibid., 27.
7. Ibid.
8. Ibid., 28.
9. Ibid., 37–38.
10. Ibid., 38.

time. We also can't claim some groups did not have "real" marriages just because their marriage practices were not "typical."[11]

Claiming *that* would be like insisting that all Americans are white and dismissing the counterexamples by saying that if you're not white you're not a "real" American. Appealing to what is most *common* for the sake of identifying what's *essential* is not just unsound, it's the source of much of the harms that minorities endure.

Marriage as Essentially Contested

The complex variability we face when we look at marriage leads me to suspect that in its actual usage, the term "marriage" is what the philosopher W. D. Gallie would call an "essentially contested concept." According to Gallie, there are some terms we not only use in competing ways but *should* use in competing ways, because they function in our language to organize social disagreements and discussions about matters of value—for him, discussions about what is best or deserves praise—with the goal of advancing or perpetuating certain kinds of achievements.[12] If we insist on a fixed definition with precise boundaries, what we are basically doing is using definitions to shut down moral debate and silence opposing perspectives.

Gallie uses the notion of "art" as an extended example to clarify what he means. When it comes to art, people often disagree about whether something qualifies, and the disagreements can't be resolved just by consulting a dictionary. But we all agree on a number of things that qualify as works of art: Beethoven's *Ninth Symphony*, Michelangelo's *David*, Frank Lloyd Wright's *Darwin Martin House*, Leo Tolstoy's *War and Peace*. These exemplars or paradigms of art help to unify our understanding.[13] But what about Jackson Pollack's giant canvases of swirling and spattering paint? When they first appeared on the scene, some said they weren't art at all, while others insisted they were. Over time, the consensus has gravitated toward treating them as art, but a few still disagree.

And then there's the case of the Piero Manzoni, who purportedly canned his own excrement. He produced ninety cans, labeling them as "Artist's Shit" in English, French, German, and Italian. The one numbered 004

---

11. Ibid., 28.
12. Gallie, "Essentially Contested Concepts," 180.
13. Ibid., 182.

was purchased by the Tate Art Gallery in London.[14] Is this art? Some say yes, but I suspect there is a strong contingent of nay-sayers.

So what's going on here? Gallie thinks that when it comes to art, there are a number of paradigms—core examples—that all of us would call art. And when we call them art, we are making a *value judgment* about them. We aren't just describing something. To call a human creation "art" is to say it has achieved something (although there are greater and lesser works of art such that artistic achievement comes in degrees).

The paradigms of art are creations we agree deserve this positive appraisal. But they are complex and varied. They have things in common, but also numerous differences. And we don't all agree on what it is *about* the paradigms that makes them worthy of the label "art." Is it the novelty and innovation that matters most, or the skill exhibited in the execution? Is it the beauty of the creation or its symbolic power? Can the self-referential irony and social commentary of an artist canning and labeling his own excrement elevate the product to the level of art?

In other words, our disagreements over what is art are really disagreements over what it is about the paradigms of art that makes them worthy of the positive appraisal we attach to the term. Positive appraisal, in other words, is part of the very *meaning* of "art." And the dispute is about what deserves that positive appraisal and what doesn't.

And so, in addition to the paradigms of art there are borderline cases—cases of human creativity that have some of the features of the paradigms, but not all. While some think the features possessed by Manzoni's ironic exercise in creative canning are features that make the outcome deserve the label "art," others are convinced that what makes something deserve that label are features of the paradigms *missing* from Manzoni's *merda*.

If we impose some dictionary definition of art onto this discussion, we are basically trying to shut down a debate about value judgments by definitional fiat. But surely that's not the way to resolve disputes about what is good and right. Hence, we must allow for the definition of "art" to be contested.

This doesn't mean anything goes. We can't ignore the shared paradigms. Hence, if we define art in a way that excludes the *Mona Lisa*, we misuse the word. And we can't ignore the positive value that attaches to the term. And so, if we define art in a way that includes things nobody would sincerely attach positive value to, we misuse the word. And in the case of art, there is agreement about the broader class of things to which art belongs:

---

14. Milner, "The Tate Values Excrement," para. 2–3.

art is something *made* by someone. What we disagree about is what distinguishes works of art from more mundane human creations.

Others have noted that it isn't just concepts with *positive* appraisive meaning that can be essentially contested. Newton Garver has argued that "violence" is essentially contested,[15] and I have argued that "rape" is.[16] In the case of marriage, however, the appraisive meaning of the word is positive, at least within Christian communities. To be called a marriage, rather than a case of domestic cohabitation or "living in sin," is to confer a positive evaluation.[17] And there is debate about what warrants that positive label. Does a same-sex partnership, characterized by loyalty and devotion and mutual love, cemented by vows of monogamous fidelity and lasting for a lifetime, *deserve* to be called a marriage?

This isn't a question about what is possible. It's a question about values. When someone says, "This relationship doesn't fit the definition of marriage, end of story," it looks like they are trying to shut down a moral debate by definitional fiat.

Of course, when it comes to marriage we have our *paradigms*, characterized by a range of features. And heterosexuality is a feature of those paradigms. But what this means is that however we define "marriage," we need to do so in a way that *includes* traditional heterosexual marriages. If we adopt a definition such that *only* same-sex unions count as marriages, we misuse the term. But including all the paradigms is not the same as limiting ourselves to them. If marriage has a positive connotation, we can ask which features of the paradigms justify this positive appraisal. If other relationships deserve that sort of approval, we should expand our concept to include them.

Imagine a couple that has lived in isolation for decades. Suppose that when they first fell in love, they lacked access to any institutions that might officiate a wedding ceremony, but they made vows to one another and have considered themselves married for twenty years. And suppose they embody many features of paradigmatic marriages: they love one another and support one another and have formed a partnership in life. Their relationship

15. Garver, "Violence and Social Order," 220.
16. Reitan, "Rape as Essentially Contested," 43–66.
17. This is not the case in every community. In some circles "marriage" has acquired a negative connotation. If so, then "marriage" might be what I have called a "bifurcated essentially contested concept" (in Reitan, "Moving the Goalposts," 91): competing communities each use the term in an essentially contested way—but while one community attaches a positive meaning to it and asks which features of the paradigms justify the positive judgment, another community attaches a negative meaning and asks what makes marriage so bad. Since my focus is on the Christian community where "marriage" has a positive connotation, I will not explore these complexities here.

might not be a *paradigmatic* marriage, since they never said "I do" before an official of the church or the state. But should we call their relationship a marriage anyway?

What would we say to someone who insists that their relationship *can't* be a marriage because it's "part of the definition of marriage" that couples make vows before witnesses and an authorized officiant? Should that be the final word? I doubt the couple would appreciate having the last twenty years of their relationship downgraded by definitional fiat. Likewise, we shut down legitimate ethical inquiry when we say, "Marriage is between a man and a woman *by definition*, so same-sex relationships just *can't* be marriages."

Complex Paradigms

Recently I attended the wedding of a young couple. Since they were evangelical Christians, the pastor stressed the importance of putting Christ first in their relationship. "We are taught that God is love," the pastor said, "and so the love you have for each other can only endure if it's rooted in the God who *is* love. It's in Christ we learn the meaning of God's love, and so it's as disciples of Christ that the love you have for one another will flourish through the years." Or something along those lines. I didn't memorize the exact words. I was too busy marveling at the beauty of the couple and the perfect weather for a garden ceremony, not to mention the expression on my daughter's face as she watched with rapt delight.

I do remember some things, though. I remember that the vows included both the traditional promises of mutual care in good times and in bad, and more personal promises—one of them about nurturing a spirit of fun. And because I was writing this book, I also noticed how many times offspring were mentioned during the ceremony. It happened once, in passing, toward the end of the homily. There was no marriage vow about baby-making. The vows that led the pastor to pronounce them husband and wife were entirely about *how the two of them were going relate to each other* in the years ahead. And these vows of faithful love were not conditioned by fertility. When the couple promised to stick it out even through hardships, they didn't say, "Unless the hardship is infertility, in which case all these promises are null and void."

This wedding wasn't unique. It was characteristic of Christian weddings I've attended, where mutual love takes center stage in the vows, in the sermon, and in the toasts and speeches at the reception. At the ceremonies where Christian marriages are actually *formed*, it's almost as if everyone takes it for granted that the defining feature of Christian marriage is the kind of commitment a couple has to one another. After attending just about any Christian wedding today, you'd be forgiven for coming away with the impression that what makes a marriage a marriage is that a couple has made a lifelong commitment of faithful and exclusive love. And this, of course, is something same-sex couples *can* do, whether or not you think they should.

Those in the marriage equality movement, however, have typically had something much more practical in mind: legal rights. The political movement for marriage equality has been about securing for same-sex couples equal access to the distinct bundle of rights that come with civil marriage, rights that have long been available to heterosexual couples.

Others consider the broader social aspects of marriage. Philosopher Ralph Wedgwood, for example, argues that marriage has a social meaning, because when a couple marries they "give a signal to their community that they wish their relationship to be viewed in the light of . . . generally shared assumptions about what married life is like." For Wedgwood,

> . . . marriage's social meaning makes it possible for couples to communicate information about their relationships in a particularly effective way. This is important because people do not only care about tangible benefits (such as money or health care or the like); they care about intangible benefits as well. In particular, people care deeply about how they are regarded by others—which inevitably depends on the information about them that is shared in their community.[18]

And what does Wedgwood take to be the "generally shared assumptions about what married life is like"? He describes them as follows:

> . . . normally, marriage involves sexual intimacy (which in heterosexual couples often leads to childbirth); it involves the couple's cooperation in dealing with the domestic and economic necessities of life (including raising children if they have any); and it is entered into with a mutual long-term commitment to sustaining the relationship.[19]

Wedgwood concedes that heterosexuality has also been an underlying assumption about marriage until recently, but he argues that the sex of each partner is not something one needs the social institution of marriage to communicate. A person's sex is usually well-established and readily communicated apart from marriage. And so the communicative function

---

18. Wedgwood, "The Meaning of Same-Sex Marriage," para 9–10.
19. Ibid., para. 7.

of marriage is not served by hanging on to the assumption that married couples are heterosexual.

More importantly, Wedgwood notes that the traditional social meaning of marriage has changed over time based on considerations of justice. The marital partnership used to be generally understood as a *hierarchical* one in which the woman is subordinated to her husband. Marriage is not superfluous for communicating such a message—but most of us have decided, based on standards of justice, that this message shouldn't be communicated, let alone put into practice.

By contrast, changing our understanding of marriage to include same-sex couples does not substantively affect what is communicated by marriage: it continues to convey the message that the couple wants to be treated by society as kind of loving partnership, or family. But unless that change is made, the capacity of gay and lesbian couples to signal society about how they want to be regarded is compromised. So for Wedgwood, justice in this case calls for a change that has minimal impact on the social meaning of marriage.

Setting the matter of justice aside for the moment, it should be clear that it is *possible* for society to structure itself so that same-sex couples can readily communicate their intent to be seen by society as a loving partnership and family unit. If marriage is about such social communication, then there is nothing impossible about making marriage available to same-sex partners. It is also possible, of course, for same-sex couples to serve as the locus for larger family units: they can and often do raise children together.

So: same-sex couples *can* relate to one another in the way married couples vow to do on their wedding days. The state *can* confer on them the legal rights that come with being civilly married. Society *can* treat same-sex couples as family units in the way that they do heterosexual married couples, and *can* make marriage available to same-sex couples as a means of efficiently signaling their desire to be treated in this way. All of this is possible.

And most of what I have said about civil marriage is also true of Christian matrimony. Most who advocate for marriage equality in the church are seeking something it is entirely *possible* for churches to give: officiating at a ceremony where the couple vows mutual love and commitment, and then supporting them in their effort to live up to those vows. These are things a church *can* do, whether or not we think it should.

So when conservatives say that marriage equality is "impossible," they need to confront the fact that in a number of rather straightforward ways, marriage equality is clearly possible. And those who are asking for marriage equality are generally asking for these very things. To answer, "It can't be done," makes sense only if those asking for marriage equality are asking for access to the *one* feature of paradigmatic marriages that really is impossible for same-sex couples: to become a reproductive pair. That, of course, is something no same-sex couple can be. Everything else—the vows and commitments, the legal and social recognition—is just as possible. And when same-sex couples ask for access to marriage, it's *these* possible things they're asking for, not the one impossible thing.

So, what Matt Walsh and others like him are actually doing when they call same-sex marriage impossible is lifting up one specific feature of the marriage paradigms and insisting it would be *wrong* to judge a relationship as possessing the unique value we associate with marriage if the couple lacks this feature. To declare that marriages between same-sex couples aren't "real" is a veiled way of making a *moral judgment* in the guise of a descriptive one. What they mean is that same-sex relationships don't deserve the positive value judgment that goes with the name "marriage." Even though same-sex relationships can have all kinds of things in common with paradigmatic heterosexual marriages—in fact, almost everything—there is one thing they can't have in common with them. What Walsh and others are really saying, then, is that the positive value of marriage depends on *this one thing*. Without it, the positive judgment that goes with being called a marriage is gone.

The one thing, of course, is procreative potential. The language of necessity obscures what is fundamentally a moral claim: the institution of marriage *should* be reserved for couples who form a procreative pair-bond.

It is perfectly legitimate for someone to make this moral claim and try to defend it. What is not legitimate is to shut down the inquiry by defining the question out of existence. It is not legitimate to invoke a rigid definition in order to preemptively silence those who wish to make a contrary case. That won't settle what is fundamentally a moral dispute.

The question is what worth we should attach to a romantic, sexual pair-bond between two people of the same sex who make the same vows, the same commitments of lifelong love and care and fidelity, that heterosexual couples make to each other when they marry. Does that relationship have value? Is it the same kind of value possessed by a comparably-situated heterosexual pair? Of course, same-sex couples can't procreate, but there are infertile heterosexual couples who we call married—that is, to whom we attach the kind of value that goes with the label "marriage." Should we do the same for same-sex couples?

There may be those at this point who will say I am willfully ignoring an important possibility: What if the marriage of two people is not something *people* do but something *God* does? If God never joins together people of the same sex, then same-sex marriage will be impossible for us to bestow, because we cannot make God do something God refuses to do.

Let me make two points about this. First, it is possible for same-sex couples to make marital vows, for churches to witness and support them, for legal authorities to recognize them and bestow rights on them, and for the couples to live their lives as loving partners in accordance with their vows, even if God does not approve of any of this and even if God does not dip into creation to forge a metaphysical union that transcends what humans can do. If "marriage" names a divinely-created union and God never makes same-sex unions, then presumably humans *ought* not to treat same-sex couples as married. But we *can* treat them as married, even if we shouldn't.

Secondly, if we assume that marriage is something God does, the question becomes what God would and would not do—a question about God's will. Human judgments about God's will are fallible and riddled with disagreement. Christians strive to understand God's will in a number of ways, including prayer, reading and interpreting Scripture, and studying the tradition. But if you accept that God is love, then the deepest truth about God's will is that it is a loving will. And so, whether or not God would marry same-sex couples depends, ultimately, on whether doing so expresses love.

And that takes us back to the same conclusion I've been pushing from the start: we cannot address whether or not we should make marriage available to same-sex couples without paying attention to how its availability or lack thereof affects gays and lesbians for good or ill. If there is evidence to suggest that it would be unloving to withhold marriage from same-sex couples, then there is evidence to suggest that God, who is love, would not withhold marriage from same-sex couples. While that evidence needs to be weighed against the evidence gleaned from other sources such as Scripture and tradition, *it needs to be weighed*.

This means we need to think carefully about what marriage *does* for those who participate in it. If marriage is good for people, why? If sex outside of marriage is damaging, why? What is the impact of marriage on human sexuality? What is its impact on human happiness and on our efforts to develop our moral character, especially our capacity for love?

The Goods of Marriage

Humans don't need marriage to make babies. Some babies result from rape. Less grimly, a teen couple that hooks up for five minutes after a party can make a baby without saying vows and in fact without ever seeing each other again. For producing babies, regularly measuring basal temperature will be more useful than commitment and fidelity, and as a strategy could be used as effectively by a married couple deciding optimal times to have sex and by a lesbian woman and her gay friend deciding when to employ the turkey baster.

The point is this: if there is a significant relationship between marriage and procreation, it isn't at the level of making children. It's at the level of *raising* them. While it's as easy to make babies outside of marriage as within it, children do better when they grow up in a stable, loving home where they are nurtured by a parenting team rather than a single parent. The marriage vows, by encouraging couples to stay together and nurture love over time, helps promote (if not guarantee) this superior childrearing environment. Likewise, the community support in keeping those vows, the public accountability to them, makes it more likely that married couples will stick together through the years it takes to raise a child.

Since most adult human beings are heterosexual and most are fertile during the time of life when they experience the strongest sexual urges, encouraging everyone to form enduring partnerships, cemented by vows and community support, *before* having sex can be good for any children that result. While the advent of reliable contraceptives could change our judgments about *how* important this is, no contraceptive is perfect. Still, if marriage were *just* about providing a healthy environment for the children that result from heterosexual sex, reliable contraceptives would weaken the case for limiting sex to marriage. But do Christians really think that marriage is *just* for the sake of children?

In 1996, the Evangelical Lutheran Church in America issued a statement on sexuality that, among other things, sought to unpack the church's shared beliefs about the value and purposes of marriage. Part of their understanding was rooted in the conviction that "human sexuality is a powerful, primal force in personal and communal life," and that because of its potential for volatility and abuse "both church and society seek to order sexual expectations and expression."[20] Marriage is central to this ordering:

> Marriage provides the structure of security and stability within which spouses may fully enjoy and risk sexual expression. The binding legal contract of marriage reinforces its "staying power" when it is threatened by sin. Within marriage, spouses can learn to exercise mutual, faithful love.[21]

---

20 Church Council of the ELCA, *A Message on Sexuality*, 2.
21. Ibid., 3.

The message also recognizes that while "the intimacy and companionship it provides the couple" is important, "[t]he wider community is symbolically present when a couple publicly exchanges vows." Not only does the broader community "pledge to support the marriage" but the couple is reminded "that their marriage will affect the wider community."[22]

These themes about the goods of marriage are hardly unique to the ELCA. They are widely endorsed both within and beyond Christianity, and so warrant deeper reflection. First of all, there is the notion that marriage helps to create a safe space for expressing and enjoying our sexuality. Christians have long argued that human sexuality involves at its best a kind of self-giving vulnerability that, apart from a covenant of trust and commitment and mutual love, is dangerously susceptible to exploitation and heartbreak.

Our sexuality has the potential to unite us with another person, to forge intimacy and delight of a uniquely powerful and meaningful kind. But it also has the potential to be tied to human drives toward domination, objectification, and violation. It has the potential to be treated as nothing but momentary recreation—a pleasure pursued in something like the way we pursue the thrill of five minutes on a rollercoaster, without thought to the fact that the ride in this case is another human being whose emotional self is bound up with their sexuality.

There is a radical difference between one person using another for personal pleasure (even if the use is mutual) and two people taking delight in each other as embodied persons in and through their sexuality. In the former case, each person treats the other as a thing, an object used for selfish ends. The philosopher Immanuel Kant saw the potential for this as the greatest moral danger in human sexuality, and he saw marriage—in which each person gives themselves as a whole person to the other, and sex takes place in the context of such mutual giving—as a pathway to avoiding this danger.[23] While his case for this is challenging and controversial, the core idea is one he drew from the Christian tradition in which he was raised. The idea remains powerful even today, amidst all the forces of pop culture: in addition to nurturing a healthy child-rearing environment, marriage institutionalizes the covenant of mutual love that serves as a safeguard against abuse and allows human sexuality to more safely realize its potential for bonding people together in love. Marriage, as a public institution where couples are held accountable for their vows, aims to lift human sexuality out

---

22. Ibid., 4.
23. Kant, *Metaphysics of Morals*, 96–97.

of the arena in which it is fraught with risks of abuse and harm, and into an arena where it can flourish.

But this idea has two aspects. It isn't just about protecting people from the harms of exploitative sexuality. It's also about the deep emotional love that transcends the sexual lives of couples and depends for its survival and growth on much more than a couple's sex-life. Marriage doesn't just keep sex from degrading into exploitation. It aims to locate sex within a broader shared life where it can realize its potential to nurture love.

The giddy and sometimes intoxicating feelings of first love do not last. And while those feelings provide strong incentives to care for another person, many couples find it hard to maintain that caring attitude as the honeymoon of first love fades. Those heady feelings (what Kant calls "pathological love"[24]) *can* give way to new emotions that are more enduring but every bit as romantic—in the sense that they bond two people together, are connected with sexual intimacy, and motivate mutual care. But the transition can be difficult, and without a commitment to stay together many relationships do not survive it. Without the vows of marriage it is easy for couples to part ways when the urgency of new love wanes.

But from the standpoint of Christian ethics, the most important function of the marriage vows may be their capacity to encourage couples to work through conflicts and disputes and stick together, continuing to care for one another, as years of familiarity expose the partner's inevitable flaws. All of us are imperfect, and the better we know someone, the more clearly we see their failings. When we live with someone every day, illusions are shattered and the reality of imperfection becomes impossible to ignore.

To love in the Christian sense is to maintain an attitude of care and good will that does not wait on moral worth, but may, through its transforming power, plant the seeds of moral growth. Marriage can serve as a crucible for learning how to love in this way. As the feelings of first love ebb and the trials of life crash in, as imperfections become more glaring and grating, the vows to love for better or worse, in sickness and in health, kick into full gear and call a couple to be better than they imagined they could be: more loving, more open to the spirit of grace, more capable of channeling the love Christ showed the world.

Marriage offers a uniquely potent framework for growing in our capacity to love.

These goods of marriage do not just benefit the couple. A community organized around the institution of marriage benefits in at least two obvious ways. The first has to do with the volatile power of human sexuality—its

24. Kant, *Fundamental Principles*, 17.

potential for inspiring murderous jealousies and power struggles (especially in love triangles—or rectangles!), the shattering heartbreaks when one person plays with another's emotions to gain sexual access only to walk away. Jonathan Rauch has argued that marriage is "unmatched" as a way for "domesticating men," keeping them "at home and out of trouble"—the kind of trouble that you see when "unattached males gather in packs."[25] But this is too narrow and gender-specific an understanding of how marriage works to stabilize communities. Jealousies and unstable love triangles can exist in lesbian relationships where no men are involved, and the disturbances that these things can cause are evident any time a love betrayed culminates in murder headlines.

All of this is at least partially calmed by the power of marriage to bind sexual expression to love and commitment and stable relationship pairs. Even apart from the effect this has on limiting the spread of sexually transmitted diseases and unwanted pregnancies, the social practice of encouraging people to express their sexuality within loving pair-bonds stabilizes the community. But even more important is the love learned by living up to marital vows throughout life's challenges—by seeking out the spirit of grace and discovering the capacity to work through conflicts rather than walk away. The lessons of this aren't limited to the marital relationship. Those who learn in their marriages how to set aside accusation in favor of self-disclosure, replacing "you-statements" with "I-statements," have developed a community-building skill useful in all their relationships. If marriage helps teach us how to love, that lesson isn't restricted to the spouses. It may bring us a step closer to the beloved community.

Of course, a good marriage also contributes significantly to the quality of life of those who enter into it, while a bad marriage can be a source of misery—especially if there is abuse, exploitation, or betrayal. But a marriage in which both parties are faithful to their promises of mutual love and care is a lifelong benefit. It offers an anchor in a restless world. It provides a partner with whom to face life's challenges and celebrate life's joys, a guard against loneliness, a source of comfort and security and support in times of trial. And these realities are not just good for the individuals involved but for society. As Jonathan Rauch puts it,

> All by itself, marriage is society's first and, often, second and third line of support for the troubled individual. Absent a spouse, the burdens of contingency fall immediately and sometimes crushingly upon people who have more immediate problems of their own (relatives, friends, neighbors), then upon

---

25. Rauch, "For Better or Worse?" 22.

charities and welfare programs that are expensive and often not very good. From the broader society's point of view, the unattached person is an accident waiting to happen. Married people are happier, healthier, and live longer; married men have lower rates of homicide, suicide, accidents, and mental illness. In large part, the reason is simply that married people have someone to look after them, and know it. [26]

Elsewhere, Rauch highlights the significance of this purpose of marriage for the same-sex marriage debate when he puts the point this way: "Legally speaking, marriage creates kin. Surely society's interest in kin-creation is strongest of all for people who are unlikely to be supported by children in old age and may well be rejected by their own parents in youth."[27]

In short, marriage is good for people—both those who marry and the broader society. If so, then the Christian call to love one another provides a strong reason to build and sustain such an institution. Human sexuality has the potential for enormous beauty and the capacity to do enormous harm. Compassionate Christian love cries out for a way to channel human sexuality toward the former and away from the latter.

What can be said about marriage in general can be said about same-sex marriage. If we love our gay and lesbian neighbors as ourselves, then, all else being equal, we would want to extend to them the array of goods marriage makes available. If we love the children being raised by same-sex couples, we would want to extend to their caregivers the stabilizing power of marriage. If we love the members of the gay community, then we would want for them an institution that offers that community the stabilizing effects that heterosexual marriage provides the straight majority. And insofar as stabilizing an embedded subculture benefits the wider society, we would want to make same-sex marriage available for that reason as well.

But denying gays and lesbians the goods of marriage doesn't just deprive them of those goods. It's one thing to go without marriage because, say, you never meet the right person or you choose to remain single. It is another thing for the broader society to *shut you out*. That message of marginalization is damaging to human welfare above and beyond the opportunity costs of going without marriage's benefits.

Andrew Sullivan expresses this point with considerable force when he speaks of his upbringing in a conservative Catholic home, where he learned that the most important moment in your life wasn't graduation day or your first job or home. "The most important day of your life was when you got

26. Rauch, "Who Needs Marriage?" 308.
27. Rauch, "For Better or Worse?" 23.

married." Why? Because the most important aspect of life is family, and your wedding day is the day you start a family of your own. Sullivan describes what it was like to have the dawning realization that this was not going to be a part of *his* life:

> When I looked toward the years ahead, I couldn't see a future. There was just a void. Was I going to be alone my whole life? Would I ever have a "most important day" in my life? It seemed impossible, a negation, an undoing. To be a full part of my family I had to somehow not be me. So like many gay teens, I withdrew, became neurotic, depressed, at times close to suicidal. I shut myself in my room with my books, night after night, while my peers developed the skills needed to form real relationships, and loves. In wounded pride, I even voiced a rejection of family and marriage. It was the only way I could explain my isolation.[28]

To deny gays and lesbians access to same-sex marriage is to shut them out of participating in one of society's most central institutions. It is to tell them that they don't belong, that they will never be full and equal members of society. If we are called to love our gay and lesbian neighbors, we need truly compelling reasons to marginalize them in this way. Absent such reasons, opposing same-sex marriage is a failure of Christian love.

Patriarchal vs. Egalitarian Marriage

Marriage has its critics. Some question the idea that marriage is the valuable institution I have claimed it is. Is it really suited to conferring the range of goods I've been sketching out?

One of the most important lines of criticism points out that, historically, the patriarchal subordination of women has systematically undermined the power of marriage to protect women from the risks of sexual vulnerability. Some Christian thinkers argue that the extent to which marriage has been infected by patriarchal norms has rendered women susceptible to sustained sexual exploitation at the hands of husbands who can abuse them with relative impunity.[29]

I'm highly sympathetic to this concern. If marriage has the power to create a safe space for sexual expression and become a crucible for cultivating love and a source of human happiness, it has that power only absent oppressive hierarchy. Wives who are expected to "submit" to their husbands' sexual

---

28. Andrew Sullivan, "The M-Word," 323.
29. See, for example, Gudorf, *Body, Sex, and Pleasure*, 163–65.

whims may quickly find that, rather than being a safe space to nurture their sexual selves, marriage has become a nightmare of sexual servitude. When men are invested with final authority in a marriage, the mutual negotiation of needs and interests that care demands may quickly give way to a dynamic of domination, in which the man uses his wife to satisfy *his* needs without any regard for hers, and the woman learns to suppress herself and her needs in such a way that she no longer shares herself with her husband.

But some of the same points I have raised to challenge the idea that heterosexuality is essential to marriage, despite it's historic centrality, apply to patriarchal hierarchy as well. If marriage is an essentially contested concept, then we need to ask which features of the marriage paradigms justify the positive appraisal that attaches to the term. If we think patriarchal hierarchy undermines the goods of marriage (as I do), then the proper conclusion is that we *must exclude* patriarchy from our understanding of marriage if we want to continue thinking of marriage in positive terms. Not only *can* we define marriage in a way that excludes patriarchy, but we must if we want to attach to marriage the positive value that Christians want to attach to it.

Some conservative Christians deny this, insisting that gender hierarchy has positive value and is essential to healthy Christian marriage. One advocate of this view is Douglas Wilson who, in *Fidelity: What It Means to Be a One-Woman Man,* explains his perspective as follows:

> ... however we try, the sexual act cannot be made into an egalitarian pleasuring party. A man penetrates, conquers, colonizes, plants. A woman receives, surrenders, accepts. This is of course offensive to all egalitarians, and so our culture has rebelled against the concept of authority and submission in marriage. ... But we cannot make gravity disappear just because we dislike it, and in the same way we find that our banished authority and submission comes back to us in pathological forms. This is what lies behind sexual "bondage and submission games," along with very common rape fantasies. Men dream of being rapists, and women find themselves wistfully reading novels in which someone ravishes the "soon to be made willing" heroine. Those who deny they have any need for water at all will soon find themselves lusting after polluted water, but water nonetheless.[30]

In short, Wilson thinks that pursuing gender equality in marriage amounts to repressing something inescapable—which supposedly leads, in Freudian fashion, to dysfunctional expressions of it. "True authority and true submission," Wilson claims, "are therefore an erotic necessity. When

---

30. Wilson, *Fidelity*, 86–87.

authority is honored according to the word of God it serves and protects—and gives enormous pleasure. When it is denied, the result is not 'no authority,' but an authority which devours."[31] The idea is that men *need* to have authority over "their" women, and when feminists and other supporters of gender equality deny them the chance to meet this need in the benign patriarchy of a head-of-household family, they're going to get it by fantasizing about raping women, or maybe by actually doing it. Likewise, women who don't get to submit to benevolent patriarchs are going to fantasize about being raped or dominated.

To be blunt, this message makes my nauseous. And it's crazy-talk.

Part of the problem is it assumes that the male desire to have authority over women is an essential part of being a man as opposed to a culturally malleable one. It isn't. I know this because I am a man and I don't have this desire. Somehow, being socialized by egalitarian Norwegian parents, I ended up not wanting to wield patriarchal authority, benevolent or otherwise, in my intimate relationships.

Wilson might say I'm in denial—but that's easy to say. If I'm in denial, it's a denial that hasn't produced any bondage and submission games or rape dreams. It has, instead, generated a relationship with my spouse characterized by mutual respect and care, where the relational dynamic isn't "authority and submission" but egalitarian partnership.

What does Wilson offer in support of his essentialist view of gender differences? Mainly metaphors about sex. But do these metaphors describe the reality of sex, or do they create and nurture a certain *perception* of a reality that's far more malleable? What would our culture be like if we talked about sex in terms of the woman "enveloping" while the man is "enveloped" or "consuming" while the man is "consumed"? Are these metaphors any less descriptive of the reality of sex? Don't metaphors and other cultural constructs help shape what sex becomes?

Wilson might point to biological arguments for generalizable differences between human males and females on both physiological and psychological levels. But what do these differences show? Even if there are psychological generalizations that can be made about the sexes, there will always be people who defy them and suffer when they are culturally *expected* to conform.

Furthermore, psychological dispositions can be *both* accentuated *and* muted by culture. Let's grant that there is a tendency for the more testosterone-laden sex to be more aggressive when they don't get their way. If so, that creates a danger—a risk of women being exploited in heterosexual

---

31. Ibid., 87.

relationships, their needs trampled by the more aggressive male. What happens when you combine such male aggressiveness and its attendant danger with a gender-role division that instructs women to submit to their husbands and tells men they have the authority to get their way? Isn't that just a recipe for women's needs and interests being even more consistently suppressed in favor of their husbands' preferences? For men primarily interested in getting their way, this may sound great. But for Christians who aspire to live by the love ethic—and who notice that women are their neighbors, too—this sound pretty terrible.

A gender pattern that affirms male authority and female submission makes it *less* likely, not more likely, that husbands will respect the needs of their intimate partners. It doesn't matter if endorsing that relationship pattern is paired with an injunction for men to be *benign* monarchs over their wives. Yes, such an injunction may soften the harmful effects of hierarchy—and for that reason, we may need to enjoin men in this way so long as patriarchy persists. But it doesn't follow that the hierarchy lacks harmful effects. Kings who were invested with authority to rule, unconstrained by others with equal power to impose checks on that authority, would sometimes listen to the moral message that they should use their power benignly. But not always. After all, power corrupts, as they say.

In a world where male authority and female submission is the cultural norm, women are more vulnerable to exploitation by their husbands. Many good men will try their best to resist the temptation to exploit their wives. But in such a culture, women will be more *dependent* on the good will of their husbands because of their increased cultural *vulnerability* to exploitation. And if there is a biological tendency for men to be more aggressive in the pursuit of their desires, there will also be a temptation to take advantage of their wives' vulnerability.

Advocates of patriarchy insist that falling prey to such temptation would be wrong, that men have a duty to be benevolent rather than abusive patriarchs. But patriarchal Christians like Wilson also believe in *original sin*. And we don't realistically deal with sin by setting up social institutions that increase the temptation to sin and make it easier to get away with it. Rather, we do so by setting up conditions which make it easier to "avoid the near occasion of sin" and harder to violate and abuse others.

If we want those with a disposition toward domination and oppression not to dominate and oppress, setting up social institutions where domination and oppression are made easier isn't the way to go. Instead, we need to set up social institutions that discourage domination and oppression. We need gender socialization that mutes dispositions to dominate in those who have them (not always men, whatever the generalized effects of testosterone) and builds up in those who are more easily cowed (both men and women) the self-worth and dignity required to stand up to oppression or walk away from it. If exploitation is a danger, then marital ideals that feature equality, not hierarchy, are the wiser and more loving choice; and communities that hold married couples accountable to these egalitarian ideals are doing more to prevent exploitation and harm than are those that remind women to be obedient.

John Kronen and I have argued that same-sex marriage may actually help undermine the patriarchy that has, for so long, compromised the capacity of marriage to achieve the goods discussed above. Our argument is this: a patriarchal mythology evolved around the monogamous sexual union such that it came to be "conceived as a hierarchical contract between an inferior and a superior, in which the inferior gives up her individuality in return for the leadership and protection that the superior can provide."[32] The sex act itself is interpreted in ways that symbolize the hierarchy: "the woman's body is physically taken; her flesh becomes the man's flesh. He 'claims' her."[33] But same-sex relationships, by their nature, challenge this mythology of essential hierarchy:

> When confronting a gay relationship, at least between men of comparable maturity and social status, one must understand the sexual union in one of two ways: either one man "takes on the woman's role," in which case it is possible for men to be submissive in sex, to be "taken"; or both are equal partners, in which case there is no need for a dominant-submissive sexual relationship. Confronting lesbian relationships, one must either accept that one woman adopts the "man's role," or that there is an equal exchange. No matter which interpretation one accepts, the myth that male dominance and female submission are an essential part of human sexuality explodes.[34]

In short, patriarchal gender hierarchy threatens the goods of marriage, while same-sex marriage challenges the very coherence of such hierarchy. This not only helps explain the link between sexism and homophobia but also why advocates for egalitarianism in marriage seem more prone to accept same-sex marriage. But for my purposes here it means this: from the standpoint of the love ethic there is a strong, multi-level case for extending marriage to same-sex couples. Not only does it promote the welfare and moral growth of gays and lesbians and the children raised by them, and

32. Kronen and Reitan, "Homosexuality, Misogyny, and God's Plan," 225.
33. Ibid.
34. Ibid.

not only does it appear to have broader social benefits, but it may benefit the institution of Christian marriage itself—by challenging a dangerous mythology of patriarchal hierarchy that has, for too long, infected Christian marriage with forces that threaten to deprive it of its capacity to bestow the goods it is capable of bestowing.

What we have, then, is a strong presumptive case for same-sex marriage grounded in the goods that such marriage bestows and the moral imperative to love our neighbors as ourselves. Combined with the harms that categorically condemning homosexuality imposes, and the fact that the most conservative Christian alternative to a ban on gay sex is a requirement that it be restricted to a marital context, and one conclusion becomes inevitable: Christian love would call for making same-sex marriage available to gays and lesbians absent some sufficiently powerful Christian argument to the contrary.

The remaining question, then, is whether such a sufficiently powerful contrary argument exists.

9

The Scriptures of a Loving God

I've tried to paint a picture of what it's like for gays and lesbians to live in societies that deny them access to legal marriage and condemn every expression of their sexuality. Although Western societies have been moving fitfully away from this model of exclusion, this is the kind of society conservative Christians think gays and lesbians *should* live in. And because so many gays and lesbians have grown up in such a society, we know what it's like for them.

My argument so far has been that by endorsing such a society, conservative Christians endorse something that harms their gay and lesbian neighbors. In such a society, gays and lesbians learn from a young age that they'll never be equal and fully accepted members of their community. Most who try to change their intimate feelings fail, but in the process some trap themselves and their spouses in miserable heterosexual marriages they hoped would "fix" them. If they do form a loving partnership, society will condemn it. Every effort to nurture the bonds of love will be seen as evidence of their commitment to sin. While their straight friends can hope to fall in love and have their partnerships celebrated and supported by the wider community, the best sexual minorities can hope for is to find such support in a marginalized subculture while erecting walls of secrecy and isolation from those who would condemn them.

Some internalize the message that their deepest impulse toward love and intimacy is an affront to God. And when promises of change prove empty, they come to see that impulse as a sign that their very nature is a perversion, a blight on the world. Others, struggling to live in self-denial, cling to the praise of the very Christian conservatives who deny them what so enriches their heterosexual peers—a pattern reminiscent of abused children living for intermittent scraps of parental affection. As the only real payoff for their sacrifice, they wear the mantle of "costly discipleship" so tightly they hardly notice it costs them their ability to focus on discipleship.

Some, unable to suppress their deep instinct for sexual and romantic intimacy, pursue it in contexts where healthy constraints on sexuality are absent. Since their sexuality as a whole is condemned, they make no fine-tuned distinctions between appropriate and inappropriate expressions. Loving monogamy becomes no better than casual sex—except that the latter can be explained away as momentary weakness rather than commitment to sin. In such a world, we shouldn't be surprised when closeted pastors and politicians are caught with their pants down in pathetically tawdry sex scandals.

Other minorities, such as blacks and Jews, are raised by families like them in the ways that mark them off for marginalization. They have the opportunity from childhood to know solidarity with others who are similarly marginalized. Their homes and religious communities offer coping skills and at least some measure of refuge from society's stigmatization.

But sexual minorities routinely grow up in profound isolation. Fearing rejection even from their own families and churches (at least if they admit who they are), they retreat into the closet—a metaphor for hiding one's true self from the world and living a pretense. And because intimacy is about sharing oneself with others, the closet impedes intimacy across relationships—with parents, siblings, coworkers, friends, teachers, and pastors. Deprived of one kind of intimacy by the categorical condemnation of homosexuality, the closet takes away the rest. Sometimes the isolation and rejection can be almost too much to bear, and all it takes is a final gesture of denunciation or scorn to spark an act of self-obliteration.

Despite all of this, many gays and lesbians make their way to a subculture that accepts them. They shake off self-loathing and the condemnation of their sexuality, and they come to see faithful partnerships as having a worth that other expressions of their sexuality lack. They fall in love, form marriage-like partnerships, and work to sustain them despite a society that not only withholds the social supports and accountability marriage provides but can be overtly hostile. Many have the devotion to do that work, and with the security of those relationships and a gay subculture that steps in to partially fill the gap, many escape suicidal loneliness.

But this bulwark against despair is something conservatives think *they ought to be deprived of*. Admittedly, many are sincere about trying to make alternative support systems available: ex-gay communities and spiritual friendship networks that aim to help those without the gift of celibacy to endure a life of ongoing suppression of their sexual and romantic selves. But these alternatives lack what Christian marriage has: the multiple-level intimacy in which physical love is integrated with other forms of closeness in a way that forms a deeper and more holistic connection between *embodied spirits* than is possible without that physical dimension. And because they lack a framework for expressing sexuality that lifts sexuality out of the realm of animal lust and into a space of human meaning, these alternatives set up those gays and lesbians who lack the gift of celibacy not only for failure, but for failure of a particularly debasing kind: momentary sexual relief in meaningless encounters. As we have seen, such failure can lead to genital-slashing self-loathing.

What conservatives on this issue cannot consistently support is the bulwark against despair that does the most good: a community that supports and celebrates expressions of a homosexual orientation within the context of enduring monogamous love. Conservatives can't consistently say that homosexuality is always a sin and yet be glad there's a subculture where despairing gays and lesbians are embraced for who they are and encouraged to live out their sexuality with a self-affirming identity. They can't consistently say that homosexuality is always a sin and yet be happy for their gay and lesbian neighbors who form life-enriching same-sex relationships. To think homosexuality is always a sin is, on pain of inconsistency, to think there should be no such subculture and no such relationships.

Suppose someone said something like the following about your most intimate partnership: "No matter how much it enriches your life and no matter how hard you have worked to nurture love and intimacy within it, it would be better if your relationship ceased to exist." And then suppose they follow it up with something like this: "But even though I think this relationship that means so much to you is a moral blight on the world, *I still love you.*"

Wouldn't your natural response be to say, "No, you don't"?

The portrait I'm painting doesn't *look* like a society that loves the gays and lesbians in its midst. The practical implications of condemning homosexuality, which come to vivid life when we listen compassionately to our gay and lesbian neighbors, are hard to reconcile with the Christian command to love our neighbors, including our gay and lesbian ones, as ourselves.

And yet.

And yet, defenders of the conservative Christian view will say, I've left out something crucial. And for many, the most crucial thing that I've left out is what the Bible says.

The Conservative Biblical Argument in Overview

The objection is this: everything I've argued so far is fatally flawed because it fails to wrestle with what Scripture teaches. Conservative Evangelicals will typically put it this way: the Bible clearly teaches that homosexuality is a sin, and the Bible is the Word of God. While the Bible clearly calls us to love our neighbors—including gays and lesbians—as ourselves, what follows is that condemning their romantic partnerships *must* (somehow) be consistent with loving them. Were these things *inconsistent*, the Bible wouldn't tell us to do both.

There are different ways to develop this argument. One way is to argue that human welfare requires obedience to God; and since God prohibits homosexual sex, abstaining from it is necessary for human welfare. One fundamentalist ministry insists that "if you love your neighbor as yourself you will warn them about trampling God's Word under foot, and living to please themselves rather than pleasing God." Telling gays and lesbians to end their "gay lifestyle" is therefore an act of love, whatever the earthly costs, because pursuing same-sex relationships "will lead to their downfall at the time of judgement."[1]

This argument is deeply flawed. While it is true from a Christian standpoint that our welfare depends on aligning our wills with God's will, the argument here makes it seem as if God's will is some arbitrary force we need to accommodate, like the force of gravity: a force indifferent to our good that we have to pay attention to (and teach others to pay attention to) if we want to flourish. If we say this, what we are essentially saying is that what makes it so "loving" for us to demand that gays and lesbians suppress their sexuality is that such suppression is the only way to appease a dangerous superpower who will otherwise smite them. But to say that is to present ourselves as loving at the cost of painting God as an unloving tyrant.

God's will is not an indifferent force. God's will is a loving will. To explain why it's loving for *us* to condemn homosexuality *given* that God condemns it is to beg the question at hand. The real question is why a God of love would condemn it despite the apparently unloving implications. If it isn't loving to condemn it, a loving God wouldn't condemn it.

---

1. Pilgrim's Light Ministries, "Homosexuality and Loving Your Neighbor," para. 21–22.

But maybe the biblical argument isn't supposed to explain why it's loving to categorically condemn homosexuality. Maybe the aim is simply to give us reason to think *that* it's loving, leading to the following understanding of the biblical argument: whatever reasons there are to think that condemning homosexuality is unloving, the Bible gives us reason to think otherwise when it teaches that homosexuality is a sin. The Bible would teach this only if the God of love condemns homosexual acts. But given the costly discipleship this condemnation imposes on gays and lesbians, God would condemn it *only if doing so were ultimately beneficial.*

The argument, then, is this: We may not know *why* it is good that gays and lesbians suppress their sexuality, but we can know *that* it is good based on what the Bible teaches. Since we know *that* it is good, the loving thing to do is encourage those who can't change their orientations to live celibate lives. Despite the hardships this imposes, we must trust that it's what love demands. Our failure to see why isn't a reason to doubt the demand. It's just a sign of our limits. God has no such limits, so we should be humble and trust God's judgment above our own.

Although this argument is couched in the language of humility, the idea that we can escape the domain of human judgment, deferring to God's judgment, is problematic. First of all, we need to make a human judgment about what the Bible teaches. Secondly, we need to make a human judgment about what kind of text the Bible is. More precisely, we need a theory about *how the Bible is related to divine revelation.*

Even granting a tight relationship between divine revelation and the Bible, the precise nature of that relationship remains a matter of uncertainty, complexity, and dispute. For example, there's a difference between saying the Bible *contains* divine revelations and saying it *reports* them. Many biblical verses (such as Gen 6:13) sound like reports *about* divine self-disclosure, as if human authors were telling readers what God said, rather than God speaking to us directly.

And then there are texts—such as many psalms—that read most naturally as *human responses* to a self-disclosing God: words of praise, adoration, even confusion about God's ways. We can speak of such passages as inspired by God in the way a lover inspires a love poem; but it makes little sense to think of them as something *God* said. Biblical texts can be inspired by a self-disclosing God without *being* the self-disclosure of God.

If this is true in the Book of Psalms, where else might the Bible feature, not divine revelation, but human responses *to* divine revelation by historically situated human beings? If and when Scripture shares human reports about and responses to divine revelation, how susceptible to error are these reports and responses? Would God guarantee inerrancy? Why? If *critical* engagement with the ideas of ancient authors does more to bring us into a living relationship with God than rote appropriation of their ideas, God might favor insightful-but-fallible Scriptures. But suppose God does want inerrant Scriptures, just as God wants a world without genocide. Maybe the same things that keep God from stopping horrors like the Holocaust keep God from stopping cultural prejudices from creeping into inspired biblical testimonies. Perhaps God's respect for free will extends even to Scripture's human authors.

What we think about these things, and why, determines our theory about the Bible. Any such theory is a *human* theory. Since human theories are subject to error, the theory that the Bible isn't subject to error is a human theory about the Bible that *is* subject to error.

The point is this: many say that, since the Bible clearly teaches that homosexuality is a sin, we must conclude that homosexuality is a sin. But those who say this are offering both a fallible human judgment about what the Bible teaches and a fallible human judgment about what the Bible *is*. These judgments underwrite a conclusion whose practical implications have been driving gays and lesbians to the brink of despair. For those committed to neighbor-love, the obligation to assess these judgments is urgent. It can't be escaped by deferring to God's authority, because the claim that God's authority supports these judgments is a contestable human claim, not a matter of divine authority.

The Clobber Passages

Among biblical scholars and interpreters, there is no consensus that the Bible teaches a timeless moral condemnation of all homosexual sex. To many, however, it looks as if there *ought* to be such a consensus. Doesn't Leviticus say that a man sleeping with a man as with a woman is an abomination (Lev 18:22)? Doesn't Paul say that both male and female same-sex acts are the unnatural fruits of degrading passions (Rom 1:24–27)?

But when the meaning of these and other passages is investigating in their original languages and in light of such things as historical context, what may seem obvious to contemporary readers becomes more controversial. Some scholars, such as Robert Gagnon, nevertheless conclude that the texts are best read as implying the traditional condemnation of all homosexual sex.[2] But others disagree.

Since biblical scholars don't all agree on what these texts mean, I won't pretend that I can come in from the outside—a philosopher, not a biblical

---

2. Gagnon, *The Bible and Homosexual Practice*.

scholar—and settle matters. But it is important to recognize the controversy. Since the conservative reading of relevant biblical texts (which takes them to categorically condemn homosexuality) is the most entrenched and obvious, I want to devote what space I can to explaining why not everyone accepts this reading.

The Bible says very little about homosexuality. It says nothing about sexual orientation, nothing about same-sex marriage as an enduring relationship, and *almost* nothing about same-sex sex acts. However we interpret the relevant texts, condemnation of these acts can hardly be called a recurring or emerging scriptural theme in the manner of, say, the call to love our neighbors as ourselves. Most biblical authors never mention it.

There are two exceptions: the authors of Leviticus and Paul. Some will also cite the story in Genesis (Gen 19:1–11) in which angels visit Sodom and receive an ugly welcome. In that story, Lot welcomes the angels into his home but the men of Sodom clamor at the door, demanding that the visitors be thrown out for them to rape. A horrified Lot offers the mob his daughters instead. When the mob attacks, the angels pull Lot to safety and blind the men. Later, God destroys the cities of Sodom and Gomorrah.

To see how irrelevant this story is, imagine reading a story about a Parisian woman being gang-raped in New York City and thinking, "How awful. I guess that, since what happened to her is so awful, consensual sex in the context of a loving heterosexual marriage is a sin!" Such a conclusion makes no sense. And if you consult other biblical texts for an interpretation of the "sin of Sodom," what you learn is that the Sodomites were "arrogant, overfed, and unconcerned; they did not help the poor and needy" (Ezek 16:49).

But there are biblical texts that do speak to homosexual sex. Two appear in Leviticus and three in Paul's letter (although two are passing remarks). Out of thousands of pages and hundreds of thousands of words, that's it.

The two passages from Leviticus are these:

> Leviticus 18:22: "Do not have sexual relations with a man as one does with a woman; that is detestable."

> Leviticus 20:13: "If a man has sexual relations with a man as one does with a woman, both of them have done what is detestable. They are to be put to death; their blood will be on their own heads."[3]

---

3. The NIV translation, which I am using throughout, uses "detestable" where other translations use what has become the more familiar label of "abomination."

These passages seem pretty straightforward—although they only refer to *male* homosexual acts and (in the original Hebrew) use language that seems to be specifically about anal penetration,[4] raising questions about lesbian sex[5] and the range of gay sex that doesn't involve such penetration.[6] But these complexities of the texts aside, there are reasons to question their timeless applicability. The Holiness Code of Ancient Israel, found in Leviticus, includes diverse commandments that Christians (and many Jews) do not regard as authoritative: the commandment not to mate different kinds of animals (no mules!) or eat meat with blood in it (no bloody steaks!) or wear garments made of two kinds of yarn (no more cotton-polyester blends!).

Of course, Leviticus also contains commandments with more timeless authority, such as prohibitions against robbing your neighbor and making your daughter work as a prostitute. The point is that we cannot conclude that a commandment is authoritative for Christians just because it appears in Leviticus. Much of Leviticus is motivated by purity concerns that Jesus challenged (see Matt 15:10–20). In his letters, Paul stresses repeatedly that justification comes through Christ, not through obedience to the old law; and he speaks of chastising Peter for expecting gentile Christians to follow Jewish practices (see Gal 2:11–16). There is clearly no simple relationship between Israel's purity laws and contemporary Christian practice.

But it isn't just purity standards that can be seen as time-bound rather than timeless. Consider the requirement, in Deuteronomy 22:28–29, that if a man rapes an unpledged virgin he must marry her. In the patriarchal world of ancient Israel, a woman's survival depended on finding a husband, but a rape victim would be hard-pressed to find one. Given these realities, the Deuteronomy requirement demands that the man who jeopardized a woman's survival must provide for her. But the only thing this rule would do today is chain rape victims to their rapists. Based on cases like these, even those who think *all* biblical commands reveal God's will might borrow a line from Martin Luther, who argued that we cannot simply "look and see whether this is God's word, whether God has said it; rather we must look and see to whom it was spoken, and whether or not it is addressed to you."[7] Perhaps some commands were addressed *to the ancient Israelites* because of historical and cultural contingencies that no longer obtain.

---

4. Numerous scholars are convinced that anal penetration is the primary focus of concern, including Olyan, "And with a Man"; Walsh, "Leviticus 18:22 and 20:13"; and Thurston, "Leviticus 18:22."

5. It's so specific to male homosexuality that Talmudic authors treated lesbian sex as in a different moral category. See Greenburg, *Wrestling with God and Man*, 86–96.

6. See Boyarin, "Are There Any Jews," 336–37.

7. Martin Luther, "How Christians Should Regard Moses," 170.

A similar point is this: just because a command *presupposes* certain cultural realities does not mean it *endorses* them. Jesus treated some ancient laws, such as those on divorce (Mark 10:2–5), as concessions to human sinfulness rather than ideals to live by. There is something deeply wrong with a culture in which a rape victim's only hope for survival lies in her abuser being forced to marry her. Ancient laws that function as time-bound concessions to such horrific social realities don't call for us to perpetuate those horrific realities. Rather, they call us to work for a world where those laws are obsolete.

The point is that, even assuming the conservative view that every biblical injunction comes from God, the task of deciding which laws apply beyond their ancient context is hardly straightforward. These concerns arise for the Levitical texts condemning male homosexuality, although in a different way than they arise in the Deuteronomy text.

Some scholars argue that the Levitical aversion to male penetration of other men is rooted in the patriarchy of ancient Israel, which saw men as occupying a higher status than women, a status degraded by sex acts that treated men "like women." If so, the prohibition on men penetrating other men would not be a *concession* to patriarchal hierarchy but an *expression* of it—a rule justified based on assuming that women have less value than men.[8] The biblical authors, on this reading, were not just making a concession to a culture that presupposed the subordinate status of women but were presupposing it themselves. Many (including myself) think these kinds of patriarchal justifications say more about ancient human prejudices than about divine revelation, and that a holistic reading of Scripture dictates against treating such patriarchy as an expression of divine will. But for now, I want to focus not on reasons for doubting the inerrancy of these texts, but on reasons for doubting the interpretation of them as positing a timeless norm.

One important point here is that the Hebrew word invoked to condemn men lying with men is *tôēvah*, usually translated as "abomination." Saul Olyan indicates that, although the term may not always mean the same thing, "Usage in general suggests the violation of a socially constructed boundary, the undermining or reversal of what is conventional, the order of things as the ancient might see it."[9] Jerome Walsh sees it as signifying a failure to separate distinct kinds of things, and most especially "to protect the boundaries between Israelites, who are to be Yahweh's 'holy' people (i.e. 'set

---

8. See Nissinen, *Homoeroticism in the Biblical World*, 43–44; and Boyarin, "Are There Any Jews," 341.

9. Olyan, "And With a Man," 180 (fn 3).

apart, separate'), and the various peoples surrounding them who, in Israel's view, indulged in all these prohibited dietary, sexual, and cultic practices."[10]

Jay Michaelson, picking up on this idea, suggests that what was *tôʿevah* for the ancient Israelites depended on the cultural divisions in place at that time. It was all about preserving the "boundary between Israelite and foreigner."[11] More significantly, Michaelson finds *tôʿevah* used in Scripture to reference foreign cultic behavior and idolatry; and given the context of Leviticus and its concern about Molech worship, he thinks the prohibition against male anal sex was about of its role in Canaanite cultic practice and idolatry.[12] Historian John Boswell likewise argues that the use of the term *tôʿevah* implies a concern about idolatry and remaining distinct from neighboring peoples.[13] Put simply, same-sex anal sex on this view was associated with the idolatrous sexual practices of neighboring peoples and was condemned for that reason.

Others, while agreeing that the condemnation is time-bound and that *tôʿevah* is about violating boundaries, have a different understanding of which boundaries are at issue. L. William Countryman argues that ancient Jewish ethical norms were organized around property rights and purity, and that the latter forbade the crossing of boundaries by mixing things that don't go together. Countryman sees *tôʿevah* as a concept tied to these purity standards, arguing that in homosexual sex, "the male who fulfills the 'female' role is a combination of kinds and therefore unclean, like a cloth composed of both linen and wool."[14] Jerome Walsh agrees.[15] But if this is right, we have to wrestle with the fact that the ancient Israelite understanding of which boundaries must be preserved for purity's sake are not ones Christians find inviolable. And so we have reason to doubt, absent other evidence, that the Levitical injunctions are timeless moral laws—especially when the cost to gays and lesbians is so high.

But what about the passages in Paul? The passing remarks in 1 Corinthians 6:9–10 and 1 Timothy 1:9–10 run up against translational challenges that make it difficult to base a compelling case on them.[16] The key Greek terms are *malakoi* and *arsenokoitai*. The former, in its common Greek usage,

---

10. Walsh, "Leviticus 18:22 and 20:13," 207.
11. Michaelson, *God vs. Gay?* 63.
12. Ibid., 63–65.
13. Boswell, *Christianity, Social Tolerance, and Homosexuality,* 100–101.
14. Countryman, *Dirt, Greed, and Sex,* 26.
15. Walsh, "Leviticus 18:22 and 20:13," 207.
16. See Helminiak, *What the Bible Really Says,* 105–7.

The Scriptures of a Loving God 181

literally meant "soft" and was sometimes used to mean "effeminate."[17] The latter is hard to pin down since it is not a common Greek word but one that many think Paul coined himself.[18] While there are scholars who say *malakoi* and *arsenokoitai* taken together refer sweepingly to the "passive" and "active" partners in any instance of male homosexual sex,[19] others think the terms refer respectively to catamites and pederasts—that is, prepubescent boys and the adult men who used them sexually in the pederasty common at the time.[20] Others think the terms refer to male prostitutes and their clients.[21] On either of these narrower readings, the passages say nothing about same-sex monogamy.

But what about Romans 1:26-27? The passage reads as follows:

> Because of this, God gave them over to shameful lusts. Even their women exchanged natural sexual relations for unnatural ones. In the same way the men also abandoned natural relations with women and were inflamed with lust for one another. Men committed shameful acts with other men, and received in themselves the due penalty for their error.

What Paul is describing here is what happens to those who "exchanged the truth about God for a lie, and worshiped and served created things rather than the Creator" (Rom 1:25). When people turn from God and worship things of this earth, their passions become disordered. "Unnatural" sexual relations *express* these disordered passions, whereas the root sin—the focus of Paul's concern—is idolatry. But even if idolatry is his main concern, isn't Paul clearly communicating a negative view of homosexual sex here? After all, he links it to other offenses that result when people turn from God, including murder and gossip and slander (Rom 1:29-30). Of course, this is right. The question is not whether Paul has a negative view of the unnatural acts he lumps together with these other wrongs. The question is what behavior he was specifically referencing.

Some point out that what Paul appears to be talking about here is a sexual passion so unrestrained that men and women just can't limit themselves to the opposite sex. As Walter Wink notes, there is no way Paul's

---

17. Richie, "An Argument," 723-24.

18. Ibid., 725. See also Malick, "Condemnation in 1 Corinthians," 484.

19. Malick, "Condemnation in 1 Corinthians," 484-85. Older articulations of the view include Barrett, *Commentary*, 140; and Conzelmann, *1 Corinthians*, 108.

20. Examples include Richie, "An Argument," 727; and Fee, *First Epistle to the Corinthians*, 243-44.

21. Scroggs, *The New Testament and Homosexuality*, 106-9; Boswell, *Christianity, Social Tolerance, and Homosexuality*, 107.

remarks could have been informed by the concept of sexual orientation, since that idea "was not available in his world." Instead, Paul "seemed to assume that those he condemned were heterosexuals who were . . . 'exchanging' their regular sexual orientation for that which was foreign to them."[22] Paul took it for granted that homosexual behavior sprang, not from a different orientation of the sexual desires, but from an excess of lust that couldn't be contained to the normal parameters. But this describes something very different from loving same-sex monogamy, where sexual expression is just as restrained as it is in heterosexual marriage.

Add to this the following fact: interpreters widely agree that in this part of Romans, Paul's portrait of those who turn from God highlights tropes characteristic of the gentile world at the time—gentile offenses that Jewish readers would resonate with.[23] If so, Paul's mention of unnatural same-sex relations would orient readers toward the same-sex activities visible *in that world*. Faithful homosexual monogamy wouldn't be in the picture. In the Greco-Roman world, same-sex sex was rampantly and visibly *extra-marital*: married men had young male lovers on the side, while slave boys serviced male clients in brothels to the point of inspiring female prostitutes to complain about the competition.[24]

In Paul's culture, homosexual sex was always the indulgent sexual use of another's body for personal pleasure outside of marriage. It would be natural to assume that homosexual sex sprang from uncontrolled sexual appetites, not from a homosexual orientation that might be channeled into a marital context. When Paul advised Christians to marry rather than burn with lust, his cultural context wouldn't have allowed him to fathom that for some, a heterosexual marriage would provide no guard against burning with lust since such a marriage would bind them to someone completely outside the sphere of their sexual desires. He couldn't have fathomed that there were some for whom only a *same-sex* marriage could do this work.

Put simply, the argument is this: what Paul had in mind in Romans 1 was not committed monogamy between persons of a homosexual orientation, but promiscuous and abusive homosexual sex pursued out of excessive lust. That Paul considers *such* behavior shameful provides little reason to conclude that same-sex marriage is likewise shameful.

Finally, we need to situate this passage within the broader context that reveals its rhetorical aim. At the start of Romans 2 Paul says, "Therefore you

22. Walter Wink, "Homosexuality and the Bible," 36.

23. Cranfield, *Critical and Exegetical Commentary*, 105. Helminiak, *What the Bible Really Says*, 94–97; Stuhlmacher, *Paul's Letter to the Romans*, 33–38.

24. Scanzoni and Mollenkott, *Is the Homosexual My Neighbor?* 66; Graham-Murray, *History of Morals*, 64–66.

are inexcusable, O man, whoever you are who judge, for in whatever you judge another you condemn yourself; for you who judge practice the same things" (Rom 2:1). In other words, *all of us* have turned from God and have disordered and excessive desires; so none of us has any right to judge anyone else. Not only does this serve as a telling indictment of those who use the Romans passage to single out gays and lesbians for condemnation, but it raises questions about just what sort of authority we should attach to Paul's invocation of gentile perversions. David Helminiak argues that this invocation is a rhetorical "ploy": Paul uses common Jewish prejudices against gentiles in order to put himself "in the middle of a petty name-calling bout. He seems to be playing a game of we're-better-than-you. Paul is quoting Jewish prejudice! And he seems to be supporting it. Ah, but he quotes it precisely to counter and reject it."[25]

Helminiak argues that Paul quite deliberately includes examples not only of gentile sinfulness but also of gentile impurity (their violation of Jewish purity standards), since both would be taken by Jewish readers as ugly fruits of gentile idolatry.[26] The aim is to paint gentiles as "dirty," and sexual deviance is one of the easiest ways to do that. But the rhetorical purpose is to transcend the separation between gentile and Jew, to expose the root sin of idolatry as common to all, and to reject the idea that obedience to Jewish law is the path to justification.[27] This reading of Romans fits well with the idea that the ancient Jewish condemnation of homosexual sex was about purity standards or idolatry, but it also raises the question of whether Paul's apparent endorsement of that condemnation is more than just a rhetorical move.

None of these arguments offer a decisive case against traditional interpretations. But when experts disagree about how to interpret a text, it starts to make sense to decide which interpretation to accept based on such broader considerations as the urgings of Christian love. Whatever the disagreements about passages like Romans 1:26–27, there can be no doubt that Scriptures teaches us to love our neighbors as ourselves. In the light of this, if one interpretation fits better with the love ethic, we have a reason to favor

---

25. Helminiak, *What the Bible Really Says*, 98.

26 In fact, Jeramy Townsley, in "Paul, the Goddess Religions, and Queer Sects," has argued that idolatry was the primary target of Paul's attention in Rom 1:26–27. According to Townsley, the era in which Paul was writing "witnessed the wide growth of goddess sects whose cross-gender and sexual practices violated patriarchal norms, giving Paul graphic imagery to refer the audience back to them" (708). He concludes that "Paul's context for the entire periscope of Rom 1:18–32 is idolatry, and the vv. 26–27 refer to the gender and sex-variant practices of the goddess cults" (728).

27. Ibid., 98–101.

it—a reason that isn't divorced from Scripture but springs from something at its heart.

Holistic Interpretations

Were the clobber passages the whole of the biblical case against same-sex marriage, I think reasonable doubt would be enough to favor a revised interpretation of them, given that these interpretive decision are made "in a context in which children are killing themselves," as Jay Michaelson notes.[28] But when interpreting Scripture, looking at isolated passages is never the whole story.

The Bible is a collection of writings in diverse styles by various authors over centuries. To talk about what "the Bible says" given this reality is a bit like talking about what a college library says. We're most warranted in using that phrase with respect to messages that emerge when we read the Bible as a whole.[29] And so it isn't enough to study isolated texts. We need to look at broader scriptural themes.

Some scholars think these themes provide a solid case against homosexuality. Craig Koester argues that if we read the Scriptures broadly, we find a consistent message about a special order between males and females, what we might call a "heterosexual order." This order emerges in Scripture as part of God's design plan for creation—especially as evidenced in the Genesis narrative, which specifies that God created human beings male and female (Gen 1:27) and intended them to form a special kind of bond (Gen 2:18–24). Koester thinks Jesus affirms this Genesis theme when he condemns divorce (especially in Mark 10:6–9), and that Paul's teachings on marriage (especially 1 Corinthians 7) draw together Jewish Scripture and Jesus' teachings to reinforce the theme of a heterosexual order that finds fruition in heterosexual marriage.[30]

Koester's effort to trace out a heterosexual order in the Bible gets its initial traction from how he reads the creation stories in Genesis, especially the second chapter. According to the story found there, after God made the first human he decided it would not be good for that human to be alone. Not finding a suitable companion among the creatures in the Garden, God

---

28. Michaelson, *God vs. Gay*, 58.

29. Every such holistic reading depends on a human act of intellectual synthesis even more subject to doubt than interpretations of isolated texts. Hence, we may be *most* justified in using the phrase "the Bible says" when we are *least* justified in being confident we're right.

30. Koester, "The Bible and Sexual Boundaries," 378–83.

created a helpmate. Of course, the first human in the story is male, and the helpmate female. Does this imply that for all time, every human must cleave to a helpmate of the opposite sex? For a gay man, a woman won't make for a suitable helpmate—as evidenced by the litany of failed heterosexual marriages in which gay men hoped the love of a good woman would make them straight. But another gay man *will* be a suitable helpmate, as the many loving partnerships among my gay friends demonstrates. Likewise for lesbian women.

Must we assume, based on the details of the Genesis story, that all the gay men unsuited for the kind of helpmate God gave Adam are obligated to go through life without any helpmate rather than with one of the same sex, and all the lesbians unsuited for the kind of helpmate God gave Eve are obligated to go through life alone? Does that lesson show the most fidelity to a story where God says, "It is not good for Adam to be alone"?

Consider the fact that God gave to Adam a helpmate with a propensity to be fooled by serpents. Were I to learn that my wife had no such propensity, should I conclude that my marriage isn't a real biblical marriage, because the helpmate God gave to Adam *had* this propensity? Of course this is silly, but the point is that some biblical interpretations come to seem obvious only because of familiarity rather than any intrinsic obviousness. We often read morals into stories that have multiple possible meanings, and the Bible is full of such "polysemic" stories. To what extent do Koester and others read their heterosexual presuppositions into Genesis and build their holistic argument from there?

But let's set such worries aside and grant that the Bible, in a holistic way, teaches that God designed humanity with two sexes, male and female—and tied reproduction exclusively to heterosexual pairings—for a reason. In other words, let's assume that this isn't just some random fact about God's creation that has no normative implications, but that there is a purpose to this design plan. Perhaps the most significant challenge to Koester's holistic argument targets, not the idea that the Bible portrays such a heterosexual order, but the idea that this order offers grounds for condemning homosexual relationships.

The problem is this: we can accept that a heterosexual ordering of the human species is a deliberate feature of God's design plan—a species-level pattern intended to achieve some purpose—without concluding that everyone is obligated to "opt in" to this pattern. Christians have never condemned a life of singleness, even though it might be unwise for those who lack the gift for it. For those who have the gift (or orientation?), a single life is morally acceptable even though it does not conform to the pattern in which "a man leaves his father and mother and is united to his wife, and they become one flesh" (Gen 2:24). Singleness, for those suited to it, does nothing to *disrupt* the purported heterosexual order. Hence, such an order offers no basis for prohibiting a single life.[31]

More profoundly, deviations from a prevailing pattern are sometimes part of an even larger pattern, one in which not only the prevailing pattern but also the deviations play a role. As noted in the last chapter, John Kronen and I have argued that homosexual relationships challenge the plausibility of misogynistic myths that threaten the goods of marriage.[32] If we're right about this, strong prohibitions against same-sex relationships may actually *damage* God's larger design plan—even assuming that a heterosexual order is an important dimension of that plan. Whatever we think of this hypothesis, the point is that *deviating* from a pattern isn't the same as opposing it. Even if a pattern exists for some good purpose, it doesn't follow that every deviation is wrong—and some deviations may serve a purpose in a larger pattern of which both the dominant pattern and the deviations are important parts.

A holistic biblical case against same-sex marriage therefore requires more than just biblical evidence of a heterosexual order. We need an account of the purpose of that order—one that shows that homosexuality threatens it. Stanton Jones tries to offer such an account, and since what he says represents a common evangelical view it deserves some attention. According to Jones, "God has a big purpose in mind" for sex and marriage, a purpose made clear in Ephesians 5, where Paul tells wives to submit to their husbands the way the church submits to Christ, and for husbands to love their wives the way Christ loves the church.[33]

Paul is making an analogy here between the hierarchical relationship of husbands and wives that prevailed in Paul's patriarchal culture, and the hierarchical relationship that exists between Christ and the church. Perhaps Paul is rightly concerned that patriarchy makes women vulnerable to exploitation. But rather than reject the patriarchy, he offers an analogy in which the party higher in the hierarchy serves and cares for the one below. Be that as it may, Jones says this passage teaches us that the big purpose of marriage is "to model concretely here on earth what God wants in the relationship between Christ and his bride, the church."[34]

But this goes way beyond what Ephesians 5 actually says. From the fact that Paul uses one thing as an analogy to teach us about another, we

---

31. Kronen and Reitan, "Homosexuality, Misogyny, and God's Plan," 216.
32. Ibid., 222–27.
33. Jones, "Loving Opposition," 21.
34. Ibid.

cannot infer that *God* designed the first thing from the beginning of history for the cosmic purpose of serving as an analogy to teach us about the other thing. If Paul thought this, why did he seem to treat marriage as a second-rate alternative to celibacy for those who lacked the gift for the latter (1 Cor 7:1–7 and 32–35)?[35]

Furthermore, Jones's interpretation of Ephesians 5 involves a cosmic endorsement of patriarchal hierarchy. But there are biblical reasons to question that reading. While Paul tells slaves to obey their masters, he also says that in Christ there is neither slave nor free. While he tells women to obey their husbands, he also says that in Christ there is neither male nor female. One way to make sense of these dissonant juxtapositions is to see Paul as making concessions to entrenched cultural realities. Perhaps Paul sees slavery and patriarchy as so deep-seated that defiance by slaves and wives would only inspire repressive responses, and so he focuses instead on urging masters and husbands to be benevolent until human societies can move closer to that kingdom of God where there truly is neither slavery nor patriarchal oppression.[36]

Beyond the size of Jones's interpretive leap and the plausibility of other interpretations, there is the question of whether Jones's account of marriage's purpose makes sense. His idea is that although we are "utterly different from God," God wants union with us. And he thinks this "can be uniquely modeled on earth through the union of two different kinds of beings, male and female."[37]

If this is what marriage is supposed to do, the differences between male and female don't seem nearly enough, since they are completely trivial compared to the difference between humanity and God. And we tend to seek spouses who are like us in many ways. My wife is far more like me than most men. If I wanted a relationship that modeled the gap of difference between humanity and God I'd do better to choose a poor, uneducated black Muslim man in Africa than a middle class, highly educated white preacher's daughter in the US. Or perhaps, even better, a hamster! If God really wanted marriage to model the relationship between humanity and

---

35. Furthermore, there's Paul's endorsement of mutual submission between husband and wife (1 Cor 7:4), which raises questions about whether Paul consistently adhered to a hierarchical head/body relationship between spouses.

36. Of course, if we reject biblical inerrancy, another possibility emerges. Perhaps Paul was a creature of his time, gripped by cultural prejudices, but was also inspired by God. And so divine insights defying his prejudices would break through to shatter them—generating luminous moments in Scripture where divine wisdom vividly refutes Paul's own merely human presuppositions. I will explore challenges to inerrancy in the next section.

37. Jones, "Loving Opposition," 21.

God, one wonders why he found all the beasts in the Garden unsuitable companions for poor Adam.

But the deeper problem is this. For marriage to model the relationship between Christ and the church there must be a hierarchy—a head and a body. If men are always the head, marriage won't help teach them how to be the body of Christ, even if it might give them the chance to practice being Christ-like (assuming they don't succumb to sin and exploit their privilege). And if women are always the body, marriage won't teach them the lessons, available to their husbands, about being Christ-like. And insofar as their husbands will never be sinless as Christ, it is almost certain that women will submit to husbands who won't always resist the temptation to exploit their privilege. Husbands will never be adequate stand-ins for Christ, and women who marry abusive men may learn more about what it's like to be the church of Satan.

This hardly seems like a plausible strategy for teaching humanity about how to relate to Christ—hardly the sort of plan we'd independently expect to spring from the mind of a perfect God. What Jones offers, then, isn't a holistic biblical case for a heterosexual norm. What he offers is a dubious interpretive leap to an inherently implausible conclusion.

So: holistic biblical interpretations aimed at supporting the traditional condemnation of homosexuality are no more immune to doubt than standard readings of the clobber passages. But perhaps this doubt can be mitigated if we *combine* these holistic readings with conservative interpretations of the clobber passages. Put another way, perhaps there is a kind of mutual reinforcement between conservative readings of those passage and those conservative holistic readings of Scripture that find there a divinely-ordained heterosexual order. Perhaps the latter offers a lens for reading the former, which in turn supports the latter. David Malick, for example, argues that in Romans 1:26–27, Paul uses language that evokes both Leviticus and the Genesis creation story in a way that makes it reasonable to assume Paul had in mind a timeless violation of the natural heterosexual order laid down by God in creation.[38]

But if we start to look at holistic context, it's also the case that both the clobber passages and these holistic themes of a heterosexual order fall within an even more important holistic theme: the love ethic itself. And this theme raises important questions about any reading of the second chapter of Genesis that is more impressed by the supposed moral implications of the heterosexual order than by the compassionate God who looks at Adam and says, "It isn't good that he should be alone." This theme raises important

---

38. Malick, "Condemnation in Romans."

questions about readings of the clobber passages that have borne so many poisoned fruits for gays and lesbians.

But let's set aside all this interpretive controversy and grant, for the sake of argument, that Romans 1:26–27 fits so well with broader themes about a heterosexual order that the most faithful interpretation of Paul's intent is this: he means to say that all homosexual sex violates the heterosexual design God built into the world. For argument's sake, let's even grant that Jones is right about what Paul takes the plan for marriage to be. Does it follow that *we* should believe it?

That depends on which theory of the Bible we adopt.

The Question of Inerrancy

According to one of my favorite philosophers, Aristotle, some people are "by nature slaves" who are best off "under the rule of a master."[39] Aristotle is among history's greatest minds, and his writings are among the towering intellectual achievements in the Western world. I have drawn more life lessons from his *Nicomachean Ethics* than any other philosophical work. But such reverence for Aristotle does not require me to agree with his claim that some people are natural slaves. On this point, I think Aristotle was misled by cultural prejudices. He had blind spots I don't have, not because I'm smarter, but because I live at a time in history that affords me the perspective to see what he didn't see.

Similarly, it is possible to revere Paul and his writings while thinking he had cultural blind spots. To conclude that something must be true just because Paul said it, you need more than just reverence for Paul and his epistles. You need a theory of the Bible according to which no human error or cultural blind spot ever finds expression there. That is, you need to embrace the doctrine of inerrancy, or what I'll call "inerrantism." Inerrantism's hallmark is that whenever a biblical author intends to say something, the author's intended meaning is true.[40]

For reasons already discussed, inerrantists might see some scriptural laws as time-bound rules that don't apply today. But if Paul condemns homosexuality based on its perceived conflict with God's design of the world, that isn't some time-bound basis for condemning it. So on that conservative reading, Paul *intends* to express a timeless moral truth. Combine that with

---

39. Aristotle, *Politics* 1.5, 1254b18–19, trans. Jowett (pp. 1133).

40. This is not the same as literalism. Inerrantists may think the intended meaning of a passage is not the literal one.

inerrantism and we're led to conclude that this condemnation *is* a timeless moral truth.

But inerrantism has problems. First, there are the practical challenges of reconciling inerrantism with the actual content of Scripture. For example, the Gospels offer conflicting accounts of key events in Jesus' life—forcing inerrantists into some serious interpretive gymnastics. Some try to weave the contrasting narratives into a larger, more convoluted story; but as Bart Ehrman points out, the result is often a failure to do justice to the intended meaning of each text:

> When that is done, the messages in both Mark and Luke get completely lost and glossed over. Jesus is no longer in deep agony, as in Mark (since he is confident as in Luke), and he is no longer calm and in control as in Luke (since he is in despair as in Mark). He is somehow all things at once.... When readers then throw both Matthew and John into the mix, they get an even more confused and conflated portrayal of Jesus, imagining wrongly that they have constructed events as they *really* happened.[41]

While one *could* reconcile the divergent texts by supposing Jesus underwent precipitous mood swings that no Gospel authors talk about, this portrait of Jesus is at odds with what each author was trying to convey. We end up with a story at odds with *every* Gospel author rather than just some of them. "To approach the stories in this way," Ehrman notes, "is to rob each author of his own integrity as an author and to deprive him of the meaning that he conveys in his story."[42] Ehrman's argument is that inerrantists, unable to accept contrasting views of biblical authors, impose uniformity by distorting biblical voices in ways that fail to respect them. A theory about the Bible that drives readers to such disrespect is not a theory that respects the Bible.

But let's suppose inerrantists can overcome this problem. There remains the question of why we should favor this theory over rival ones. Consider the following theory: everything in the Bible is there because God wants it to be there for the purpose of leading us to divine truths. Surely this offers a high view of Scripture. But it does not posit inerrancy.

Suppose I create a packet of materials on a political candidate that includes his inflammatory claims alongside research findings contradicting those claims, as well as quotes that show the candidate contradicting himself. If everything in the packet has been chosen by me, does it follow that I

---

41. Ehrman, *Jesus, Interrupted*, 69–70.
42. Ibid., 70.

endorse every claim that appears in it? Of course not. My message has little to do with the claims in the packet and everything to do with the overall lesson, never directly stated, that emerges from the whole: the candidate is untrustworthy.

Take a different example. Suppose several people saw me at an event where I did something significant. Suppose I collect their eyewitness accounts, which conflict on some details but agree on others. I choose these accounts, rather than telling you what happened myself, because I want you to get a sense of what happened based not on my assurances but on the independent testimony of others. Since no witness is perfect, I offer several accounts that, collectively, give a reliable sense of what happened even if some isolated claims are mistaken. In this case, it would miss my point to pick out one isolated claim and insist that, since it was part of the collection of witness accounts, it must be something I endorsed.

Or suppose that, instead of witnesses to a single event, I include a series of reports over time—a kind of chronicle of a community's evolving understanding of me. Some reports include misunderstandings that are cleared up by later reports. Maybe I include the early reports because I want to communicate something about how easily my actions are misunderstood, and I want my audience to learn that lesson through something more powerful than rote assurances. I want to *show* them the danger, rather than merely tell them about it. In such a case, anyone who took the collection of reports as inerrant, rather than as an evolving picture, would not just miss part of my message. They'd end up attributing to me the early errors *along with* the later corrections, making me seem erratic and contradictory in ways I'm not.

Those who revere Scripture and look to it for guidance aren't thereby committed to the view that every sentence in the Bible is something God wants us to believe. Rather, different theories about the Bible—positing different ways that God might communicate to us through human-authored texts—imply very different way of approaching the Bible for guidance. If we uncritically embrace the wrong theory, our approach could guide us to the wrong conclusions.

Determining which theory offers the best understanding, given Scripture's content and history, is beyond what I can do here. For what it's worth, I think the actual content of Scripture puts inerrantism out of the running. Armed with a rigid idea of what kind of text deserves respect—namely, one whose assertions are uniformly true—inerrantists try to force Scripture into a mold that doesn't suit it. The result is that they fail to respect Scripture for what it actually is. Instead of adjusting their idea of what deserves respect to suit the substance of Scripture, they distort Scripture to suit their idea of what deserves respect.

But defending that view would require its own book. The point here is that we can be skeptical of inerrancy and still believe that God communicates to humanity through Scripture. We can be sincere Christians who revere the Bible while not believing that the intended meaning of every sentence ought to be embraced. Christianity, after all, is not *about* obedience to the Bible. It's about being disciples of Christ. The Bible offers our oldest preserved stories and reflections about Jesus. It offers the sacred writings of the Jewish tradition Jesus was born into and laid claim to as his own. To treat the Bible as nothing but bunk would thus be incompatible with Christian life. But there are many options between the extremes of bunk and inerrancy.

Consider Martin Luther. Although he introduced into Western theology the notion of "Sola Scriptura" (the idea that the chief authority for Christians is the Bible) and thus paved the way for the later emergence of inerrantism, Luther was no inerrantist. Luther likened Scripture to the manger and swaddling clothes in which the baby Jesus lay.[43] That manger contained the holy child, but it also contained straw. Likewise, Luther thought the Bible contains the gospel but also straw. He once called James "an epistle of straw" on the grounds that "it has nothing of the nature of the Gospel about it."[44] In his Old Testament introduction, Luther offers the following advice on how to deal with the heap of laws one finds there: "All other laws ought to be measured by faith and love. That is to say, the other laws are to be kept where their observance does not conflict with faith and love; but where they conflict with faith and love, they should be done away entirely."[45]

Luther thinks isolated parts of Scripture have to be interpreted (even "done away entirely") in light of what emerges as central when you read Scripture holistically. And what is central? For Luther, the answer is *Christ*. On Luther's high view of Scripture, the "true test" of any texts is "whether or not they inculcate Christ." If they don't, then they are "not apostolic" even if "St. Peter or St. Paul does the teaching."[46] For Luther, those parts of the Bible that inspire faith in Christ and allegiance to the law of love are Scripture. The rest may be useful in the manner of straw in the manger but should not be confused with Christ.

George MacDonald makes a similar point when he says that the Bible "nowhere lays claim to be regarded as the Word, the Way, the Truth. The Bible leads us to Jesus, the inexhaustible, the ever unfolding Revelation of

---

43. Luther, "Preface to the Old Testament," 236.
44. Luther, "Preface to the New Testament," 362.
45. Luther, "Preface to the Old Testament," 240.
46. Luther, "Preface to the Epistles of St. James and St. Jude," 396.

God."[47] C. S. Lewis follows MacDonald's lead in one of his letters, adding an interesting warning:

> It is Christ Himself, not the Bible, who is the true word of God. The Bible read in the right spirit and with the guidance of good teachers, will bring us to him. . . . But we must not use the Bible (our fathers too often did) as a sort of Encyclopedia out of which texts . . . can be taken for use as weapons.[48]

In his *Reflection on the Psalms*, Lewis directly challenges inerrantism, arguing that God uses human authors in Scripture and that the "human qualities of the raw materials show through." He goes on:

> Naïvety, error, contradiction, even (as in the cursing Psalms) wickedness are not removed. The total result is not "the Word of God" in the sense that every passage, in itself, gives impeccable science or history. It carries the Word of God; and we . . . receive that word from it not by using it as an encyclopedia or an encyclical but by steeping ourselves in its tone or temper and so learning its overall message.[49]

What we find here is a portrait of the Bible in which God works through flawed human authors in all their flaws. God breaks into the human perspective, blazing out from behind human prejudices, shattering cultural presuppositions, but not preventing those things from finding expression on the page. When God works through human authors, the human element remains. And so we have, for example, a brilliant apostle who elsewhere parrots the patriarchal assumptions of his age, but in a luminous moment makes the culture-defying pronouncement that in Christ there is neither male nor female. If we prayerfully immerse ourselves in the Bible as a whole, we can begin to distinguish the human from the divine—but not by ourselves. We do so in conversation with the broader community of faith, guided by the insights of its wisest voices.

And why shouldn't the revelation of a personal God of love come to us in that way—in a way that requires us to enter into loving and respectful dialogue with other persons in order to discern God's will, rather than simply reading it off an inanimate page? A Bible that points beyond itself to Christ *needn't* be inerrant, even if we think it could be. Lewis's point is that a look at Scripture's content shows us it isn't. It retains its humanness—and the human is fallible.

47. MacDonald, *Unspoken Sermons*, 52–53.
48. Lewis, *Collected Letters*, 246.
49. Lewis, *Reflections on the Psalms*, 111–12.

Beyond this, there are reasons to question inerrancy rooted in the love ethic itself.

Love and Scripture

In my personal spiritual journey, I have become increasingly convinced that the doctrine of inerrancy clashes with the scriptural love ethic because it encourages us to focus on a book. But if the core message of the book is that our allegiance belongs to a God of love who exists beyond its pages, and if the core ethic of that book is not about obedience to rules that can be listed in a book but about love for neighbors who exist in the world beyond its pages, then inerrantism encourages a direction of focus opposed to what the book is trying to teach.

Consider a story from my struggles as a parent. When my daughter was several months old, my wife and I decided it was time to train her to sleep through the night on her own. The parenting books we'd read encouraged this and gave advice on how to do it—advice that worked well with our son. The strategy is to let the baby scream in the crib, but come in every few minutes to say comforting words without picking the child up, until the child falls asleep. In theory, after a few nights the baby learns to fall sleep on her own without being rocked or held.

I say *in theory* because, although it worked with our son, our daughter was different. The first night, we took turns getting up and saying comforting words by her crib *all night long*. She screamed relentlessly from when we put her to bed until 6 AM—at which point, bleary-eyed and nauseous, I carried her from her crib to her ExerSaucer—whereupon she promptly fell asleep.

The next night was the same. And the night after that. After the fourth night of blood-curdling screams of abject betrayal for hour after hour after hour (I was convinced my ears or my daughter's head—or both—would explode), my wife and I decided kids are different. What works with others just wasn't right for her. And so we started once again rocking her to sleep.

We could have stuck with the advice of the experts, continuing night after night for as long as it took. Extreme sleep deprivation played some role in our decision not to do that, but the deeper motive was that we love our daughter. Hearing her relentless anguish inspired a desire to comfort her. We resisted that desire at first because we thought, based on expert advice, that doing so was best for her. But at some point that changed. The tenor of her cries communicated something no expert, speaking in generalities, can know. And it wasn't just her cries at night. During the day she was different. A less joyful child.

We paid attention to our daughter and, based on what we saw, became convinced that no good could come from perpetuating her suffering. She needed to know we were there for her more urgently than she needed to learn to fall asleep by herself. What might be good for other kids wasn't good for *this* one. We could have decided to ignore what compassion and empathy were telling us. Or we could have bought earplugs. Perhaps, had we done so, she would still have become the self-assured, determined, funny and relentlessly loving ten-year-old she is today (who, by the way, puts herself to sleep and sleeps through the night). Or perhaps a remorseless campaign of ignoring her cries and dismissing her negative personality changes would have poisoned some part of her childhood with long-term effects.

But as loving parents we couldn't persist down that path. If we continued to prioritize the authoritative teachings of the so-called experts, it would have been because we were turning off our empathy, stifling our compassion, and in general hardening our hearts in ways at odds with what parental love is supposed to be about.

I think the relevance of this story is clear. Suppose we agree there are biblical verses whose clear meaning is that homosexual acts are always sinful, no matter the context. If we also accept inerrantism, we're forced to conclude that appearances are often deceiving, and that what appears harmful when we attend compassionately to our gay and lesbian neighbors isn't actually harmful at all. And so, based on this theory about how the Bible is related to divine will, we'll need either to ignore the lessons drawn from sensitive, compassionate, and empathetic attention to our gay and lesbian neighbors, or we'll need to refrain from practicing such attention at all.

Accepting this view about the Bible would force us to do one of two things: *stifle the urgings of our most loving impulses*, making us increasingly resistant to the influence of compassion and empathy; or *limit the scope of our compassion and empathy*, extending it only when doing so doesn't have implications at odds with what our theory of the Bible teaches.

Do we have the right theory about a book if the book teaches us to love our neighbors as ourselves, but our *theory* about the book demands that we stifle the character traits most intimately associated with love? If our theory of the Bible leads us to *plug up our ears with Bible verses* so we don't hear the anguished cries of our gay and lesbian neighbors, isn't that a reason to rethink our theory? Put more forcefully, how many gays and lesbians, crushed by the weight of traditional teachings, have to *kill themselves* before we decide our theory about the Bible isn't the best fit with the idea that God is love—and hence with the content of the Bible itself?

I take the Bible seriously. But the Bible says that God is love—and while Scripture can urge love and testify to it with powerful stories, love is *really present* in human relationships. I take the Bible seriously. But the Bible says that Jesus—a person, not a book—is the fundamental revelation of God. And in the Bible, Jesus says he comes to us in the form of the neighbor in need—"even the least of these" (Matt 25:37–40).

My gay and lesbian neighbors have come to me. How can I fail to see there the face of Christ? *There* is the revelation of God. Any theory of the Bible that requires me to ignore them in favor of the unsurprising discovery that biblical authors expressed their culture's heterosexist presuppositions does an injustice to the Bible's heart.

I'm not saying rules don't matter as long as we have love in our hearts. I'm not saying we can just cultivate love and then do as we will. On the contrary, if what we will is to treat the Bible as a rule book no matter how much our neighbors cry out in anguish, then it doesn't matter how much love is in our hearts. We are failing to live up to the law of love. If what we will isn't shaped by compassionate attention to our neighbors, then it doesn't matter how much love is in our heart. Our behavior is sure to be out of tune with what love demands.

It's not enough to have inner loving motives. Love has rules, and some of those rules—such as those against rape and enslavement and murder—are absolute. The question is how we discern what those rules are. If the Bible teaches us to love our neighbors as ourselves, and if the Bible itself says that Christ comes to us in the neighbor in need, how can we ignore the fact that, as Dale Martin puts it, "the church's stand on homosexuality has caused oppression, loneliness, self-hatred, violence, sickness, and suicide for millions of people"?[50] Can it really be that the best strategy is to prioritize specific Bible verses over compassionate attention to the neighbors whose lives have been damaged by rigid allegiance to those verses?

Whatever our theory of Scripture, Christians must maintain the primacy of Christ and the core understanding of God that emerges in the Gospel narrative: a God whose love is so unconditional that, while we yet were sinners, God became incarnate and died for us. This message of divine love and the call to reflect it in our human relationships must be the lens through which we read Scripture and develop our theories about it.

The Bible teaches love. It does not teach the doctrine of inerrancy. At the very least, this means we should never use the Bible as a weapon to beat our gay and lesbian neighbors down. But more than this, it means that if allegiance to a doctrine of inerrancy gets in the way of love, it is inerrancy, not love, that needs to go.

---

50. Martin, *Sex and the Single Savior*, 50.

10

Natural and Unnatural

I was standing in an airport with my best friend, waiting on an arriving flight, when my last objection fell away. Maybe it's better to say it faltered into awkward silence.

At the time, I was a philosophy graduate student studying ethics, and I was drawn to the natural law tradition. St. Thomas Aquinas, who did more than anyone to develop that ethical tradition, was a powerful philosophical inspiration for me. And St. Thomas called homosexual behavior "the unnatural vice"[1] (although he later clarified that other sexual acts, such as bestiality, masturbation and non-vaginal heterosexual intercourse also qualified[2]).

I can't remember how, precisely, our conversation turned to homosexuality. "It's weird, though, isn't it," I said, "given how our sexual organs are designed, that some people are only attracted to members of the same sex?"

John looked at me sharply. "What do you mean?"

"I mean, the sexual organs are designed to make babies." I spoke in a clinical tone, as if the only thing at stake were intellectual curiosity, not my friend's life. "But the desire for gay sex . . . it's cut off from procreation. In gays and lesbians, the sexual desire is at odds with the natural function of the sexual organs."

---

1. Aquinas, *Summa Theologica*, I-II, Q. 94, Art. 3.
2. Aquinas, *Summa Theologica*, II-II, Q. 154, Art. 11.

Like me, John is a philosopher. And so he responded, not with defensiveness, but with arguments. We stood under the airport's sterile institutional light, in a place of flat surfaces and square angles, human artifice and vague chemical smells, and we spoke about what's natural and unnatural. I don't remember everything we said—although I suspect it touched on many of the issues I will explore in this chapter. But I do remember John's final remark: "What seems unnatural to me," he said, "is that we aren't all bisexuals. Why is it that I'm only able to feel this sort of love for men, and you're only able to feel it for women? That *limitation* in our capacity for love is what strikes me as unnatural."

The thought silenced me. At the time I still intuitively thought of sex as involving *coitus*: a penis penetrating a vagina. I thought of young people who'd engaged in all kinds of sexual acts as virgins if they hadn't had vaginal intercourse. For me, romantic love piggy-backed on a physical act whose biological purpose was to bring sperm and egg into contact.

But for John, romantic love wasn't just something that rode on the back of coitus. Romantic love was the deeply human connection that expresses itself in and through the physical intimacy of sex but is far more than the physical act and, perhaps for that reason, isn't confined to a single *form* of sex. John's point was this: the "unitive" end of sexual expression—the bonds of intimate human love it helps forge—can be achieved apart from vaginal intercourse; and it is beautiful, rich in value, whether or not it can make babies.

But in saying this, John was opposing himself to a tradition of Christian moral thought, rooted in the natural law theory and defended vigorously by Roman Catholics, that takes homosexual sex to be a violation of the natural order precisely because it is cut off from the "procreative end of sex."

The Theory of Natural Law

Sometimes the natural law theory is seen as a Christian alternative to the love ethic. Conceived in that way, it might seem I don't need to explore it in a book focusing on what *the love ethic* says about homosexuality and same-sex marriage. But there's at least one understanding of natural law theory wherein it is not an alternative *to* the love ethic but an integral piece *of* it. While the love ethic tells us *to* love, natural law purports to tell us *how*.

When Roman Catholic thinkers say that homosexuality is "unnatural," they don't mean one never finds it among non-human animals. If they did, their argument would quickly collapse in the face of all the contrary evidence.[3] Nor do they deny that gays and lesbians have unchosen homosexual dispositions that make homosexual sex more "natural" for them than heterosexual sex in terms of being in tune with their innate dispositions. Roman Catholics typically acknowledge that there are "homosexual persons" with a stable and unchosen attraction only to members of the same sex. They call for such persons to be treated with respect.[4] Within the natural law tradition, calling something unnatural is not a synonym for calling it artificial (the product of human artifice) or contrary to inborn inclinations. So what does it mean?

When I explain natural law theory to my students, I usually begin with some key ideas from Aristotle, who powerfully shaped St. Thomas Aquinas's understanding of natural law. One of these ideas is the notion that things in the world are *naturally ordered to an end*: their natures give them powers or faculties suitable for achieving certain ends. They have, in Aristotle's words, a function or purpose.[5] In much the way that a cell phone has a design structure that gives it powers suited to the end of communication, so do living organisms and their parts have natures that invest them with the capacity to attain specific goals. When things have this sort of purposive nature, they have a "teleology." And when things have a teleology, it's as if they were designed especially to do certain things—as if that's what they were made *for*.

Natural law theorists, following Aristotle, understand the concepts of "good" and "bad" as tied to this idea of teleology. As Timothy Hsiao puts it, on the natural law theory "something is good by *functioning as it should*."[6] Or, in Edward Feser's words, "what is good for a thing is determined by the ends for the sake of which its natural faculties exist."[7] So, a hammer is a *good* hammer if it performs its function well—if it possesses the "virtues" that equip a hammer to do what hammers are designed to do, namely drive in nails. Aristotle thought the same idea extends to anything with a teleology—including plants and animals and people. Our human teleology provides an objective basis for deciding which qualities count as human "virtues" (traits that help humans to actualize our purposes and do what we are designed to do) and which count as "vices" (traits that interfere with these purposes). In other words, by looking at human teleology we can figure out what makes *people* good.

3. See Bagemihl, *Biological Exuberance*.
4. US Catholic Bishops, *Marriage*, 23.
5. Aristotle, *Nicomachean Ethics* 1.7, 1097b–1098b, trans. Ross (pp. 942–43).
6. Hsiao, "Defense of the Perverted Faculty Argument," 751.
7. Feser, "The Role of Nature," 69.

But not just in the moral sense. For Aristotle, some virtues are "intellectual" rather than moral: they help us actualize our potential as rational beings in a non-moral sense.[8] More significantly, at least for the love ethic, the person who cultivates human virtues has what is most essential for *human flourishing*. Aristotle didn't distinguish sharply between what makes us good people and what is good *for* us. When we live in accord with our natures, cultivating virtue and avoiding vice, we promote our own welfare. Vice, then, isn't just bad for *other* people. It's bad for the vicious themselves. And it isn't just bad for them because those around them will become angry or God will punish them. Just as the worst part about being in pain is that it hurts, the worst part about being vicious is that you're vicious. Viciousness *is* the affliction. It compromises your welfare all by itself, without help from punitive gods or governments.

Aquinas found all of this quite congenial, especially since he believed all things are created by an intelligent designer who made everything *for a reason*. Just like a hammer was made for some purpose by us, everything in the natural world was made for some purpose by God. On the natural law theory, something is good if it corresponds with "nature" in this sense: it has a place within the created order and is properly *fulfilling the purpose* which its nature suits it to fulfill. This idea is most easily seen in relation to bodily organs: eyes are made for seeing, hearts for pumping blood. Their natures give them powers that suit them to fulfill these ends.

In the natural law tradition, to call an activity unnatural is to say it conflicts with this natural ordering—by, for example, disrupting it. When natural law theorists talk about the "unnatural use" of a bodily organ (such as a penis), they mean it is being used in a way contrary to its purpose.

But drawing moral conclusions from this is not straightforward. When we eat steak, we are using muscular tissue for a purpose contrary to the one it served for the cow. Are we behaving wrongly? The same question arises when we eat the stems and roots and leaves of plants. It becomes quickly obvious that living creatures can't live good lives—can't realize their purposes—if they studiously respect the natural purposes of every other living thing.

Natural law theorists address these concerns by looking at a larger picture, a broader natural order. Aquinas took the notion that goodness or value was rooted in being or existence as such and paired it with the idea that some things had more being than others, leading him to conclude that in the broader natural order animals and plants exist for the sake of humans,

---

8. Aristotle, *Nicomachean Ethics* 1.13, 1103a3–6 (p. 952).

since humans have more being and so more inherent worth.[9] While cow muscles have the purpose of promoting locomotion in cows, the whole animal exists as part of a broader system directed toward meeting human needs. So we can eat them.

Environmentalists who reject the anthropocentrism here will often still embrace the basic form of the solution, by invoking the idea of larger natural systems, such as ecosystems, which have a structure that defines what is good for them. Allowing foxes to fundamentally compromise the natural ends of rabbits might prove good for the forest ecosystem. Hence, we don't have to anguish over whether saving bunnies is worth letting foxes starve. Despite my daughter's tears, we should let the bunnies die.

Another kind of problem arises when medical science intervenes to remove diseased organs. Is it wrong to surgically remove someone's gall bladder for the sake of promoting overall health? On the one hand, it's hard to think of a more final way to compromise the gall bladder's ability to perform its function. On the other hand, if the gall bladder is malfunctioning and can't be fixed, its continued presence in the body might compromise the healthy functioning of the broader system, in this case the patient.

Put simply, the natural purposes of things often clash, and natural law theory seeks to resolve these conflicts by looking at broader systems. But this doesn't always yield answers. Sometimes it's a hard call whether removing an organ or leaving it in place is better for the patient. And while we nod sagely when animal predation is justified because it keeps the prey population in control, it would be a tad more controversial to apply similar logic to human diseases that could curb exponential population growth.

Here is where it can be helpful, within the Christian tradition, to view natural law theory not as a distinct theory but as a way of working out the love ethic. It is this way of appropriating natural law that I mean to wrestle with here. What natural law does, on this understanding, is tell us how to love our neighbors as ourselves by giving us a framework for understanding what is good for us and them. The natural teleology of organs, organisms, and larger systems tells us what is good for these things. The law of love tells us it is *our neighbors*—treated as whole persons, not as collections of organs, and not as just pieces of larger systems—whose good is the primary object of moral concern.[10] We should care about the health of our neighbor's organs, not because we're supposed to love kidneys and intestines for their own sakes, but because we're supposed to love our neighbors—and

---

9. Aquinas, *Summa Theologica*, I-I, Q. 96, Art. 1–2.

10. Whether nonhumans animals as well as humans can qualify as neighbors is a question I will not take up in this book.

healthy organs are good for them. While we should care about larger natural systems, this is again for the sake of the neighbors we are called to love.

It's the welfare of our neighbors, not their parts or the larger systems of which they are a part, that Christian love pursues. And so it is the natural teleology of our neighbors that we should care about—not that of their parts or the broader systems of which they are a part, save as those things impact our neighbors. But while it is easy to agree about the purpose of an organ such as the eye, it is harder to agree about the purpose of a human being. Aristotle thought the natural human function was to be excellently rational, which he thought found its highest attainment in the contemplative life.[11] At least some Christians would say our human powers orient us toward participation in the kingdom of God: the community presided over by God and characterized by the agapic love of every community member for every other.

Even if we can settle this question, we face the challenge of what to do when, in our fallen world, the good of one neighbor clashes with that of another. What do we do when one neighbor is attacking another? What do we do if caring for an injured neighbor means exposing a child in our care to dangers we could protect them from? What about when a pregnant woman's life is threatened by her pregnancy, and aborting the fetus seems the only way to save it? Purely consequentialist solutions—doing what has the highest probability of achieving the most good—are problematic for reasons addressed in chapter 3. A Christian pacifist could argue that nonviolent interventions in cases of violent attacks—even when they have a low chance of success—show love for *both* aggressor *and* victim in a way that violent interventions don't, and so should be preferred even when violence has a higher chance of doing more good. But does relying on nonviolent remedies when they're unlikely to work show sufficient love for victims? Similar issues arise in connection with life-threatening pregnancy cases.

In short, when we draw on ideas from natural law theory to decide how best to love our neighbors, we are stepping into controversial terrain littered with puzzles and dilemmas. Roman Catholic leaders have a tendency, based on their view of themselves as the historic repository of divine revelation, to articulate the solutions they prefer with considerable authority. But while the wisdom of Roman Catholic thinkers is considerable, they are not infallible. And on the issue of homosexuality, I think they are mistaken in ways that damage the welfare of the gay and lesbian neighbors they intend to love.

---

11. Aristotle, *Nicomachean Ethics* 10.7, 1177a13–23, trans. Ross (p. 1104).

Homosexuality as Sin against Nature

When natural law theorists say that homosexual acts are unnatural, what they typically mean is that these acts violate the natural purposes of the reproductive organs. Janet Smith, in *Humanae Vitae: A Generation Later*, puts it this way:

> First, it must be understood that the sexual organs are naturally ordered to procreation and nothing can render them not ordered to procreation. This ordination, whether capable of being actualized or not, is inherent. This is equivalent to saying that eyes that are being used to see, eyes that are closed, and blind eyes are still ordered to seeing; eyes blind at birth and eyes blinded by some deliberate act are still ordered to seeing. ... Only eyes can be "given" or restored to the power of seeing because only eyes do that kind of work; ears and noses do not. The same is true of sexual organs; sexual organs, whether fertile or infertile, temporarily or permanently, by the choice of the individual or not, are ordered to procreation. They are organs of the reproductive kind....[12]

Smith argues further that while there is "no shame in having an organ that cannot perform its functions ... there may be shame and immorality involved if one deliberately deprives an organ of the ability to perform its proper function."[13]

Based on this perspective, Roman Catholic thinkers object to a range of sexual practices: contraceptive use, permanent sterilization, masturbation, and any sex that doesn't involve coitus. The latter, of course, includes all same-sex sex. In all of these cases, the natural reproductive end of the sexual organs is thwarted. In developing this perspective, Catholic thinkers sometimes point out that the reproductive organs are different from other bodily organs in that they can only perform their function with the help of another person. To achieve the reproductive end, male and female organs must be brought together in sexual intercourse. As Feser puts it, these organs "fit together like lock and key."[14] There is a sense in which male and female organs are incomplete without one another—and unlike other animals, human beings know this. "We *know*," Feser says, "that qua male or female each

---

12. Smith, *Humanae Vitae*, 80.
13. Ibid.
14. Feser, "Role of Nature," 72.

of us is in some unusual way incomplete."[15] Without the piece that the other sex provides, none of us can achieve the natural end of reproduction.

In an amusing formulation of this idea, Matt Walsh invokes the cartoon character, Captain Planet:

> A man and a woman can get together and make a person. They can, between the two of them, conceive a human child. If I have to put this in terms that my fellow nostalgic millennials will comprehend: a man and a woman can combine their powers, much like the kids from Captain Planet, and bring forth into the world another sentient being. Only this being hopefully won't be a spandex-clad vigilante who goes around assaulting people for littering in a public park.[16]

The basic thinking is this: most human powers—the power to walk and talk and digest potatoes—are powers we have in the way Superman has his powers. He's got them all by himself. But our reproductive power is activated only when a man and woman have sex. In this sense, it's more like the power the Captain Planet kids have. They don't have it on their own, but they each bring a piece to the puzzle. It's as if the organ for reproduction were divided into two parts, with one part given to one sex and the other part to the other. Only by uniting the pieces can the reproductive function of either part be realized.

But homosexual sex does not bring together the two halves of this whole. It fails to create a complete reproductive organ and therefore lacks the procreative power that heterosexual sex possesses. Roman Catholic thinkers conclude that these sex acts "are contrary to the natural law" because they "close the sexual act to the gift of life. They do not proceed from a genuine affective and sexual complementarity. Under no circumstances can they be approved."[17]

The question, however, is why the non-procreative character of same-sex sex matters *morally*. From the standpoint of the love ethic, it's the neighbor's good, not the good of their organs, that matters. Although the sex organs and their use in sexual intercourse clearly serve a reproductive purpose, sex is not just about procreation. It's also about love, about the romantic bonding of two people that my friend John talked about in that airport hallway. And this isn't just something gay men in airports believe. It's something the Roman Catholic Church teaches.

---

15. Ibid., 73.
16. Matt Walsh, "There is No Such Thing," para. 25.
17. *Catechism of the Catholic Church*, no. 2357 (p. 566).

Our sexual powers are, according to Roman Catholic teaching, directed toward two natural ends: the procreative and the unitive. These are also the purposes of marriage, the only context in which these sexual powers are properly actualized. Human sexual expression, within the context of marriage, binds together husband and wife in a communion of persons, and their love overflows into the generation of new life.[18]

Sometimes, natural law critics of homosexuality structure their arguments as if the sexuality of gay couples can't be about anything other than hedonistic gratification since it isn't about making new life.[19] But this leaves out the unitive end. If human sexuality has two natural ends, one procreative and the other unitive, why is it wrong for gays and lesbians to pursue only the unitive end?

This question acquires more force when we think about it in the light of the love ethic. Roman Catholics don't just *concede* that the unitive end of marriage is good for married couples. They wax eloquent about it. The US Catholic Bishops argue that "we humans are directed to relationship" and that it is "only in relationship that we achieve a true wholeness as a communion of persons."[20] Such communion finds its fullest expression in the conjugal love nurtured in marriage. Quoting the Song of Solomon, they marvel at the beauty of marital love:

> "My lover belongs to me and I to him" (Song 2:16; see Song 6:3). With all the dignity and simplicity of poetry, the Bride in the Song of Songs sings of the unitive meaning of married love.
> "You have ravished my heart, my sister, my bride. . . . How beautiful is your love!" (Song 4:9-10). So responds the Bridegroom of the Song, overcome with the wonder of conjugal love that is extended to him by the Bride. This is the love that is strong as death . . . .[21]

Love as strong as death! If gays and lesbians can pursue the unitive end of sexual powers in a lifelong covenant of mutual fidelity and love, why should they be denied this wondrous end of the sexual powers just because the reproductive end is unavailable? The effect of a homosexual orientation is to separate in gays and lesbians what, in heterosexuals, is united. While my wife and I can pursue the unitive and procreative ends through the very same activity, gays and lesbians have to choose. Those with whom they can pursue the procreative end are people with whom they can't cultivate

18. US Catholic Bishops, *Marriage*, 11-13.
19. Finnis, "Homosexual Conduct is Wrong," 499-500.
20. Us Catholic Bishops, *Marriage*, 12.
21. Ibid., 12-13.

romantic attraction and the feelings of conjugal love, and vice versa. But if we care about the whole person, why should we deny *both* ends to gays and lesbians just because they can't pursue them together? Doesn't it do more to promote their good to make available a marital relationship within which they can cultivate the unitive end?

The sex organs aren't the only ones with multiple functions. Our mouths, for example, serve the ends of both communication and food consumption (as well as other things). If I use my mouth for communication, the fact that I am not also, at the same time, consuming food doesn't mean I'm violating the natural purposes of my mouth. And if I can no longer consume food orally and have to live via intravenous nutrition, no one would accuse me of doing something wrong if I continue to use my mouth to speak. So why shouldn't gays and lesbians be free to pursue the unitive end in same-sex marriages, even if they can't at the same time pursue the procreative one?

Roman Catholic thinkers typically answer by appeal to two claims, what I'll call the Inseparability Thesis and the Complementarity Thesis. Both claims are, I think, problematic.

The Inseparability Thesis

By the Inseparability Thesis, I mean the idea that one cannot separate the two purposes of marriage (loving union and procreation) without doing violence to the nature of human sexuality and the marital union. As the Catechism of the Catholic Church puts it, these two purposes "cannot be separated without altering the couple's spiritual life and compromising the goods of marriage and the future of the family."[22]

According to the US Catholic Bishops, this inseparability cuts in both directions. They do not merely think that the procreative aim is harmed if mutual self-gifting love is absent (because children are then brought into the world in less-than-ideal conditions). They also think that conjugal love itself is undermined if the couple's intimacy isn't directed toward reproduction.

It is this latter claim that is crucial for making the case that same-sex marriage is unacceptable. We might all agree that procreative sex should be linked to a commitment to nurturing bonds of love, so that children are more likely to have two parents who love each other and stick together. It doesn't follow from this that conjugal love can't be pursued in the absence of procreative sex. Why think that?

---

22. *Catechism of the Catholic Church*, no. 2363 (p. 568).

Considerable human experience tells us that the unitive end of sex can be achieved without heterosexual coitus. Sex is not just about bringing reproductive organs together. Far more is involved. When my high school girlfriend and I kissed for hours on my beanbag chair, what we were doing was clearly sexual. But while it involved our mouths, our necks and ears (nibbled on), our hair and hands (much entangling), and the nerve endings along virtually every bit of exposed skin, our reproductive organs were not directly engaged, let alone linked together to form a "complete" reproductive system. Had we foolishly had intercourse, the connection of our reproductive organs would have supplemented, not replaced, all the touching and kissing and other expressions of physical closeness.

Any sexual activity that is more than just a perfunctory procreative performance is like that. It involves the whole body and mind, creative and imaginative touching that in some ways reminds me of what it's like to make improvisational music with another musician. Were it restricted to genital contact, I doubt it would have the power to build and nurture love.

In fact, if there is any lesson about sexuality I can take from my juvenile relationship, it's that a powerful bond can be formed *without the reproductive organs ever coming into contact*. While I fought it and denied it for a long time, I was deeply in love with my high school girlfriend by the time our relationship finally crashed against the rocks of life transitions and growing pains. While the dimension of sexual activity conducive to reproduction—vaginal intercourse—may be *part* of unitive sex, unitive sex is much more than just this; and not only does genital coitus fail by itself to achieve the unitive end, but the unitive end is served by these broader dimensions of sex even when genital contact is absent.

The stories of same-sex couples only reinforces this insight. There is no single way in which gays and lesbians express sexual intimacy (and there are many myths, such as that all gay men have anal sex). What is clear is that sexual closeness of the sort that bonds couples together can neither be reduced to vaginal penetration nor limited to relationships that include it. Gays and lesbians can experience the same kind of love that heterosexual couples enjoy, where sexual closeness is part of a broader pattern of intimacy that nurtures and expresses love.

Only those who haven't been paying attention to their gay and lesbian neighbors can deny this. I have followed my gay and lesbian friends through the stages of romantic life, from the intensity of new love to the joy of making vows of lifelong fidelity, from the hardships that test a relationship to the transformation and deepening of love over a lifetime. And it looks just like the kind of unitive bonding I see among my heterosexual friends. It matches up with what I have experience *from the inside* in my own relationships, including my marriage. To imagine that all of this is pretense, that gays and lesbians are by the thousands engaged in a vast ruse, is beyond absurd. The reasonable and charitable interpretation here is simply this: gays and lesbians fall in love, form intimate bonds, and become connected in the same ways that heterosexual couples do—ways that are nurtured when sexual closeness is linked to partnership and mutual care and all those things couples do outside the bedroom to strengthen their bonds.

Despite this contrary evidence, the US Catholic Bishops insist on the Inseparability Thesis, which they express in the following way:

> The unitive meaning is distorted if the procreative meaning is deliberately disavowed. Conjugal love is then diminished. This love is, by its nature, faithful, exclusive, and intended to be fecund. As Pope Paul VI says, "It is not confined wholly to the loving interchange of husband and wife; it also contrives to go beyond this to bring new life into being." Without its ordering toward the procreative, the unitive meaning of marriage is undermined.[23]

Unfortunately, this statement is ambiguous. There's an important difference between a love that is "diminished" if it's separated from procreation, and a love that is "undermined" by such separation. The latter is what the Bishops have to say to support their condemnation of same-sex marriage. After all, one thing could be less wonderful than another, all else being equal, and still be wonderful. And if the less wonderful thing is all that's available to you, it's being less wonderful than what is available to others is no reason to bar you from accessing the goods you can enjoy.

So the Bishops have to cleave to the stronger view that taking reproduction out of a conjugal union removes what is good from it, even if the other aspects are still earnestly pursued. This means they have to hold one of two things. Either they have to claim that mutual faithful intimacy of the sort they praise in marriage isn't *possible* when the procreative element is removed, or they have to say that such mutual faithful intimacy is stripped of its *value* when the procreative element is removed (even though it is still mutual and faithful and loving). Either it ceases to exist or is drained of its goodness. But it's hard to justify the former when same-sex couples have relationships that, in terms of their unitive aspects, look just like loving heterosexual marriages. If they opt for the latter, they face the formidable challenge of defending the claim that removing the procreative potential from a loving union erases the *immense positive value* that (according to them) attaches to a successful conjugal union *with* such potential.

23. US Catholic Bishops, *Marriage*, 15–16.

But the case they make for the Inseparability Thesis falls far short of supporting any such assertion. Here's the heart of what they say:

> In their marriage promises, the spouses pledge love and fidelity for as long as they live. The transmission of life is a sublime, concrete realization of this radical self-gift between a man and a woman. The mutual married love of man and woman "becomes an image of the absolute and unfailing love with which God loves man[kind]," because as mutual self-gift, it is at the same time creative self-gift. The unitive and the procreative meanings of marriage are joined because they are two aspects of the same self-giving.[24]

The idea seems to be this: when a man and woman give themselves completely to each other, this mutual giving can manifest in a very concrete and astonishing way—in new life. This feature helps to make conjugal love a deeper and fuller reflection of God's love, which manifests itself in the creation of the world. Human conjugal love—at least between a fertile man and woman—is designed by God to be creative like God's love is creative. If the procreative end is missing, it's not creative in such a concrete way. But notice that they say procreation is a "sublime, concrete realization of this radical self-gift." The mutual self-gifting *culminates* in new life, but is not *constituted* by it. That is, the mutual self-gifting can occur apart from new life actually coming about.

This point is driven home by a key concession that the US Catholic Bishops make. Specifically, the Bishops note that while an infertile couple "may be tempted to think that their union is not complete or truly blessed," this temptation is false. "The marital union of a man and a woman is a distinctive communion of persons. An infertile couple continues to manifest this attribute."[25] Put simply, they concede that a conjugal union *remains* a conjugal union, complete and blessed and rich in value, even if it cannot produce offspring. Infertile couples will not experience the "sublime, concrete realization" of their love, but they can still *have the love*.

Hence, the Bishops have to concede that the unitive and procreative ends of marriage are separable in the following sense: it is fully possible to realize a valuable conjugal union even if that union *cannot* overflow into the creation of new life.

Roman Catholic thinkers, recognizing the possible challenge that their embrace of infertile couples generates, are quick to point out a difference between infertile straight couples and same-sex ones. Catholic political

24. Ibid., 17.
25. Ibid., 15.

philosopher Ryan Anderson summarize the basis for this distinction in the following way:

> ... a marriage is a comprehensive union marked by one-flesh union—the coordination of the spouses' two bodies toward the single biological end of reproduction. That coordination—and thus the one-flesh union—takes place *whether or not* it achieves its biological end in the fertilization of an egg by a sperm some hours later.[26]

As Timothy Hsiao puts it, "A good or permissible action need only realize the direction to the end provided by teleology."[27] If something is broken or defective that prevents this end from being realized, no wrong has been committed.

We might flesh out this idea in terms of the notion that male and female sex organs are incomplete parts of a whole. The idea is this: when an infertile couple engages in vaginal intercourse, they bring together the parts of the reproductive system into a complete whole and so are still engaging in an act that is reproductive in kind—the sort of act that can produce babies when the timing is right and the systems are working properly. The problem is that the systems aren't working. But infertile couples are still doing something *oriented toward* reproduction, since they are "putting together" the system whose natural purpose is reproduction. But same-sex couples are not.

This clearly is a difference, but what implications does it have? Broad attention to human experience teaches us that, whether by disability in the case of infertile couples, or by inability in the case of same-sex ones, the unitive end of sex can still be pursued and achieved even absent procreative potential. What the US Catholic Bishops argue is that the value of conjugal love is *enriched* by its potential to overflow into the creation of new life—but they concede that it *retains* value even when this potential is tragically stripped away by disability in the case of infertile couples. But if it retains its value when cut off from procreation through some disability, why would it lose its value when it is found among those who lack the ability?

Imagine there's a species of persons who lack ears. Unlike humans, they have no sense of hearing. Unlike the deaf, this isn't a disability. They just aren't designed to hear. Suppose these persons are systematically denied jobs as music critics because they lacked the power to hear. They aren't being denied it because of a disability. They're just members of a species without hearing. But if their inability to hear is the reason we withhold music critic

---

26. Anderson, "Four Responses," para. 6.
27. Hsiao, "Defense of the Perverted Faculty Argument," 752.

jobs from them, then consistency demands that, for the very same reason, we withhold music critic jobs from the deaf—even though, in their case, the lack of hearing *is* a disability. It makes no difference whether the lack of hearing is a "natural" inability or a disability.

Likewise, if our reason for withholding marriage from same-sex couples is that they don't form a procreative unit, then why shouldn't we also withhold marriage from infertile couples for the same reason? And if we *don't* withhold marriage from infertile couples, isn't that because we think it is perfectly possible for them to have marriages that are fulfilling and meaningful even absent procreation? In other words, isn't it because we think the unitive end of marriage has value apart from whether it can culminate in new life? If it has such value, then it has such value whether it is found among those whose procreative potential has been disabled or among those who never had it to begin with.

To extend the deafness example, imagine an art museum that includes art with both visual and auditory dimensions. Suppose we think the deaf will gain something from visiting this museum, based on the merits of the visual dimensions of the art, even though the auditory dimensions are inaccessible to them. If so, wouldn't the same reasoning extend to those who lack ears? Suppose someone said, "The deaf have organs that are *oriented toward* hearing even though they can't actually hear, and this means their purely visual experience of the art will have a value it just won't have for those earless folks." Wouldn't we dismiss this as mere prejudice?

The US Bishops note that there is something beautiful available to fertile heterosexual couples: a conjugal love that can overflow into new life. And this is surely right. But when they concede that infertile couples can still have blessed marriages, they acknowledge that even if their conjugal love can't culminate in new life, it still has great value. But gays and lesbians are in a situation where they can pursue one of the natural ends of sex but not both together. There may be reasons why, given that situation, they should not pursue a *heterosexual* marriage in which the procreative end of sex is pursued despite the fact that the unitive end can't be. We have many examples of gays and lesbians who've done that. Such marriages, lacking the unitive bond, tend to fall apart. If the marriages produce children, those children have to face the hardship of the all-but-inevitable collapse of a marriage devoid of conjugal love.

But pursuing the unitive end by choosing a same-sex partner seems to put gays and lesbians into a similar situation as infertile straight couples. How can the distinction between disability and inability matter for whether such unions have value? Imagine again the art museum with works that have both visual and auditory dimensions. But now suppose our earless people actually have an organ that can *either* see *or* hear but not both. Let's suppose, for some reason, that the auditory dimension of the art can't be appreciated without access to the visual dimension, but the visual can be appreciated on its own. Now imagine a policy of the following sort: the deaf are permitted into the museum because they can appreciate the visual dimension and "at least they have organs that orient them toward the auditory dimension even though those organs aren't working." But the alternative humans aren't allowed in, since they don't have the organs that orient them toward the full experience even though they have what it takes to get as much out of the experience as the deaf.

Can any sense be made of such a policy? If the visual experience is genuinely wonderful by itself, wouldn't it be unloving to exclude these alternative humans? Wouldn't we view it as a prejudice? Roman Catholics speak eloquently about the joys of marriage. When they encounter those who, because of a disability in their reproductive organs, can only pursue the unitive end, they do not conclude that they should be barred from pursuing this end or that its value is lost because it won't overflow into new life. Why, then, should they conclude that the unitive relationships of gays and lesbians have no value, and gays and lesbians should be barred from pursuing the unitive end, just because the procreative end cannot be simultaneously pursued?

Perhaps the most charitable interpretation of the Roman Catholic argument, then, is this: they sincerely think that the unitive end of sexual intimacy is parasitic on engaging in an act that by its nature is oriented toward reproduction (even if some disability might prevent it from achieving this end). In other words, the Inseparability Thesis amounts to the following hypothesis: the fact that vaginal intercourse is by nature oriented toward reproduction is what *makes* sex unitive, and if that orientation toward reproduction is missing then the unitive power of sex is lost as well.

Timothy Hsiao attempts to defend this idea, insisting that "it is on account of its procreative purpose that sex is *capable* of uniting persons as persons."[28] Why? Because a union "is formed by the coordinated activity of its constituent members to a common end that completes them."[29] Unity between persons, he says, "requires that an aspect of their humanity biologically coordinate toward a common goal." In sex, that common goal is reproduction. The idea, in short, is that the act of sex cannot unite two people unless the act is directed toward something other than union as such, an

---

28. Ibid., 753, emphasis added.
29. Ibid.

aim that calls for a coordinated effort. It's this common effort in pursuit of a shared goal that unites the parties.

This is an interesting hypothesis. It is certainly true that we can unite people by pursuing some common goal apart from union itself. But it is also clear from human experience that we can pursue union directly. For example, when my daughter and I hug, this act contributes directly to the bond between us, even though the act of hugging has no common goal beyond sustaining and expressing love. The rich data of human experience tells us that through acts of physical closeness—hugging, snuggling, kissing—we promote closeness as whole persons in an immediate way, at least when those gestures of physical closeness are part of a relationship featuring other forms of intimacy. Why then suppose that the distinctive closeness we call romantic love can't be nurtured and sustained through sexual intimacy (within a broader context of human closeness) apart from common pursuit of the reproductive end?

All we need to do is look at happy gay and lesbian couples, and we will see that they have actually attained the unitive end *despite the fact that their unions aren't oriented toward reproduction*. In short, Hsiao's thesis about how and why sexual intimacy can promote unity might have some plausibility in the abstract, but as soon as we consult the evidence of human experience, it becomes apparent that the unitive end of sex is achievable apart from pursuing procreation.

This fact offers a stumbling block for other theoretic defenses of the Inseparability Thesis. Edward Feser, for example, maintains that "the unitive end of sex builds on the procreative in just the way the conceptual structure of human perceptual experience builds on the sensory element."[30] What he's saying here is that while human sex is more than procreation, the *something more* builds on the basic biological function of sex and so depends on it. Based on this idea, Feser concludes that homosexual acts "have no tendency toward procreation at all, and the emotions associated with them direct the unitive drive, which can by nature be fulfilled only by a human being of the opposite sex, toward an improper object."[31] Feser's claim here is that since the unitive end builds off the procreative one, the drive to pursue union with someone of the same sex is misdirected, pushing gays and lesbians toward someone with whom that unitive drive *cannot* be fulfilled.

But given the evidence provided by loving same-sex couples, it clearly *is* possible to fulfill the unitive end of sex with a partner of the same sex. Hence, Feser's conclusion can only be sustained by prioritizing the

---

30. Feser, "The Role of Nature," 75.
31. Ibid., 76.

implications of *his theory about the nature of human sexuality* above *the lessons gleaned from compassionate attention to gays and lesbians*. But any such prioritization strikes me as a move similar to one we looked at in the last chapter—namely, prioritizing allegiance to a theory about the Bible over the lessons of compassionate attention to our gay and lesbian neighbors. Such priorities are not what the law of love demands. When the natural law theory is invoked in this way, it represents a theory in competition with the ethic of love, not a theory in the service of it.

The Complementarity Thesis

Roman Catholic thinkers believe—as do many conservative Evangelical Christians—that there is an essential complementarity between men and women that suits them for being united in loving pair-bonds. As the US Bishops put it in their pastoral letter on marriage:

> Marriage, this clinging together of husband and wife as one flesh, is based on the fact that man and woman are both different and the same. They are different as male and female, but the same as human persons who are uniquely suited to be partners or helpmates for each other. The difference between man and woman, however, cannot be restricted to their bodies, as if the body could be separated from the rest of the human person. The human person is a union of body and soul as a single being. Man and woman are two different ways of being a human person.[32]

They maintain that "their differences serve to relate them to each other" in a way that brings them together. Male and female are "complementary" and "harmonizing" ways of being human and "of responding to the vocation of love."[33]

They offer two things as evidence for this complementarity. First, they offer the same interpretation of the Genesis creation story that Craig Koester does. On this interpretation, the fact that God made a *female* helpmate for Adam means that no same-sex helpmate can ever be a suitable helpmate for *any* human being, whatever their personal qualities, and so if gays and lesbians can't form an opposite-sex pair-bond they are condemned to endure what God said it was not good for Adam to endure. The difficulties of relying on such a contestable interpretation to defend a thesis with such painful implications has been well rehearsed already.

32. US Catholic Bishops, *Marriage*, 10.
33. Ibid.

The second thing they offer is a kind of extension of the notion that male and female reproductive organs fit together to produce a complete reproductive system.

> While human persons are more than biological organisms, the roots of marriage can be seen in the biological fact that a man and a woman can come together as male and female in a union that has the potential for bringing forth another human person. This kind of union fills the need for the continuation of the human race. Since human beings exist at more than a biological level, however, this union has further personal and spiritual dimensions. Marriage does not exist solely for the reproduction of another member of the species, but for the creation of a communion of persons.[34]

Although there are different kinds of communions of persons, the communion of husband and wife is "unique" in that they "exist for each other" through a gifting of their whole selves to one another. What is important to note here is that the complementarity of the sexes is treated as essential for the *existence* of such an intimate union of mutual self-giving. Again, this is a fine hypothesis, but it's one we can and should test by attending to the relationships of gays and lesbians. When we do, it becomes apparent that the hypothesis is false. To cling to the hypothesis in the face of this evidence—especially when the hypothesis is used to preclude gays and lesbians from access to the goods of marriage—is to care more about a certain theory than about our actual gay and lesbian neighbors, and so to fall short with respect to love.

I'm tempted to leave the argument at that, because it strikes me as sufficient in light of what has already been said. But this Complementarity Thesis—this idea that the unitive love found in marriage is impossible apart from the holistic complementarity between male and female—is too deeply entrenched in Christian communities.

So let's explore the thesis a bit further. The idea is that biological differences between men and women affect them at more than just the physical level. Men are naturally endowed with masculine traits, women with feminine ones, at a psychological level. And these traits complement each other—presumably in the sense that, in relationships, masculine strengths make up for feminine weaknesses and vice versa. The idea, in short, is that differences between men and women go beyond obvious physical traits, extending to differences in native abilities and psychological characteristics that are distributed such that men and women "complete" each other: when

---

34. Ibid.

they come together, they bring together distinct "ways of loving" that generate a kind of "fit" on an interpersonal level that two men or two women simply can't achieve.

This idea won't take you to the conclusion that you need a man and a woman to achieve the unitive ends of marriage unless you assume that men never possess the "feminine" strengths, and women never possess the "masculine" ones. If you think the distributions are merely probabilistic (women are more commonly possessed of more of the feminine ones, etc.), you open the door to two men or two women being comparably well-situated to complement one another (while some heterosexual couples fail to achieve such complementarity). Furthermore, if you think the distributions of "masculine" and "feminine" traits are strongly influenced (not necessarily determined) by culture, there may be cultural contexts in which the sex-based distribution doesn't hold true even in general.

So those who say that sexual complementarity is essential for the marital bond need to hold that these "gendered" qualities *can't* cross the borders of biological sex. They need to hold that women, by virtue of their sex, *can't* possess the "masculine" strengths, since those are the exclusive province of men; and men *can't* possess the feminine ones.

You rarely hear the point put so starkly, because when put that way it is obviously false. Ordinary human experience tells us that the sorts of character traits that can contribute to building mutual love and life-partnership are diverse, that few people have all of them, that any two people will likely complement one another in some ways but not others, and that no character trait is the exclusive province of men or women.

All of us know, from our experience of the rich, messy complexity of humanity, that men and women come in all shapes and sizes. Even if we think there are general differences between the sexes in their "ways of loving," these generalities aren't universal. And even if we think these general differences are rooted in something biological rather than being just a cultural construct, we must concede that culture and other forces can exaggerate or diminish them.

If we want to bring together people who are at once "different and the same," we can do that in ways that pay no attention to gender. We might do it in terms of Myers-Briggs personality scores. Pair off an INTJ with an ESFP and you'll likely achieve more complementarity of divergent traits than is found in many heterosexual marriages. And if you think the virtues linked to "masculinity" and "femininity" are especially important, it might make more sense to pair people off in terms of how they score on personality tests that measure how masculine or feminine they are, rather than pairing them off by whether they are biologically male and female.

Back when I was in college, as part of a psychology course, I took a test like that. It was supposed to measure how "feminine" or "masculine" I was based on conventional understandings. My test pegged me as androgynous. Absolutely smack-dab in the middle of the scale. I recently took some masculine/feminine personality tests online, to see if anything has changed over the years. The first one pegged me as . . . androgynous. The second one determined I was 53 percent feminine, 47 percent masculine. So I guess not much has changed. Biologically, I'm male. In terms of sexuality, I'm heterosexual. In terms of personality, I'm androgynous.

This fact raises some personal questions I have for those who insist that a marriage requires the complementarity that goes with gender difference. After all, I'm not a "masculine" husband. I am (apparently) an androgynous one. So, although my wife has a husband in terms of plumbing, she apparently doesn't have a "husband" in the full complementarian sense. Knowing what I know about my personality—about my failure to be "masculine" in my character and hence my inability to be a "husband" in the complementarian sense—was my decision to become a husband wrong? Did I deny my wife a "husband"?

Whatever virtues I have as a spouse—and I believe I have a few—they don't fall into the traditionally "masculine" cluster. They aren't in the distinctly feminine cluster, either. They're just mine. What makes me a good husband (to the extent that I achieve this) is the love and acceptance and support I show my wife. I'm not a take-charge husband (we're equal partners in decision-making). I'm clueless when it comes to handyman tasks (my wife likes power tools more than I do). My wife, a triathlete, is physically stronger than me (a fact that does not intimidate me; I think it's pretty cool). If it came down to defending the family from an aggressor, not only is my wife more likely to act decisively (she doesn't have my long history of flirting with Christian pacifism), but her self-defense and kick-boxing training (not the cardio type, but the type where you smash things) makes her the better choice.

If my wife and I complement each other, it isn't because I bring the masculine and she brings the feminine. It's because we are different human beings with different psychological qualities. She has ADD, which makes her easily distracted and flustered when there's lots of noise and chaos going on. I'm fine with chaos and keep an even emotional keel through the noise and confusion of taking care of the kids. I'm relentlessly goofy at home in a way my wife is not—and I think this adds to our relationship. Is it masculine to be goofy? I know too many goofy women and girls (one of them my daughter) to say that. Put simply, when we look beyond plumbing, what I bring to my role as a husband isn't anything distinctly tied to *maleness*.

But that hasn't stopped me from forming a bond of love with my wife. And those who want to claim that my marriage can't achieve an authentic union because my wife and I don't bring our respective packages of complementary gendered traits are ignoring the fact that we have a loving union that has weathered some significant trials. And there are plenty of couples like us. To say the unitive end of marriage is impossible without the traditional distribution of gendered traits amounts to a failure to pay attention.

But perhaps the Complementarity Thesis shouldn't be read as *describing* what is required for a successful pair-bond but as imposing a moral demand for all pair bonds: only those heterosexual couples who exhibit traditional distributions of gendered traits are acceptable. If so, does this mean men and women who don't conform should be barred from marriage? Then it won't just be gays and lesbians who are forced to endure what God said in Genesis was not good for Adam to endure. I doubt these are implications many would find acceptable. But perhaps the point is that all men and women are morally required to adopt gender-specific roles in their marriages, whatever their native dispositions. If so, that would push men and women into pre-established roles that don't always suit them. Even if these roles complement one another, they don't always complement the personalities of the people trying to fill them. Trying to force people into specific complementary marital roles can go a long way toward damaging both individuals and their marriages. A sexual ethic so committed to pushing people into rigid molds as the price for life-partnership and romantic love is an ethic hard to reconcile with the law of love, with a creation story in which God says it is not good for Adam to be alone, and with a Christian vision of the kingdom of God in which there is neither male nor female.

Respect for Dignity

There is one final dimension of Roman Catholic natural law thinking that needs serious attention—specifically, the argument that the dignity of the human person is degraded by homosexual sex. This argument ties natural law ideas to the love ethic in a very direct way: according to Roman Catholic thinking, acting on a homosexual orientation violates human nature in a way that diminishes gays and lesbians themselves. Thus, a call to celibacy is an act of love.

Edward Feser expresses this idea in the following (rather strident) terms:

> Now, since the natural ends of our sexual capacities are simultaneously procreative and unitive, what is good for human beings

vis-à-vis those capacities is to use them only in a way consistent with these ends. This is a *necessary* truth, given the background metaphysics. It *cannot possibly* be good for us to use them in a way contrary to those ends, whether or not an individual person thinks it is, any more than it can possibly be good for a tree to fail, because of disease or damage, to sink its roots into the ground. . . . That a desire to act in such a way is very deeply entrenched in a person only shows that his will has become corrupted.[35]

Put less stridently, if the natural law framework and the account of sexuality that Feser develops are accurate, it would follow that gays and lesbians who pursue lifelong monogamy with a person of the same sex are ultimately harming themselves (and their partners). But if this is true, we would expect that this would be discernible in some way, that their lives would display some deficiency, either physically, psychologically, or spiritually. Put another way, were homosexual activity "against" the human nature of those with a homosexual orientation, we would expect there to be evidence that self-rejecting gays and lesbians are better off, at least in the long run, than self-accepting ones. Is there?

It is important here to stress that clear evidence of the harms of *promiscuity* among gays and lesbians is not evidence that same-sex monogamy harms them, and hence not evidence that expressing a homosexual orientation in a same-sex marriage violates their nature. The question is whether there is any support for the hypothesis that gays and lesbians who reject and suppress their sexuality do better overall in life than those who accept their sexuality in the same terms that Christian heterosexuals do—as a gift to be reserved for the context of a loving marriage.

The empirical evidence pertaining to mental health certainly does not support this, as we saw in chapter 5. Although gays and lesbians have higher rates of mental health problems, these are correlated with social stigma and its internalization and diminish to the extent that gays and lesbians can avoid this stigma, resist internalizing it, and pursue enduring relationships with same-sex partners.

In terms of physical health, there are serious health costs associated with promiscuous expressions of homosexuality, just as with promiscuous expressions of heterosexuality. Insofar as gays and lesbians have been denied the social supports of marriage, they have predictably had less permanence and more promiscuity in their relationships. But when expressed in the context of monogamous love, sexual intimacy is no more a health threat for

---

35. Feser, "The Role of Nature," 76. Emphasis in original.

same-sex partners than for heterosexual ones. From this evidence, the best conclusion is that monogamy—heterosexual or homosexual—does more to promote our natural ends than does promiscuity. Social policies that encourage monogamy would thus promote our natural ends, and *withholding* same-sex marriage could on those grounds be viewed as problematic.

Of course, these conclusions only apply to empirical data about mental health and physical health. They don't speak to *spiritual* health—which, for Christians, is the most important measure of welfare. But the key aspect of spiritual health, for Christianity, is the nature of one's relationship with God. Do we have reason to believe that self-rejecting gay and lesbian Christians, who stifle all their romantic impulses, have a healthier relationship with God than those self-accepting gay Christians who express their sexuality in a marital context?

Not at all. As a Lutheran, when I think about a healthy relationship with God I can't help but turn to Luther. Luther stresses that the essence of a healthy Christian relationship with God is not found in good works, but in an attitude of trust—what Luther means by faith. Someone's outward behavior can be impeccable while lacking such trust. In fact, for Luther, such impeccable behavior is often a sign that the person is fixated on her own works, trusting in them instead of God. There's a big difference between obeying a list of rules and handing yourself to God and saying, "I'm in your hands! Make of me what you will." Luther argued that without that act of trust, doing what you think God requires becomes a hollow exercise prone toward a self-righteous moralism devoid of grace. In other words, obedience to God's will isn't so much a way of establishing a healthy God-relationship as it is an *effect* of such a relationship. When it comes to establishing such a relationship, our main contribution is to trust in God enough to open ourselves to the flood of divine grace.

This view is not idiosyncratic to Luther but reaches back to Augustine and even further, to Paul. While there are continuing disagreements about the relationship between grace and faith and works in the Christian tradition, these disputes are relatively minor compared to the points of agreement: to do good works we need God's grace, and for that grace to flow, we need to trust God's goodness enough to open ourselves to the tide-rush of divine love.

I've had extensive contact over the years with gay and lesbian Christians—both those who are self-accepting and those who are self-rejecting. I've paid attention to their religious lives. And it seems clear, from the lives of religious devotion exemplified by many self-affirming gays and lesbians, that it is possible for them to trust in God's benevolence in the indicated sense while remaining self-affirming. By contrast, as we've already seen in chapter 7, self-rejecting gays and lesbians often feel rejected by God, and it isn't until they conclude that God does *not* condemn them for who they are and who they love that they find themselves responding to God with the love and trust that transforms their lives.[36] It is particularly telling that among religious gay men with AIDS, those who remain committed to religions of origin typically critical of homosexuality exhibit higher levels of death anxiety than those pursuing alternative religious paths. In effect, they are less capable of trusting in God's benevolent love.[37]

The inner turmoil brought on by persistent homosexual desire in the face of the (supposedly) divinely decreed rejection of it, combined with the failure of persistent prayer and other spiritual efforts to change their sexuality, have a tendency to undermine trust in God. It's no wonder so many gays and lesbians who grow up in Christian communities that condemn homosexuality ultimately reject not merely that condemnation, but Christianity itself.[38]

Others adopt a pretense of heterosexuality that has all the marks of works righteousness. Despising who they are, many who go through ex-gay ministries without success decide to pretend to be cured. While some part of them knows it's a lie, it's a lie they tell themselves and hence one they become defensive about. They tell themselves that so long as they are outwardly pure, it doesn't matter what longings linger in their hearts. They resent those who don't make the same sacrifice, sometimes becoming the most vocal denouncers of homosexuality. The result is a kind of works righteousness: they've latched onto sexual purity as the path to salvation. In the personal narratives of my gay and lesbian Christians friends, the restoration of faith comes with the rejection of the idea that homosexuality is a sin—often experienced as an epiphany in which God's unconditional love breaks through the barrier imposed by traditional teachings.[39]

In short, natural law thinkers who say homosexual behavior violates the dignity of gay and lesbian persons must face head-on the evidence that on multiple levels gays and lesbians who affirm their sexuality and express it in monogamous partnerships live healthier and more productive lives than those who reject and struggle with it. They must give us compelling reason to embrace the following unlikely claim: a person's dignity is better served by adopting a self-understanding that drives some to such extremes

36. For more on this, see Ritter and Terndrup, *Handbook*, ch. 13.

37. Franks et al., "Exploration of Death Anxiety."

38. See, for example, Ellis and Wagemann, "The Religiosity of Mothers and Their Offspring."

39. In addition to the qualitative research cited in chapter 7, see also Yip, "Leaving the Church to Keep My Faith."

as slashing their own genitals than by adopting one that brings a sense of wholeness and integrity. Put another way, they must justify their commitment to pursuing the welfare of gays and lesbians according to a measure of welfare—derived from their understanding of the nature of human sexuality—that is sharply at odds with what the actual lived experiences of gays and lesbians would lead us to conclude.

Sustained attention to the experiences and lives of gays and lesbians is a relatively new phenomenon in history. The concept of sexual orientation, which helps in both telling and understanding gay and lesbian stories, is new. Empirical study of human sexuality beyond its most common forms is new. The Roman Catholic theory of human sexuality predates all this, and so was not shaped by the realities of gay and lesbian sexuality that only become apparent when such attention is paid. To show love for gays and lesbians, it's not enough to do what this theory says is best for them. In other words, it's not enough to cling to a theory about the nature of human sexuality originally developed at a time in history when gays and lesbians had no public voice with which to critique that theory, and then ignore the cries of gays and lesbians who now do have such a voice.

Defenders of the natural law perspective who want to be faithful to the love ethic need to show, somehow, that it is more loving to act in ways that bring lifelong distress, out of respect for an abstract theory about what is required for human dignity, than to act so as to promote a lived experience of wellness at the expense of discarding a theory that was created without the benefit of any sustained attention to gay and lesbian lives. They have the formidable task of explaining why a commitment to loving the neighbor should be *more* attentive to such a theoretic human construct than to the anguished cry of the gay man who is driven to suicide based on the conviction that, paradoxically, his very nature is unnatural.

11

Slippery Slopes

A 2004 Family Research Council pamphlet, *The Slippery Slope of Same-Sex Marriage*, begins with the story of a Missouri farmer who wanted to marry his horse. After describing the farmer's passionate devotion to his mare, the pamphlet makes the following assertion:

> The Missouri man and homosexual "marriage" proponents categorically reject the definition of marriage as the union of a man and a woman. Instead, the sole criterion for marriage becomes the presence of "love" and "mutual commitment." But once marriage is no longer confined to a man and a woman, it is impossible to exclude virtually any relationship between two or more partners of either sex—even non-human "partners."[1]

This kind of argument is hardly unique, although more serious conservative critics of same-sex marriage are less concerned about interspecies wedlock than about undercutting the monogamy norm and eroding incest taboos. One-time Supreme Court nominee Robert Bork has argued that "the rationale for same-sex marriage would equally support group marriage, incest, or any other imaginable sexual arrangement."[2] Political commentator Stanley Kurtz agrees: "Among the likeliest effects of gay marriage is to take us down a slippery slope to legalized polygamy and 'polyamory' (group

---

1. Dailey, *The Slippery Slope of Same-Sex Marriage*, 2.
2. Bork, "The Necessary Amendment," 17.

marriage)."[3] And this view isn't limited to the political right. Anita Wagner Illig, an activist for polyamory, has said she thinks Kurtz is right about the slippery slope. "We just disagree," she adds, "as to whether it's a bad thing."[4]

So, is same-sex marriage a "slippery slope" to things most Christians would be loath to accept? Does setting aside the heterosexuality requirement mean that abandoning the monogamy norm is not far behind?

The Logic of Slippery Slopes

Crack open any critical thinking textbook and you're likely to find the slippery slope included in a list of fallacies, with an explanation of the fallacy along the following lines:

> The fallacy of the slippery slope is an argument that objects to a position on the erroneous belief that the position, if taken, will set off a chain of events that inevitably will lead to an undesirable outcome. . . . Regardless of the desirability or undesirability of the final event, all slippery slope fallacies involve hasty conclusions because they fail to adequately consider the complex factors involved in causal chains.[5]

But it's one thing to say that if we legalize same-sex marriage our society *will* become—by some mysterious causal chain—a sexual free-for-all in which ranchers start having group marriages with their cows and siblings. It is something else to say that if we legalize same-sex marriage, we are deprived of a principle basis for objecting to those who want to create such incestuous, multi-party, multi-species marital bacchanals. For ease of reference, let's say that people who say the former are postulating a *causal* slippery slope, while those who endorse the latter are endorsing a *reasons-based* slippery slope.

Only those who say the former are guilty of the slippery slope *fallacy* as traditionally defined, because only they are making a sweeping claim about inevitable chains of cause-and-effect that are at best hard to prove and at worst clearly false. All we need to do to show that there is no such inevitable causal chain is look at progressive churches that have been conducting

---

3. Kurtz, "Beyond Gay Marriage," 26. For those unfamiliar with the polygamy/polyamory distinction, the former refers to someone having more than one marriage at a time, whereas the latter refers to groups of more than two forming a single "group marriage."

4. Quoted in Cheadle, "After Gay Marriage," para. 5.

5. Soccio and Barry, *Practical Logic*, 348–49.

same-sex marriage ceremonies for decades without ever displaying the slightest inclination to anoint sibling-goat-group-marriages.

But in its slippery slope pamphlet, the Family Research Council isn't saying that such churches will inevitably get swept up by the desire to perform interspecies marriages. What they're saying is that if anyone ever does get that inclination, these churches will have no principled grounds for saying no. This means the Family Research Council is not positing a fallacious causal slippery slope. What they are doing is claiming there's a reasons-based slippery slope: embrace same-sex marriage, and you're left without any reason to oppose bestiality.

Is that true? Of course not. There are abundant reasons to oppose bestial marriage even if you think same-sex marriage is fine. Maybe you think, along with most people, that marriage is about the mutual love, support, sharing of selves, and partnership in life that other human beings can offer us but horses can't. Maybe you think human sexuality is debased unless it is expressed in a context where two people give themselves to each other's care in an honest and open sharing of selves and lives—and maybe you think horses can't do that with each other, let alone with a human. Maybe you think marriage involves an exchange of vows of mutual fidelity and love—vows that both parties need to understand and affirm, so that any party that can't do that can't participate in a marriage. Thinking these things won't stop you from supporting same-sex marriage but will surely rule out a marriage between Farmer Bob and his horse.

So although the Family Research Council does not commit the causal slippery slope fallacy as described in critical thinking texts, their reasons-based slippery slope argument is disastrously unsound. But as terrible as their argument is, there's something they get right: if you are committed to the view that marriage should be available to same-sex couples, you are also committed to *your reasons* for adopting that view. And those reasons might have implications for other positions. This is why reasons-based slippery slope arguments aren't *automatically* fallacious, even if some of them are very bad arguments indeed. The question is whether any other reasons-based slippery slope arguments are any better.

When Robert Bork says that the "rationale for same-sex marriage" would also support such things as group marriage and incest, he's claiming that the reasons for supporting same-sex marriage don't stop there, but justify these other things. Stanley Kurtz agrees.[6] Whether they are right

---

6. Although most of Kurtz's essay makes the vague connections (between the gay rights movement and movements for polygamy and polyamory) typical of causal slippery slope fallacies, he also claims (without defending the claim) that "Once we say that gay couples have a right to have their commitments recognized by the state, it becomes

depends on exactly what our reasons for supporting same-sex marriage actually are. Perhaps the most serious mistake of those who warn about a slippery slope is to make dubious and uncharitable assumptions about this "rationale for same-sex marriage." Bork, for example, thinks the rationale is "the anarchical spirit of extreme personal and group autonomy" that could variously be labeled "moral chaos, relativism, (or) postmodernism."[7] In other words, Bork is convinced that same-sex marriage supporters think morality is all relative anyway, so anyone should be free to do as they please sexually; and whatever they decide to do, we should accommodate it by calling it marriage. That rationale *would* generate a slippery slope.

But if Bork thinks this is the actual rationale that's been driving increased public and legal support for same-sex marriage, he hasn't been paying attention. It's certainly not the rationale I've been developing here. Perhaps there are some who think of marriage in this way. But while in any pluralistic society there will be diverse reasons for supporting a movement, no valid argument can focus on the reasons *some* people have and then saddle *everyone* with the bad consequences of commitment to those reasons. For example, if someone opposes abortion rights because he thinks male control over women's bodies should be absolute, this doesn't warrant tarring every abortion opponent with the right-to-rape implications of this horrible rationale.

This book develops a rationale for supporting same-sex marriage that's rooted in the demands of Christian love, and so the key issue at hand is whether *that* rationale generates a reasons-based slippery slope. But before looking at this issue, I want to consider the most influential secular rationale for same-sex marriage—what I'll call the equality argument. Unlike my love-based argument, the equality argument is directed only toward *civil* marriage, that is, marriage conferred by the state and defined largely in terms of a cluster of legal rights. The love-based argument certainly serves as a reason for Christians to support same-sex civil marriage, but it also (and especially) applies to the *Christian* marriages that pastors preside over and churches celebrate and support.[8] In a pluralistic society like ours, where

---

next to impossible to deny that same right to polygamists, polyamorists, or even cohabiting relatives and friends." See Kurtz, "Beyond Gay Marriage," 31.

7. Bork, "Necessary Amendment," 17.

8. If my arguments are sound, Christians have reasons to make same-sex marriage available within their own communities *whether or not the state offers same-sex civil marriage*. More strongly, it may be the *moral responsibility* of Christians to offer same-sex marriage even in repressive homophobic societies where doing so is dangerous, where making the goods of marriage available to our gay and lesbian neighbors means risking ourselves for their sakes.

freedom of religion is affirmed, public policy decisions about marriage will ultimately have to be made based on principles that transcend particular sectarian values and beliefs and can be generally affirmed. One such principle is the principle that citizens should be treated equally under the law: they should not be subjected to legal discrimination absent a compelling state interest. By the equality argument, I mean the case for same-sex civil marriage that appeals to this principle.

I want to begin with this equality argument for two reasons. First, were this argument to have the slippery-slope implications Bork and Kurtz are worried about, a Christians commitment to monogamy might then clash with a principle many find essential for a fair civil society—a conclusion that could force Christians to make some very difficult decisions. But since (as I will argue) the equality argument does not have these troubling implications, Christians aren't pushed into this ethical corner. Second, a careful look at why the equality argument *doesn't* generate these troubling slippery slopes will help us see why the love-based argument doesn't create such slippery slopes either.

The Equality Argument

A 2004 editorial in *The Economist* captured well the motivation behind the growing public support for same-sex marriage rights. "The case for allowing gays to marry," wrote the editors, "begins with equality, pure and simple. Why should one set of loving, consenting adults be denied a right that other such adults have and which, if exercised, will do no damage to anyone else?"[9]

With these words, *The Economist's* editors reflected a burgeoning pattern of argument that would increasingly shape both legal and public debates about same-sex marriage—so much so that the movement for same-sex marriage came to be called the marriage *equality* movement. This emphasis on equality has been a consistent theme in the courts, although it has often been supplemented by other arguments that focus on individual liberty. It's telling, however, that the seminal 1993 decision of the Hawaiian Supreme Court, in *Baehr v. Lewin*, rejected appeals to liberty and privacy while supporting same-sex civil marriage based on equal protection and non-discrimination.[10]

---

9. "The Case for Gay Marriage," 9.

10. For an excellent discussion of this case, within its legal context, see Deitrich, "Lessons of the Law," 141–44.

Put briefly, the equality argument rests on three premises: first, that traditional marriage laws discriminate against gays and lesbians; second, that discrimination is permissible only when it serves a compelling state interest; and third, that no such compelling state interest exists for discriminating against gays and lesbians.

There are some who challenge the premise that traditional marriage laws are discriminatory. They argue that these laws give everyone the same opportunity, namely the right to marry someone of the opposite sex; and they impose on everyone the same constraints, including and especially that no one may marry a person of the same sex. Since everyone faces the same opportunities and constraints, no one is being discriminated against.

But imagine a school lunch policy that makes a free lunch available to everyone without restriction—namely a peanut butter sandwich. Everyone is given the same opportunity: a free peanut butter sandwich. And everyone faces the same constraint: if you want a free lunch, it can only be a peanut butter sandwich. But even though everyone faces the same opportunities and constraints, the policy discriminates against children with peanut allergies. The reason is clear enough: the benefit that the program was designed to make available—namely a free meal—is made available in a form that makes it inaccessible to these allergic children. Or suppose a city makes its public records available only in a designated reading room. And suppose this reading room is located on the fourth floor of a building without an elevator. Those who rely on wheelchairs for mobility can justly complain that they are being discriminated against, even though everyone is subject to the same opportunity and constraint.

Likewise, traditional marriage makes a valuable social good available in a form that excludes gays and lesbians. The capacity to have your intimate romantic partnership legally recognized—and to get the array of legal rights that go with that recognition—is a public good that's highly prized. When the state restricts marriage to heterosexual couples, it denies gays and lesbians the chance to receive something that heterosexuals take for granted: social and legal support for their intimate pair-bonds.

The legal discrimination in this case is uniquely difficult to justify because of the reasons the state has for being in the marriage business. If we look at what motivates the state to make marriage available—to confer the cluster of legal benefits that civil marriage confers on couples—we find that they actually *favor* extending marriage to same-sex couples. I've addressed some of these reasons in a different context, but they are worth reiterating. One reason for the state to be in the marriage business is to promote a stable child-rearing environment. But there are children being raised by same-sex couples, and the welfare of those children would be served by introducing the stabilizing power of marriage into their homes.

Another reason for the state to be in the marriage business is that civil marriage is a stabilizing force on society. The legal benefits of civil marriage encourage couples to form and sustain stable partnerships, and the prevalence of such partnerships helps to shield society from the more volatile effects of human sexuality run amok. And in this age of AIDS, the stabilization of human sexual activity also plays a role in promoting public health. To deny gays and lesbians access to civil marriage is to limit these stabilizing benefits, including the public health benefits.

A third reason for the state to be in the marriage business is that civil marriage establishes a kind of "default support person" for adult members of society as they confront life's hardships. Without the support of a spouse, as Jonathan Rauch points out, the role of providing support falls on less immediate family and friends, who have their own problems, as well as on charities and government programs that are already overtaxed, underfunded, and ineffective.[11]

Put simply, civil marriage isn't just about the good that it does for the couple, but the good that it does for society. The state is in the marriage business for the sake of these broader social goods. If same-sex marriage didn't serve those goods, that could potentially justify legal discrimination. But since making marriage available to same-sex couples actually *serves* the broader social interests that motivate the state conferral of the goods of marriage, the presumptive duty to observe equality under the law remains in force.

Careful readers will notice that there are some points of connection between this secular rationale for same-sex civil marriage and the love-based rationale for Christian same-sex marriage. Both arguments stress that some people—gays and lesbians—have a homosexual orientation that they did not choose and that resists change. For them, the distinctive goods of marriage are available only if they are free to pursue marriage with members of the same sex. But whereas the legal equality argument stresses the legal discrimination that results when marriage is restricted to heterosexual pairs, the love-based argument focuses more on the harms to human flourishing that result. Some of those harms are, of course, directly tied to discrimination, to being shut out from access to such an important social institution and the goods that come with it: the sense of marginalization, the loss of a stable, socially-supported relationship in which to nurture their sexuality. But some of those harms—the conflicted identity and spiritual costs,

---

11. Rauch, "Who Needs Marriage?" 308.

for example—go beyond what discrimination alone can produce. And the psychological burdens of being expected to suppress their most vivid and embodied impulse toward love and intimacy can drive some to despair in a way that is not adequately captured by saying they're being discriminated against.

So while the love-based argument is attuned to issues of discrimination and shares this feature with the equality argument, it goes beyond that issue to the more complex and far-reaching harms that discrimination in this uniquely important area of human life has the potential to produce.

Again, like the equality argument, the love-based argument pays attention to the purposes of marriage, which include the child-rearing benefits, but extend beyond them to the mutual support that a marriage provides, and the channeling of sexuality into stable partnerships that protect against the risks and potential volatility of sexual expression. But in the case of the equality argument, the focus is on the social benefits of marriage. The joy and love of the married couple is almost incidental. In the love-based argument, these interpersonal benefits take center stage. The broader social benefits of same-sex marriage are relevant insofar as we are concerned about how other neighbors will be affected. Since these effects are largely positive, love does not face a moral dilemma in this case.

Finally, as with the legal equality argument, the love-based argument claims that withholding marriage from same-sex couples stands in need of justification. In other words, the burden of proof rests with those who say that gays and lesbians should be excluded from the goods of marriage. But whereas the equality argument only has to contend with secular justifications rooted in public welfare concerns, the love-based argument, given its Christian context, must contend with possible justifications that appeal to divine revelation and God's design plan for the natural order.

But given the parallels between the two arguments, the reasons why the legal equality argument is immune to slippery slope challenges help show why the love-based argument is similarly immune. Hence, I want to consider the two arguments in tandem. I will first explain why the legal equality argument does not produce a slippery slope to non-monogamy, and then build off of these considerations to show why the love-based argument doesn't bear such fruits. I will then make a similar case with respect to incest fears.

The Failure of the Slippery Slope to Non-Monogamy

There are two distinct but related reasons why the equality rationale for same-sex civil marriage fails to generate a slippery slope to non-monogamy.

First, the equality argument arises only because there exists a class of people—gays and lesbians—who are denied access to the goods of marriage when marriage is restricted to heterosexual pairs. The discrimination exists only because some people have a stable homosexual orientation that makes it impossible for them to access the goods of marriage when it is made available only in a heterosexual form.

If everyone had a heterosexual orientation, a law restricting marriage to heterosexual couples would preclude everyone from doing something no one had any interest in doing anyway. If everyone had a bisexual orientation, then a law restricting marriage to heterosexual couples would put the same limit on everyone, and that limit would affect everyone in essentially the same way. No individual would be deprived of the chance to access the goods of marriage, since it would be available in a form that everyone, given their bisexual orientation, could take advantage of. While we might ask why this constraint should be imposed, at least the constraint wouldn't discriminate against a class of people. But we live in a world where some people have a homosexual orientation. And so, legally limiting civil marriage to heterosexual couples does discriminate against a class of people.

The same is not true about a law that says one can only have a single spouse at a time, thereby denying me the right to marry both Mary and Martha at the same time. Of course, most of us have a sexuality that makes it possible to fall in love with multiple people at once. But the reason why it is possible for me to fall in love with both Mary and Martha is because I have the ability to fall in love with Mary, and I have the ability to fall in love with Martha. And this means that a law requiring me to marry only *one* of them does not prevent me from marrying someone I can love. I can have a marriage with someone I love; I just can't have more than one such marriage at once (or a group marriage that includes more than one partner at once). The fact that I can fall in love with more than one person at a time doesn't keep me from being able to access the social goods of marriage.

In order for a monogamy requirement to discriminate against a class of people, there would need to exist people with the following bizarre sort of sexual orientation: they are unable to feel any romantic or sexual attraction to *individuals*, but can only feel it toward groups of two or more. Suppose the following were true of me: if Mary walks into a room alone, I'm incapable of feeling any romantic interest or attraction. If Martha walks in, it's the same. But if Mary and Martha walk in together, my sexual interest suddenly comes alive for the pair *as a pair*. No matter how beautiful they are individually, it won't do any good—because one of my essential erotic cues is that there be two of them. It's only when both are present that my romantic side bursts forth, complete with an interest in long conversations, walks on the beach, bicycle rides together on a brisk fall day, . . . but only with the two of them together. Take one away and all this interest vanishes completely. And it's been this way since adolescence. Since my first sexual awakening, as other boys began to notice girls, I felt nothing for any individual girl. Not a one. But then I saw a pair together, and my heart leapt for the pair *as a pair*.

Not only don't I have this kind of "polyamorous orientation," but *no one* does. Anyone who is sexually and romantically attracted to both Mary and Martha is individually attracted to each. This is why, in societies where polygamy is allowed, the husband with multiple wives is able to visit each wife in turn and still function sexually even though only one of them is present. And since there is no such polyamorous orientation, *there is no class of people against whom a monogamy norm discriminates.*

But let's suppose, contrary to common human experience, that there is such an odd sexual orientation. If so, there would still be no slippery slope from same-sex marriage to non-monogamy. In the same-sex marriage case, the state could not justify discriminating against gays and lesbians because the state's reasons for being in the marriage business are actually served by expanding marriage to that class. But the same would not be true if some minority had a polyamorous orientation.

The state is in the marriage business in part to promote the kind of stability in sexual partnerships that is good for children and good for society. And the simple fact is this: the monogamous pair-bond is inherently more stable than larger groupings. That's not to say that monogamous pair bonds are perfectly stable. Every couple faces destabilizing forces brought on by the complexities of interpersonal dynamics. But adding a third person to a relationship multiplies those complexities enormously. When you have two people, Abe and Betty, there is one relationship to deal with. Add a third person, Cathy, and you now have six relationships: Abe's relationship to Betty, Betty's relationship to Cathy, Cathy's relationship to Abe, Abe's relationship to the Betty-Cathy pair, Betty's relationship to the Abe-Cathy pair, and Cathy's relationship to the Abe-Betty pair.

Of course, all of us have multiple relationships in our lives, and hence have a range of complications to face. But marriage is supposed to be a life partnership characterized by the mutual commitment to share the challenges of life together, to support one another, to be in each other's corner through the years, to divide the responsibilities of making a home, and to make crucial decisions as a team. And that sort of relationship involves distinctive stresses and conflicts, as well as payoffs. A three-person life-partnership faces challenges that exponentially magnify these stresses and conflicts: potential for jealousy, for playing off one partner against the other, for two teaming up and browbeating the third, for alliances that disempower, etc.

There are ways to manage this multiplication of relational dynamics and complexities to maintain stability, but they typically involve imposing hierarchies and formalized roles and rules that can inhibit genuine intimacy and mutual sharing. Without such intimacy-inhibiting strategies, the magnified complications and pitfalls of adding another party to the marriage would make those marriages less stable over time. Of course, if the state cared about marriage only for the sake of social stability, it might achieve the same stability achieved through the monogamy requirement by legislating hierarchies and formalized rules and roles on marital groups. But why magnify state intrusions into marriage when a monogomy norm will achieve the same result without such intrusion and without the stifling effects on marital intimacy?

Since no individuals are being discriminated against by a monogamy norm, the state's burden for justifying such a restriction is substantially lower than would be the case were discrimination involved. And the fact that such a restriction promotes marital stability is, it seems, a sufficient reason for the state to restrict official, state-sanctioned marriage to pairs.

But whatever we think about the state's interests, Christians clearly care about more than social stability when it comes to marriage. They care about what the marital relationship itself provides for those who participate in it. The stability that a pair-bond has (and larger groupings lack) is good for people: it stabilizes their lives and increases the chances they will have someone they can rely on to be there through the travails of life.

But from the standpoint of Christian love, there is something even more important. Christians have reason to want to nurture the communion of persons that marriage is designed to nurture: a loving partnership of mutual care characterized by a spirit of grace, in which the spouses learn how to move past disappointments and imperfections, forgive one another, work through conflicts, and revive or rebuild loving feelings when they (inevitably) fade. Marriage seeks to nurture this sort of love by building on the romantic and sexual inclinations that are intrinsic to our human nature, using those inclinations as a starting point but elevating them to something more through vows of fidelity and accountability to a supportive community.

Christians have reason to support such a communion of persons both because it is good for spouses, but also because it can serve as a crucible for learning how to love in the Christian sense and, in its best moments, as a foretaste of the beloved community. If Christian love is so unconditional and full of grace that it even extends to enemies, then it isn't something that fallen human beings do easily or naturally. But human beings do, quite naturally, fall in love. When expressed in a loving partnership, their sexuality quite naturally helps to forge bonds of intimacy and inspire mutual sharing. A marriage calls on couples to nurture those bonds even through the hardships and conflicts that test them, the challenges that might end other kinds of human friendships and associations. In the process, it expands our capacities for loving others in the way that Christian love demands.

As a human phenomenon, this has limits. Marital vows do not call on spouses to endure escalating cycles of abuse. An abusive marriage is not a crucible within which we can learn to love, because it is so broken that what it teaches victims will have more to do with fearful submission to tyranny than genuine care, and what it teaches perpetrators is to mistake controlling possessiveness for love.

But despite these limits, a pair-bond has the potential to bring both joy and moral growth. Larger groups are at best more fragile, more limited, more prone to the destructive forces that strip the marriage of its capacity to serve as a learning environment for love. But there may even be reason to wonder whether something larger than a pair can even *form* the kind of relationship that a marriage is supposed to be, let alone sustain it over a lifetime.

We can only look directly into the eyes of one person at a time. We can only process the deep personal stories of one person at a time. We can only kiss the lips of one person at a time. In many ways, human intimacy is a one-person-at-a-time kind of thing. To forge marital intimacy with more than one person therefore demands a *division* of our time and attention. But if we take seriously the Roman Catholic notion that marriage is a mutual giving of the whole self to another, we face the question of whether this marital way of relating is even possible when there are more than two people involved. Either someone is left out, or the gift of self is divided. Or, perhaps, fear that the gift won't be reciprocated—that the sharing will go toward another party in the group—inspires an inevitable withholding.

Critics might claim that the same considerations count against having children, or against having more than one child. If it is possible for parents to divide their love between two or more children, why can't they do the same with multiple spouses?

Let me first consider the argument that having children compromises the marital goal of mutual self-giving. Of course, the investment that parents make in their children can create complications in a marriage. But the understanding of marriage as a mutual giving of selves in life partnership does not mean that each spouse gives up their own projects and goals. Rather, it means that each spouse claims the projects and goals of the other as their own, at least in the sense of extending mutual support, encouragement, empathetic celebration of successes and mourning of failures. But it also means something else: taking on joint projects, pursuing goals together *as a team*, as an active expression of a shared life. The parenting of children is one such project, and perhaps the most paradigmatic one. It is something that both parents, when they are married, do together as partners in life. In other words, married spouses give themselves to each other in life partnership and then, as one paradigmatic expression of that life partnership, work on the shared project of nurturing and guiding and caring for their children.

But what about the argument that, if we can successfully parent more than one child, it follows that we can successfully partner with more than one spouse? This would follow if the nature of the parent-child relationship were the same as that of spouses. But it is not. The problem with a husband (say) who has two wives is that while each wife may be giving her whole self to her husband, the husband is forced to divide his attention—generating inequality and a lack of mutuality in the relationships. But the parent-child relationship is not *supposed* to be mutual and equal. Parents and children aren't supposed to share their whole selves with one another in life partnership. Ideally, parents give deep loving care and guidance, and children give respect, gratitude, and deference to parental wisdom. And the aim is for the child to eventually go out "on their own," an aim *at odds* with life partnership.

That one can only give one's full attention to one child at a time does not prevent deep love and care for each child, even if it would prevent one from having a relationship of mutual and egalitarian self-giving with each child. Since the latter is not what parenting aims to achieve, its failure to achieve it is not the kind of problem that such failure is in the case of marriage

Maybe it's naïve to suppose that any two people ever share themselves wholly with each other. Maybe there is only so much that we can share with another person without losing our sense of self and our emotional wholeness. But even so, what we *can* share faces the prospect of being doled out partly here and partly there when a marriage includes more than one partner. Perhaps it is true that even what we can safely share is rarely shared fully with a life partner. But at least this can be a relationship-defining aspiration when we form a marriage with one person. Add more spouses, and even that aspiration needs to be set aside.

What we have here is a love-based answer to a question posed by same-sex marriage opponent Hadley Arkes. Arkes frames the slippery-slope argument in the following way:

> The traditional understanding of marriage is grounded in the "natural teleology of the body"—in the inescapable fact that only a man and a woman, and only two people, not three, can generate a child. Once marriage is detached from that natural teleology of the body, what ground or principle would thereafter confine marriage to two people rather than some larger grouping?[12]

The answer is clear: not only is confining marriage to two people a more stable arrangement, but a two-person marriage may be the only setting in which two people can even aspire to give themselves to one another in loving partnership over a lifetime. Insofar as Christians have reasons rooted in the love ethic to encourage this marital way of relating, they have reasons to stand for monogamy—reasons entirely untouched by same-sex marriage.

The Failure of the Slippery Slope to Incest

Any time one argues that a particular social taboo should be set aside because enforcing it is damaging and the taboo itself lacks justification, one opens the door to the question, "What else might be like that?" In the arena of marriage, there are a range of taboos. Perhaps the most powerful is the taboo against incestuous marriages—that is, marriages between very close relatives. When it comes to marriages between a parent and child, the long history of an asymmetrical relationship featuring dependence and authority raises serious questions about whether any such marriage can avoid being deeply exploitative, let alone achieve the marital way of relating in the face of long-entrenched habits of a contrary kind.

But the taboo against incestuous marriage is not just against parent-child marriages. It also extends to sibling marriages. In these cases, it's at least possible to imagine adult siblings entering into a consensual relationship devoid of hierarchy and exploitation. Does lifting the taboo against same-sex marriage have any implications for this taboo against sibling marriage?

I can imagine critics of same-sex marriage advancing an argument similar to Hadley Arkes's: If we separate marriage from "the natural teleology of the body," it's no longer about making babies. And the only reason to discourage siblings from marrying is that they might produce children more prone to heritable diseases. Without the taboo, widespread sibling marriages could result in "in-breeding" that is bad for the human species.

---

12. Quoted in Rausch, "For Better or Worse?" 21.

But if we separate marriage from procreation, there's no longer any reason to maintain the taboo.

But is this right? Once again, it may be worth starting with civil marriage and the question of whether the state still has reasons to prohibit sibling marriage once same-sex marriage is allowed. On this issue, the great nineteenth-century German philosopher Hermann Lotze has some interesting things to say. His remarks about incestuous marriage are part of a broader discussion of legal marriage that makes points similar to ones I've already made. Notably, Lotze points out that when the state extends legal standing to an intimate partnership, this is not just something that private individuals do on their own. The state, in marrying a couples, acts to recognize the relationship and "protect the rights of what is recognized."[13] And while the state may withhold such recognition from a particular relationship because it does not reflect "the moral spirit which it wishes to maintain in power in its own midst," he insists that "society has no right to execute punishment upon forms of conduct which merely contradict its ways of looking at things, and which have not as yet gone so far as to work positive harm to it."[14]

In other words, Lotze distinguishes between, on the one hand, the state allowing relationships to exist without intervening to stop them and, on the other hand, officially recognizing and protecting relationships. Civil marriage is about the latter. Lotze's point is that the state can *withhold recognition* from relationships for reasons more modest than those that would be required to *prohibit* them.

While this is right, I need to qualify it with a point I've already made: any time the state makes a social good legally available, the decision to withhold it from some people must reflect a robust respect for equal treatment under the law. This means we must distinguish between cases where a restriction on who can marry deprives a class of people of the opportunity to enjoy the social goods of civil marriage, and cases where a restriction does not have such effects. The burden of justification is much heavier in cases of the former sort than in cases of the latter.

What I've argued so far, in effect, is that restrictions against same-sex marriage are of the former type, while restrictions against non-monogamous marriage are of the latter. But what about restrictions against sibling marriages? These appear to be of the latter type as well, since it would be pretty preposterous to presume there was a siblings-only sexual orientation.

---

13. Hermann Lotze, *Outlines of Practical Philosophy*, 70.
14. Ibid., 71.

A rule against sibling marriage effectively removes a couple of individuals from one's pool of potential mates, a pool that theoretically numbers in the billions. A rule against same-sex marriage, for gays and lesbians, removes from their pool of potential mates *every person on Earth with whom they could fall in love and actually form a lasting and satisfying intimate relationship*. Given this difference, the state's burden of justification for withholding legal recognition from siblings is going to be *far* more modest than what would be required for withholding legal recognition from same-sex relationships. Social bias alone might not be enough to justify it, but the state may have reasons beyond bias.

Lotze thinks it does. According to him, the state can legitimately withhold recognition from "marriage between brothers and sisters and very near relatives . . . not because it contradicts any (not demonstrable) 'command of nature,' but because a correct moral insight condemns the admixture of different moral relations, each of which can unfold its peculiar beauty and worth only when it does so purely for its own sake."[15]

This is a pregnant passage. The idea seems to be this: there are different ways that people relate to one another, and each species of relationship has its own "peculiar beauty and worth." The sibling relationship has a potential to be a distinctive kind of beautiful and valuable relationship, but only if it is clearly distinguished from relationships of the marital kind. Likewise, the distinctive fruits of the marital way of relating might be compromised if it is "admixed" with the form of relatedness distinctive of siblings.

When I reflect on my relationship with my sister, I find Lotze's claim intuitively right. My sister and I couldn't be what we are for each other were we trying to be what spouses are. And what we are for each other has value. Although it would take considerable work to unpack all the features of the sibling relationship, I suspect readers with siblings or sibling-like friendships can see the point readily enough.

Of course, there's the question of whether the state has an interest in "protecting" this sibling way of relating against things that might compromise it; and if so, whether this interest is compelling enough to withhold legal recognition from sibling marriages. It might not be compelling enough if doing so resulted in legal discrimination against a class of individuals. But it doesn't. As such, even if we think Lotze's concern about allowing different kinds of relationships to blossom is a relatively mild one, it may be enough to justify a state policy of withholding marriage from siblings.

And if we think about it, the state may have more than just "mild" reasons to maintain a sharp distinction between sibling relationships and

---

15. Ibid.

marital ones. Consider the following: siblings typically grow up with unprecedented access to one another. If we'd prefer that children limit sexual activity and exploration before reaching a certain level of maturity, we'd have a reason to try to limit sexual opportunities among adolescents (especially at those times when they are newly awakening to their sexual feelings). But to impose external limits on sexual opportunities among siblings, who grow up in the same home, could require draconian measures of supervision that would in the same stroke undermine the kind of closeness that, for example, my sister and I enjoyed growing up. *Internal* constraints offer a more promising approach.

Maintaining a strong, deeply ingrained taboo—sufficient to make siblings balk at the very idea of sex with one another—may be the best thing a society can do to discourage siblings from unwise and developmentally damaging sexual exploration with one another. An internalized taboo may be the only thing that can do this work while at the same time enabling siblings to form the close sibling (non-sexual) intimacy that characterizes the best sibling relationships. But can such a strong taboo be established and maintained if the state extends marriage to adult siblings who defy that taboo? It seems likely that the kind of powerful taboo required to produce self-policing among adolescent siblings may break down if the state treats sibling-marriage as equivalent to marriages among non-relatives.

At this point, a critic might argue that I've opened the door to justifying a taboo against same-sex intimacy, and thereby against same-sex marriage. After all, children of the same sex typically enjoy less adult supervision and hence greater sexual access to one another as they grow up. External rules designed to prevent sexual exploration with their same-sex friends would, in the same stroke, impede strong bonds of platonic friendship of the sort that all children need to develop as they grow—friendships that last a lifetime. Why not, then, argue that for the same reasons we should maintain a robust taboo against incest, we should maintain a robust taboo against homosexual sex?

There are several reasons why this parallel argument doesn't work. One has to do with the scope of the taboo. A taboo against sibling sex, inculcated early on, has the potential to encourage a heterosexual boy, upon sexual awakening, to direct his sexual interest toward every single girl at his school except his sister(s), and every girl at church, and every girl at band camp, etc. Likewise, a heterosexual girl is instructed by the taboo to direct her interest toward any boy in town but her brother(s). The taboo against same-sex intimacy, by contrast, instructs a gay adolescent to completely *stifle his sexuality and shut down all of his sexual feelings toward everyone.*

The former has a realistic chance of working at a cost so trivial that it is easily justified. The latter? Because a homosexuality taboo is so total in its scope for those it targets, it's more likely to inspire rebellion than the required total shutdown of all sexuality—and if it does work, it has the risk of inspiring self-loathing, since the effect of the taboo is to communicate the message that the very sexuality of the child is defective. A taboo which comes at the cost of increasing the suicide rate among adolescents is suspect no matter what good it might do.

Furthermore, the level of sexual access among those growing up in the same household is considerably higher than what exists among friends of the same sex, even if it is true that our society is structured such that adolescent heterosexual contact is more controlled and patrolled than is same-sex contact.

But this leads to the most important point: we don't eliminate homosexual attraction by pretending that every adolescent is straight. If there is a reason why young gays and lesbians have greater sexual access to one another, it's because we live in a heterosexist society that assumes kids are straight and guards against premature sexual contact *on that assumption*. Children who defy that assumption do have the potential for greater sexual access to those they are attracted to than do their heterosexual peers (although this implication is diminished by the fact that most of their peers won't be gay and so won't reciprocate sexual interest).

But a taboo against gay sex won't help in this situation, and not just because it demands such complete suppression of adolescent gay and lesbian sexuality that it is more likely to inspire rebellion than compliance. The deeper issue here is that these taboos drive gay and lesbian adolescents into the closet. And the closet quite effectively impedes social efforts to constrain premature sexual exploration among gay and lesbian teens.

In a society accepting of homosexuality, young gays and lesbians will be more likely to self-identify without fear of social stigma. Their parents will thus know that the rule against closing the bedroom door should be enforced when Joe has Bob over rather than when he's playing with Kathy. The most likely effect of the taboo is to strengthen the illusion that all adolescents are straight, thereby lulling adult supervisors into the false confidence that when it's just boys or just girls behind closed doors, there's nothing to worry about.

In short, there is a strong, multi-level disanalogy between incest taboos and taboos against homosexual sex. The state's burden of justification when it comes to restricting incestuous marriage is much lower than for same-sex marriage, because only the latter discriminates against a class of people. The more modest burden means that considerations of the sort Lotze raises are sufficient to justify a policy that permits same-sex marriages but prohibits incestuous ones.

But if these considerations are sufficient for the state, they are even more powerful when it comes to Christians motivated by love. An entrenched social taboo against mixing sex into sibling relationships protects children from themselves during a developmentally sensitive time of their lives. It helps ensure that sibling relationships are able to become what relationships of that kind are distinctively suited to become. If there are lessons to be learned about how to love that come out of the marital way of relating, there are likely also lessons to be learned from other ways of relating. This is evidently true for parent-child relationships, which teach different lessons about love than do marital ones. But it is also true of sibling relationships. There are, if you will, characteristic "sibling" virtues that flourish only when siblings relate as siblings rather than as lovers. A strong taboo against the "admixture of different moral relations" helps to actualize sibling relationships not only because it protects them from the distorting effects of sexual and romantic intimacy, but also because they aren't stifled by the kind of external policing that might otherwise have to be invoked to protect children from themselves.

All of this seems to be for the good of the neighbors we are called to love. In a world with many potential mates, excluding the tiny fraction related by close blood ties won't compromise anyone's ability to find a suitable mate. Thus, incest taboos protect the integrity of sibling relationships and protect adolescents from the harmful impact of their own foolishness without imposing a heavy cost. If we love our neighbors as ourselves, a norm that does this much good at little cost is a norm we should embrace. But a deeply entrenched social norm against all same-sex sex is not like this. The costs for gays and lesbians can be life-crushing and are not counterbalanced by comparable goods.

I've already addressed why taboos against homosexual sex, if they are meant to protect children from themselves, are likely to backfire. But for the sake of completeness I should also consider the less urgent question of whether there is some distinct kind of relationship that a taboo against homosexual intimacy would protect. The only candidate would seem to be platonic same-sex friendship. But unlike sibling relationships, which are created by unchosen familial ties, platonic friendships are chosen from a very large pool of potential friends, and new friends can be made at any point in life. Experience teaches that gays and lesbians are perfectly capable of cultivating platonic friendships with members of the same sex even as they form a loving partnership with someone of that sex—just as heterosexuals are able to have opposite-sex friendships while also cultivating a heterosexual marriage. If anything, gays and lesbians have to learn to be better at forming platonic friendships with people who belong to the sex that their orientation attracts them to, simply because the friends they make growing up will mostly be heterosexuals who won't reciprocate romantic interest.

Of course, sometimes gays and lesbians start out "just friends" with someone whom they come to fall in love with. Wouldn't this create a problematic "admixture" of relationship types? Wouldn't a strict taboo against homosexual relationships "protect" these friendships? First, even if such a taboo did protect these friendships, it would come at the high cost of denying gays and lesbians any access to the marital kind of relationship. Furthermore, friends becoming romantically involved is something that also happens among heterosexuals, and no one treats this as a reason to systematically forbid heterosexual romantic love. It may be true that the "platonic friendship" way of relating becomes displaced by the marital way of relating in these cases, but there is not much risk that this change will deprive either party of platonic friends. By contrast, there is a genuine danger in the case of sibling relationships simply because the number of siblings any individual has is small and essentially fixed. But even those who have a small circle of platonic friends have the potential, at any point in life, to cultivate more. So even if the blossoming of romance within what had previously been a platonic friendship means losing a friend, this is not near as weighty a matter as losing a brother or sister. Furthermore, many married couples appear to be good friends in addition to being spouses. Arguably, friendship has a flexibility that allows it to blend with romantic love in a way that simply isn't true for other familial relationships.

In sum, creating strict taboos designed to prevent the transformation of friendships into marriages has far less to justify it than taboos against marrying close blood relatives. Something far more modest than a taboo seems appropriate—such as, say, the warnings and cautions that we in fact see: if you turn a friendship into a romance, you may lose that friendship, so think carefully before you take that step.

12

Disagreeing in a Spirit of Love

In these pages I have offered my reasons, rooted in the Christian love ethic, for setting aside traditional teachings on homosexuality and supporting same-sex marriage. I'm not foolish enough to think my arguments are the final word on these matters. There are Christians just as committed to the love ethic as I am who will remain unpersuaded. But the arguments here show, I think, at least this much, if not more: Christians who reject the traditional condemnation of homosexuality can appeal to distinctively *Christian* values in making their case, and so can't be simply dismissed as sell-outs to secular culture. At the very least, I hope I have challenged fellow Christians to wrestle honestly with what it means to love their gay and lesbian neighbors and to avoid approaches having more to do with divisive ideology than an ethic of love.

The disagreements will continue, and so must the conversation. But I need to qualify this in an important way. Many of my gay and lesbian friends are tired—tired of defending their most intimate relationships, tired of revisiting the same biblical clobber passages over and over, tired of conversations where they have to brace themselves in the event that someone decides to call them abominations.

Just like straight people, gays and lesbians want to live their lives and love their partners without being persistently called to justify those lives and loves. Heterosexuals who don't want to debate this issue can just mind their own business and focus on their personal lives and families. But for gays and lesbians, the debate is *about* their personal lives and families. Even if they try to mind their own business, they are in danger of being sucked back into the debate.

Christians must be sensitive to the fact that the debate is about the fate of actual people. While love demands that gay and lesbian voices be heard and reckoned with in the debate, many have contributed what they're ready to contribute and now want to focus on living their lives. To keep challenging them to defend the legitimacy of those lives goes beyond *debating* the ethical issues.

There's a difference been dialogue aimed at advancing insight and consensus and the pretense of dialogue used as a tool to disrupt gay and lesbian lives. The latter is something we do when we're so sure we're right—so sure they have no legitimate claim on those lives—that we've abandoned dialogue in favor of imposing our values on them. If we're wrong we disrupt lives in the service of error, a risk those committed to the love ethic should be hesitant to take. If our aim is actual dialogue, there are plenty of conversation partners to choose from without having to badger those gay and lesbian neighbors who have had enough.

With that qualification in mind, an important question remains. In the face of ongoing disagreements that impact human lives, opposing sides will inevitably come into conflict on matters of policy and practice. Amidst such conflict, how do we show love for our opponents?

There are two sides to this question. First, how do we conduct loving conversations amidst such disagreement? We can always share our stories in a spirit of love. But in the face of disagreement, we don't just share stories. We debate the issues, making our case and challenging one another. How do we do that in a spirit of love?

Second, there is the fact that sometimes, while disagreements persist, we need to act—but what we feel called to do clashes with the aims and projects of those who disagree with us. How do we show love for those who not only think our choices are wrong, but are brokenhearted by them? How do we show love when our choices, born out of love, force those who disagree with us to make painful choices of their own—for example, to leave a beloved church?

Disgust and Other Irrelevant Emotions

A few years back, Thabiti Anyabwile (currently the pastor of Anacostia River Church in Washington DC) argued in a Gospel Coalition essay that conservative Christians should make more use of the following strategy when debating homosexuality and same-sex marriage: they should try to fire up visceral disgust against same-sex activity.

In the essay, Anyabwile explains why he advocates this strategy. Years ago he was privy to a well-argued, eloquent, and essentially conservative defense of same-sex marriage rights, one that left him stumbling for a response. In hindsight, he thinks the most effective retort would have involved inviting others to focus on the details of gay sex in a manner intended to elicit disgust. To exemplify his strategy, Anyabwile offers an example:

> We are talking about one man inserting the male organ used to create life into the part of another man used to excrete waste. We are talking about one man taking the penis of another man into his mouth, or engaging in penis-to-penis grinding.
>
> We are talking about a woman using her mouth to stimilute the nipples, vulva, clitoris or vagina of another woman, or using her hand or other "toys" to simulate sexual intercourse.
>
> We are talking about anilingus and other things I still cannot name or describe.[1]

Anyabwile recommends this explicit strategy for two reasons. First, he thinks it will be effective. Second, he identifies the "gag reflex" with our moral sense at work. Since many people condemn what disgusts them, I suspect Anyabwile is right on the first point, at least with some people. But is the disgust response really a good indicator of moral truth?

If people are disgusted by someone inserting "the male organ used to create life" into another organ "used to excrete waste," I wonder how many are disgusted by the fact that the very same male organ used to create life *is* an organ designed to excrete waste. If it's disgusting for humans to bring these things together in a temporary way, does that make it even more disgusting that God (or evolution, with God's consent) brought them together in a much more permanent and essential way? Is God guilty of moral wrongdoing?

The point is this: disgust is hardly the best guide in moral matters. I love sardines. I've been known to eat them in front of witnesses. Some are disgusted before I even open the can. I'm sure at least some readers will experience something of a gag reflex if I describe sardine-eating with the same explicit detail Anyabwile uses with respect to gay sex:

> We are talking here about a man, at lunch, plunging his fork into the silvery skin of a small fish, a fish that has been canned with the bones still inside its body. We are talking about lifting

1. Thabiti Anyabwile, "The Importance of Your Gag Reflex," para. 26–28.

that punctured fish corpse up towards human lips, the floppy tail dripping olive oil as it ascends. We are talking about the man shoving the entire body, skin and bones and all, into his eager mouth and systematically grinding the oily, fishy flesh into mush, allowing the aroma to rise into his sinuses, before reflexively swallowing.

Thankfully, although this description might inspire visceral revulsion in some readers, I doubt anyone has thereby concluded that sardine-eating is morally wrong. It certainly didn't inspire me to reach any such conclusion when, a few years back, I was following a wooded path up to a Buddhist monastery in Korea, and I encountered street vendors selling something called beondegi: silkworm pupae that are steamed or boiled. Koreans bought paper bags of them, crunching them like popcorn as they strolled.

I was disgusted. But why should what *other* people eat disgust me? Here's what I suspect is happening: eating is such a universally human phenomenon that when I think about the beondegi-eaters I find myself instantly imagining myself in their place, sympathetically sinking my own teeth into the pupa's steamed little body. What is happening here is a kind of *partial* empathy: I put myself into the beondegi-eater's situation while retaining my own preferences, my own cultural biases and assumptions and dispositions.

I suspect something similar is at work with sex. One of the most eye-opening discoveries I made after developing friendships with gays and lesbians was this: the visceral disgust many heterosexuals have toward gay sex is matched by a comparable disgust many gays and lesbians feel when they contemplate having (or actually do have) heterosexual sex. To be more precise, when any of us imagines participating in not-our-kind-of-sex, we tend to have a yuck-reaction.

But what all of this shows is that there are forces shaping our disgust responses that have nothing to do with morality—such things as upbringing, socialization, and familiarity. Amidst the variation there is, I suspect, a common element to disgust: it's related to our concepts of health and cleanliness, especially with respect to our bodies. We are universally disgusted by maggot-ridden excrement and rotting corpses because it's been hard-wired into our DNA. But with other things, like canned fish and moth pupae, ideas about health and cleanliness are shaped by contingent forces like culture and familiarity. Thus, something as perfectly healthy as eating beondegi will disgust us if we come from a culture that strongly links bugs with uncleanliness.

But disgust is a powerful aversion that, even if it's about health and cleanliness, can be easily confused with other strong aversive responses such as moral aversion. This makes it uniquely dangerous to invoke disgust as a way of winning a moral argument: it can be effective even though it is unreliable. More seriously, disgust has been used historically to perpetuate social injustice. As Richard Beck notes,

> ... disgust properties have always been imputed onto despised groups. More, disgust creates justifications for violence and social scapegoating. From kids being bullied on playgrounds to acts of genocide, disgust justifies exclusion, violence, and extermination.[2]

Many Americans used to be disgusted by interracial marriages, not because their moral sense detected wrongness and communicated this through gag reflexes, but because a racist system molded the capacity for disgust into the service of injustice. Any emotional reaction with such a history of being used to justify injustice is not one we should trust as a moral guide.

Invoking disgust in moral arguments is, in short, a morally fraught strategy, even when it succeeds. It doesn't succeed by illuminating the truth, but by playing on our tendency to confuse different kinds of aversion—a tendency that has been used historically to perpetuate injustice.

Manipulative vs. Truth-Oriented Persuasion

What is true of appeals to disgust is true of many other common strategies of argument: appeals to ridicule and flattery, straw-man objections that criticize distorted caricatures of opposing views rather than the views themselves, and ad hominem attack that target the person holding a view rather than the merits of the view. These strategies, like appeals to disgust, can often be effective in debates but are unreliable indicators of what is true and right and good.

Long ago, Plato argued that our goal in discussions should be to instruct rather than merely persuade.[3] The appeal to disgust is a good example of mere persuasion: it's a tactic that can be effective, but for reasons that have nothing to do with a propensity to expose the truth. If we love each other, we will care about how we debate one another. We won't try to trick each other with misleading strategies, especially ones that can as readily work as tools of oppression. We will, instead, rely on methods of persuasion that illuminate truth and encourage insight.

2. Beck, "On Love and the Yuck Factor," para. 17.
3. Plato, *Gorgias*, 453d–461b (pp. 237–38).

Strategies of *mere* persuasion typically rely on human psychological glitches such as our tendency to confuse visceral disgust with moral aversion. We have many such glitches, some of which evolved as cognitive shortcuts under conditions very different from those we face today. Consider an example. If you spend much time watching twenty-four-hour cable news, you'll hear frequent reports about child abductions. You'll learn the names and faces of the children and hear from their anguished parents. But here's the problem: in ancient societies you'd be exposed to such stimuli only if a *child-abduction epidemic* were ongoing in your community. And in many ways, our brains haven't changed much since those ancient times.

This is why, not long after our children were born, my wife stopped watching cable news. Although her rational mind knew there was no child-abduction epidemic in our town, the news reports produced the anxiety appropriate to such an epidemic. Her conscious mind told her the children were safe, but her instinctive mind—designed for a world without mass media—didn't believe it. On a visceral level, the news convinced her our children were in mortal peril.

Our glitchy brains make us ripe for psychological manipulation, and some have made a science of mastering manipulative techniques. When the advertisers for male body spray create an ad showing women throwing themselves at young men who use the spray, they aren't just telling a visual joke that's in poor taste. They're subconsciously shaping the expectations of their audience by exploiting mental tendencies suited to another time and place, a world where you'd repeatedly see such things only if they repeatedly happened. If a tribal adolescent boy saw a peer slap tree sap on his neck only to become the amorous target of every woman in the tribe, he'd make himself sticky with sap in no time. Adolescent boys today are stinking up junior high hallways because they have the same ancient brains.

It isn't just advertisers. Political careers are made or broken based on rhetorical skills that are more about flattery and fear-mongering than truth. But deliberately using these tactics to win debates fails to show the kind of respect for our neighbors that love demands. It's a case of what Kant called treating someone as a mere means. While all of us occasionally lapse into ways of arguing that are imperfect, we should strive to argue fairly, avoiding manipulation and in favor of arguments that aim to increase insight and understanding.

When we debate such issues as same-sex marriage, our objective should not be to defeat our opponent using any rhetorical means available. Even if we're convinced we have the truth on our side, our aim should be to spread that truth, not to win. And this means we should rely on means of persuasion that serve the truth—by honestly offering our reasons for thinking as we do. If those reasons are as strong as we think, our words may plant seeds of critical reflection, even in the face of defensive impulses. If our reasons are not as strong as we think, then perhaps sharing them with someone who isn't already convinced will help expose their weaknesses.

If we care more about truth than about winning, we won't want to win debates by deliberately confusing our opponents so much they miss the weaknesses in our arguments. If we care more about truth than about winning, we'll be grateful when our opponent shows us where we're wrong. If we care more about truth than about winning, we won't want to win if truth isn't on our side, and so won't rely on persuasive techniques that are as effective in the service of lies.

Anyone devoted to an ethic of love *should* care more about truth than about winning. If our aim is victory, right or wrong, what we care about is being a winner—and our neighbor becomes at best an obstacle and at worst a tool for stroking our egos. But if we enter a debate with the aim of explaining why we believe what we believe as clearly and powerfully as we can, our aim is to share with our neighbor something genuinely good: our experience, our research, our best thinking, our most compelling insights into a truth that transcends us.

To give our neighbors that good, it isn't enough to convince them of something that happens to be true. We do nothing to orient them toward truth if we simply play off their insecurities or push their emotional buttons or pull off some logical sleight-of-hand that makes an unsound argument seem sound. Even if they end up believing the truth, we've done nothing to help them see the truth. If the truth sets us free, it's *seeing* the truth that does this, not believing what happens to be true by some accident or trick that could as easily have led us to believe a lie.

Appeals to misleading emotions are one potent form of manipulation, and the appeal to disgust is just an example. Consider a more complex case involving shame, fear of ridicule, and the desire for belonging. Suppose I'm in a conversation about same-sex marriage, and one member of the group—call her Jane—shifts uncomfortably before asking how I deal with the biblical passages that condemn homosexuality. Imagine I respond as follows: "You don't actually think homosexuality is wrong, do you? I mean, that's ridiculous! This is the twenty-first century. You're smarter than that, right?"

Such a comment is designed to manipulate Jane with the fear of appearing a fool. It shuts down the open sharing of perspectives rather than inviting it. A hint of flattery—"you're smarter than that"—is really a basis for invoking the specter of public shame. More often than not, the person most influenced by such a tactic is not Jane but the fence-sitting bystander. Let's call him Joe. The more Joe witnesses those with a given view being shamed and silenced, the more he gravitates to the socially safest choice. At its worst this strategy can generate an arms-race of shame, where each side escalates the social costs of rejecting their view to ensure that siding with them is the socially safest choice.

While such manipulative use of emotional responses is inimical to debating issues in a spirit of love, this does not mean that our discussions and debates should be divorced from our feelings. Not every emotion is an irrelevant emotion. Sometimes a compelling story generates an emotional response because it has stimulated our capacity for empathy. We are suddenly in the shoes of another person, feeling what it's like to be them. Our eyes tear up because we vicariously feel their suffering. We smile because we suddenly understand their joy.

That kind of emotional resonance is crucial for loving our neighbors as ourselves. We can't make wise decisions about how to love our neighbors if we can't empathize and thereby discern the truth about what their situation is like for them. Sometimes, in disagreements and debates, what we have to offer is a way of looking at an issue that invites and encourages this sort of empathy. The emotions that result are hardly irrelevant, because they are *part* of the insight into truth. If I didn't feel some vicarious anguish at the story of a mother who can't produce enough milk to feed her baby, that means I'm not seeing the *truth* about her situation.

Likewise, there are some emotional responses *to* the experiences of others—compassion for those who suffer, anger at injustice—whose absence betrays a failure to appreciate what is going on. While our emotions are tricky, a strong intellectual tradition sees them as having cognitive content: emotions are *about* something.[4] Anger, for example, is a response to a perceived wrong. If injustice does not anger us, if it's just some fact about the world that our intellect says is wrong, then a part of us has failed to *see* that it's wrong. Our emotional selves have become blinded to the injustice, and so we aren't discerning the injustice with our whole selves. In discussion or debate, part of our aim might be to awaken others' *emotional* selves to a truth they have failed to see (even if their intellects have discerned it). In other words, we might not limit ourselves to an intellectually dispassionate case. We might look for an analogy or image or narrative that helps expose the *outrageousness* of the injustice. This is not an appeal to an irrelevant emotion. It's a way of helping the heart, and not just the mind, to see.

---

4. See, for example, Solomon, *Not Passion's Slave*; and Nussbaum, *Upheavals of Thought*.

But because emotions can be misled, it is best to wed such emotion-evoking arguments to more intellectual ones, to argue in a way that awakens the heart along *with* the mind, as opposed to awakening the heart alone.

Christian love, whatever else it is, is emotional. Loving our neighbors as ourselves entails feeling for them and with them. Any strategy of debate that treats these feelings as irrelevant is at odds with the very nature of Christian love. But truth-oriented arguments that extend to our emotional selves are not the same as manipulative ones that evoke emotions so as to confuse and obscure and misdirect. Love calls for the former, and rules out the latter.

Personal Attacks and Playing Nice

In heated debates, sometimes things get personal. Someone walks away feeling embarrassed or humiliated. At least sometimes, these hurt feelings result because someone in the debate has committed what logic and critical thinking texts call the "ad hominem fallacy": the practice of attacking the person who holds a view or advances an argument rather than criticizing the view or argument itself.

Usually, this rhetorical tactic does little to persuade the person under attack. Rather, it's about making that person look bad in the hope that onlookers will be less likely to take them seriously. One of the most common kinds of ad hominem attacks seeks to expose opponents as hypocrites. But a person's hypocrisy has little to do with whether their views are accurate. A serial adulterer who condemns adultery isn't wrong about adultery. The self-righteous finger-pointing of hypocrites is a moral failing, and the aim of such finger-pointing is often to distract from personal failures. But when the pot calls the kettle black, the pot is right about the kettle.

Consider some of the responses to Kim Davis, the Kentucky county clerk who refused to issue marriage licenses to same-sex couples. If we interpret her motives charitably, she appears to have been inspired by religious conviction. Based on her understanding of Christian teachings, she believed it would violate her moral obligations to materially participate in establishing same-sex marriages. And so Davis risked legal action and job loss for the sake of conscience. Some, such as gay commentator Dan Savage, have questioned whether this was in fact her motive, suggesting that it was instead about "cashing in" on "a big pile of sweet, sweet bigot money out there waiting for her."[5] And if the issue is whether Davis should be admired as a martyr for her faith, such questions of motive are relevant. But if the issue is

---

5. Savage, "And Now I Have to Say," para. 9.

whether her position on same-sex marriage is correct, questions of motive are beside the point.

Even less relevant is Davis's history of failed marriages, featuring multiple divorces and remarriages. Jesus does say in Scripture that those who divorce and remarry are guilty of adultery (Matt 19:4–9). Perhaps there is an inconsistency between her willingness to remarry after divorce and her unwillingness to issue same-sex marriage licenses; but this doesn't imply that her stance on same-sex marriage is wrong. Nor does it tell us when agents of the state need to set aside religious convictions for the sake of doing their jobs, and when they can be given space to exempt themselves from assigned tasks based on conscience. Many details—such as why she was previously divorced and when she became a Christian—are relevant for deciding whether her marital history undermines the view that conscience inspired her actions. But in my experience, those who brought this issue up on social media seemed decidedly disinterested in these details. It was more about relishing the personal attack, about slapping the "hypocrite" label on a visible public representative of a view they condemn.

I don't know much about Davis, but here is one interpretation of her checkered history and her refusal to issue same-sex marriage licenses: She had a turbulent life. She looked for meaning in all the wrong places, including a series of failed marriages. But then she experienced a religious conversion that gave her a stability and sense of purpose she'd never known. She started afresh, building her life—and a new marriage—on the bedrock of a faith wedded so deeply to conservative sexual teachings that she couldn't disentangle her life-saving faith from those teachings. And so, when the state asked her to issue a same-sex marriage license, she experienced that as a demand to betray the faith that had saved her. And so she refused.

If this is right, then painting her as a hypocritical serial divorcée for the sake of scoring points in a public debate fails to show the kind of compassion that love demands.

In many ways, ad hominem arguments are the rhetorical tactics most obviously at odds with the love ethic. Trying to win debates by making people look bad is about hurting others for the sake of personal gain. But we need to be careful not to accuse people of ad hominem attacks too broadly. If someone offers terrible arguments for harmful views, and I systematically demonstrate just how terrible the arguments are and just how harmful the views, this may have the effect of making the person look bad. But it's not an ad hominem attack. Ad hominem attacks try to make someone look bad in the hope that the negative associations will spill onto their words and ideas. If, by contrast, I expose their words and ideas as bad and this spills over onto the person standing behind them, I'm not guilty of an ad hominin attack.

Another important caveat has to do with matters of credibility. Sometimes, we have to decide whether to trust someone's word. In that case, it would be relevant that they're habitual liars. This fact doesn't tell us whether their claims in this case are false, but it does tell us that their testimony is not a good reason to believe. In the case of scientific researchers, we may need to decide whether to trust their research without having the expertise to evaluate it for ourselves. What if their findings conflict with the prevailing scientific consensus and inspire numerous critical responses? Are they breaking new ground that will change that consensus in time, and the backlash is just an expression of biased defensiveness? Or is their work untrustworthy? In cases like these, facts about the researcher—not only their credentials, but such things as allegiances and convictions that might compromise objectivity—become relevant.

In these cases where human feelings can be hurt—whether it is because we are sharing the bad news that someone's arguments are no good, or explaining why we don't attach much credibility to their authoritative claims—there is something to be said for being gentle. In part, this means creating a kind of distance between what we are criticizing and the person as a whole. This is what I try to do with my students as they make their initial forays into philosophical reasoning, and for me this is part of what it means to love them in the Christian sense. But is this always the best approach? What about when the Family Research Council uses its public platform to foment prejudice against gays and lesbians with woefully bad arguments? Should I take pains to distance them from their own bad arguments in order to protect them from having to take responsibility for their false witness against their gay and lesbian neighbors? Or should I call them out?

Doing the latter might be the best way to show love for my gay and lesbian neighbors. But there is another consideration in play as well. If, as I have argued, the Family Research Council makes unsound arguments that deliberately distort facts in the service of a divisive ideology, I *might* choose to focus solely on the merits of their arguments. And evidence that they are motivated by divisive ideology has no bearing as such on whether their arguments are sound. But it may have bearing on whether they are debating the issue in a loving way. And if part of my aim is to address what it means to love our gay and lesbian neighbors as ourselves, calling attention to those who betray the spirit of love in the way they debate the ethics of homosexuality isn't an ad hominem attack. Sometimes, calling people to task for their bad character—and making it thereby harder for them to hide from it or deny it—can be an act of love.

In debates, loving one another does not always mean being gentle or "nice." In the midst of disagreement, the Christian love ethic does not say we should "agree to disagree" in the sense of brushing over our disagreements and refusing to confront them. Nor does the Christian love ethic require us to "tolerate" opposing views in the sense of never taking steps to prove them wrong or strip them of their social influence. As we've seen, according to the love ethic, it isn't just loving motives that matter. Loving *acts* matter, too. And sometimes loving motives fail to culminate in loving acts because of mistaken beliefs. When that's true, there's a problem that needs to be fixed for the sake of the neighbors we're supposed to love.

And so if I think you're wrong about something significant, something that influences how you live in the world and how you treat your neighbors, I don't show love for you or those whose lives you affect by quietly tolerating your error. If I really think you are wrong, then out of love I ought to try to explain why. If I think your error runs deeper than a mistaken belief that's misdirecting your loving motives—if I think, instead, that love has been displaced by darker motives—I don't display a respect for the law of love by failing to point this out. And if I think many with loving motives have been misled by trusting an authority that's been feeding them falsehoods in the service of divisive ideology, exposing that may be a crucial act of love.

Love means favoring honest sharing over manipulative rhetoric. It does not mean adopting a polite tone at every turn. Sometimes a blunt statement is more honest and clear than a politely circumspect statement that obscures the point in an effort to be nice. But even if Christians aren't always "nice," they need to strive toward discourse that respects their opponent's dignity and cares more about truth than about winning.

Word Choice and the Spirit of Grace

In late September of 2016, as I was deep into the revising process for this book, a controversy erupted within the Society for Christian Philosophers. At one of their regional meetings, the eminent Christian philosopher, Richard Swinburne, gave a talk entitled, "Christian Moral Teaching on Sex, Family, and Life." Swinburne sent me the text of the talk. Its aim is to offer guidelines for philosophical reflection on the indicated teachings—and one of the topics addressed is homosexuality.

Swinburne begins his reflection on this topic by assuming that Christians have good grounds for thinking *that* God prohibits all homosexual acts, based on Scripture and tradition (not an assumption I share, and not one he defends in his brief remarks). But he also thinks there is no strong case for thinking that homosexual sex is intrinsically wrong—that is, wrong in itself. He is critical of natural law arguments that attempt to demonstrate such intrinsic wrongness.

But he thinks God might nevertheless have a reason to prohibit homosexual sex—and if God does prohibit it, such sex would be wrong for us based on the allegiance we owe to God. Swinburne sketches out a possible reason for such a prohibition. Homosexuality, he maintains, is a disability, since the loving relationships of gays and lesbians cannot lead to procreation. But while he concedes that homosexuality may become an "incurable condition" for many, he postulates that a strong and widespread social prohibition on gay sex could prevent the condition from arising in some who might be prone to it. Such a prohibition would have the good effect, then, of reducing the frequency of a disability.

Readers of this book will likely anticipate how I might object to this argument. While the causes of sexual orientation are poorly understood, homosexuality arises even amidst powerful social stigma. Hence, such stigma does not guarantee that none will be gay or lesbian. What it does do is ensure that gays and lesbians will face the hardships I've talked about, up to and including suicidal depression. We can't reliably compare the rates of homosexual orientation in societies accepting of homosexuality with those in societies that stigmatize it, since honest reporting will be repressed where stigma is high. So we can't know whether Swinburne's hypothesized "benefit" of a sweeping social prohibition is real. What we do know is that homosexuality is found in even the most repressive societies, and represents a small percentage of the population even in the most tolerant—so effects will at best be small. But suppose there *is* a small effect. Given the evidence from close attention to the lives of our gay and lesbian neighbors, the separation of the unitive and procreative ends of sex has a far less damaging impact on human life than lifelong exclusion from the goods of marriage, the lifelong social marginalization that goes with it, and a lifelong demand to wholly suppress one's sexuality whether one has the gift of celibacy or not. Given the anguished stories I have heard, it strikes me as wildly implausible that a God of love would favor such a trade-off and so issue a rigid prohibition on these grounds. It would be like supporting a public policy that marginally reduces the rate of deafness in society at the cost of making the lives of deaf people enormously more difficult—even driving some to suicidal despair.

But the controversy surrounding Swinburne's address did not turn on these kinds of objections. The controversy was sparked when a member of the audience—J. Edward Hackett—not only objected to Swinburne's remarks but published a blog post in which he called them "toxic." Central to his concern was Swinburne's use of the language of sickness—"disability," "incurable condition"—in a way he found dehumanizing.[6]

Hackett's comments invoked an unusual flurry of social media discussion among Christian philosophers. When the SCP President offered a statement of regret for hurt feelings, indicating that Swinburne's views do not necessarily represent the views of the society, and affirming the society's commitment to inclusiveness and diversity, this triggered another wave of vociferous commentary—including a demand that the SCP President apologize to Swinburne for issuing the statement.[7]

While all of this was going on, I had the chance to meet Swinburne for the first time. From the SCP conference, his next stop was the university where I teach. I welcomed him, had lunch and dinner with him, and had the honor to moderate one of his lectures and introduce him at another. The man I met was warm, gracious, thoughtful, and brilliant. Throughout his visit, I was receiving various social media invitations to join in the outrage against Swinburne's remarks. Instead, I tried to help him (without success) to figure out how to use his new phone.

Obviously, I do not agree with Swinburne's position on homosexuality. And the concerns Hackett raises about word choice are not trivial. To call a homosexual orientation a "disability" and an "incurable condition" is to evoke the notion of sickness and to relegate something as central as how a person loves to the status of a medical condition. When I first heard of this language choice, it made me cringe.

But it's important to notice something. When Swinburne calls homosexuality a disability, he is making a point similar to one I make in chapter 10 when I compare same-sex couple to infertile couples and note that for gays and lesbians the unitive and procreative ends of sex are separated. When he says homosexuality can become an incurable condition, he is conceding that many if not most gays and lesbians cannot be expected to change their orientation—a point I stress in chapter 4. He makes use of these claims in ways very different from how I use of them, but the issue here is not with the claims themselves but with the words he uses to express them. I would not use such language, because I know how it has been used to abuse sexual minorities. I know that many gays and lesbians have been kicked out of their parents' homes with the word "sick" ringing in their ears. I've held the hands of gay friends who were still scarred by abuse that was couched in the language of "sickness."

---

6. Hackett, "Richard Swinburne's Toxic Lecture," para. 4.

7. Feser, "Michael Rea Owes Richard Swinburne an Apology" (Sept. 26, 2016), http://edwardfeser.blogspot.com/2016/09/michael-rea-owes-richard-swinburne.html.

But someone lacking that sort of experience might have no idea how this word choice—especially when paired with a defense of the traditional Christian teaching—could stir up painful crud among gay and lesbian listeners. Underlying this word choice is the same issue I think of as the deepest problem with the substance of Swinburne's argument: it hasn't seriously reckoned with the lived experiences of our gay and lesbian neighbors. And unlike the abstract questions in analytic philosophy of religion or epistemology that have been the focus of Swinburne's career, Christian ethics demands such careful reckoning with human stories.

But the truth is that all of us are limited in whose stories we have heard, in what we have experienced and attended to with care. Swinburne displays the kind of lack of familiarity with the LGBT community that is unsurprising in an elderly Christian philosopher who has spent his career focused primarily on traditional questions in the analytic philosophy of religion, travels in circles where most gays and lesbians probably remain in the closet, and has not spent a long time considering these issues. Many if not most philosophers in his field spend more time obsessing about things like modal logic and probability theory than they do reflecting on how word choices are related to human feelings. While this is perhaps a human failing, all of us have failings and we need to treat each other with grace.

And this is the key point I want to make. Oblivious use of terms that hurt can easily inspire anger, and anger can energize meaningful discourse. But anger is volatile, and is most likely to inspire productive sharing and insight when it is paired with grace. Grace calls for recognizing the inevitability of human limitations and trying to help each other move past them rather than holding them against one another. And this means treating the oblivious use of hurtful words as an opportunity to share stories about why they hurt, not to repudiate and shame.[8]

I remember, years ago, being at a discussion on homosexuality and the church where I used the phrase "gay lifestyle." A gay man in the discussion explained the associations that term had for him and the reasons it grated so badly. I don't know how many times he'd made that point. Probably many, many times. But for me it was the first time. His sharing was personal. And I stopped using the term. I doubt things would've gone so smoothly if he'd said, instead, "How many times do I have to tell you people that there is no *#$@! gay lifestyle!"

I'm not saying that the words we use don't matter. What I'm suggesting is that we need to try to engage one another in a spirit of grace,

---

8. The knowing and malicious use of words that hurt is another matter. In such cases, repudiation and shame may be entirely fitting.

understanding where other people come from and trying to share our contrary insights and experiences honestly and directly, resisting the urge to repudiate and shame except when we encounter deliberate maliciousness. As a recent study showed, there are ways to inspire people to be less prejudiced against members of an "outgroup"—but it's not done by calling them bigots.[9]

If a spirit of grace should shape our response to those who express ideas or use language we find harmful, a similar point applies to Hackett. Hackett's response to Swinburne may not have been an ideal expression of grace. But the call to cultivate a spirit of grace extends not just to failures to choose the right words but also to failures to show the spirit of grace—especially in moments of deep hurt. The spirit of grace sees through the anger to the hurt that inspires it, and reaches for the compassionate response. As one friend recently pointed out to me, it is "a privilege to be able to rise above the emotions of being attacked."[10] Especially for those who are systematically subjected to social marginalization and abuse, demanding a gracious response to *one more straw on the back* can display a deep lack of empathy. The gracious response may, in these cases, be the proper work of allies.

A spirit of grace calls us to be sensitive enough to those we argue with to choose our words with care—to seek ways of making our points that don't open old wounds. This is part of what the concept of political correctness gets right. But all of us will fail in this endeavor. Sometimes it is too important to say what we need to say clearly and powerfully, and we don't know how to say it in a way that won't trigger hurt and anger. Sometimes we are just oblivious, because we don't know others' stories. Sometimes, swept up in a moment of outrage, our arguments include rhetorical excesses that don't illuminate truth. It is important to forgive these failures, since all of us have them. That is what the concept of political correctness gets wrong.

Because we are human, we fall short in manifold ways that come out when we debate issues we care deeply about. While a spirit of grace does not preclude us from pointing out these failures, it does require that we not attribute more to the failures than is really there—wicked motives where there is only ignorance, habitual hypocrisy when there is only a moment of passionate excess. Most importantly, while the spirit of grace does not call us to put up with unrepentant verbal abuse from our debate opponents, it does calls us to forgive inevitable lapses and missteps rather than using them as an excuse to escalate or walk away.

---

9. Broockman and Kalla, "Durably Reducing Transphobia," 220–21.

10. Jendi Reiter, personal correspondence.

Fallibility, Humility, and the Art of Listening

Although we are more likely to notice the shortcomings in our debate opponents, we inevitably have our own. This does not just mean we might make our point in an insensitive way. It also means we could wrong. We need to conduct our disagreements and discussions with the kind of humility that admits our own fallibility.

This does not preclude confidence. I am confident enough in my thoughts on same-sex marriage and Christian love *to write an entire book about it*. But I know that other Christians are equally confident that I'm wrong—confident enough to write books of their own. The mere existence of such opposing perspectives shouldn't be enough for anyone to give up their considered views or stop acting on them. But it should encourage us to approach ongoing discussions and debates in a way that acknowledges the dignity and humanity of our opponents and expresses an openness to being moved by their thoughts and experiences. We need to listen.

To be honest, I don't expect that Christian opponents of same-sex marriage will say something at this point that will force me to abandon my position. My views have been formed and refined through decades of discussion and reading and critical reflection, and I experienced dramatic shifts in perspective only during the early years of that process. But I also know from all those years that my opponents are continually making observations and arguments that force me to refine my perspective. Sometimes the most dramatic changes in perspective come from a series of small refinements over time. But even when that doesn't happen, if we listen to our opponents with care we are likely to grow.

We have no obligation to put up with abusive rhetoric that insults us or people we love. That is not what listening is about. It's about paying compassionate attention to sincere thoughts and arguments that reflect deeply held concerns, commitments, and values. It's about reaching beyond arguments and positions to the human feelings and needs that lie beneath. Such attention deepens understanding of where those who disagree with us are coming from and why. It may help us see precisely where they are misguided and how we can help them to discern the truth. Or it may help us see where we have been misguided and how our thinking must be revised.

Furthermore, authentic listening is sometimes the only path to finding *integrative* solutions to our conflicts—solutions that integrate the deepest values and needs of everyone involved. Put concretely, listening to conservative opponents of same-sex marriage may help me discern ways to stand up for my gay and lesbian neighbors without leaving my conservative neighbors feeling as if their integrity has been violated. It is one thing to argue that my conservative neighbors ought to support same-sex marriage, something else to endorse policies that require them, while they remain unconvinced, to provide photography services for a same-sex wedding.[11] It is one thing to argue that it would be harmful for a therapist to counsel a gay client in ways premised on the wrongness of homosexuality, another thing to implement professional standards of therapeutic service that force conservatives to either leave the profession or act contrary to their deepest convictions.[12]

Sometimes legal requirements may be the only way of protecting LGBT persons from systemic discrimination. But sometimes they result from a failure to appreciate alternatives—ones that become apparent only once we listen to one another with care. There may be insoluble dilemmas where someone will be trampled no matter what we do, but those motivated by love should make sure such dilemmas are more than just *apparent* before taking action. Authentic listening can help us do that.

But there is something intrinsic to listening that is more important than all of these beneficial effects. Love aims for fellowship, and listening that is sincere, compassionate, and empathetic is a crucial constituent of such fellowship. Fellowship exists when we share who we are with one another. Debate and disagreement do not preclude such fellowship unless we stop listening. Discussing our differences and wrestling with them is, in fact, a *way* to build fellowship if we do so in way that features both honest sharing and earnest listening. Where that happens, fellowship is possible even amidst deep disagreement.

Perhaps the most serious problem with personal attacks and put-downs lies in this: when I put you down I am not sharing myself with you, but rather encouraging you to close in on yourself and refuse to share with me. But the kind of niceness that avoids controversy is just as much an impediment to fellowship. If Christian love seeks fellowship, and if fellowship is about sharing ourselves with one another, we need to be prepared to have the hard conversations—at least when we are emotionally ready for them and sufficiently confident that the conversation will be defined more by grace than verbal abuse.

---

11. This example is, of course, inspired by an actual case. For a discussion of the case sympathetic to the photographer, see Conor Friedersdorf, "Refusing to Photograph a Gay Wedding."

12. For a discussion of this issue, see Cox, "When Religion and Sexual Orientation Collide."

Fallible Choices

Love in the face of disagreement is not just about pursuing difficult conversations in loving ways. Sometimes we need to act on our convictions, and we confront those with incompatible aims. It can be tempting to think that churches can just put off concrete action and policy decisions until disagreements have been resolved. But churches typically have a status quo—existing policies or practices, for example, that prohibit same-sex union ceremonies and bar the ordination of partnered gays and lesbians. To refuse to act amounts to preserving that status quo. If a congregation says they will make no decisions pending further study, what they are saying is that they will continue to operate, for the time being, as if same-sex relationships are immoral and partnered gays and lesbians are unfit for ministry. To delay in the name of more prayerful discourse is to decide, albeit temporarily, in favor of the conservative position.

For the sake of stability and cohesion, it can be wise to delay changes pending study and deliberative reflection. Valuable institutions, built over generations, can be destroyed overnight by hasty changes. This is the deep truth behind conservatism. But if consensus does not emerge from deliberative processes, indefinite delay for the sake of more study, more conversation, more prayerful reflection, only *looks* as if it preserves neutrality amidst conflict. In reality, it always favors the status quo. And when the issue is about real people crying out against the harms or injustices the status quo purportedly inflicts, such a default presumption is suspect. If the harms or injustices are real, then love demands action on behalf of victims, not indefinite study motivated by fear of change. Sometimes, inertia and habit keep us from addressing injustice. This is the deep truth behind progressivism.

What is true on the collective level is also true for individuals. We are fallible, and awareness of that fallibility should inspire us to study and reflect before we act. But we can always read another book or have another conversation. If the issue is the purported harms of the status quo, every delay carries the risk of allowing real harms to continue unopposed. It isn't easy to find the virtue between the extremes of timidity and impetuousness. There is no formula. But at some point, deciding not to act against the status quo amounts to deciding in favor of it. At that point of decision, it is no longer impetuous to act, and continued delay is just timidity.

The problem is that sometimes disagreement lives on beyond that point, and those who are neither impetuous nor timid find themselves facing off, each side equally convinced they have the truth. While loving conversation and debate should continue even then, there is also a sense in which the debate is now over. We have moved into a new phase where actions are being taken and policies implemented, where the status quo is being changed or reaffirmed. Those who have voiced their concerns about harm or injustice are getting their answer, and some in the community remain convinced it is the wrong one.

What does love look like in the midst of such a conflict? In my experience with the ELCA's struggle over same-sex unions and the ordination of partnered gay and lesbian clergy, I have had wrestled with this question both from the side of those who have lost a contested policy decision and from the side of those who have won. When I first became convinced that the traditional condemnation of homosexuality was harming my gay and lesbian neighbors, I had to confront significant policy realities that were in place within the ELCA: the policy that excluded partnered gays and lesbians from being ordained, and the lack of any policy for recognizing same-sex partnerships. While the ELCA had not explicitly prohibited pastors from performing holy union ceremonies (as, for example, was done by the United Methodist Church), the ELCA Conference of Bishops issued the following statement on such unions in 1993:

> We, as the Conference of Bishops of the Evangelical Lutheran Church in America, recognize that there is basis neither in Scripture nor tradition for the establishment of an official ceremony by this church for the blessing of a homosexual relationship. We, therefore, do not approve such a ceremony as an official action of this church's ministry. Nevertheless, we express trust in and will continue to dialogue with those pastors and congregations who are in ministry with gay and lesbian persons, and affirm their desire to explore the best ways to provide pastoral care for all to whom they minister.[13]

Because the ELCA expected all unmarried clergy to abstain from sex, and because there was no recognized same-sex marriage within the ELCA, partnered gays and lesbians were denied ordination. Even if their relationships looked like marriages—monogamous, faithful, loving, and cemented by public vows—they were not seen as marriages. But they *were* seen as sexual. And so all such partnered gays and lesbians were judged in violation of the chastity requirement for single clergy. The church founded by Luther, who lashed out remorselessly against the Catholic requirement for clerical celibacy, effectively required this very thing of gay and lesbian clergy.

From my perspective, this policy created a double-standard that turned gays and lesbians into second-class citizens. Those who felt the call to ministry were forced to make a choice their heterosexual peers didn't

---

13. Task Force for ELCA Studies on Sexuality, *Journey Together Faithfully*, 5.

face, between pursuing that call and pursuing (or preserving) an intimate life partnership. After much study, discussion, and reflection, I reached a point where I knew I had to act. I became active in efforts to change existing policies, and when the ELCA voted not to change them at the 2005 ELCA General Assembly, I faced a difficult choice.

Some of my friends, including my gay best friend, were committed to remaining part of the ELCA, to continue to fight for change from within. But I felt called to something else. There were, of course, entire congregations that defied the rules, ordaining partnered gay clergy and performing holy union ceremonies. Had I lived anywhere near them, I might have joined their civil disobedience. But a solitary lay person is not positioned to disobey these policies. And so, instead, I wrote a manifesto of sorts, distributed it widely, and left the ELCA. My family and I drove an hour to and from church every Sunday to attend one of the few open and affirming churches in the state, a United Church of Christ congregation. Spiritually, I missed the ELCA's theology and liturgy. Personally, I missed my congregation. But I made a symbolic stand: ELCA policies did not make *me* a second-class citizens, but it did that to its LGBT members. To stand in solidarity with them, at the margins of the church, I chose to exclude myself.

Four years later, those who had remained within the church to continue the struggle found a way to prevail. The ELCA established a denominational policy that allowed individual congregations to decide for themselves whether they would perform union ceremonies and ordain partnered gay and lesbian clergy. And so I returned home even as others were leaving in protest.

There were those in 2005 who questioned my decision to leave. How could I claim to love my opponents in a policy dispute if I was willing break fellowship with them over it? Wasn't the decision to walk away a decision to withhold who I am from them, a decision to make *agreeing with me* a condition for fellowship? Moreover, how could I really claim to love gay and lesbian Lutherans if I left the ELCA instead of staying to fight for their equality?

Similar challenges might be leveled against those conservative Lutherans who left the ELCA in 2009, when the new policies were implemented. When, if ever, is walking away from your faith community consistent with Christian love?

I can only answer for myself, but I think my answer may apply to others. Let me use the language of a dinner table, set with a feast, to explain my decision. For me, the feast the church offers should be radically inclusive in its invitation. Basic safety might impose some regrettable limits, but the feast we offer is not ours but Christ's, who died for the sins of the world. The feast is the feast of God, who gave life not because we deserved it, but as a free gift.

While I belonged to the ELCA, it was *my* table. And for me, love requires that I welcome my LGBT neighbors to my table on an equal footing with my straight neighbors—for all the reasons I've talked about here. I could not justify inviting them to anything less than the full feast. In walking away from that table, my aim was not to withhold my welcome from those who chose to stay, but to find a table I could call my own that fully welcomed my gay and lesbian neighbors. I walked away not because I was closing off fellowship from those I was leaving behind, but because I wanted to extend a welcome, an openness to fellowship, that was wider and more inclusive than what I could honestly offer so long as I remained at that other table and called it mine.

The story of those who walked away in 2009 can't be precisely the same, since they were leaving in favor of tables with a more restrictive welcome. But that doesn't mean their decision wasn't made with a sincerity of conscience that deserves my respect. They were convinced that the new policies would do harm both to them and to the wider ELCA community. Perhaps the way to put it is this: they believed the feast had been poisoned. They walked away from the table, not to close off fellowship with those they left behind, but so that when they invited others to join them at their table, they wouldn't be inviting them to what they took to be a poisoned feast.

Because I believe that offering an unqualified welcome to gays and lesbians does not poison the feast but only makes the whole feast more broadly available, my loving motives call me to extend that unqualified welcome at my table. Those same motives call me to find a new table if I cannot extend that welcome where I am. They call me to explain my position to those who disagree, to listen to their case, and to explain fairly and thoughtfully where I find it uncompelling. But they don't call me to support policies that effectively demand opponents to act against their conscience—to serve what they honestly believe is poisoned food—*unless my LGBT neighbors would otherwise go hungry.*

The ELCA policy that is now in place allows individual congregations to perform same-sex holy union ceremonies and to ordain clergy who are in such unions. The policy does not foist partnered gay and lesbian clergy on unreceptive congregations or require a member of the clergy to perform these same-sex union ceremonies if their individual conscience has yet to be convinced that doing so is loving and right. As such, the policy allows congregations to extend the kind of welcome that I think love demands, while at the same time respecting the freedom of conscience of those who dissent. But such a policy is not uncontroversial. For those gay and lesbian

Lutherans who live in a small town, with only one Lutheran church for hundreds of miles, this policy might well mean they are denied the full feast. The only way to avoid this outcome would be to enact a policy requiring some clergy and congregations to act against their conscience. Those unwilling to do so would then have to choose between leaving the ELCA or engaging in civil disobedience.

For anyone with my convictions, this situation creates a dilemma not easily or immediately solved. When it comes to issuing mandates to clergy, we need to keep in mind that clergy have voluntarily adopted a role that makes them an agent of a broader communion. They have agreed to represent the values of that communion in their role as agent. This fact means the broader communion *does* have the authority to establish rules and impose requirements on clergy acting in their role. If they cannot in good conscience follow those rules or meet those requirements, they are free to leave that role. But a decision to stay but to defy the rules through civil disobedience can also be a choice that displays integrity—if that decision is rooted in continued allegiance to the community's deepest values combined with the pastor's conviction that the rules do not reflect those values.

For example, a United Methodist pastor may be convinced that the current ban on same-sex holy unions is at odds with the most fundamental values of the Methodist communion, and so may be convinced that performing union ceremonies in defiance of the rules shows greater fidelity to the values they've been called to represent than does obedience.[14] Likewise, were the ELCA to require pastors to be willing to preside over same-sex holy unions on the same terms under which they are willing to perform heterosexual marriage ceremonies, a pastor who sincerely believes that the ELCA's deepest values conflict with the rule could, with integrity, disobey rather than resign.

Some clergy, however, may find themselves at odds with the values of the church at a deeper or more systemic level. In that case, they can no longer in good faith act as agents of the church. The point is that while love calls us to respect the freedom of conscience of our neighbors, such respect does not mean the church cannot impose requirements on clergy—since clergy are agents of the church. Similar constraints apply to agents of the state, which raises serious questions about whether it was appropriate for Kim Davis to refuse to issue marriage licenses while still seeking to function in her assigned role—at least if we accept the argument that precluding same-sex marriage discriminates against gays and lesbians in a way at odds

---

14. This is in fact how United Methodist Pastor Jimmy Creech approached matters. See his memoir, *Adam's Gift*.

with the state's obligations. Since the state depends on its agents to carry out its obligations, it must impose on them requirements reflecting those obligations. Citizens whose values preclude meeting the requirements of a given role are thus not qualified for the role, even if, as private citizens, they should remain free to express their values unconstrained by coercive laws.

At the same time, the state's interest in accommodating freedom of conscience might justify reassigning someone like Kim Davis to a job that doesn't require her to act against her conscience, rather than simply firing her. If this is true for the state, it is even more true for a community organized around the law of love, when its agent face a crisis of conscience.

It is often difficult, however, to enact policies that reflect the right balance between respect for individual conscience and fidelity to community values. I doubt there is a formula for it. There will always be some who are dissatisfied with existing policies, who don't think the best solution is to leave either the church or their role, and whose dissatisfaction is serious enough that it would defy their integrity to simply shut up and put up. In these cases, nonviolent protest and civil disobedience, combined with an ongoing commitment to civil discourse, have an important role to play as a resource for loving protest, one that needs to be appreciated by those both in and out of power.

Loving protest of established policies and practices sets aside violent methods, not only because of the harm these methods inflict, but for the same reason loving discourse sets aside manipulative rhetoric: *violence is blind to truth*. Violence can be just as effectively used to silence prophets as it can be to silence liars. If they see themselves as bearers of a truth not represented in current policies, both love and humility call them to act in the service of that truth in a way that sets aside violence. For those who find themselves in power, both love and humility call them to design policies that make room for conscientious objection within the limits set by community values. And where this balance is hard to strike, both love and humility call for an approach to enforcing policies that makes civil disobedience and nonviolent protest living options. This does not mean there should be no costs for breaking rules, but it does mean that the penalty for disobedience must not be designed to push those with dissenting convictions into silent submission.

All the while, loving discourse must continue. In a world where it has become painfully simple to "unfriend" those whose views and ideas offend us, this may be the hardest thing we are called to do: to listen to our opponents with the sincerity that reaches for the human being behind the words, even when we find their perspective dangerously harmful, even when their arguments are riddled with manipulative rhetoric, even when they violate our rules or punish us for doing what our deepest values demand.

We are limited creatures. We cannot endlessly endure verbal put-downs and abuse. We may not be able to pursue fellowship with every opponent, every person who rejects our perspective. But when we encounter opponents who are committed to honest sharing and listening and who pursue their cause in consciously nonviolent ways, what we face is not a threat but an opportunity. To the extent that we can both respond to and create such opportunities, we will nurture fellowship across the gap of conflict and disagreement, building the bridges of love that can help transform a polarized world into the kingdom of God.

Or perhaps it is better to say that when we are *open* to such fellowship, when we stop fighting it, God works in us and through us to bring about the triumph of love.

Bibliography

Abel, Gene G., et al. "Self-Reported Sex Crimes of Nonincarcerated Paraphiliacs." *Journal of Interpersonal Violence* 2 (1987) 3–25.
Amato, Paul R. "The Well-Being of Children with Gay and Lesbian Parents." *Social Science Research* 41 (2012) 771–74.
American Psychological Association. "Guidelines for Psychological Practice with Lesbian, Gay, and Bisexual Clients." *American Psychologist* 67 (2012) 10–42.
———. *Lesbian and Gay Parenting*. Washington, DC: American Psychological Association, 2005.
American Psychological Association Task Force on Appropriate Therapeutic Responses to Sexual Orientation. *Report of the American Psychological Association Task Force on Appropriate Therapeutic Responses to Sexual Orientation*. Washington, DC: American Psychological Association, 2009. Online: http://www.apa.org/pi/lgbc/publications/therapeutic-resp.html.
Anderson, Ryan T. "Four Responses to the 'What about Infertility?' Argument." *The Catholic World Report* (August 17, 2015). Online: http://www.catholicworldreport.com/Item/4101/four_responses_to_the_what_about_infertility_argument.aspx.
Anyabwile, Thabiti. "The Importance of Your Gag Reflex When Discussing Homosexuality and 'Gay Marriage.'" *The Gospel Coalition*. Online: https://blogs.thegospelcoalition.org/thabitianyabwile/2013/08/19/the-importance-of-your-gag-reflex-when-discussing-homosexuality-and-gay-marriage.
Aquinas, Thomas. *Summa Theologica*. Benziger Bros. ed. Translated by Fathers of the English Dominican Province. Westminster, MD: Christian Classics, 1947. Online: http://www.ccel.org/ccel/aquinas/summa.html.
Aristotle. *Nicomachean Ethics*. Translated by W. D. Ross. In *The Basic Works of Aristotle*, edited by Richard McKeon, 927–1112. New York: Random House, 1941.
———. *Politics*. Translated by Benjamin Jowett. In *The Basic Works of Aristotle*, edited by Richard McKeon, 1114–1316. New York: Random House, 1941.
Aulen, Gustav. *The Faith of the Christian Church*. Translated by Eric H. Wahlstron and G. Everett Arden. Philadelphia: Muhlenberg, 1948.
Bagemihl, Bruce. *Biological Exuberance: Animal Homosexuality and Natural Diversity*. New York: St. Martin's, 1999.

Bailey, Michael, et al. "Heritable Factors Influence Sexual Orientation in Women." *Archives of General Psychiatry* 50 (1993) 217–23.

Barnes, David M., and Ilan H. Meyer. "Religious Affiliation, Internalized Homophobia, and Mental Health in Lesbians, Gay Men, and Bisexuals." *American Journal of Orthopsychiatry* 82 (2012) 505–15.

Barrett, C. K. *A Commentary on the First Epistle to the Corinthians.* 2nd ed. London, A. & C. Black, 1971.

Barth, Karl. *The Doctrine of Reconciliation.* Vol. 4.2 of *Church Dogmatics.* Edited by G. W. Bromiley and T. F. Torrance. Translated by G. W. Bromiley. Edinburgh: T. & T. Clark, 1958.

Barton, Bernadette. "'Abomination'—Life as a Bible Belt Gay." *Journal of Homosexuality* 57 (2010) 465–84.

Bauer, Jack J., et al. "Narrative Identity and Eudaimonic Well-Being." *Journal of Happiness Studies* 9 (2008) 81–104.

Baumeister, Roy F. "Gender Differences in Erotic Plasticity: The Female Sex Drive as Socially Flexible and Responsive." *Psychological Bulletin* 126 (2000) 347–74.

Beck, Richard. "On Love and the Yuck Factor." *Experimental Theology.* Online: http://experimentaltheology.blogspot.com/2013/08/on-love-and-yuck-factor.html.

Becker, John M. "Exclusive: Dr. Robert Spitzer Apologizes to Gay Community for Infamous 'Ex-Gay' Study." *Truth Wins Out* (April 25, 2012). Online: http://www.truthwinsout.org/news/2012/04/24542.

Besen, Wayne. "Yale Professor Says James Dobson 'Cherry Picked' His Research in *Time Magazine* Article." *Truth Wins Out* (December 14, 2006). Online: https://www.truthwinsout.org/pressrelease/2006/12/38.

Birkett, Michelle, and Dorothy L. Espelage. "LGB and Questioning Students in Schools: The Moderating Effects of Homophobic Bullying and School Climate on Negative Outcomes." *Journal of Youth and Adolescence* 38 (2009) 989–1000.

Bork, Robert H. "The Necessary Amendment." *First Things* 145 (2004) 17–21.

Boswell, John. *Christianity, Social Tolerance, and Homosexuality: Gay People in Western Europe from the Beginning of the Christian Era to the Fourteenth Century.* Chicago: University of Chicago Press, 1980.

Boyarin, Daniel. "Are There Any Jews in 'The History of Sexuality'?" *Journal of the History of Sexuality* 5 (1995) 333–55.

Broockman, David, and Joshua Kalla. "Durably Reducing Transphobia: A Field Experiment on Door-to-Door Canvassing." *Science* 352 (2016) 220–24.

Bussee, Michael. "Statement of Apology by Former EXODUS Leaders." *Beyond Ex-Gay.* Online: http://www.beyondexgay.com/article/busseeapology.html.

Carey, Benedict. "Psychiatry Giant Sorry for Backing Gay 'Cure.'" *New York Times* (May 18, 2012). Online: http://www.nytimes.com/2012/05/19/health/dr-robert-l-spitzer-noted-psychiatrist-apologizes-for-study-on-gay-cure.html.

"The Case for Gay Marriage," *The Economist* 370 (Feb 26, 2004) 9.

Catechism of the Catholic Church. 2nd ed. Washington, DC: Libreria Editrice Vaticana—USCCB, 2000.

Cheadle, Harry. "After Gay Marriage, Why Not Polygamy?" *Vice* (March 29, 2013). Online: http://www.vice.com/read/after-gay-marriage-why-not-polygamy.

Church Council of the Evangelical Lutheran Church in America. *A Message on Sexuality: Some Common Convictions.* Chicago: Evangelical Lutheran Church in America, 1996. Online: http://download.elca.org/ELCA%20Resource%20 Repository/SexualitySM.pdf.

Conzelmann, Hanz. *1 Corinthians: A Commentary on the First Epistle to the Corinthians*. Translated by James W. Leitch. Philadelphia: Fortress, 1975.

Coontz, Stephanie. *Marriage, a History: How Love Conquered Marriage*. New York: Penguin, 2005.

Corvino, John. "Are Gay Parents Really Worse For Children? How a New Study Gets Everything Wrong." *New Republic* (June 10, 2012). Online: https://newrepublic.com/article/104001/john-corvino-are-gay-parents-really-worse-children-how-new-study-gets-everything.

Corvino, John, and Maggie Gallagher. *Debating Same-Sex Marriage*. Oxford: Oxford University Press, 2012.

Countryman, L. William. *Dirt, Greed, and Sex: Sexual Ethics in the New Testament and Their Implications for Today*. Minneapolis: Fortress, 2007.

Cox, Michelle R. "When Religion and Sexual Orientation Collide." *Counseling Today* (May 1, 2013). Online: http://ct.counseling.org/2013/05/when-religion-and-sexual-orientation-collide.

Cranfield, Charles E. B. *A Critical and Exegetical Commentary on the Epistle to the Romans*. Edinburgh: T. & T. Clark, 1975.

Creech, Jimmy. *Adam's Gift: A Memoir of a Pastor's Calling to Defy the Church's Persecution of Lesbians and Gays*. Durham, NC: Duke University Press, 2011.

Crouch, Simon R., et al. "Parent-Reported Measures of Child Health and Wellbeing in Same-Sex Parent Families: A Cross-Sectional Survey." *BMC Public Health* 14 (2014). Online: http://www.biomedcentral.com/1471-2458/14/635.

Dailey, Timothy J. *The Slippery Slope of Same-Sex Marriage*. Washington, DC: Family Research Council, 2004. Online: http://downloads.frc.org/EF/EF04C51.pdf.

Deitrich, Jonathan. "The Lessons of the Law: Same-Sex Marriage and *Baehr v Lewin*." *Marquette Law Review* 78 (1994) 121–52.

Diamond, Lisa M. *Sexual Fluidity: Understanding Women's Love and Desire*. Cambridge: Harvard University Press, 2008.

Dobson, James C. *Bringing Up Boys*. Carol Stream, IL: Tyndale House, 2001.

———. "Q&A—Attitudes of Christians Towards Homosexuality." *Dobson Digital Library*. Online: http://www.dobsonlibrary.com/resource/article/80220f7b-b3d3-4be7-9538-1c41f65d5751.

———. "Two Mommies is One Too Many." *Time* 168 (December 18, 2006) 123.

Drescher, Jack, and Kenneth J. Zucker, eds. *Ex-Gay Research: Analyzing the Spitzer Study and Its Relation to Science, Religion, Politics, and Culture*. Binghamton, NY: Harrington, 2006.

Eckert, Elke D., et al. "Homosexuality in Monozygotic Twins Reared Apart." *British Journal of Psychiatry* 148 (1986) 421–25.

Edwards, David. "Karen Santorum: Gays 'Vilify' My Husband" *Raw Story* (January 16, 2012). Online: http://www.rawstory.com/2012/01/karen-santorum-gays-vilify-my-husband.

Ehrman, Bart. *Jesus, Interrupted*. New York: HarperOne, 2009.

Ellis, Lee, and Bruce M. Wagemann. "The Religiosity of Mothers and Their Offspring as Related to the Offspring's Sex and Sexual Orientation." *Adolescence* 28 (1993) 227–34.

Erickson, W. D., et al. "Behavior Patterns of Child Molesters." *Archives of Sexual Behavior* 17 (1988) 77–86.

Espelage, Dorothy L., et al. "Homophobic Teasing, Psychological Outcomes, and Sexual Orientation among High School Students: What Influence Do Parents and Schools Have?" *School Psychology Review* 37 (2008) 202–16.

Emery, Erin. "Family Arrested at Rally." *Denver Post* (May 3, 2005). Online: http://www.denverpost.com/ci_2702491.

Ettelbrick, Paula. "Since When is Marriage a Path to Liberation?" In *Same-Sex Marriage: Pro and Con,* edited by Andrew Sullivan, 122–28. New York: Vintage, 2004.

Eversley, Melanie. "Post-Election Spate of Hate Crimes Worse Than Post-9/11, Experts Say." *USA Today* (November 14, 2016). Online: http://www.usatoday.com/story/news/2016/11/12/post-election-spate-hate-crimes-worse-than-post-911-experts-say/93681294.

Fee, Gordon. *The First Epistle to the Corinthians.* Grand Rapids: Eerdmans, 1987.

Feser, Edward. "Michael Rea Owes Richard Swinburne an Apology." Online: http://edwardfeser.blogspot.com/2016/09/michael-rea-owes-richard-swinburne.html.

———. "The Role of Nature in Sexual Ethics." *National Catholic Bioethics Quarterly* 13 (2013) 69–76.

Finnis, John. "Homosexual Conduct Is Wrong." In *Morality in Practice,* 8th ed., edited by James P. Sterba and Peter Bornschein, 499–501. Boston: Wadsworth, 2013.

Franks, Kent, et al. "Exploration of Death Anxiety as a Function of Religious Variables in Gay Men with and without AIDS." *OMEGA-Journal of Death and Dying* 22 (1991) 43–50.

Freund, Kurt. "Should Homosexuality Arouse Therapeutic Concern?" *Journal of Homosexuality* 2 (1977) 235–40.

Freund, Kurt, et al. "Heterosexuality, Homosexuality, and Erotic Age Preference." *Journal of Sex Research* 26 (1989) 107–17.

Freund, Kurt, and Robin J. Watson. "The Proportions of Heterosexual and Homosexual Pedophiles among Sex Offenders against Children: An Exploratory Study." *Journal of Sex and Marital Therapy* 18 (1992) 34–43.

Friedersdorf, Conor. "Refusing to Photograph a Gay Wedding Isn't Hateful." *The Atlantic* (March 5, 2014). Online: http://www.theatlantic.com/politics/archive/2014/03/refusing-to-photograph-a-gay-wedding-isnt-hateful/284224.

Gagnon, Robert A. J. *The Bible and Homosexual Practice: Texts and Hermeneutics.* Nashville: Abingdon, 2001.

Gallie, W. B. "Essentially Contested Concepts." *Proceedings of the Aristotelian Society* 56 (1956) 167–98.

Garver, Newton. "Violence and Social Order." In *Philosophy of Law, Politics, and Society: Proceedings of the 12th International Wittgenstein Symposium,* edited by Ota Weinberger et al., 218–23. Vienna: Holder-Pichler-Tempsky, 1988.

Gates, Gary J. "How Many People Are Lesbian, Gay, Bisexual, and Transgender?" Los Angeles: Williams Institute, 2011. Online: http://williamsinstitute.law.ucla.edu/wp-content/uploads/Gates-How-Many-People-LGBT-Apr-2011.pdf.

Gonsiorek, John C. "The Empirical Basis for the Demise of the Illness Model of Homosexuality." In *Homosexuality: Research Implications for Public Policy,* edited by John C. Gonsiorek and James D. Weinrich, 115–36. Newbury Park, CA: Sage, 1991.

Gonsiorek, John C., and James R. Rudolph. "Homosexual Identity: Coming Out and Other Developmental Events." In *Homosexuality: Research Implications for Public Policy*, edited by John C. Gonsiorek and James D. Weinrich, 161–76. Newbury Park, CA: Sage, 1991.

Graham-Murray, James. *A History of Morals*. London: Library 33, 1966.

Green, Richard. "The Immutability of (Homo)Sexual Orientation: Behavioral Science Implications for a Constitutional (Legal) Analysis." *Journal of Psychiatry and Law* 16 (1988) 537–75.

Greenburg, Steven. *Wrestling with God and Man: Homosexuality in the Jewish Tradition*. Madison, WI: University of Wisconsin Press, 2004.

Grenz, Stanley J. *Theology for the Community of God*. Grand Rapids: Eerdmans, 1997.

Griffith, Robert. "Homosexuality, A Christian Perspective." Online: http://www.glow.cc/lead/griffith.htm.

Groth, A. Nicholas, and H. Jean Birnbaum. "Adult Sexual Orientation and Attraction to Underage Persons." *Archives of Sexual Behavior*, 7 (1978) 175–81.

Gudorf, Christine E. *Body, Sex, and Pleasure: Reconstructing Christian Sexual Ethics*. Cleveland, OH: Pilgrim, 1994.

———. *Victimization: Examining Christian Complicity*. Philadelphia: Trinity, 1992.

Gutierrez, N. "Customer Review: I was a subject in this study." Amazon.com review of Jones and Yarhouse, *Ex-Gays?* Online: https://www.amazon.com/review/R1GMKDM1DDLZHK/ref=cm_cr_dp_title?ie=UTF8&ASIN=083082846X&channel=detail-glance&nodeID=283155&store=books.

Hackett, J. Edward. "Richard Swinburne's Toxic Lecture on Christian Morality at the Midwest Meeting of the Society of Christian Philosophers." *Philosophical Percolations* (Sept. 24, 2016). Online: http://www.philpercs.com/2016/09/richard-swinburnes-toxic-lecture-on-christian-morality-at-the-midwest-meeting-of-the-society-of-chri.html.

Haldeman, Douglas C. "Sexual Orientation Conversion Therapy for Gay Men and Lesbians: A Scientific Examination." In *Homosexuality: Research Implications for Public Policy*, edited by John C. Gonsiorek and James D. Weinrich, 149–60. Newbury Park, CA: Sage, 1991.

Harris, J. Irene, et al. "Religious Attitudes, Internalized Homophobia, and Identity in Gay and Lesbian Adults." *Journal of Gay & Lesbian Mental Health* 12 (2008) 205–25.

Helminiak, Daniel. *What the Bible Really Says about Homosexuality*. Tajique, NM: Alamo Square, 2000.

Herek, Gregory. "Facts about Homosexuality and Child Molestation." Online: http://psc.dss.ucdavis.edu/rainbow/HTML/facts_molestation.html.

Hershberger, Scott L., and Anthony R. D'Augelli. "The Impact of Victimization on the Mental Health and Suicidality of Lesbian, Gay, and Bisexual Youths." *Developmental Psychology* 31 (1995) 65–74.

Hill, Wesley. *Spiritual Friendship: Finding Love in the Church as a Celibate Gay Christian*. Grand Rapids: Brazos, 2015.

Hines, Melissa. "Prenatal Endocrine Influences on Sexual Orientation and on Sexually Differentiated Childhood Behavior." *Frontiers in Neuroendocrinology* 32 (2011) 170–82.

Hines, Melissa, et al. "Androgen and Psychosexual Development: Core Gender Identity, Sexual Orientation, and Recalled Gender Role Behavior in Women and Men with Congenital Adrenal Hyperplasia (CAH)." *Journal of Sex Research* 41 (2004) 75–81.

Hooker, Evelyn. "The Adjustment of the Male Overt Homosexual." *Journal of Projective Techniques* 21 (1957) 18–31.

Hsiao, Timothy. "A Defense of the Perverted Faculty Argument against Homosexual Sex." *Heythrop* 56 (2015) 751–58.

Human Rights Campaign. "Professional Organizations on LGBTQ Parenting." Online: http://www.hrc.org/resources/professional-organizations-on-lgbt-parenting.

Jenny, Carole, et al. "Are Children at Risk for Sexual Abuse by Homosexuals?" *Pediatrics* 94 (1994) 41–44.

Jones, Mike. "The Problem We Have With Sin." *Tulsa World* (July 17, 2016). Online: http://www.tulsaworld.com/opinion/mikejones/mike-jones-the-problem-we-have-with-sin/article_db85dbfe-bc1a-5520-97ce-929833c6e6a5.html.

Jones, Stanton L. "The Loving Opposition." *Christianity Today* 37 (1993) 19–25.

Jones, Stanton L., and Mark A. Yarhouse. *Ex-Gays? A Longitudinal Study of Religiously Mediated Change in Sexual Orientation.* Downers Grove, IL: IVP, 2007.

———. *Homosexuality: The Use of Scientific Research in the Church's Moral Debate.* Downers Grove, IL: IVP, 2000.

———. "A Longitudinal Study of Attempted Religiously Mediated Sexual Orientation Change." *Journal of Sex and Marital Therapy* 37 (2011) 404–27.

Kant, Immanuel. *The Fundamental Principles of the Metaphysics of Morals.* Translated by Thomas K. Abbott. New York: Macmillan, 1949.

———. *The Metaphysics of Morals.* Translated by Mary Gregor. Cambridge: Cambridge University Press, 1991.

Kendler, Kenneth S., et al. "Sexual Orientation in a U.S. National Sample of Twin and Nontwin Sibling Pairs." *American Journal of Psychiatry* 157 (2000) 1843–46.

King Jr., Martin Luther. "Advice for Living." *Ebony* 13 (November 1957) 106.

Kirk, Alan. "'Love Your Enemies,' the Golden Rule, and Ancient Reciprocity (Luke 6:27–35)." *Journal of Biblical Literature* 122 (2003) 667–86.

Klein, Fritz. *The Bisexual Option.* 2nd ed. New York: Routledge, 2013.

Koester, Craig. "The Bible and Sexual Boundaries," *Lutheran Quarterly* 7 (1993) 375–90.

Kralovec, Karl, et al. "Religion and Suicide Risk in Lesbian, Gay, and Bisexual Austrians." *Journal of Religion and Health* 53 (2014) 413–23.

Kronen, John, and Eric Reitan. "Homosexuality, Misogyny, and God's Plan." *Faith and Philosophy* 16 (1999) 213–32.

Kurtz, Stanley. "Beyond Gay Marriage." *The Weekly Standard* 8 (August 4/11, 2003) 26–33.

Kuyper, Lisette, and Floor Bakker. *De Houding ten Opzichte van Homoseksualiteit* (Acceptance of Homosexuality in the Netherlands). The Haag: Sociaal Cultureel Planbureau, 2006.

Landsbaum, Claire. "Every One of Donald Trump's Cabinet Picks So Far Opposes LGBT Rights." *New York Magazine* (November 30, 2016). Online: http://nymag.com/thecut/2016/11/so-far-every-member-of-trumps-cabinet-opposes-lgbt-rights.html.

Lenz, Ryan. "NARTH Becomes Main Source for Anti-Gay 'Junk Science.'" *The Intelligence Report* (Spring 2012). Online: https://www.splcenter.org/fighting-hate/intelligence-report/2012/narth-becomes-main-source-anti-gay-%E2%80%98junk-science%E2%80%99.

LeVay, Simon. "A Difference in Hypothalamic Structure between Heterosexual and Homosexual Men." *Science* 253 (1992) 1034–37.

Lewis, C. S. *Collected Letters, Vol. III: Narnia, Cambridge, and Joy 1950–1963*. Edited by Walter Hooper. New York: Harper Collins, 2007.

———. *Reflections on the Psalms*. San Diego: Harcourt, 1986.

Lotze, Hermann. *Outlines of Practical Philosophy: Dictated Portions of the Lectures of Hermann Lotze*. Translated by George T. Ladd. Boston: Ginn & Company, 1885.

Lutes, Jeff. *A False Focus on the Family*. Lynchburg, VA: Soulforce, n.d. Online: https://www.scribd.com/document/16099510/A-False-Focus-on-My-Family.

Luther, Martin. "How Christians Should Regard Moses." In *Luther's Works Volume 35: Word and Sacrament 1*, edited by E. Theodore Bachmann, 161–74. Translated by E. Theodore Bachmann. Philadelphia, Muhlenberg, 1960.

———. "Preface to the Epistles of St. James and St. Jude." In *Luther's Works Volume 35: Word and Sacrament 1*, edited by E. Theodore Bachmann, 395–98. Translated by Charles M. Jacobs and E. Theodore Bachmann. Philadelphia: Muhlenberg, 1960.

———. "Preface to the New Testament." In *Luther's Works Volume 35: Word and Sacrament 1*, edited by E. Theodore Bachmann, 357–62. Translated by Charles M. Jacobs and E. Theodore Bachmann. Philadelphia: Muhlenberg, 1960.

———. "Preface to the Old Testament." In *Luther's Works Volume 35: Word and Sacrament 1*, edited by E. Theodore Bachmann, 235–51. Translated by Charles M. Jacobs and E. Theodore Bachmann. Philadelphia: Muhlenberg, 1960.

MacDonald, George. *Unspoken Sermons*. London: Alexander Strahan, 1867.

Mahaffy, Kimberly A. "Cognitive Dissonance and Its Resolution: A Study of Lesbian Christians." *Journal for the Scientific Study of Religion* 35 (1996) 392–402.

Malick, David E. "The Condemnation of Homosexuality in 1 Corinthians 6:9." *Bibliotheca Sacra* 150 (1993) 479–92.

———. "The Condemnation of Homosexuality in Romans 1:26–27," *Bibliotheca Sacra* 150 (1993) 327–40.

Malyon, Alan K. "Biphasic Aspects of Homosexual Identity Formation." *Psychotherapy: Theory, Research, and Practice* 19 (1982) 335–40.

———. "The Homosexual Adolescent: Developmental Issues and Social Bias." *Child Welfare* 60 (1981) 321–30.

———. "Psychotherapeutic Implications of Internalized Homophobia in Gay Men." *Journal of Homosexuality* 7 (1982) 59–69.

Mandell, Nina. "GOP Presidential Candidate Rick Santorum Says Gay Community is Waging Jihad on Him." *New York Daily News* (August 29, 2011). Online: http://www.nydailynews.com/news/politics/gop-presidential-candidate-rick-santorum-gay-community-waging-jihad-article-1.944678.

Martin, A. Damien, and Emery S. Hetrick. "The Stigmatization of the Gay and Lesbian Adolescent." *Journal of Homosexuality* 15 (1988) 163–83.

Martin, Dale. *Sex and the Single Savior*. Louisville, KY: Westminster/John Knox, 2006.

Mehta, Herman. "Christian Pastor Celebrates Nightclub Massacre: 'There's 50 Less Pedophiles in This World.'" *Friendly Atheist*. Online: http://www.patheos.com/blogs/friendlyatheist/2016/06/12/christian-pastor-celebrates-nightclub-massacre-theres-50-less-pedophiles-in-this-world.

Meyer, Ilan H., and Laura Dean. "Internalized Homophobia, Intimacy, and Sexual Behavior among Gay and Bisexual Men." In *Stigma and Sexual Orientation: Understanding Prejudice against Lesbians, Gay Men, and Bisexuals*, edited by Gregory M. Herek, 160–86. Thousand Oaks, CA: Sage, 1998.

Michaelson, Jay. *God vs. Gay? The Religious Case for Equality*. Boston: Beacon, 2011.

Milner, Catharine. "The Tate Values Excrement More Highly than Gold." *The Telegraph* (June 30, 2002). Online: http://www.telegraph.co.uk/news/uknews/1398798/The-Tate-values-excrement-more-highly-than-gold.html.

Moore, Kristen Anderson, et al. "Marriage from a Child's Perspective: How Does Family Structure Affect Children, and What Can We Do about It?" *Child Trends Research Brief* (June 2002) 1–8.

Morrow, Susan L., and A. Lee Beckstead. "Conversion Therapies for Same-Sex Attracted Clients in Religious Conflict: Context, Predisposing Factors, Experiences, and Implications for Therapy." *The Counseling Psychologist* 32 (2004) 641–50.

Muehlenberg, Bill. "SCOTUS Declares War on Marriage and Family." *BarbWire* (June 26, 2015). Online: http://barbwire.com/2015/06/26/scotus-declares-war-on-marriage-and-family.

Munoz-Plaza, Corrine, et al. "Lesbian, Gay, Bisexual and Transgender Students: Perceived Social Support in the High School Environment." *High School Journal* 85 (2002) 52–63.

Needham, Belinda L., and Erika L. Austin. "Sexual Orientation, Parental Support, and Health During the Transition to Young Adulthood." *Journal of Youth and Adolescence* 39 (2010) 1189–98.

Nestingen, James A. "Is There a Law? Lutheranism and Homosexual Practice." Lecture. *American Lutheran Publicity Bureau Conference on Christian Sexuality*, Kansas City, MO, October 2002. Published as "The Lutheran Reformation and Homosexual Practice." In *Christian Sexuality: Normative and Pastoral Principles*, edited by Russell E. Saltzmann, 18–37. Minneapolis: Kirk House, 2003.

Netherlands Institute for Social Research. "Acceptance of Homosexuality in the Netherlands." Summary of Kuyper and Bakker, *De Houding ten Opzichte van Homoseksualiteit*. Online: http://www.scp.nl/english/Publications/Summaries_by_year/Summaries_2006/Acceptance_of_homosexuality_in_the_Netherlands/Acceptance_of_homosexuality_in_the_Netherlands.

Nissinen, Martti. *Homoeroticism in the Biblical World: A Historical Perspective*. Minneapolis: Fortress, 1998.

Nussbaum, Martha C. *Upheavals of Thought: The Intelligence of Emotions*. Cambridge: Cambridge University Press, 2001.

Nygren, Anders. *Agape and Eros*. Translated by Philip S. Watson. Philadelphia: Westminster, 1953.

Olyan, Saul. "'And with a Man You Shall Not Lie the Lying Down of a Woman': On the Meaning and Significance of Leviticus 18:22 and 20:13." *Journal of the History of Sexuality* 5 (1994) 179–206.

Paris, Jenell Williams. *The End of Sexual Identity: Why Sex Is Too Important to Define Who We Are*. Downers Grove, IL: IVP, 2011.

Parsons, Jeffrey T., et al. "Alternatives to Monogamy Among Gay Male Couples in a Community Survey: Implications for Mental Health and Sexual Risk." *Archives of Sexual Behavior* 42 (2013) 303–12.

Pilgrim's Light Ministries. "Homosexuality and Loving Your Neighbor as Yourself." *Pilgrim's Light for the Path.* Online: https://pilgrimslight.wordpress.com/2012/05/18/homosexuality-and-loving-your-neighbor-as-yourself/ (accessed 10/3/16).

Pillard, Richard C. "Sexual Orientation and Mental Disorder." *Psychiatric Annals* 18 (1988) 52–56.

Piper, John. "The Tornado, the Lutherans, and Homosexuality." *Desiring God* (August 19, 2009). Online: http://www.desiringgod.org/articles/the-tornado-the-lutherans-and-homosexuality.

Plato. *Gorgias*. Translated by W. D. Woodhead. In *The Collected Dialogues of Plato*, edited by Edith Hamilton and Huntington Cairns, 229–307. Princeton: Princeton University Press, 1961.

Post, Stephen. "Disinterested Benevolence: An American Debate over the Nature of Christian Love." *Journal of Religious Ethics* 14 (1986) 356–68.

Proulx, Annie. *Brokeback Mountain.* New York: Scribner, 2005.

Putnam, Frank M. "Ten-Year Research Update Review: Child Sexual Abuse." *Journal of the American Academy of Child and Adolescent Psychiatry* 42 (2003) 269–78.

Ramsey, Paul. *Basic Christian Ethics.* New York: Scribner's Sons, 1950.

Rauch, Jonathan. "For Better or Worse?" *The New Republic* 214 (May 6, 1996) 18–23.

———. "Who Needs Marriage?" In *Beyond Queer: Challenging Gay Left Orthodoxy*, edited by Bruce Bawer, 296–313. New York: Free, 1996.

Regnerus, Mark. "How Different are the Adult Children of Parents Who Have Same-Sex Relationships? Findings from the New Family Structures Study." *Social Science Research* 41 (2012) 752–70.

Reitan, Eric. "Gay Suicide and the Ethic of Love: A Progressive Christian Response." *The Humanist* 71 (2011) 24–27. Original published in *Religion Dispatches* (October 18, 2010). Online: http://religiondispatches.org/gay-suicide-and-the-ethic-of-love-a-progressive-christian-response.

———. "Moving the Goalposts: The Challenge of Philosophical Engagement with the Public God Debates." *Philo* 13 (2010) 80–93.

———. "Rape as an Essentially Contested Concept." *Hypatia* 16 (2001) 43–66.

Richie, Cristina. "An Argument against the Use of the Words 'Homosexual' in English Translations of the Bible." *Heythrop Journal* 51 (2010) 723–29.

Ritter, Kathleen Y., and Anthony I. Terndrup. *Handbook of Affirmative Psychotherapy with Lesbians and Gay Men.* New York: Guilford, 2002.

Rivers, Ian. "The Bullying of Sexual Minorities at School: Its Nature and Long-Term Correlates." *Educational and Child Psychology* 18 (2001) 32–46.

———. "Recollections of Bullying at School and Their Long-Term Implications for Lesbians, Gay Men, and Bisexuals." *Crisis: Journal of Crisis Intervention and Suicide Prevention* 25 (2004) 169–75.

———. "Social Exclusion, Absenteeism and Sexual Minority Youth." *Support for Learning* 15 (2000) 13–18.

Rodriguez, Eric M., and Suzanne C. Ouellette. "Gay and Lesbian Christians: Homosexual and Religious Identity Integration in the Members and Participants of a Gay-Positive Church." *Journal for the Scientific Study of Religion* 39 (2000) 333–47.

Rosenbaum, Janet Elise. "Patient Teenagers? A Comparison of the Sexual Behavior of Virginity Pledgers and Matched Nonpledgers." *Pediatrics* 123 (2009) 110–20.

Rostand, Edmond. *Cyrano de Bergerac*. New York: Heritage, 1954.
Sanders, Geoff, and Lynda Ross-Field. "Neuropsychological Development of Cognitive Abilities: A New Research Strategy and Some Preliminary Evidence for a Sexual Orientation Model." *International Journal of Neuroscience* 36 (1987) 1–16.
———. "Sexual Orientation, Cognitive Abilities and Cerebral Asymmetry: A Review and a Hypothesis Tested." *Italian Journal of Zoology* 20 (1986) 459–70.
Sarantakos, Soterios. "Children in Three Contexts: Family, Education, and Social Development." *Children Australia* 21 (1996) 23–31.
Sartre, Jean-Paul. *Anti-Semite and Jew*. New York: Schocken, 1948.
Savage, Dan. "And Now I Have to Say Something about Kim Davis." *The Stranger* (Sept. 1, 2015). Online: http://www.thestranger.com/blogs/slog/2015/09/01/22793219/i-suppose-i-should-say-something-about-kim-davis.
Scanzoni, Letha, and Virginia Ramey Mollenkott. *Is the Homosexual My Neighbor? Another Christian View*. San Francisco: Harper and Row, 1980.
Schuck, Kelly D., and Becky J. Liddle. "Religious Conflicts Experienced by Lesbian, Gay, and Bisexual Individuals." *Journal of Gay & Lesbian Psychotherapy* 5 (2001) 63–82.
Schultheis, Emily. "Trump Talks to '60 Minutes' about Same-Sex Marriage, Abortion and the Supreme Court." *CBS News* (November 13, 2016). Online: http://www.cbsnews.com/news/trump-promises-pro-life-justices-supreme-court-same-sex-marriage.
Scroggs, Robin. *The New Testament and Homosexuality: Contextual Background for Contemporary Debate*. Philadelphia: Fortress, 1983.
Scutti, Susan. "Asexuality Is Real: How a Rare Orientation Helps Us Understand Human Sexuality." *Medical Daily* (May 7, 2015). Online: http://www.medicaldaily.com/asexuality-real-how-rare-orientation-helps-us-understand-human-sexuality-332346.
Secretary of the Evangelical Lutheran Church in America. *2013 Pre-Assembly Report: Report of the Secretary*. Chicago: Evangelical Lutheran Church in America, 2013. Online: http://download.elca.org/ELCA%20Resource%20Repository/02c_Report_of_the_Secretary_20130806e.pdf.
Singer, Jefferson A. "Narrative Identity and Meaning Making Across the Adult Lifespan." *Journal of Personality* 72 (2004) 437–60.
Smith, Janet. *Humanae Vitae: A Generation Later*. Washington, DC: Catholic University of America Press, 1991.
Soccio, Douglas J., and Vincent E. Barry. *Practical Logic: An Antidote for Uncritical Thinking*. 5th ed. Fort Worth, TX: Harcourt Brace, 1998.
Solomon, Robert C. *Not Passion's Slave: Emotions and Choice*. Oxford: Oxford University Press, 2003.
Southern Baptist Convention. "Resolution on Homosexual Marriage." New Orleans: Southern Baptist Convention, 1996. Online: http://www.sbc.net/resolutions/614/resolution-on-homosexual-marriage.
Spitzer, Robert L. "Can Some Gay Men and Lesbians Change Their Sexual Orientation? 200 Subjects Reporting a Change from Homosexual to Heterosexual Orientation." *Archives of Sexual Behavior* 32 (2003) 403–17.
Sprigg, Peter. *The Top Ten Myths about Homosexuality*. Washington, DC: Family Research Council, 2010.

Stuhlmacher, Peter. *Paul's Letter to the Romans.* Louisville, KY: Westminster/John Knox, 1994.

Sullivan, Andrew. "It's the Gays' Fault." *The Atlantic* (April 1, 2010). Online: http://www.theatlantic.com/daily-dish/archive/2010/04/its-the-gays-fault/188648.

———. "The M-Word." In *Same-Sex Marriage: Pro and Con*, edited by Andrew Sullivan, 322–24. New York: Vintage, 2004.

Suppe, Frederick. "Curing Homosexuality." In *Philosophy and Sex*, 2nd ed., edited by Robert Baker and Frederick Elliston, 391–420. Buffalo, NY: Prometheus, 1994.

Swinburne, Richard. "Christian Moral Teaching on Sex, Family and Life." Lecture. *Midwest Society of Christian Philosophers Conference*, Springfield, MO, September 23, 2016.

Tashman, Brian. "Conservatives React to Gay Marriage Ruling: End Times! God's Wrath! Civil War!" *Right Wing Watch* (June 26, 2015). Online: http://www.rightwingwatch.org/post/conservatives-react-to-gay-marriage-ruling-end-times-gods-wrath-civil-war.

Task Force for ELCA Studies on Sexuality. *Journey Together Faithfully, Part Two: The Church and Homosexuality.* Chicago: Evangelical Lutheran Church in America, 2003.

Thacker, Paul D. "Fighting a Distortion of Research." *Inside Higher Ed* (Dec. 19, 2006). Online: https://www.insidehighered.com/news/2006/12/19/gilligan.

Throckmorten, Warren. "The Jones and Yarhouse Study: What Does it Mean?" Patheos: Warren Throckmorten (October 27, 2011). Online: http://www.patheos.com/blogs/warrenthrockmorton/2011/10/27/the-jones-and-yarhouse-study-what-does-it-mean.

Thurston, Thomas. "Leviticus 18:22 and the Prohibitions of Homosexual Acts." In *Homophobia and the Judeo-Christian Tradition*, edited by Michael L. Stemmeler and J. Michael Clark, 7–24. Dallas: Monument, 1990.

Townsley, Jeramy. "Paul, the Goddess Religions, and Queer Sects: Romans 1:23–28." *Journal of Biblical Literature* 130 (2011) 707–28.

Treadway, Leo, and John Yoakam. "Creating a Safer School Environment for Lesbian and Gay Students." *Journal of School Health* 62 (1992) 352–57.

United States Conference of Catholic Bishops. *Marriage: Love and Life in the Divine Plan.* Washington, DC: United State Conference of Catholic Bishops, 2009. Online: http://www.usccb.org/issues-and-action/marriage-and-family/marriage/love-and-life/upload/pastoral-letter-marriage-love-and-life-in-the-divine-plan.pdf.

Volf, Miroslav. *Exclusion and Embrace: A Theological Exploration of Identity, Otherness, and Reconciliation.* Nashville: Abingdon, 1996.

Wagner, Glenn, et al. "Integration of One's Religion and Homosexuality: A Weapon against Internalized Homophobia?" *Journal of Homosexuality* 26 (1994) 91–110.

Walsh, Jerome T. "Leviticus 18:22 and 20:13: Who is Doing What to Whom?" *Journal of Biblical Literature* 120 (2001) 201–9.

Walsh, Matt. "There is No Such Thing as Marriage Equality." *The Blaze* (Oct 7, 2014). Online: http://www.theblaze.com/contributions/there-is-no-such-thing-as-marriage-equality.

Walton, Gerald. "'Fag Church': Men Who Integrate Gay and Christian Identities." *Journal of Homosexuality* 51 (2006) 1–17.

Warwick, Ian, et al. "Sexuality and Mental Health Promotion: Lesbian and Gay Young People." In *Young People and Mental Health*, edited by Peter Aggleton et al., 131–46. Chichester, UK: Wiley and Sons, 2000.

Wattles, Jeffrey. "Levels of Meaning in the Golden Rule." *Journal of Religious Ethics* 15 (1987) 106–29.

Wedgwood, Ralph. "The Meaning of Same-Sex Marriage." *New York Times* (May 24, 2012). Online: http://opinionator.blogs.nytimes.com/2012/05/24/marriage-meaning-and-equality/?_r=0.

Weeks, Jeffrey. "Questions of Identity." In *The Cultural Construction of Sexuality*, edited by Pat Caplan, 31–51. London: Routledge, 1989.

Weil, Simone. *Gravity and Grace*. Translated by Arthur Wills. Lincoln, NE: University of Nebraska Press, 1997.

Whitam, Frederick L., et al. "Homosexual Orientation in Twins: A Report on 61 Pairs and Three Triplet Sets." *Archives of Sexual Behavior* 22 (1993) 187–206.

White, Mel. *Holy Terror: Lies the Christian Right Tells Us to Deny Gay Equality*. Reprint ed. New York: Magnus, 2012.

———. *Stranger at the Gate: To Be Gay and Christian in America*. New York: Penguin, 1995.

Wilson, Douglas. *Fidelity: How To Be a One-Woman Man*. Moscow, ID: Canon, 1999.

Wink, Walter. *Engaging the Powers: Discernment and Resistance in a World of Domination*. Minneapolis: Fortress, 1992.

———. "Homosexuality and the Bible." In *Homosexuality and Christian Faith*, edited by Walter Wink, 33–49. Minneapolis: Fortress, 1999.

Yip, Andrew K. T. "Leaving the Church to Keep My Faith: The Lived Experiences of Non-Heterosexual Christians." In *Joining and Leaving Religion: Research Perspectives*, edited by Leslie J. Frances and Yaacov J. Katz, 129–45. Leominster, UK: Gracewing, 2000.

Index

abstinence, 79–80, 81–82, 117, 133, 136–37, 140. *See also* celibacy
ad hominem fallacy, 247, 251–53
adoption, 94–95
adultery, 9, 84, 85, 251, 252
agape, xv, 44, 50–51
allies, ix, 15–16, 17, 258
Amato, Paul, 93–94
American Academy of Child and Adolescent Psychology, 92
American Academy of Pediatrics, 92
American Psychoanalytic Association, 92
American Psychological Association (APA), 66, 67, 73, 74–75, 82, 92, 93
American Family Association, 3
Andersen, Hans Christian, 8
Anderson, Ryan, 210
Anderson, Steven, 97, 102
anthropocentrism, 201
Anti-Semite and Jew (Sartre), 22–23, 24, 25
anti-semitism, 23, 24, 25, 30, 102
Anyabwile, Thabiti, 244–45
Aquinas, Thomas, 4, 47 n16, 197, 199–200
argument
   and emotion, 249–51, 253
   fairness in, 57, 104, 105, 247, 248–49, 251, 252, 253
   fallacious, 224–25, 226, 247, 251

Aristotle, 109, 189, 199–200
Arkes, Hadley, 235–36
art, 152–54
Aulen, Gustav, 43–44

Baehr v Lewin, 227
Barth, Karl, 44
Barton, Bernadette, 132–33
Beck, Richard, 247
beloved community, 49, 55, 110, 139, 163, 234
Bible. *See* Scripture
bestiality, 20, 197, 225
bisexuality, ix, 24, 25, 66, 67, 68, 70, 75, 76, 82, 85–86, 98, 100, 142, 197, 231
Bork, Robert, 223, 225, 226, 227
Boswell, John, 180
Bringing Up Boys (Dobson), 27–28
"Brokeback Mountain" (Proulx), 80
bullying, 6, 20, 82, 83, 86, 89
Bussee, Michael, 76–77

celibacy, 76, 79, 80–81, 136, 146, 187, 218, 262. *See also* gift of celibacy.
child molestation, 28, 91–92, 97–105, 132, 140. *See also* pedophilia.
Child Welfare League of America, 92
Christ, xi, 3, 11, 19, 22, 39, 44, 51, 52, 53, 54, 55, 56, 58, 62, 129, 130, 131, 134, 140, 155, 162, 178, 186,

Christ *(continued)* 187, 188, 192, 193, 196, 263. *See also* Jesus
Christian love
  and abuse, 50, 53, 56, 90
  acts vs motives, 58, 117–18, 254
  antithetical to ideologies of division/hate/othering, 13, 17–18, 29, 30, 31, 32, 33, 54, 102, 243
  and attention, xvi, 16–17, 48–49, 62, 120–22, 259
  and conflict, 57, 244, 262–67
  and the crucifixion, 35, 51–57
  and debate/disagreement, 33, 144, 244, 247–51, 252, 261
  and emotions, 109, 251
  and empathy, 16–17, 48–49, 120
  of enemies, xv, 39, 45, 54, 234
  and fallibility, 58–59, 259, 261
  and fellowship, 11, 38, 39–40, 41, 49–50, 55, 57, 260, 263–64, 267
  and God's love, 24, 30, 43–44, 50–51
  and the Golden Rule, 120–21
  and hatred of sin, 8, 21–22, 107–9, 110, 112–13, 116–17, 118–20, 122–23, 138
  and identity, 125, 139, 146–47
  and listening, xvi, 8, 16, 57, 139, 140, 146, 259–60
  and love of God, 42–43, 44
  and marriage, 9–10, 116–17, 149, 150, 159, 162–65, 168, 169–70, 218, 226, 229–30, 233–34, 236
  and mutuality, 49–50, 52
  and natural law, 198, 201–2, 204, 205, 214, 215, 218, 222
  vs niceness 253–53
  and obedience to God, 44–45
  redemptive power of, 54
  and repudiating evil, 56, 57, 58
  and respect for value, 50–51
  and sacrificial suffering, 52–53, 54
  and science, 62–66
  and Scripture, 174–75, 176, 177, 183–84, 188–89, 192, 194–96
  self-giving, 44–45
  and self-love, 42, 47, 60
  unconditional nature of, xv, 50, 51, 54, 234
  universal scope of, 45–48
  and violence, xvii, 55–57, 59, 202, 266
Christian pacifism, 202, 217
civil disobedience, 263, 265–66
complementarity of the sexes, 204, 214–18
conjugal love, 205, 206, 208, 209, 210, 211
contraceptives 160, 203
conversion therapy, 5, 71, 72, 73. *See also* ex-gay ministries, reparative therapy, SOCE
Coontz, Stephanie, 150–52
Corvino, John, 94, 96
costly discipleship, 53, 114, 116, 137, 138, 140, 142, 146, 172, 175
Countryman, L. William, 180
cross, xv, 35, 42, 43, 51–57. *See also* crucifixion
crucifixion, 35, 54, 56
culture, secular, 2–3, 9, 14, 243
Cyrano de Bergerac (Rostand), 125–26, 128, 139

Davis, Kim, 251–52, 265, 266
discrimination, 2, 31, 82, 88, 126, 227–30, 231, 233, 238, 260
disgust, 13, 17, 21, 244–47, 248, 249
divine commands, 44, 45
divine revelation, 175, 179, 192–93, 196, 202, 230
Dobson, James, 26–29, 30, 33, 92–93, 108
domestic violence, 53

Ehrman, Bart, 190
The End of Sexual Identity (Paris), 31–32, 129
eros, 44
essentially contested concepts, 152–55, 166
Ettelbrick, Paula, 13
Evangelical Lutheran Church in America (ELCA), 1, 2, 3, 10, 11, 160, 161, 262, 263, 264, 265

ex-ex-gays, 76
ex-gay ministries, 70, 73, 74, 76–77, 112, 113, 132, 134–35, 136–37, 142, 144, 173. *See also* conversion therapy, reparative therapy, SOCE
Ex-Gays? (Jones and Yarhouse), 74
Exodus International, 76–77, 132. *See also* ex-gay ministries

faith, xv, xvi, 3, 4, 10, 11, 31, 114, 116, 121, 133–34, 135, 141, 143, 144, 145, 146, 192, 220, 221, 252
fallibility, 58, 59, 159, 176, 193, 259, 261
Family Research Council, 28, 64, 72, 82, 91, 97, 102, 108, 223, 225, 253
fellowship, 11, 31, 33, 40, 42, 49–50, 51, 55, 57, 60, 115, 118, 142, 260, 263–64, 267
feminism, 52, 167
Feser, Edward, 199, 203–4, 213–14, 218–19
Fidelity: What It Means to Be a One-Woman Man (Wilson), 166
Focus on the Family, 26–27, 29–30
free will, 176
freedom of conscience, 264–266
Freund, Kurt, 71–72
friendship, 4, 8, 21, 49, 50, 53, 234, 238, 246
  platonic, 80, 239, 241–42
  spiritual, 80, 173
  with God, 47 n16

Gagnon. Robert, 176
Gallie, W. D., 152–53
Gandhi, Mahatma, 29, 59
Garver, Newton, 154
genocide, 176, 247
gift of celibacy, 80–81, 82, 89, 131, 137, 173, 255. *See also* celibacy
Gilligan, Carol, 92–93
God's love, 19, 30, 43, 44, 45, 51, 136, 155, 209
God's will, 44, 47, 159, 174, 178, 193, 220

Golden Rule, 26, 120–21
Good Samaritan, 17, 45, 48
gospel, 39, 53, 192, 196
Gospel Coalition, 244
grace, 10, 11, 13, 24, 112, 135, 146, 162, 163, 220, 233, 234, 257–58, 260
Grenz, Stanley, 44
Griffith, Robert, 111–12, 116
Gudorf, Christine, 52–53, 114

Harrington, Zach, 20
hate crimes, x
hell, 21, 122, 132, 142–43
Herek, Gregory, 97, 98
heterosexist neglect, 88, 89
heterosexual privilege, 29, 65, 115–16
heterosexual order, 184–86, 188–89
Hill, Wesley, 80
HIV/AIDS, 21, 77, 140, 221, 229
Holiness Code, 178
homosexual orientation/homosexuality
  causes of, 20, 65–66
  change of. *See* conversion therapy, ex-gay ministries, reparative therapy, Sexual Orientation Change Efforts (SOCE)
  and choice, 25, 61, 63–64, 66, 68, 70, 126, 229
  effects of condemnation/stigma, 5–7, 10, 15, 16, 22, 25–26, 32, 37, 78–79, 83–87, 90, 103–4, 111, 114–15, 122–23, 126–27, 129, 131, 136–37, 138–39, 142, 170, 171–73, 221, 255
  definition of, 67
  and disability, 255–56
  and discrimination, 229, 231
  and hedonistic self-gratification, 3, 69, 205
  and heterosexual marriage, 70, 72, 78, 96, 135, 140, 142, 171, 185
  and identity, 24, 31, 128–31, 138, 139
  and integration with Christian faith, 114, 128, 133–34, 135, 140, 145–46

homosexual orientation/homosexuality *(continued)*
　and mental health, 5, 64, 73, 81–83, 87–89, 117, 126–27
　and natural law, 199, 205, 218–19, 221–22
　and othering, 31
　and parenting, 28, 64, 91, 92–96
　and pedophilia, 20, 28, 64, 90–91, 97–105, 108
　and Scripture, 177, 182
homophobia, 21, 132, 169
　internalized, 82, 86 n. 14 & 15, 87, 145
Hsiao, Timothy, 199, 210, 212–13
Humanae Vitae: A Generation Later (Smith), 203
Humanist (magazine), 20
hypocrisy, 251–52, 258

ideologies of division/hate, x, 13, 17, 22–24, 29, 30, 31, 32, 33, 34, 102, 108, 112, 116, 243, 253, 254
identity, xvi, 124–26, 128–29, 138, 229
　Christian, 129, 130, 131, 134
　dissonance, 133
　integration, 133–34, 137, 145, 146
　and race, 84, 128, 139
　self-affirming, 138–39, 173, 220
　self-rejecting, 138–39, 219, 220, 221
　sexual, 13, 24, 31, 32, 67, 68, 70, 75, 76, 127–31, 146
idolatry, 180, 181, 183
Illig, Anita Wagner, 224
incest, 20, 223, 224, 225, 230, 236–42
inerrancy/inerrantism, 175–76, 179, 187 n36, 189–94, 195, 196
infidelity, 9, 113
inseperability of natural ends of sex, 206–14
InterVarsity Christian Fellowship, 21
Israel, 178, 179, 180

Jesus, xi, xv, 10, 16, 17, 32, 42, 45, 51, 52, 53, 54, 55, 56, 60, 111, 112, 120, 134, 178, 179, 184, 190, 192, 196, 252. *See also* Christ.

Jones, Mike, 107–8
Jones, Stanton, 63, 74–76, 77, 79, 112–16, 134, 137, 140–43, 144, 145, 146, 186–88, 189
junk science, 73

Kant, Immanuel, 46, 161, 162, 248
King, Martin Luther Jr., 29, 49, 59
kingdom of God, 49, 55, 57, 187, 202, 218, 267
Koester, Craig, 184–85, 214
Kronen, John, 169, 186
Ku Klux Klan, 15
Kurtz, Stanley, 223, 224, 225, 227

Lewis, C.S., 193
liberation theology, 52
The Little Match Girl (Anderson), 8
Lotze, Hermann, 237–38, 240
"The Loving Opposition" (Jones), 112, 140
Luther, Martin, 10, 178, 192, 220, 262

MacDonald, George, 192–93
Malick, David, 188
marginalization, 10, 13, 17, 82, 88, 89, 102, 164, 172, 229, 255, 258
marriage
　and abuse/exploitation, 9, 91, 234, 165–66, 168, 169, 234
　and complementarity, 214–18
　as constraint on sexuality, 8, 12, 14, 182
　criticism of, 12–13, 165–66
　definition of, 148–49, 152, 154–56, 223
　and divine will, 3, 158–59
　egalitarian, 166–68, 169
　equality, 4, 13, 14, 149, 156, 157–58, 227
　exclusion of gays and lesbians from, 61, 63, 80, 86, 89, 117, 164–65, 171, 228, 230
　and friendship, 241–42
　goods of, 105, 159–65, 166, 169, 186, 206, 215, 226 n8, 229, 230, 231, 255

as healthy space for sexual expression, 9, 13, 80, 104, 131, 146, 160, 161–62, 165, 173, 219–220
and heterosexual order, 184–88
history of, 150–52
incestuous, 236–39, 240
interracial, 247
and mental health, 81–82
purposes/ends of, 186–88, 205, 206, 208, 209, 210, 211, 212, 215, 216, 218, 230
and parenting, 93, 160
patriarchal, 165–70, 186–87
polygamous/polyandrous, 223–24, 231–33, 234–36
and procreation, 155, 158, 159–60
rights, 156, 226
and sexual holiness, 147
social meaning of, 156–57
as source of security and comfort, 89, 163–64, 229
as space to nurture love, 160, 162, 234
stabilizing power of, 160, 163, 164, 219, 228–29
traditional, 27, 32, 228
See also homosexual orientation, same-sex marriage
Martin, Dale, 196
Metropolitan Community Church, 145, 146
Michaelson, Jay, 180, 184
monogamy, 5, 8, 9, 27, 79, 81–82, 84, 90, 105, 127, 131, 147, 154, 169, 172, 173, 181, 182, 219–20, 221, 223–24, 227, 231–33, 236
Muehlenberg, Bill, 3

National Association for Research and Therapy of Homosexuality (NARTH), 73, 82
natural law, 8, 111, 147, 149, 197, 198–202, 203–4, 205, 214, 218–19, 221, 222, 255
Nestingen, James, 3, 5, 10
Nicomachean Ethics (Aristotle), 189
Nonviolence, 55, 56, 59
Nygren, Anders, 44, 50–51

Obama, Barack, ix
Obergefell v Hodges Supreme Court decision, ix, 2–3
Olyan, Saul, 179
open and affirming church, 39, 136, 145, 146, 263

parenting, 7, 26, 27–29, 50, 64, 66, 83, 92–96, 99, 160, 194–95, 206, 234–35, 240
Paris, Jenell Williams, xiii, 31–32, 33, 129–31, 141, 146
pathological love, 162
patriarchy, 12, 28, 165–70, 178, 179, 183 n26, 186–87, 193
Paul, St., 10, 43, 80–81, 129, 131, 146, 176, 177, 178, 180–83, 184, 186–87, 188, 189, 192, 220
Pedophilia, 28, 64, 90–92, 97–105, 108, 112. *See also* child molestation
Peter, St., 178, 192
Phelps. Fred, 19, 27, 32, 33, 34, 107
philosophy, xvi-xvii, 4, 197, 257
Plato, 247
political correctness, 258
polyamory, 223–24, 225 n6, 232
polygamy, 150, 223, 224 n3, 225 n6, 232
pornography, 8
postmodernism, 226
pride, 60, 128
promiscuity, 5, 8, 9, 81, 84, 136, 140, 182, 219–20
Proulx, Annie, 80
Pruett, Kyle, 92–93

Rauch, Jonathan, 163–64, 229
Racism, 23, 26, 30, 60, 84, 102, 127–28, 129, 138, 139, 247
Ramsey, Paul, 42, 45, 47, 48
Reflection on the Psalms (Lewis), 193
Regnerus, Mark, 94
Reitan, Jake, 29–30
Reitan, Phil, 29–30
Reitan, Randi, 29–30
relativism, 14, 226

reparative therapy, 74. *See also* conversion therapy, ex-gay ministries, SOCE
reproductive organs, 203, 204, 207, 212, 215. *See also* sexual organs
Roman Catholic Church
  US Bishops, 205, 206, 208, 209, 210
  Catechism of, 206
  celibacy for clergy, 79, 262
  and pedophilic priests, 103
  teachings of, 198–99, 202, 203, 204, 205, 209–10, 212, 214, 218, 222, 234
romantic love 25, 38, 78, 86, 89, 104, 117, 130, 134, 137, 145, 198, 213, 218, 242
Rostand, Edmond, 125

same-sex marriage
  as alternative to celibacy, 137
  benefits of, 164–65, 170, 228–30
  and child welfare, 95–96
  Christian support for, 8–9, 11, 226
  and loving debate, 248, 249, 251–52, 259–60
  legalization of, ix–xi, 2–3, 12, 13, 89, 91, 96, 224
  natural law and, 8, 206, 208, 219, 220
  and patriarchy, 169
  possibility of, 148–50, 158–59
  and relativism, 14, 226
  Scripture and, 8, 177, 182, 184, 186
  and slippery slope arguments, 223–27, 231–36, 236–42
Santorum, Rick, 148, 149, 151
Sarantakos, Soterios, 93–94
Sartre, Jean-Paul, 22–23, 24, 25
Savage, Dan, 251
scapegoating, 17, 23, 24, 25, 26, 33, 247
Scripture
  clobber passages, 40–41, 57, 143, 176–84, 243
  and God's will, 159, 174, 193, 195
  and inerrancy, 175, 176, 189–94, 195–96
  holistic interpretation of, 179, 184–89, 192
  and revelation, 175–76, 192, 193, 196
  theory of, 176, 189, 190–91, 195, 196, 214
  as weapon, 41, 59, 193, 196
sexual holiness, 9, 32, 147
sexual orientation, 24, 63–70, 72–78, 82, 84, 89, 98, 100, 101, 102, 112, 114, 126, 134, 177, 182, 222, 231, 232, 237, 255. *See also* homosexual orientation/homosexuality
Sexual Orientation Change Efforts (SOCE), 70, 71, 75–77. *See also* conversion therapy, reparative therapy, ex-gay ministries
sexual organs, 197, 203. *See also* reproductive organs
sin
  and atonement, 54, 76
  bondage to, 23, 54
  of calling behavior sinful, 119, 120
  and compassionate attention, 122–23
  and emotion, 109–10
  as enemy of love, 110
  hatred of while loving sinner, 8, 21–22, 107–10, 113, 116, 119–20, 123, 138
  and idolatry, 181, 183
  original, 168
  and repentance, 117, 143
  of Sodom, 177
  and stigmatization, 83
singleness, 81, 164, 185–86
slippery slope
  and bestiality, 223, 225
  causal vs. reasons-based, 224
  fallacy of, 224, 225
  fear of, 91
  and incest, 223, 236–42
  and non-monogamy, 223–24, 227–36
Smith, Janet, 203
Society for Christian Philosophers, 255–56
Sola Scriptura, 192

Index

Soulforce, 29, 36, 39, 40, 57, 58
Southern Baptist Church, 36, 37, 60, 85
Southern Poverty Law Center, x, 73
Spitzer, Robert, 73, 74
Sprigg, Peter, 28, 64–65, 72–73, 77, 79, 82, 88, 89, 91, 92, 93–94, 97, 98–99, 100–102
stigma, 6, 64, 73, 82–83, 85, 86, 87–88, 89, 90, 94, 98 n41, 103, 104, 105, 126, 127, 130, 131, 139, 172, 219, 240, 255
Stranger at the Gate (White), 16, 135
Suarez, Francisco, 4
Sullivan, Andrew, 103–4, 164–65
Suppe, Frederick, 70–71, 72
suffering, 16, 46, 47, 48, 51, 52–54, 57, 113–16, 121–22, 127, 133, 146, 167, 195, 250
suicide, 5, 9, 15, 20, 87, 122, 134, 164, 196, 222, 240
Swinburne, Richard, 254–58

taboos, x, 223, 236–37, 239–41, 242
Tea Party, ix
teleology, 199, 201, 202, 210, 236
Throckmorten, Warren, 75
Trump, Donald, ix–x

United Church of Christ, 263

utilitarianism, 46–47

victimization, 52–53
Victimization: Examining Christian Complicity (Gudorf), 52
violence, x, xvii, 8, 13, 29, 31, 36, 47 n17, 52, 53, 55–57, 59, 60, 89, 113, 154, 196, 202, 247, 266
Volf, Miroslav, 49

Walsh, Jerome, 179, 180
Walsh, Matt, 149, 158, 204
Walton, Gerald, 134
Wedgwood, Ralph, 156–57
Weeks, Jeffrey, 128
Westboro Baptist Church, 19, 22, 26, 27, 34
Weil, Simone, 48
white privilege, 60, 128
Wilson, Douglas, 166–67, 168
Wink, Walter, 55–56, 181–82
White, Mel, xi, 16, 39, 135, 141
Wildmon, Tim, 3
works righteousness, 221
worship, 11, 16, 38, 39, 40, 43, 146, 180, 181

Yarhouse, Mark, 63, 74–76, 77, 79, 113

Printed in Great Britain
by Amazon